LAW FOR JOURNALISTS

Visit the *Law for Journalists* Companion Website at

www.pearsoned.co.uk/practicaljournalism

to find valuable **student** learning material including:

- Discussion questions to highlight topical issues and debates within the subject.
- Regular updates on major legal changes affecting the book.
- Links to relevant sites on the web.
- An online glossary providing definitions of key legal terms.

The Elliott & Quinn Series
for the best start in law

This renowned author team draw on their extensive experience to bring an unbeatable selection of texts that provide total clarity on the core areas of law.

ISBN: 9781405847339

ISBN: 9781405835282

ISBN: 9781405846714

ISBN: 9781405846721

Sourcebooks of carefully selected cases, commentary and articles are also available to accompany books in the series.

The Elliott & Quinn Series is supported by extended companion websites that include regular updates to the law and a range of resources from interactive questions, exam advice and weblinks, for students to use throughout their course.

For further information or to order these books, please visit:
www.pearsoned.co.uk/law

LAW FOR JOURNALISTS

Frances Quinn

PEARSON
Longman

Harlow, England • London • New York • Boston • San Francisco • Toronto
Sydney • Tokyo • Singapore • Hong Kong • Seoul • Taipei • New Delhi
Cape Town • Madrid • Mexico City • Amsterdam • Munich • Paris • Milan

Pearson Education Limited

Edinburgh Gate
Harlow
Essex CM20 2JE
England

and Associated Companies throughout the world

Visit us on the World Wide Web at:
www.pearsoned.co.uk

ISBN: 978-0-582-82311-2

British Library Cataloguing-in-Publication Data
A catalogue record for this book is available from the British Library

Library of Congress Cataloging-in-Publication Data
A catalogue record for this book is available from the Library of Congress

10 9 8 7 6 5 4 3 2 1
10 09 08 07

Typeset in 9.5/12pt Giovanni by 35
Printed and bound by Ashford Colour Press Ltd in Gosport

The publisher's policy is to use paper manufactured from sustainable forests.

Brief contents

Full contents

How does the law work in reality?

Law in practice boxes provide handy tips, from experts in the area, on how to use, and avoid falling outside of, the law when you are researching and writing your story.

Examples of actual cases provided throughout highlight how the law has been applied to real-life cases.

What are the main points I should know after reading this chapter?

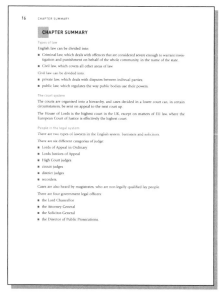

Look to the **Chapter summaries** at the end of each chapter to see the key points that you should know after finishing your reading.

Do I understand the chapter I have just read?

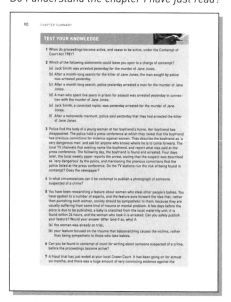

Use the **Test your knowledge** sections, at the end of each chapter, to check you understand the topic.

Where can I find out more about the topics in the book?

Explore interesting and relevant websites on the web using the **List of online resources** at the end of each chapter. Use the **Further reading** section at the end of the book to point you to further sources that allow you to delve deeper into the subject.

Forgotten the meaning of a legal term?

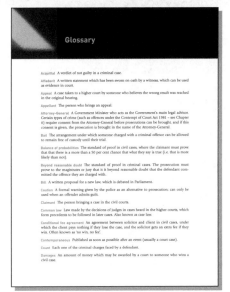

Turn to the **Glossary** at the end of the book to remind yourself of its meaning.

Want to discuss topical issues and questions raised in the book, stay up to date with all the major changes in the law, and search the internet for helpful sources?

Use the **Companion Website**, at www.pearsoned.co.uk/practicaljournalism to find extensive sources designed to assist you with your study, including discussion questions and answer guidance, web links to useful resources, an online glossary and regular updates on major legal changes affecting the book.

Acknowledgements

Thanks to Pat Bond, formerly of Pearson Education, who first came up with the idea for this book – there've been times in the past few years when I've cursed you for it, Pat, but thanks anyway! Michelle Gallagher was my editor during the first stages of the book, and a constant source of support and enthusiasm – thank you. Thanks are also due to my current editor, Zoë Botterill, and her assistant, Cheryl Cheasley, who were a mine of good ideas during the writing of the book – I really appreciate all the hard work you both did.

Thanks to all the people who generously shared their experience and knowledge, and patiently answered my questions, particularly Rod Dadak of Lewis Silkin, former magistrate John Shillum, Freedom of Information campaigner and journalist Heather Brooke, Tony Jaffa of Foot Anstey, barristers' clerk Deborah Anderson, and of course, my consultant editor, Ken Eaton. Thanks too to journalist and lecturer Janice Bhend, for introducing me to Ken.

Finally, thanks to all the friends and family who put up with me moaning about how this book would never be finished, and most of all, to my husband, Mike Jeffree, for support, advice and always knowing when to open a bottle of wine.

PUBLISHER'S ACKNOWLEDGEMENTS

Appendix 1, © Press Complaints Commission, London; Appendix 2, © 1996, HMSO.

Tables

TABLE OF CASES

TABLE OF STATUTES

TABLE OF STATUTORY INSTRUMENTS

TABLE OF TREATIES

LAW AND THE LEGAL SYSTEM

As a journalist, there are two main reasons why you need to learn about the law. The first is that there are legal rules which affect what you can and cannot publish, and clearly, you need to know what these are. The second is that the law and legal proceedings will often form part of the subject matter of the stories you write. This is most obviously the case on local papers, where reporting the local courts is an important part of the news coverage, but legal issues and court cases are also covered by national papers, women's magazines and the trade press, even if not always to the same extent. For that reason, you need to have a basic knowledge of the legal system, and how it works. That forms the subject of this section, while later sections look at how the law will affect you in your daily work.

How law is made

If you asked the average person where to find out 'the law' on a particular subject, most would probably assume that, somewhere, it must all be written down: the answer to every question from 'Can my neighbour build a shed that blocks my view?' to 'Is it legal to sneak into a celebrity's wedding and take pictures?' In fact, there is no single set of written rules that make up 'the law'; instead, there are seven different sources of law which interact with each other. For that reason, in many court cases, the courts are asked to decide not just whether someone has broken a law, but what the law actually is on a particular issue. In this chapter, we look at where law comes from and how it is made.

Note that in this book, English law refers to the courts of England and Wales, as the Scottish system is different. In addition, there are some differences in Northern Ireland, which are pointed out where relevant in the text.

SOURCES OF LAW

The seven sources of law are:

- statute;
- delegated legislation;
- case law;
- European Union (EU) law;
- international treaties;
- custom;
- equity.

In this context it is also important to know about the effect of the European Convention on Human Rights, which has now been incorporated into English law in the Human Rights Act 1998. Although not a separate source of law, it has an important effect on the way in which law is interpreted. It is important to realise that human rights law, developed under the European Convention, is not the same thing as European Union (EU) law (for more information on this, see p. 9).

■ Statute

Statutes are laws passed by Parliament, and are also known as Acts of Parliament. They take precedence over any other type of law, except EU law. Parliament can make or cancel any law it chooses, and the courts must apply that law. This is not the case in many other countries, such as the USA, where the courts can refuse to apply legislation that they consider goes against the country's constitution.

How Acts of Parliament are passed

The Bill stage: All statutes start out as a Bill, which is essentially a proposal for a new law or a change in the law. There are three types:

■ Public Bills: These are put forward by the Government, and form the basis for most legislation. In many cases, a consultation document called a Green Paper is published beforehand (the name comes simply from the colour of the paper it is printed on). A Green Paper explains why the Government is looking at the law in a particular subject area, and gives general details of the options they are considering. The Government then invites anyone who might be affected by the plans to give their views on the proposals. Pressure groups in the relevant area will usually give a response, for example, but the paper may also ask for views from ordinary members of the public who are likely to be particularly affected by a change in the law; for example, if considering changes to particular areas of the welfare services, responses might be invited from users of those services. The Government can then choose which – if any – of the views expressed should influence the final content of the Bill. Usually, it will produce a White Paper which details the conclusions it has come to after the consultation process.

■ Private Members' Bills: These are put forward by an individual Member of Parliament (MP) (who is not a Cabinet member). Pressure on parliamentary time means there are only limited opportunities to do this, and around half of Private Members' Bills come from a ballot, held once each Parliamentary session, for the chance to put forward a Bill. Members who get this chance then have to persuade the Government to allow sufficient Parliamentary time to get the Bill passed; this rarely happens, and as a result, Private Members' Bills are more useful as a way to draw attention to an issue, which may later be taken up in a Public Bill, than they are as a way to change the law straight away. Some important legislation has been made this way, however – the Abortion Act 1967, for example, started as a Private Members' Bill.

■ Private Bills: These are put forward by individuals, local authorities or companies, and essentially concern specific local issues: for example, Railtrack, which runs the tracks for Britain's railways system, might use a Private Bill if it wanted to build a new railway line. Anyone who might be affected by the decision has to be consulted. If the Bill is passed, it only applies to the specific area cited in the Bill, and does not give any general powers applicable to the whole country. Only a handful of Private Bills come before Parliament every year, usually relating to large construction projects.

First reading: The title of the Bill is read to the House of Commons, to notify the House of the proposal.

Second reading: The proposals are debated by the House of Commons, and amendments may be suggested and voted on. MPs then vote on whether the Bill should go on to the next stage.

Committee stage: The Bill is referred to a House of Commons Committee, which will scrutinise it in detail, and may make further amendments.

Report stage: The Committee reports back to the House of Commons, and any amendments are discussed and voted on.

Third reading: The Bill goes back to the House of Commons for a vote on whether to accept or reject its proposals.

House of Lords: The Bill then passes to the House of Lords, where it goes through a similar three-reading process. If the House of Lords suggests any changes, these are passed back for the House of Commons to consider, and the Commons either accepts the suggestions, rejects them and says why, or suggests alternative amendments. If no agreement can be reached, the Commons can use special procedures to pass legislation without the Lords' approval (this is often referred to as using the Parliament Acts). In practice, the House of Lords usually gives up on changes that the Commons clearly does not want, but the Parliament Acts were used, for example, in passing the Hunting Act 2004.

Royal Assent: The final stage is for the Queen to give her consent to the new law (in practice this is never refused).

The Bill then becomes an Act of Parliament, though this does not necessarily mean that all or even any of provisions take effect immediately: the Act may specify future dates when particular provisions take effect or allow the Government or a particular minister to decide when this should happen.

Where a piece of legislation is unlikely to be objected to by any of the major political parties, a simpler process can be used, with the first three readings in the Lords followed by three in the Commons, and a final reference to the Lords only if there is disagreement.

■ Delegated legislation

Some types of legislation require very detailed rules, often of a technical nature; examples would be the law on health and safety at work, or the enormous number of road traffic provisions. Rather than using up Parliamentary time making these detailed rules, Acts of Parliament often create a framework for the law on a particular issue, putting general rules into place without necessarily specifying exactly how they should work in particular situations.

Acts drawn up in this way will include provisions for who should make the detailed rules – usually a government department or Secretary of State, local authorities, or public or nationalised bodies. These rules are known as delegated legislation, and there are three types:

■ Statutory Instruments are drawn up by government departments.

■ By-laws are made by local authorities, public bodies and nationalised bodies. For example, rules on what can and cannot be done in a specific park will usually be made in the form of by-laws drawn up by the local authority.

■ Orders in council are regulations which are made by the Government at a time of national emergency (such as in wartime).

Delegated legislation is also used where rules may need to be changed quickly in response to circumstances, and the Parliamentary procedure is considered too slow-moving and cumbersome to cope with these demands, or where local knowledge is required to make the detailed rules (local by-laws are examples of this). However, they carry as much legal force as statutes themselves.

Case law

Case law (sometimes called common law) comes from the decisions made by judges in certain legal cases. The courts are arranged in a hierarchy (see Figure 1.1 The hierarchy of the courts), and it is decisions made in the higher courts (from the High Court up) which can make law, through what is called judicial precedent (see below). Cases reach these courts through a system of appeals, which provides a route for parties who believe their case has been decided wrongly in the lower courts to take them to higher courts. In most cases permission is required for such appeals, which ensures that the higher courts mostly hear cases which raise important issues of law (the House of Lords, for example, hears fewer than 100 cases a year).

Deciding a case involves two stages: first, establishing what actually happened (often referred to as the facts of the case); and second, deciding how the law applies to the facts. In many cases the latter will be obvious, but there are situations where the law is unclear. For example, if a statute states that 'vehicles shall not be allowed in parks', it is obvious that you cannot drive a car or van round the park – but can you ride a pushbike or use a skateboard? Where these dilemmas arise, it is up to the court deciding the case to determine what the words of the statute actually mean. When a higher court does this, the decision forms what is called a precedent. Once a higher court has set a precedent by interpreting a legal provision in a particular way, that approach should be followed in all the courts that are lower in the hierarchy, and only a higher court can authorise a different approach.

The idea behind case law is that justice requires that like cases be treated alike; once a court has decided what a statutory provision means and/or how it applies to a particular set of facts, later cases with similar facts should be treated in the same way, rather than each judge interpreting the law according to their own sense of justice. For example, if the imaginary case referred to above went to the House of Lords, and it decided that for the purposes of the legislation, a skateboard was a vehicle, other courts faced with cases involving skateboards used in parks would be expected to take the same view. Case law accounts for a huge proportion of English law – for example, the law of negligence, which essentially creates the right to sue for loss or injury caused by someone else's carelessness, is almost exclusively a creation of case law.

EU law

Laws made by the EU are rapidly becoming one of the most important sources of law for the UK, because the terms of membership of the EU mean that they take precedence over any other source of law. However, although it is widely believed that the EU can dictate the law on anything, in fact there are only specific areas which can be affected by EU law. The EU can, for example, make legislation on transport, agriculture and many of the rules regulating how industry behaves, but it does not legislate in the areas of family or criminal law; these are still made solely by the UK Parliament and courts.

As well as producing new law which must be applied here, the EU affects UK law in a second way, in that the courts must interpret and apply UK law in such a way as to avoid conflict with EU law. For example, in the case of *Marshall* v *Southampton and South West Hampshire*

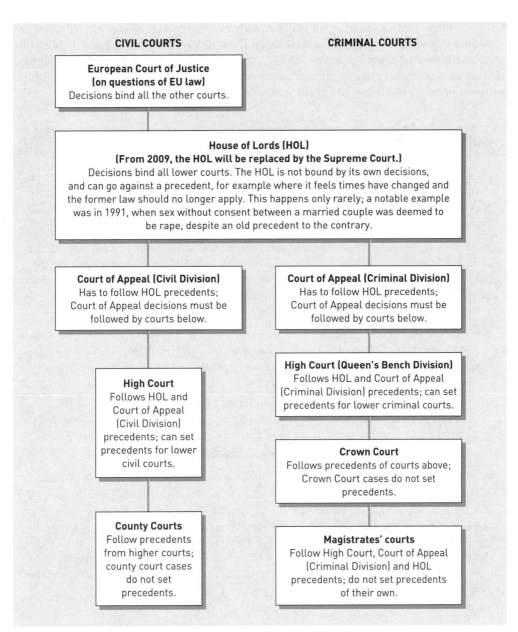

Figure 1.1 **The hierarchy of the courts**

Area Health Authority (1986), an NHS dietician challenged her employer's policy of making employees retire at that state pension age, which was 60 for women but 65 for men. This was legal under the relevant UK legislation, but the House of Lords found that it conflicted with an EU law requiring equal treatment for male and female employees. Where this happens, it is expected that Parliament will amend the domestic legislation to conform with the EU law.

The UK courts can decide questions involving EU law, but there is also a specialist court, the European Court of Justice (ECJ), which oversees the development of EU law (see p. 8).

A UK court faced with a question on EU law can refer it to the ECJ, which will tell the court what the EU law on the matter is; the UK court then decides the case. The idea behind this procedure is that the central overview the ECJ can give helps make sure EU law is interpreted in the same way throughout the different member states of the EU. The ECJ also hears disputes involving breaches of EU law by either member states or EU institutions.

Which European court?

There are two major European courts that are commonly referred to in the British media: the European Court of Justice, and the European Court of Human Rights. These are completely separate institutions, but it is not unusual for journalists to use phrases like 'taking a case to Europe' as though the two courts are one and the same thing.

The European Court of Justice (ECJ) is the court of the EU and sits in Luxembourg. Its main job is to ensure that EU law is understood and applied in the same way throughout the member states. Most cases are brought before it by member states, EU institutions or courts in member states; it rarely hears cases brought by individuals.

In general the ECJ hears three kinds of case:

- complaints from EU institutions or member states that a particular member state is not correctly applying EU law; for example, in 1979 the European Commission successfully complained that the UK had not implemented an EU regulation requiring certain lorries to be fitted with tachographs;
- challenges by member states or EU institutions to EU legislation, alleging that, for example, proper procedures were not followed when a particular piece of law was made;
- referrals from member state courts that are faced with a case involving EU law, and want the ECJ's advice on how the law should be interpreted.

The European Court of Human Rights (ECHR), on the other hand, deals with claims concerning breaches of the European Convention on Human Rights (see Chapter 5); it is not, as often thought, an institution of the EU. The court sits in Strasbourg, and can accept claims made by one state against another, or by individuals against a state. In the past, individuals who claimed that the UK had breached their rights under the Convention had to take their case to Strasbourg, but since the Human Rights Act 1998 came into force, claims can be brought in the UK courts, though it is still possible to take a case to the European Court of Human Rights as a last resort.

International treaties

In many countries, signing an international treaty automatically incorporates the provisions of the treaty into the law within that country. In the UK however, Parliament has to turn the provisions into legislation. The Taking of Hostages Act 1982 is an example of a statute created to put into domestic law the provisions of an international treaty signed by the UK.

Custom

When English law was in its early stages, the decision on whether something was or was not lawful would often be influenced by traditional local practice – if a landowner attempted to stop people taking firewood from his forests, for example, local people might argue that having been allowed to do so for many years effectively gave them a right to continue, even if such a right conflicted with the general law. These days custom can theoretically still play a role in such decisions, but in practice it arises extremely rarely.

■ Equity

Historically, equity was a system of rules which grew up in parallel to the common law to fill perceived gaps where justice could not be achieved by using the common law. For example, at one time, the common law provided that a person who had been caused loss by someone else could only claim financial compensation, which was not always an adequate solution to a problem. Equity developed its own special remedies, which could be granted at the court's discretion; for example, the injunction, which is an order to do something or not do something, and is used where compensation would not solve the problem. Equity survives now as a specific branch of law, largely concerning the ownership of property, and although it is still a source of law, very few journalists come across it in their professional lives.

■ The European Convention on Human Rights

The Human Rights Act 1998 made the provisions of the European Convention on Human Rights part of English law and, for this reason, the Convention is not, strictly speaking, a separate source of law. However, to an extent it acts like one, because it can modify the way other laws operate. As well as being applied by UK courts, human rights law under the Convention has its own court, the European Court of Human Rights, which can create case law (not to be confused with the European Court of Justice, which oversees EU law). This is discussed more fully in Chapter 5.

CHAPTER SUMMARY

Sources of law

Law is not written down in one place; it comes from seven different sources of law, which interact with each other.

Statute

This means Acts of Parliament.

Delegated legislation

This comprises detailed regulations derived from a framework set out in statute.

Case law

This is made by the decisions judges take in cases which reach the higher courts.

EU law

European law must be applied by the UK courts.

International treaties

These must be incorporated before they can become law.

Custom

Traditional customs can be a source of law, but this is rare.

Equity

Equitable rules were originally created to fill gaps in case law.

The European Convention on Human Rights (ECHR)

The ECHR acts like a source of law, as its provisions, incorporated in the Human Rights Act 1998, can modify the way UK law is interpreted.

TEST YOUR KNOWLEDGE

1 What are the seven sources of law?

2 How is case law made and why?

3 What is a Green Paper?

4 What does 'using the Parliament Acts' refer to?

5 How does EU law affect the decisions of UK courts?

6 Which European court hears cases concerning EU law?

ONLINE RESOURCES

www   The United Kingdom Parliament website has information on legislation and the legislative process, at:
www.parliament.uk

Details of current Green Papers can be found at:
www.parliament.the-stationery-office.co.uk/pa/cm/cmwib/wgp.htm

House of Lords judgments can be read at:
www.publications.parliament.uk/pa/ld/ldjudinf.htm

The European Union website is at:
www.europa.eu

For further resources and updates please go to the Companion Website for this book at www.pearsoned.co.uk/practicaljournalism

Chapter 2

The legal system

This chapter covers the way the English legal system is organised: the two main branches of law; the personnel of the legal system and their roles; and the courts which make up the system. As court cases very often form the basis of stories, a knowledge of the system will help you understand what is going on when you report on such stories, and will ensure that you use the right terminology when writing about court proceedings.

TYPES OF LAW

There are lots of different areas of law in terms of subject area, but the most important divisions are between:

- criminal and civil law; and
- public and private law.

Criminal and civil law

Criminal law deals with wrongs that are considered so serious as to be an offence against the whole community, and for this reason they are prosecuted in the name of the state (or specifically, the Queen). It also possible to bring a private prosecution, but this happens relatively rarely.

Civil law covers everything else, from road accident victims suing for compensation or neighbours fighting over who owns a fence, to newspapers being sued for libel or companies disputing tax decisions by the Inland Revenue.

In some cases, the same course of action can lead to both a criminal and a civil case. For example, someone who injures another as a result of dangerous driving may be prosecuted for the crime of dangerous driving, and sued in the civil courts by the person injured.

Criminal and civil law use completely different sets of terminology, and it is important to know which terms apply to which area of law. Not only does it look ill-informed if you refer to, for example, being found guilty of negligence, it could potentially even be libellous, since you would be suggesting that someone had committed a criminal offence, when in fact negligence is a civil wrong, which is generally considered less serious.

Public and private law

A second important distinction is between public and private law. Both public and private law are aspects of civil law.

Private law comprises disputes between individual parties, such as someone injured in an accident suing the person who caused it, or a celebrity suing a newspaper for libel.

Public law is the set of legal principles which governs the way public authorities, including the Government, use their powers. Public authorities cannot act just as they please, but can only exercise the powers given to them by law, and public law is designed to make sure these powers are not exceeded or misused. The main form of action in public law is the application for judicial review, which allows individuals (or organisations) to challenge the decisions or acts of public bodies (see p. 49).

THE COURT SYSTEM

The English court system consists of:

- magistrates' courts;
- county courts;

Know your terms

Criminal law	Civil law
When a criminal case is brought against someone, that person is described as being charged with that offence; if the case comes to court, they are described as being prosecuted.	When a civil case is brought against someone, that person is described as being sued.
Someone accused of committing a crime is called a defendant; the other side (acting for the Crown) is called the prosecution.	The person bringing the case is called the claimant (previously known as the plaintiff), and the person the claim is against is called the defendant.
Criminal cases are referred to in writing as *R v xxxxx* (the name of the person being prosecuted), but in speech this would be read as 'The Queen against xxxxx' (R stands for Regina, Latin for queen).	Civil cases are described with the names of both parties (e.g. *Smith v Jones*), with the defendant's name first. In speech this would be read as 'Smith and Jones'.
If the prosecution wins their case, the defendant is described as being found guilty, or convicted.	If the claimant wins the case, the defendant can be described as having lost, or being held liable for the relevant wrong (e.g. libel, negligence). He or she should never be described as being found guilty of (for example) negligence or libel.
A convicted defendant is sentenced.	If the claimant wins, he or she will usually be awarded a remedy. This is most often damages, which is a sum of money, but there are other civil remedies such as, for example, being reinstated in a job from which you have been wrongfully dismissed. You can say that the defendant had damages awarded against him or her; you should never say he or she was sentenced or fined.

- the Crown Court;
- the High Court;
- the Court of Appeal; and
- the House of Lords (to be replaced by the Supreme Court from 2008).

The Crown Court only hears criminal cases and the county courts only civil ones, but the others hear both civil and criminal cases.

As explained earlier, the courts form a hierarchical system, in which appeals can pass up through the courts, and decisions made in the higher courts have to be followed by those lower down. Traditionally, the House of Lords was the highest appeal court in the UK, but membership of the EU has meant the European Court of Justice is effectively the highest court for cases which concern EU law. From 2008, the House of Lords is to be replaced by the new Supreme Court, but for the purposes of this book, its role remains the same. The House of Lords also hears appeals from some other countries within the Commonwealth; when it sits in such a case it is known as the Privy Council. The functions of each court, and the hierarchy of courts for appeals, are explained in the chapters on civil and criminal procedure.

PEOPLE IN THE LEGAL SYSTEM

The main legal personnel that journalists need to know about are:

- lawyers;
- judges;
- government legal officers.

In all three cases, a knowledge of what these people do, and how to refer to them, will ensure that your reports appear authoritative.

Lawyers

The English legal profession comprises two different types of lawyer: barristers and solicitors. Traditionally, the two branches did different types of work. Today, this distinction is increasingly breaking down, but the terms 'solicitor' and 'barrister' still describe two different professionals, who each undergo a different training process and set of exams in order to qualify. Barristers are also sometimes known as counsel, but this term should not be used for solicitors. The term lawyer, however, covers both.

Traditionally, the major difference between the work of the two branches was that solicitors dealt directly with clients, while barristers were usually called on by a solicitor where necessary, either to give advice on a detailed area of law, or to represent the client in court (just as patients usually see a GP first and are referred by them to a specialist if necessary). In addition, only barristers could appear in the higher courts. However, changes made in the 1990s have broken down some of the differences between the two branches. Some clients (mostly professionals such as surveyors and accountants) can now consult barristers directly without being referred by a solicitor, and solicitors can appear in all courts, provided that they have undergone a specialist training course (solicitors who do this are often known as solicitor advocates). In fact, although it is often believed that barristers do most court work, solicitors have always done a lot of criminal court work, because 95 per cent of criminal cases are heard in the magistrates' courts, where the defendant is usually represented by a solicitor rather than a barrister.

QCs (short for Queen's Counsel) are barristers who have been in practice for at least ten years and are considered particularly talented and experienced. Becoming a QC is not, however, automatic – barristers must apply for the title, and some barristers apply several times before being granted it, while others never get it at all. Becoming a QC generally means a barrister will be offered higher-paying work.

Judges

There are six different categories of judge in the legal system, as well as magistrates, who, although they are lay people and not considered part of the judiciary, actually decide 95 per cent of all criminal cases.

Lords of Appeal in Ordinary are usually known as the Law Lords, and sit in the House of Lords (after 2008 they will sit in the new Supreme Court). There are 12 of them. They are referred to as, for example, Lord or Lady Brown.

Lord and Lady Justices of Appeal sit in the Court of Appeal. There are 37 of them. They are referred to as, for example, Lord or Lady Justice Brown. The most senior judge in the Civil Division of the Court of Appeal is called the Master of the Rolls; in the Criminal Division, the head is the Lord Chief Justice.

High Court judges sit in the High Court and hear the most serious cases in the Crown Court; there are just over 100 of them. They spend some of their time 'on circuit', travelling around the regional courts, where they may, for example, hear Queen's Bench Division cases or Family Division cases which would otherwise have to be held at the High Court in London. In the official reports of legal cases, and in law textbooks, a High Court judge called Smith would be referred to as Smith J, but for journalists, it is more usual to write Mr or Mrs Justice Smith (not Judge Smith).

Circuit judges sit in the county court and in middle-ranking Crown Court cases. There are around 650 of them, and they are referred to as, for example, Judge Simon Smith or Judge Ann Jones. Occasionally they may also sit in the Court of Appeal.

District judges hear the majority of cases in the county courts; there are around 450 of them. There are also around 100 district judges (formerly known as stipendiary magistrates) who hear the more complex and serious cases in the magistrates' courts. Both are usually referred to as, for example, District Judge Jane Brown.

Recorders are part-time judges who hear the least serious Crown Court cases and some county court cases. They are usually still working as barristers or solicitors, and the job is viewed as a kind of apprenticeship before becoming a full-time judge. They are referred to as the recorder or, for example, Mr John Smith or Mrs Mary Smith. The title of recorder is also used in a slightly different context: the Recorder of Manchester is the most senior circuit judge in the Manchester Crown Court, and similar titles are used for the same role in Liverpool, Belfast and some other cities. The title Recorder of London applies to one of the senior judges who sits at the Central Criminal Court (the London Crown Court which is better known as the Old Bailey).

Magistrates (also known as Justices of the Peace, or JPs) are lay people, drawn from the local community, who sit in the magistrates' courts, hearing both criminal and some kinds of civil cases. Though they receive training in court procedure, they are not required to be legally qualified or to know the law, but have a legally-qualified clerk to advise them. The work is voluntary (magistrates receive expenses, but no pay) and part-time – most magistrates sit for 35–70 half-days per year. Magistrates are selected by local committees, though they are officially appointed by the Lord Chancellor. When reporting cases involving magistrates, it is usual to refer to them as 'the magistrates' rather than by name, but a magistrate's name can be used if you need to refer to one specifically. In *R v Felixstowe Justices ex p Leigh* 1987 **QB 582**, *R v Evesham Justices ex p McDonagh* (**1988**), the Divisional Court of the Queen's Bench ruled that a magistrates' court could not legally withhold the name of a sitting magistrate from the press.

■ Government legal officers

There are four other important legal roles in the UK:

- the Lord Chancellor (who is also the Secretary of State for Constitutional Affairs);
- the Attorney-General;
- the Solicitor-General;
- the Director of Public Prosecutions.

The Lord Chancellor until very recently combined three roles: head of the judiciary; Speaker of the House of Lords; and member of the Cabinet. The position was traditionally taken by the most senior lawyer in the House of Lords. Although this combined role has a long history, it was increasingly seen as a problem for someone who holds a high position in the Government of the day to head up the judiciary, which is supposed to be independent of Government, and in addition, to have such a central role in the House of Lords, which is supposed to scrutinise legislation. As a result, in April 2006, the role was modified. The head of the judiciary is now the same person who holds the position of Lord Chief Justice (giving him or her the additional title of President of the Courts of England and Wales), and the House of Lords now elects a Speaker. The title of Lord Chancellor continues, and the holder, who need no longer be a lawyer, still has responsibility for the efficient running of the court system. He or she also takes the position of Secretary of State for Constitutional Affairs, which gives responsibility for important constitutional issues.

The Attorney-General and the Solicitor-General (together known as the Law Officers) are both government Ministers, though not members of the Cabinet. The Attorney-General is the main legal advisor to the Government (the Attorney-General at the time of the war in Iraq, for example, gave the Government advice on whether the war was legal under international law), and is responsible for important legal cases involving the Government, whether at home or abroad. Certain types of crime (such as offences under the Contempt of Court Act – see Chapter 6) require consent from the Attorney-General before prosecutions can be brought, and if this consent is given, the prosecution is brought in the name of the Attorney-General. The Solicitor-General is effectively the Attorney-General's deputy, and may fulfil any of his or her functions where necessary.

The Director of Public Prosecutions (DPP) is the head of the Crown Prosecution Service (CPS), and is responsible for ensuring the independent review and prosecution of criminal proceedings started by the police in England and Wales. He or she makes decisions about the most complex and sensitive cases and advises the police on criminal matters, and prosecutions for certain types of cases require his or her permission. The DPP reports to the Attorney-General.

CHAPTER SUMMARY

Types of law

English law can be divided into:

- Criminal law, which deals with offences that are considered severe enough to warrant investigation and punishment on behalf of the whole community, in the name of the state.
- Civil law, which covers all other areas of law.

Civil law can be divided into:

- private law, which deals with disputes between indivual parties;
- public law, which regulates the way public bodies use their powers.

The court system

The courts are organised into a hierarchy, and cases decided in a lower court can, in certain circumstances, be sent on appeal to the next court up.

The House of Lords is the highest court in the UK, except on matters of EU law, where the European Court of Justice is effectively the highest court.

People in the legal system

There are two types of lawyers in the English system: barristers and solicitors.

There are six different categories of judge:

- Lords of Appeal in Ordinary
- Lords Justices of Appeal
- High Court judges
- circuit judges
- district judges
- recorders.

Cases are also heard by magistrates, who are non-legally qualified lay people.

There are four government legal officers:

- the Lord Chancellor
- the Attorney-General
- the Solicitor-General
- the Director of Public Prosecutions.

TEST YOUR KNOWLEDGE

1 Define criminal and civil law.

2 Nuisance is a civil wrong. Which of these sentences about it is inaccurate?
   (a) John Smith was convicted of nuisance.
   (b) John Smith was found guilty of nuisance.
   (c) John Smith was charged with nuisance.
   (d) John Smith was sued for nuisance.
   (e) John Smith was fined for nuisance.

3 What term applies to someone who brings a civil case? What is the other side called?

4 What is the difference between the terms 'counsel' and 'lawyer'?

5 If a case is called *R v Smith*, will it be a civil or a criminal case?

6 You are reporting a court case, and want to mention a judge by name. How should you refer to him or her if they are:
   (a) a judge in the Court of Appeal
   (b) a circuit judge
   (c) a recorder
   (d) a magistrate?

7 What is the highest court in the English legal system?

8 Describe the roles of the Lord Chancellor, Attorney-General and Director of Public Prosecutions.

ONLINE RESOURCES

www The Law Society website has information on the solicitors' profession, at:
www.lawsociety.org.uk

The Bar Council website has information on the work and training of barristers, at:
www.barcouncil.org.uk

Details about the different types of judge, their training and work can be found at the Judiciary of England and Wales website:
www.judiciary.gov.uk

Information about the selection, training and work of magistrates can be found at the Magistrates Association website is at:
www.magistrates-association.org.uk

The Department of Constitutional Affairs website contains information on the legal system, including the government legal officers:
www.dca.gov.uk

For further resources and updates please go to the Companion Website for this book at www.pearsoned.co.uk/practicaljournalism

2

The legal system

Criminal courts and procedure

A society without crime might be a very pleasant place to live, but it would throw thousands of journalists out of work at a stroke. Reporting criminal trials is an everyday occurrence on local and national papers, but in almost every other area of journalism you are likely to come across the subject now and then. That means it is important to have a grasp of how the criminal justice system works, which is the subject covered in this chapter. In Section 2, you will find details of how the law restricts the way in which you report criminal investigations and trials.

THE CRIMINAL COURTS

Criminal cases are heard by either a magistrates' court, or by the Crown Court, depending on the type of offence (see the box).

Types of criminal offence

Crimes fall into three categories, based on where they can be tried:

- **Indictable offences** (or offences triable only on indictment) are the most serious crimes, and can only be tried in the Crown Court, by a jury.
- **Either way offences** can be tried in either the Crown Court or the magistrates' courts. The defendant can insist on being tried in the Crown Court; if he or she does not do so, the magistrates decide whether to try the case themselves or send it to the Crown Court, taking into account the seriousness of the offence and whether they are likely to have adequate sentencing powers if the defendant is found guilty (see below).
- **Summary offences** are tried only in the magistrates' courts. They should not, however, necessarily be seen as trivial – over the years, more and more offences have been made summary, and the category includes, for example, assaulting a police officer and drink-driving.

Magistrates' courts

All criminal cases start in the magistrates' court, where one or more initial hearings will take place before the trial itself. Around 95 per cent of criminal cases (all involving summary or either way offences) then go on to be tried in the magistrates' courts (the rest go to the Crown Court for trial).

Cases are decided by three lay magistrates, or in certain areas, by a district judge. Where the case is heard by magistrates, one of them will be the chairman, and presides over the trial; magistrates receive special training for this role. The magistrates are advised by the clerk to the justices, who usually sits in front of them. The clerk will be legally trained, and is there to advise on the law and legal procedure, but does not take part in the actual decision in the case. The maximum sentence a magistrates' court can impose is six months' imprisonment, or 12 months if passing consecutive sentences for more than one offence. If a defendant is convicted by magistrates who feel that a longer sentence is appropropriate, they can refer the case to the Crown Court for sentencing. Youth courts are a branch of the magistrates' court, and hear cases where the defendant is under 18 (for more details on criminal cases involving under-18s, see Chapter 10).

■ Crown Court

The Crown Court is where cases are decided by jury. Despite the impression given by films and TV, only around 1 per cent of cases go through this process; of the 5 per cent not decided by magistrates, a proportion of defendants will plead guilty, so no jury is needed. Where a jury does decide the case, its role is to decide whether the defendant is guilty or innocent; if the jury finds that person guilty, the judge decides the sentence (this is why juries are only used if the defendant pleads not guilty).

A jury consists of 12 people who are chosen at random from the local electoral roll. They must be between 18 and 70, though anyone over 65 can choose not to serve if called. People who are on bail, have been imprisoned in the past ten years, or received a suspended sentence, community order or probation order in the past five years are not allowed to sit on a jury, and nor are people with mental health problems that require them to be in hospital or under regular medical treatment. In the past, members of certain professions, such as lawyers, politicians, judges and doctors were exempt from jury service but this exemption was abolished by the Criminal Justice Act 2003.

There is only one Crown Court, even though it can be sitting in different places at the same time, so it is technically correct to refer to 'the Crown Court' rather than 'crown courts' or 'a crown court'. However, it is standard practice to talk about, for example, 'Maidstone Crown Court', even though technically this is the Crown Court sitting in Maidstone. For administrative purposes, the court is divided into six areas, known as circuits: Northern, North Eastern, South Eastern, Midland, Wales and Chester, and Western. Each one is run by a senior civil servant called a circuit administrator. The administrator is advised by two High Court judges.

CRIMINAL JUSTICE PROCEDURE

■ Stage one: investigating crime

Most criminal cases will begin with the role of the police, who are responsible for investigating most crimes (though some are investigated by other agencies, such as the Health and Safety Executive or the Serious Fraud Office). Police procedure during criminal investigations is regulated by the Police and Criminal Evidence Act 1984 (known as PACE) and the Criminal Justice and Public Order Act 1994, which between them specify the circumstances in which the police can stop, search, arrest, detain and interrogate members of the public.

A criminal case officially starts either when an arrest is made (see below), or when the police send the magistrates' court a document giving particulars of the alleged offence. This is called laying an information, and as a result of it the magistrates can either issue an arrest warrant or a summons, which is sent to the defendant and states what he or she is accused of, and the time and date at which he or she must attend court. Magistrates cannot try a summary offence unless the information is laid within six months of the offence being committed.

Pre-arrest powers

Nobody is obliged to answer questions put by a police officer, or to go to or be detained at a police station, unless they are lawfully arrested. However, obstructing the police is an offence, and cases suggest that there is a fine line between refusing to answer questions and obstruction: in *Ricketts* v *Cox* (1982), a defendant who was abusive and uncooperative when asked questions by two police officers investigating an assault was found guilty of obstruction.

Someone who goes voluntarily to a police station for questioning has the legal right to leave when they want to, unless they are arrested, so the often-used phrase 'detained for questioning' has no real legal meaning – a suspect is either under arrest and being questioned, or is undergoing questioning voluntarily.

Powers of arrest

Police powers of arrest were recently widened by the Serious Organised Crime and Police Act 2005. Arrests can now be made when a police officer reasonably suspects that someone has committed, is committing or is about to commit an offence, and the police officer has reasonable grounds to believe that an arrest is necessary. This will be the case where:

- the suspect refuses to give a name or address, or the officer reasonably believes the one given is false;
- the arrest will prevent the suspect suffering physical injury, harming themselves, someone else, or property, committing an offence against public decency, or obstructing the highway;
- the arrest is needed to protect a child or other vulnerable person;
- the arrest will allow the prompt and effective investigation of the offence or the suspect's conduct;
- arrest is needed to prevent the person escaping.

This very broad set of circumstances means arrest is now possible in the majority of cases where the police would wish to do so. However, in the few cases where none of the criteria is fulfilled, the police can apply to a magistrate for a warrant. This is not a common process today, and is mainly used for defendants who have failed to turn up for trial.

Police questioning

PACE states that if the police arrest someone, they must tell the person why they are being arrested. The police can then detain them for up to 36 hours, and must then either release them or charge them, unless the case is a serious arrestable offence. In that case the police can authorise a further detention of up to 12 hours, if necessary, to secure or preserve evidence. After that, the police must get permission from a magistrate to hold the suspect for further periods: the maximum is a total of 96 hours, after which the suspect must be either released or charged (except where the suspected offence concerns terrorism, in which case suspects can be detained for up to 28 days).

Where someone is held for an unreasonable time without being charged, there is an ancient form of legal action called habeas corpus, which allows that person's friends or family to get an order from the High Court requiring him or her to be released. In practice though, prolonged detention before charge or release happens fairly rarely: only 5 per cent of suspects are held for more than 18 hours, and 1 per cent for more than 24 hours.

Under the PACE Code of Practice, once someone is charged, police questioning should stop. The Code of Practice provisions are not legal requirements, but breach of them can lead to disciplinary action, and serious breaches can mean that a court will rule that evidence obtained by means of the breach cannot be used against the defendant.

Someone who is arrested and later released without ever being charged may be able to bring a civil claim against the police for false arrest or wrongful imprisonment, if the grounds for the arrest were unreasonable.

Bail

Once charged, the next question is whether the defendant should be allowed out on bail or remanded in custody. Sometimes, an arrest warrant will be 'backed for bail' when it is issued by magistrates, which means that once the suspect has been arrested and fulfilled certain formalities at the police station, he or she automatically gets bail. Where this is not the case, the police can grant bail, but if they decide not to, the defendant must be brought before magistrates by at least the day after being charged (unless that day is a Sunday, Christmas Day or Good Friday), so they can decide whether or not bail should be granted.

The general assumption is that defendants not already convicted of an offence should get bail. The Bail Act 1976 requires magistrates to give reasons for refusing bail, and to grant it unless:

■ there are substantial grounds to believe the defendant will abscond, commit other offences, interfere with witnesses or obstruct the course of justice;

■ the defendant should be kept in custody for their own protection (or is already serving a prison sentence);

■ there is not yet sufficient information to make the decision.

Where the defendant is already on bail for an indictable offence, a court is not required to grant bail even if the above requirements are not fulfilled. Under the Criminal Justice Act 2003, the same applies to a person charged with an imprisonable offence, who tests positive for a Class A drug and refuses treatment. If the defendant is charged with murder, manslaughter, rape or attempted rape or murder, and has a previous conviction for such an offence, bail should only be granted in exceptional circumstances, and the court must state its reasons. If bail is refused, the defendant has the right to apply to a judge to have the decision reversed; the prosecution also has this right where bail has been granted despite their objections.

Bail can be granted subject to conditions, such as that the defendant makes a payment (called a security) to the court which they will lose if they fail to attend a court hearing. In some cases this payment may be promised by a third person on behalf of the defendant – they do not have to make the payment (which in this case is called a surety) in advance, but if the defendant fails to appear in court and the third person cannot or will not pay, they can be jailed.

Approximately 22 per cent of the UK prison population are suspects awaiting trial who have been refused bail, known as prisoners on remand.

▓ Stage 2: prosecution

Once the investigation is complete, the Crown Prosecution Service (CPS) decides whether to prosecute the suspect, drop the case or issue a caution (in some minor cases, this decision is made by the police). A caution is a formal warning, and can only be given where the defendant admits guilt and there would be a realistic prospect of a successful prosecution. It is not, as popularly thought, a kind of get-out clause that can be used when the police think they cannot prove their case, or when the suspect might not be guilty of the particular offence in question but is thought to be a bad lot generally. Cautions are recorded, and if a person is later convicted of another offence, the caution can be cited as part of their criminal record.

In deciding whether to prosecute, the CPS uses a two-stage test:

1 Is there sufficient evidence to provide a realistic prospect of conviction? This essentially means that the evidence is such that the court is more likely to convict than not to do so. If there is not sufficient evidence, the case should not go ahead, no matter how serious or important it seems. If there is sufficient evidence, the CPS goes on to ask the second question.

2 Is a prosecution in the public interest? The reasons which can be taken into account for this test are contained in the Code of Practice for Crown Prosecutors. Factors making a prosecution more likely to be in the public interest include:

   ■ that a conviction is likely to result in a significant sentence;

   ■ that the offence was committed against someone serving the public (such as a police officer);

   ■ where an offence is relatively minor, the fact that it happens very frequently in the relevant local area.

Circumstances which can make a prosecution less likely include:

■ the defendant being very elderly or unwell;

■ a long delay between the offence taking place and the potential date of the trial.

None of these factors is conclusive; the CPS will usually need to weigh a number of factors against each other in coming to a decision.

Private prosecutions

If the CPS decides not to prosecute, a victim of crime can bring a private prosecution, but because legal aid is unavailable, this happens very rarely. Where the offence is a serious one, the Director of Public Prosecutions must be informed before a case can go ahead, and the law allows the CPS to take over private prosecutions. It will only do this if there is good reason to do so. The CPS can then continue the prosecution if it passes the two-stage test described above, or end it if there is so little evidence that there is really no case to answer, or if the prosecution is not in the public interest.

A recent example of a private prosecution was the case brought by Doreen and Stephen Lawrence, whose son Stephen was brutally killed in 1993. Charges against two youths were dropped by the CPS, which said the evidence was insufficient, so the Lawrences brought a private prosecution. The judge ordered the jury to acquit, because of lack of reliable evidence.

■ Stage 3: hearings before a trial

Almost all criminal cases begin in the magistrates' courts. Around 95 per cent of them are actually tried there; the rest go on to be tried in the Crown Court, but there will be at least one pre-trial hearing in the magistrates' courts first. Magistrates in pre-trial hearings for cases that may go on to be tried in the Crown Court are said to be acting as 'examining justices'.

Pre-trial hearings in the magistrates' courts

The type of pre-trial hearing depends on the category of offence.

Summary offences: Pre-trial hearings are optional for summary offences, but one magistrate or the magistrates' clerk may hold a hearing in which both sides can agree the main issues in the case, and identify what needs to be done in preparation for the trial itself.

Either way offences: The first step here is what is called the 'plea before venue' procedure, in which the defendant states whether they intend to plead guilty or not guilty.

If the defendant pleads guilty the magistrates hear the prosecution case (sometimes after an adjournment), and anything there is to be said in mitigation. (In other words, any information which might suggest a reduction in the sentence the magistrates would otherwise impose, such as evidence of previous good character, or that the defendant is genuinely sorry and has tried to make amends.) The magistrates then have three options:

- adjourn the case for any reports that are necessary to help decide the appropriate sentence (e.g. into the defendant's mental state, home life or employment situation);
- sentence the defendant themselves;
- send the case to the Crown Court for sentencing if their own sentencing powers are inadequate.

If the defendant pleads not guilty or does not indicate a plea, the next stage is to decide where the case should be tried. The defendant can insist on a Crown Court trial; if they do not do so, the decision is made by the magistrates, taking into account the seriousness of the offence, and whether their sentencing powers are likely to be adequate. If the case is to be tried in the magistrates' court, there may then be a pre-trial hearing to rule on points of law and the admissibility of evidence, before the actual trial happens.

If the defendant opts for Crown Court trial, or the magistrates decide that this would be appropriate, the next stage is a formal proceeding called committal (or committal for trial). This is designed to allow the magistrates to check that there is sufficient evidence to proceed to a full Crown Court trial, and to weed out any weak cases, but it is essentially an exercise done on paper; no witnesses are called. The magistrates are given written statements of the prosecution case (called depositions) and any documentary evidence, but are not required to assess this evidence unless the defence argue that there is insufficent evidence to justify a trial, or one or more of the defendants is not represented by a lawyer. If the defence argues that there is insufficient evidence, and the magistrates agree, they can dismiss the case.

Where magistrates dismiss a case for lack of evidence, the prosecution can apply to a High Court judge for a bill of indictment, which authorises the Crown Court trial to go ahead anyway. In practice this procedure is very rarely used.

For either way offences involving serious fraud and certain offences against children, there is a fast-track procedure called notice of transfer: this is explained more fully in Chapter 9.

Indictable offences: For indictable offences, there is a fast-track procedure through the magistrates' court called sending for trial. The defendant usually appears just once before the magistrates' court, and at this hearing the court decides issues concerning funding from the Legal Services Commission (what used to be called Legal Aid), whether the defendant should be given bail until the Crown Court trial, and any questions about the use of particular statements or exhibits.

In some cases there may be two hearings, where the case is adjourned after the first to confirm that the charge is the correct one. Where the defendant has not been granted bail, they will appear in court for the first hearing, but may use a video link from the prison for the second one.

There is no opportunity in the sending for trial procedure itself for the defendant to argue that there is no case to answer, but they can apply within 14 days for the charges to be dismissed on the grounds of insufficient evidence. In addition, where the defence believe that the court was not legally entitled to send the case to trial at the Crown Court, they can challenge the decision in the Queen's Bench Division of the High Court.

Bail applications

Where a defendant is to be tried in the Crown Court, the defence lawyer may ask that the defendant be granted bail until then (there can be a long delay before cases come before the Crown Court). The prosecution will be invited to put forward any objections to bail being granted (such as that the defendant is likely to abscond, interfere with witnesses or commit another offence). If bail is refused, the defendant can apply to a judge in chambers to reverse the decision.

Pre-trial hearings in the Crown Court

Once a case has been sent to the Crown Court, the next stage is a plea and direction hearing, where the defendant enters a plea of guilty or not guilty (this part of the process is known as the arraignment).

If the plea is guilty, the judge will sentence the defendant if possible, or may adjourn the case so that reports can be produced on, for example, the defendant's mental state, if it is thought this might be relevant to the sentence that should be passed.

If the plea is not guilty, the prosecution and defence will be asked to identify the key issues in the case, and provide any additional information needed to organise the trial itself, such as details of witnesses, facts that are agreed by both sides, and any questions of law that are expected to arise. The purpose of this is to encourage both sides to prepare their cases at an early stage, making it less likely that a case will fall apart at the last minute, wasting public money and court time.

For particularly serious or complex cases, there may also be a preparatory hearing which is treated as the start of the trial, even though it happens before the jury is sworn in. This hearing provides a more detailed examination of the issues in the case, to help the judge manage the trial, reduce its length and make it as easy as possible for the jury to understand.

■ Stage 4: the trial

The procedure for trial is essentially the same in both the magistrates' and the Crown Court. The prosecution's job is to prove beyond reasonable doubt that the defendant is guilty. If they do not do this, the defendant should be acquitted; the defence is not required to prove innocence.

At the beginning of the trial, the charges (sometimes called counts) are read out by the clerk of the court. The details may be different from those specified in the magistrates' court during committal, so it is important not just to repeat what it says in the report of the earlier hearing. The defendant then pleads guilty or not guilty.

Guilty pleas

If the defendant pleads guilty, the prosecution lawyer will give details of the evidence, and of the defendant's previous criminal record, if any. Social inquiry reports, which detail the defendant's circumstances and are used to help the court decide on the sentence, are read out, and defence lawyers may make pleas in mitigation. These are arguments put forward to persuade the court to be more lenient in sentencing than they otherwise would (they might, for example, draw attention to the fact that a defendant has previously been of good character, or to any evidence that they are trying to make reparation for what they have done). The court then passes sentence.

Not guilty pleas

The trial begins (after the jury has been sworn if in the Crown Court) with an outline of the case by the prosecution lawyer, who will usually be a solicitor or barrister employed by the Crown Prosecution Service. Witnesses for the prosecution are then called, and each one is questioned by the prosecution counsel (this is called examination-in-chief). After each examination-in-chief, the witness is questioned by the defence (referred to as cross-examination). If the prosecution feels it necessary to address any points brought out in cross-examination, they can then re-examine the witness.

When the prosecution has presented all its witnesses, the defence can argue that there is no case to answer, which essentially means that there is not sufficient evidence to enable any reasonable jury or magistrate to convict. If the judge or magistrates agree, a verdict of not guilty is given straight away.

If the argument of no case to answer is unsuccessful (or, as is usually the case, the argument is not put forward), the defence then puts its case, using the same procedure as the prosecution: examination-in-chief, cross-examination and, where necessary, re-examination. The defendant may give evidence, but cannot be forced to; however, where a defendant is over 14, and chooses not to give evidence, or not to answer a particular question, the prosecution can draw the jury's attention to this fact and invite jurors to draw their own conclusions about the defendant's decision.

In courtroom dramas on film and TV, a surprise witness or unexpected piece of evidence frequently proves vital, but in real life, both sides are required to disclose their evidence to each other beforehand, and to state whom they will be calling as witnesses. Witnesses who do not wish to give evidence can be ordered to do so by the court, and anyone who then refuses to do so can be jailed for up to a month, or fined. This does not usually apply, however, where the defendant is the spouse or live-in partner of the unwilling witness; in that case the witness cannot be compelled to give evidence unless the offence was committed against them or their children.

In some cases, a witness questioned in court may deny things that they prevously said in witness statements, give different evidence or refuse to give the evidence expected. In that situation, they become what is known as a hostile witness, and the side which called them as a witness may challenge the evidence given in court, and remind the witness of what was originally said.

Each side then makes a closing speech: the prosecution addresses the jury first, pointing out the reasons why it should find the defendant guilty, and then the defendant's lawyer addresses the jury, highlighting the reasons for an acquittal (in some cases, with permission, either side may address the court twice).

In the magistrates' court, the magistrates then leave the court to discuss their verdict. In the Crown Court, there is an additional stage, the judge's summing up. The judge outlines the evidence on both sides of the case and explains the law, but reminds the jury that it is its job to decide on the facts – that is, what it believed happened. The judge should also explain the concept of proof beyond reasonable doubt, and stress to the jury that it should only convict if it considers the prosecution case has been proved to this standard. However, where the judge believes that the evidence presented is clearly insufficient for the case to be proved beyond reasonable doubt, they should direct the jury to acquit the defendant.

The jury then retires to consider its verdict. If, after two hours and 20 minutes, it has not reached a decision, the judge can accept a majority verdict of 11–1 or 10–2, though a unanimous verdict is always preferred and most judges will ask juries to spend longer trying to achieve one. If the number of people on the jury has been reduced during the trial (e.g. through illness), the judge can accept a verdict of 10–1 or 9–1.

▨ Stage 5: sentencing

If the defendant is found guilty, the magistrates or the judge must decide the sentence. At this stage, any previous convictions can be revealed, and the defence can make pleas in mitigation. Cases are often adjourned at this stage so that reports can be prepared into issues that affect the decision on a suitable sentence, such as the defendant's mental state, or home or work situation.

Previous convictions and TICs

In most cases, a defendant's previous convictions should not be mentioned in court until and unless they are found guilty. However, there are some exceptions to this rule, and previous convictions can be mentioned where:

- the defendant gives a false impression as to their character;
- the defendant attacks the character of prosecution witnesses; or
- where the court believes that the information would shed important light on the case, and would not make the trial unfair (an example might be where the facts of the case are so similar to incidents which led to previous convictions that they can be taken to show a pattern of behaviour).

Sometimes a defendant found guilty will ask for other offences to be 'taken into consideration' (often called TICs). These should not be confused with previous convictions: they are in fact offences of a similar nature and seriousness, which the defendant has not been charged with, but is willing to admit to. The reason for this is that the procedure offers advantages to both sides: the police can close the relevant cases and not waste time and money investigating them, while the offender gets only a small increase in sentence, and avoids the risk of being investigated and convicted for those offences later.

TYPES OF SENTENCE

Sentences fall into seven main types:

- imprisonment;
- fines;
- community sentences;
- mental health orders;
- compensation and confiscation orders;
- binding over orders;
- absolute and conditional discharges.

Courts may also make Anti-Social Behaviour Orders (ASBOs) in criminal cases, but strictly speaking these are part of civil law and not criminal sentences.

Imprisonment

A sentence of imprisonment (also known as a custodial sentence) is viewed as the most serious punishment a court can impose. Where the defendant has been tried in the magistrates' court and the magistrates feel imprisonment is appropriate, they can only sentence up to six months for one offence, or 12 months for two or more. If the case requires a longer sentence, the magistrates will commit the defendant to the Crown Court for sentencing. If a defendant has not been in prison before, a sentence of imprisonment can only be imposed if they were represented by a lawyer in court (or were offered the chance to be and refused). Sentences usually run from the time they are stated in court, so a defendant who is sentenced to imprisonment will be taken there from the court. However, if they have been remanded into custody up until the trial, the time spent 'on remand' will be subtracted from their sentence; this can mean that some defendants sentenced to imprisonment walk free from the court.

Length of sentence

The length of a prison sentence may be fixed by law, or decided by the judge, according to a tariff system.

Fixed sentences: Only a small number of offences have fixed prison sentences (the most notable being murder, which carries a mandatory sentence of life imprisonment). There are also a few offences which carry minimum sentences in particular circumstances – for example, a third conviction for a class A drug trafficking offence attracts a minimum sentence of at least seven years' imprisonment, unless the court believes this would be unjust.

Tariff sentences: For most offences the law only lays down a maximum sentence. This gives judges and magistrates discretion to match the sentence to the seriousness of each case, but they are usually guided by what is called a tariff system. This is not a rigid scale of punishments, but a guideline as to the type and seriousness of penalties that would usually be applied for a particular offence; it is informed by guidance produced from time to time by the Court of Appeal.

When deciding a sentence, judges and magistrates use the tariff as a starting point, and then consider factors about the actual case which might suggest a more lenient sentence than that of the tariff (such as previous good character, or efforts to help the police or compensate the victim). Where there are aggravating factors which might suggest a harsher sentence than the tariff would be appropriate, the Court of Appeal has directed that courts should ignore mitigating factors and so not reduce the tariff sentence, rather than increasing it as a result of the aggravating factors.

The Criminal Justice Act 2003 introduced new rules covering cases where a short prison sentence (under 12 months) would previously have been considered appropriate. In these cases, a defendant should now be sentenced to what is called 'custody plus': up to three months in prison, followed by at least six months' supervision in the community. The court can attach conditions to the supervised period which are designed to keep the person from offending again: they may, for example, be required to do community work, get treatment for any problems which played a part in the offending or submit to a curfew. The 2003 Act also introduces intermittent custody, where, typically, offenders are allowed out of prison during the day, but must go back at night and/or during the weekends; the idea is to prevent the loss of employment or training, and the family break-ups, which can push offenders further into criminal behaviour. At the moment though, few facilities exist to allow this type of sentence.

Life sentences

Despite the name, a life sentence does not always (or even often) mean that the offender will go to prison until they die; most are released at some point. In the past, the Home Secretary made the final decision on when (or if) a person sentenced to life should be released, but in *R v Anderson* (2002), it was found to be against the European Convention on Human Rights for a politician to play this role. The Criminal Justice Act 2003 now requires the trial judge to put an offender sentenced to life for murder into one of three categories: those who have committed the most serious crimes (such as serial killers and terrorist murderers), who should stay in prison for the whole of their lives; those who should serve at least 30 years, a category likely to include murderers with sexual, racial or religious motives, or killers of police or prison officers; and the rest, who should serve at least 15 years. Once the specified minimum term has expired, the Parole Board can consider whether the person should be released, and can order this when the appropriate time comes.

Consecutive and concurrent sentences

Where a defendant has been found guilty of more than one offence, and receives more than one custodial sentence, these can be ordered to run consecutively or concurrently:

- Concurrent sentences all start at the same time, which effectively means that the defendant only stays in custody for the length of the longest one.
- Consecutive sentences run one after the other.

Suspended and deferred sentences

Custodial sentences may also be suspended for a particular period. This means that the defendant does not have to go to prison unless, during that period, they commit a further offence for which a prison sentence could be imposed. A new type of suspended sentence called 'custody minus' was introduced in the Criminal Justice Act 2003, which combines a suspended prison sentence with a period of supervision in the community, effective immediately. If you are reporting a court case where the sentence is suspended, you should always mention this in the story, and a defendant given a suspended sentence should not be referred to as being 'jailed'.

The courts can also defer passing a sentence for up to six months, where this is in the interests of justice, and the offender consents. This power is intended for use in cases where a court has reason to believe that an offender's circumstances are likely to change in the near future, with the result that no punishment will be necessary, or the appropriate punishment will become less severe; it might be used, for example, where during the deferral period the offender makes reparation to the victim, settles down to steady employment, or otherwise shows that they have changed for the better.

■ Fines

Fines can be imposed for almost any offence (unless there is a mandatory sentence of imprisonment, as for murder, for example). Where an offence is defined in statute, the maximim fine that can be imposed will be stated, otherwise it is for the court to decide. In that case, magistrates can only impose fines of up to £5,000, but in the Crown Court there is no limit. When deciding on an appropriate fine, the court must take into account the defendant's financial situation.

■ Community sentences

Defendants aged 16 or over can be given a community order, which is essentially a period of supervision in the community. Depending on the offence committed, and the offender's circumstances, conditions will normally be attached to the order: the offender can be required to do community work, get treatment for problems such as drug addiction, obey a curfew, live in a particular place and/or abstain from specified activities. Offenders under 25 may also be ordered to spend a certain number of hours at an attendance centre, where they take part in activities designed to help them avoid re-offending, such as anger management courses and employment skills training.

■ Mental health orders

Under the Mental Health Act 1983, courts can order the detention in hospital of defendants convicted of an imprisonable offence, who have a mental disorder of a type and seriousness which makes detention for treatment appropriate. They can only do this if this kind of detention is the most appropriate way to deal with the offender.

■ Compensation and confiscation orders

An offender who has physically injured someone, or caused loss or damage, can be ordered to pay compensation of up to £1,000 by a magistrates' court, and an unlimited amount if sentenced by the Crown Court. The courts can also order stolen property to be given back to its owner, or for the offender to pay back some or all of its value. Motor vehicles used for the purposes of theft can be confiscated. These orders can be made in addition to other punishments.

■ Binding over orders

The binding over order has been used since the fourteenth century, and is a way of dealing with people who are charged with minor violent offences, or breach of the peace, which essentially means behaviour which is either violent, or likely to provoke violence. It involves the defendant promising to 'be of a good behaviour' (in practice, this essentially means not doing anything that could get them arrested) for a certain period, usually a year. In most cases they will be bound over for a particular sum of money, and will have to pay that sum if they break the binding over order.

Binding over orders are sometimes given after a defendant has been found guilty of a minor offence but, in many cases, the offer of a binding over order may be made before the trial; if the defendant accepts, the charge may be dropped and no trial held. Where this happens, there is no criminal conviction, so it is important not to report the binding over as a sentence.

Absolute and conditional discharges

If a defendant is given a conditional discharge, they are free to go with no penalty – but if they commit another offence during the period which the court specifies, they can then be sentenced again for the original offence as well as the further one. This should not be confused with an absolute discharge, which is given when the magistrates or judge consider that, in the circumstances, the defendant's conduct, though against the law, does not deserve punishment. In this case the defendant is free to go without any conditions.

Anti-social behaviour orders (ASBOs)

ASBOs are civil orders issued by a court to protect the public from violent or disruptive behaviour, and in suitable cases they can be ordered by a criminal court. The Crime and Disorder Act 1998 provides that ASBOs can be issued against anyone over ten who has behaved in such a way as to cause harassment, alarm or distress to someone who they do not live with, and is likely to do so again. The ASBO may prohibit the problematic behaviour, and/or anything likely to lead to it: for example, a woman who received an ASBO for harassing local police officers was banned from going near the local police station. Although an ASBO is a civil order, breaching it can result in criminal penalties, such as a fine or imprisonment.

APPEALS AND RE-TRIALS

The end of a trial is not always the end of the case: in some circumstances, a defendant who has been acquitted may be re-tried, and there is also a system of appeals where one side or the other believes the court has made the wrong decision, or the case has not been properly conducted.

Appeals by the defendant

A defendant who has pleaded not guilty, and believes they have been wrongly convicted, can appeal to a higher court to re-examine the case. A convicted defendant can also appeal against a sentence which is alleged to be too harsh; this right exists whether the defendant pleaded guilty or not guilty.

The route through the appeals system depends on where the original case was heard.

From magistrates' courts

There are four routes of appeal from the magistrates' courts.

To the High Court, by way of 'case stated': If the defence believes the magistrates have made a mistake about the law, or acted outside their powers, the magistrates can be asked to 'state the case' to the Queen's Bench Division of the High Court. The Queen's Bench Division can confirm, reverse or vary the verdict, or order the case to be retried by different magistrates. Magistrates can refuse to state the case where the application is judged to be frivolous. If not satisfied with the result of the High Court hearing, the original defendant (now known as the appellant) can make a further appeal straight to the House of Lords, if the Divisional Court agrees that the case involves a point of law that is of public importance, and either this court or the House of Lords gives permission for a further appeal. It is important to note that the case stated procedure is only for possible mistakes about the law, or the way the magistrates handled the case; it is not used where the defendant simply believes the wrong verdict was reached.

To the Crown Court: A defendant who has pleaded not guilty can appeal to the Crown Court, on the grounds that they have been wrongly convicted, and/or too harshly sentenced. A defendant who has pleaded guilty can only appeal against the sentence, not the conviction itself. The appeal must be made within 28 days. The case will be reheard in the Crown Court by a circuit judge and two to four magistrates (not those who sat in the original case), who can either confirm the original verdict and/or sentence, or reverse the verdict, and/or alter the sentence. The Crown Court can impose any sentence which the magistrates' court could have imposed, which can sometimes mean that an appeal actually results in a higher sentence. If either side believes the appeal decision is wrong on a point of law, the case can then go to the High Court, by way of case stated, as above.

Referral by the Criminal Cases Review Commission: This is an independent body set up to review cases which may involve miscarriages of justice. Where a case has failed an original appeal (or one was not made in time), and new evidence comes to light which makes it likely that the conviction was wrong, the Criminal Cases Review Commission can refer it to the Crown Court for another hearing.

Magistrates' error: Where the magistrates accept that they have made an error (e.g. in applying the law), the Criminal Appeals Act allows them to reopen the case, and where it is in the interests of justice, have it reheard by a different set of magistrates. They can also use this power to vary a sentence.

From the Crown Court

There are three types of appeal from cases originally heard in the Crown Court.

To the Court of Appeal: A defendant who believes the Crown Court reached the wrong verdict on the facts, applied the law wrongly, or passed a sentence that was obviously too severe, can appeal to the Court of Appeal, but only with permission from the trial judge or the Court of Appeal. The Court of Appeal does not rehear the whole case, but reassesses the evidence that was given, and if necessary, any new evidence. It can confirm the conviction, quash it or order a retrial, and can also reduce a sentence (but not increase it). Where a case was heard in the magistrates' court but sent to the Crown Court for sentencing, and a sentence of over six months' imprisonment is imposed, the defendant can appeal against the sentence to the Court of Appeal. If either side believes the appeal decision is wrong on a point of law, the case can be appealed to the House of Lords, if the Court of Appeal or the House of Lords gives permission, and the House of Lords certifies that the case involves a point of law of public importance.

Referral by the Criminal Cases Review Commission: As for appeals from the magistrates' courts, above.

By case stated: As explained above.

▨ Retrials and appeals against acquittal

In the past, it was considered a general rule that once a person had been acquitted, the decision was final, and they could not be retried later for the same offence; this was known as the rule against double jeopardy. There were always some exceptions to this rule, but it has now been officially abolished under the Criminal Justice Act 2003, which allows an acquitted defendant to be retried if compelling new evidence is found. There are now several ways in which an acquittal can be reversed, a sentence increased or a retrial ordered.

Witness intimidation

Under the Criminal Procedure and Investigations Act 1996, where a defendant has been acquitted, but witnesses or jurors have been intimidated (meaning threatened or otherwise improperly persuaded to acquit), the High Court can quash the acquittal, and order the defendant to be retried. This power can only be used where someone has been convicted of interfering with a witness and/or juror, and where the court which held the original trial agrees that the acquittal would not have happened if the interference with witnesses or jurors had not taken place. (Judges can also stop a trial if, while it is taking place, it is discovered that jurors or witnesses have been interfered with, or can discharge the jury and order that the trail continues without them.)

New evidence

If, after someone has been acquitted, compelling new evidence comes to light, s75 of the Criminal Justice Act 2003 allows the Director of Public Prosecutions (DPP) to authorise an application to the Court of Appeal, which, after assessing the new evidence, can quash the acquittal and order a retrial. The DPP should only allow an application to the Court of Appeal where the new evidence is reliable, substantial and provides a high degree of proof, and the DPP must also consider whether a retrial would be in the interests of justice, taking into account the length of time which has elapsed since the original trial and the likelihood of a new trial being fair. At the time of going to press, this power had been used only once.

Appeals by way of case stated

Where the prosecution believes an acquittal is the result of a court making a mistake about the law, it can appeal to the High Court by way of case stated (see above).

Appeals from the Court of Appeal

If a case reaches the Court of Appeal, and the prosecution believes the appeal decision is wrong on a point of law, it can appeal to the House of Lords, if the Court of Appeal or the House of Lords gives permission, and the House of Lords certifies that the case involves a point of law of public importance.

Sentence review

For some more serious offences, the Criminal Justice Act 2003 allows the Attorney-General to ask the Court of Appeal to review a sentence passed by the Crown Court, which they believe is unduly lenient. The Court of Appeal can quash the sentence and pass a more appropriate one.

Stopped trials

Where a judge stops a trial part-way through (e.g. if they believe there is insufficient evidence to support a conviction), the prosecution can appeal against this decision to the Court of Appeal.

Figure 3.1 **Routes for criminal appeals**

In addition, where a person has been acquitted and the case involved a dispute over a point of law, the Criminal Justice Act 1972 allows the Attorney-General to refer the case to the Court of Appeal for its opinion on the legal point (in order to clarify it for future cases). However, this is not strictly speaking an appeal, as the defendant's acquittal cannot be quashed under this provision, and they are not required to appear before the court again.

The routes for criminal appeals are summarised in Figure 3.1.

COMMON CRIMES

Although a journalist does not need the same detailed knowledge of particular crimes as a lawyer would, it is important to understand the basics of the most common offences, and to be able to distinguish between them. In everyday language, for example, the terms 'robber' and 'thief' are virtually interchangeable, but in legal terms, robbery is a much more serious offence than theft, because it involves violence as well as dishonesty. Calling someone a robber when they have actually been convicted of theft could potentially land you in trouble for libel.

Before we look at the definitions of some common (or rather, commonly reported) offences, it may help to know that the legal definition of a crime is made up of two parts: the criminal act, known as the *actus reus*, which is what the offender must do in order to have committed the crime; and the mental element or *mens rea*, which is the mental state with which they did that act. For example, the *actus reus* of most homicide offences is the unlawful killing of another person, but whether such killing amounts to murder or manslaughter can depend on whether the killer acted intentionally or not.

An exception to this rule is what are known as strict liability offences. For these, the defendant need only have committed the relevant criminal act; the prosecution does not have to prove that they intended to do it, or even that they were at fault in any way. Some driving offences carry strict liability, and so do many of the laws which are used to regulate industry, such as those on safety at work, and food hygiene.

▧ Homicide offences

Homicide means the killing of a human being. As well as the most serious homicide offence, murder, there are two types of manslaughter, voluntary and involuntary, and a fourth offence, infanticide.

Murder is defined as the unlawful killing of another human being 'with malice aforethought'. The old-fashioned term 'malice aforethought' essentially means an intention to kill or cause very serious bodily harm. It has nothing to do with malice as we usually understand it – it is the degree of deliberateness that is legally relevant, not the reason for acting. So, in law, deliberate euthanasia performed in order to free a loved one from suffering conforms to the definition of malice aforethought as effectively as shooting someone because you hate them.

Voluntary manslaughter takes place where a defendant kills someone unlawfully, with malice aforethought, but there are mitigating circumstances which reduce their liability from murder to manslaughter. As a result it is not possible to charge someone with involuntary manslaughter; they are charged with murder, and must then put their defence at trial. If the defence succeeds, they can be convicted of manslaughter instead of murder. The three defences which can reduce murder to manslaughter are provocation, diminished responsibility and suicide pact:

- Provocation is defined as occurring where someone was provoked, by something said or done, to lose their self-control, and the provocation would have been sufficient to make any reasonable person in that position act as the defendant did. The essence of the defence is that because the provocation makes the defendant lose self-control, they cannot be said to be acting intentionally. It has been used – with some controversy – in cases where women have been killed by their husbands because they nagged them, and also in cases where women have killed their husbands after a history of domestic violence.

- Diminished responsibility applies where a defendant is suffering an 'abnormality of mind' which affects their mental responsibility for their behaviour. Medical evidence has to be put forward in such cases.

- Suicide pact applies where two people agree they will both commit suicide, and one helps the other to die (and, obviously, survives). Without a suicide pact, helping someone to commit suicide can be murder, but if there is a suicide pact, liability is reduced to manslaughter.

(Note that the above are only defences to murder, not to any other crimes.)

Involuntary manslaughter is committed when the defendant has unlawfully killed another, but without malice aforethought. This covers cases where death has been caused by gross negligence, or where the defendant commits a crime which results in the victim's death, even if they did not intend to kill.

Note that although involuntary and voluntary manslaughter are terms used in legal textbooks, when reporting cases, it is usual simply to say manslaughter, whichever type is meant (though remember that if the case is one of voluntary manslaughter, the initial charge will be murder).

Infanticide is a charge which can be used instead of murder or manslaughter in cases where a mother kills her child when it is under 12 months old, while her mind is disturbed.

■ Assaults

There is a legal hierarchy of assault charges, depending on the degree of harm done to the victim, and the state of mind of the defendant.

Wounding with intent and causing grievous bodily harm (GBH) with intent are the most serious physical assaults, carrying a maximum sentence of life imprisonment. They are committed when a defendant causes serious harm, including psychiatric as well as physical harm, or wounds the victim, which technically covers any injury that breaks the skin. The defendant must either intend to cause some physical harm or be reckless about doing so. The offence is contained in s18 of the Offences Against the Person Act 1861.

Malicious wounding and inflicting GBH are committed by inflicting serious harm or wounding. They carry a maximum sentence of five years. The offence is contained in s20 of the Offences Against the Person Act 1861.

Assault occasioning actual bodily harm (ABH) is committed where an assault causes some degree of harm that is more than merely trivial. The offence is contained in s47 of the Offences Against the Person Act 1861.

Common assault is the usual charge for the least serious physical assaults. CPS guidelines say that this should usually be the charge where injuries are limited to cuts, grazes, bruising or a black eye. It is contained in s39 of the Criminal Justice Act 1988.

■ Sexual offences against adults

Most sexual offences are now defined by the Sexual Offences Act 2003, which updated the law on rape, and created some new offences.

Rape is now defined as being committed when a man intentionally penetrates the vagina, anus or mouth of another person, with his penis, where that person does not consent to the penetration and the defendant does not reasonably believe that the person consents. Rape can be committed against a woman or a man; only a man can be charged with committing rape, but a woman can be charged as an accomplice. Any intentional vaginal, oral or anal penetration of a child under 13 is classified as rape; there is no question of consent in such cases.

Assault by penetration is committed by penetrating the vagina, anus or mouth of another person, with a part of the body other than the penis, or with any other object, where that person does not consent to the penetration and the defendant does not reasonably believe that the person consents. Again, if the victim is under 13, the intentional act is sufficient; consent is not an issue.

Sexual assault is committed by any intentional touching that is sexual, where the victim does not consent and the person touching them does not reasonably believe that they consent.

Sexual offences against children

The Sexual Offences Act 2003 provides that if, in the case of rape, assault by penetration or sexual assault, the victim is under 13, then doing the specified act (e.g. intentional penetration by the penis) is enough to lead to a conviction, and consent or lack of it is irrelevant. In addition, the Act defines a number of sexual offences which can only be committed against children, including the following:

- **Causing or inciting a child under 13 to commit sexual activity** is committed by inciting or causing someone under 13 to engage in a sexual activity.

- **Causing or inciting a child to commit sexual activity** is committed when someone over 18 incites or causes someone to engage in a sexual activity, and either the victim is under 13, or is under 16, and the defendant did not reasonably believe that person was at least 16.

- **Sexual activity with a child** is committed when someone over 18 touches someone who is under 13 sexually, or touches someone under 16 sexually, and does not reasonably believe that that person is at least 16.

Theft and fraud

This group of offences includes burglary, and a range of offences where money or other benefits are obtained by deception.

Theft is legally defined as the dishonest appropriation of property belonging to another, with the intention of permanently depriving the other of it. In most cases 'appropriation' simply means taking, but it can also cover doing anything with property that only the owner has the right to do. Theft may be described as stealing, but should not be referred to as robbery, which is a more serious offence.

Robbery is committed where a defendant commits theft, as defined above, using force or the threat of force.

Burglary is defined as entering a building as a trespasser (which essentially means without permission to be there), and stealing or attempting to steal, or inflicting or attempting to inflict GBH. Burglary can also be committed by entering as a trespasser with the intention to steal, inflict GBH, commit rape or do unlawful damage.

Aggravated burglary means committing burglary, as defined above, while armed.

Obtaining property by deception is effectively what is commonly known as fraud (and can be described as such in print). It covers, for example, using stolen or fake cheques or credit cards.

Obtaining services by deception covers frauds where the defendant obtains a service rather than tangible property – an example would be paying a hotel bill with a stolen credit card.

Obtaining a pecuniary advantage by deception relates to specific benefits that can be gained by deception, but are not covered by the previous two offences. It is committed when the defendant uses deception to: get an overdraft; take out insurance or an annuity; get a paid job or a pay rise; or win money by betting.

Making off without payment essentially covers what might be more colloquially known as 'doing a runner' – leaving a hotel, restaurant or garage, for example, without paying.

Handling covers dishonestly receiving or assisting in the disposal of stolen goods, knowing or believing them to be stolen. It is a widely-drawn offence and covers not only keeping or selling stolen goods, but doing almost anything else with them.

Law in practice Offering rewards

In high-profile cases, rewards may be offered for information leading to a conviction, and there is no problem with reporting these (in fact often it is the press that puts up the reward). However, s23 of the Theft Act 1968 states that it is an offence to offer a reward for the return of stolen goods where the implication of the offer is 'no questions asked'. This has been held to cover reports of such an offer being made, even though the offer was not made by the newspaper itself.

■ Offences related to motor vehicles

Taking without owner's consent is an offence which was created to deal with the problem of 'joyriders'. Because, as we have seen, theft requires an intention permanently to deprive the owner of their property, it was difficult to apply to joyriders, who usually abandon cars rather than keeping them, which means they are often found and returned to their owners. Therefore, this offence (often referred to as a 'TWOC') was created and is committed when someone takes a vehicle without the owner's consent. It applies to passengers as well as the driver. Although contained in the Theft Act 1968, it is not technically a form of theft, because there is no intention to deprive the owner of their property permanently, so defendants should never be referred to as 'stealing' a car, though 'taking a car' is fine. There is also a more serious version of this offence, usually called aggravated taking without consent, which applies where, for example, the defendant drives dangerously, injures someone or damages property.

Careless driving covers driving which is below the standard to be expected of a reasonable, prudent, competent driver in all the circumstances of the particular case.

Dangerous driving is committed where a driver falls considerably below the standard of driving expected of a competent and careful driver, and it would be obvious to a competent and careful driver that driving in that way would be dangerous.

Causing death by dangerous driving is committed where a defendant drives dangerously, as defined above, and as a result, causes someone's death.

Being in charge of a vehicle while unfit applies when someone is unfit to drive due to drink or drugs, and though they are not actually driving a vehicle when caught, the court believes they intended to drive (an example might be where someone is sitting in the driving seat while the car is stationary). There is a defence if it can be proved they were not intending to drive.

Driving with excess alcohol is committed when a person drives with a blood alcohol level that exceeds the legal limit.

Causing death by careless driving when under the influence of drink applies when a driver is over the blood alcohol limit and someone is killed as a result.

Driving under the influence of drugs is committed if a peron's driving is impaired by drugs; police carry out a five-point test to check this, followed by medical tests such as blood samples.

Failure to provide a specimen is committed by refusing to be tested for alcohol when asked, either at the roadside or at the police station.

Driving without insurance is self-explanatory; it is also an offence to lend a car to someone who is not insured.

CHAPTER SUMMARY

Criminal courts

Cases are heard by either the magistrates' courts or the Crown Court, depending on whether the offence is:

- indictable,
- either way, or
- summary.

Criminal procedure

A criminal case goes through the following stages:

- investigation,
- bail,
- prosecution,
- pre-trial hearings,
- trial.

Sentencing

The range of sentences includes:

- imprisonment;
- fines;
- community sentences;
- mental health orders;
- compensation and confiscation orders;
- binding over;
- absolute or conditional discharge.

ASBOs can also be ordered in criminal cases.

Appeals

Criminal appeals can go:

- to the High Court by 'case stated';
- to the Criminal Cases Review Commission;
- from magistrates' court to Crown Court or Crown Court to Court of Appeal.

Magistrates can also reopen a case to correct an error.

Acquitted defendants can be retried if:

■ compelling new evidence surfaces; or

■ witness intimidation taints the original trial.

Common crimes

Commonly-reported crimes include:

■ **homicide offences:** murder, manslaughter, infanticide;

■ **assaults:** wounding with intent, causing GBH with intent, malicious wounding and inflicting GBH, Assault occasioning ABH, common assault;

■ **sexual offences against adults:** rape, assault by penetration, sexual assault;

■ **sexual offences against children:** causing or inciting a child under 13 to commit sexual activity, causing or inciting a child to commit sexual activity, sexual activity with a child;

■ **theft and fraud offences:** theft, robbery, burglary, aggravated burglary, obtaining property, services or pecuniary advantage by deception, making off without payment, handling;

■ **offences related to motor vehicles:** taking without owner's consent, careless driving, dangerous driving, causing death by dangerous driving, being in charge of a vehicle while unfit, driving with excess alcohol, causing death by careless driving while under the influence of drink, driving under the influence of drugs, failure to provide a specimen, driving without insurance.

3

Criminal courts and procedure

TEST YOUR KNOWLEDGE

1 What is the maximum sentence a magistrates' court can impose?

2 Describe the role of the clerk to the justices.

3 Who decides the sentence for a defendant convicted in the Crown Court?

4 What are the three types of criminal offences?

5 What does 'detained for questioning' mean in legal terms?

6 What is an arrestable offence?

7 How long can the police detain a suspect before charging them?

8 Who can grant bail?

9 In what circumstances should a magistrate refuse bail to a suspect with no previous convictions?

10 Who decides whether a suspect should be prosecuted?

11 Describe the course of events in a criminal trial.

12 What are the effects on a tariff sentence of mitigating and aggravating factors?

13 Which of the following could lead to a defendant ending up in prison?

  (a) a suspended sentence

  (b) a conditional discharge

  (c) an absolute discharge.

14 When can evidence of previous convictions be used in court?

15 What is the legal definition of murder?

16 Which of these phrases is inaccurate?

  (a) John Smith was charged with murder.

  (b) John Smith was charged with manslaughter, on grounds of diminished responsibility.

  (c) John Smith was charged with diminished responsibility.

  (d) John Smith was charged with manslaughter.

17 What is the legal definition of rape?

18 What is the legal definition of theft?

19 John Smith is a pickpocket who has recently been convicted in your local court. Which of these terms can you use to describe him?

  (a) pickpocket

  (b) thief

  (c) robber.

20 A man is convicted of careless driving, but you describe the offence as dangerous driving. Why might this be a problem?

ONLINE RESOURCES

www

The Criminal Prosecution Service website carries information about the work of the CPS, and press releases about newsworthy cases:
www.cps.gov.uk

The Home Office website has information on crime and the criminal justice system, at:
www.homeoffice.gov.uk

The Government's Sentencing Guidelines website has information on sentences and sentencing policy, at:
www.sentencing-guidelines.gov.uk

For further resources and updates please go to the Companion Website for this book at www.pearsoned.co.uk/practicaljournalism

Chapter
4

Civil courts and procedure

The civil legal system handles all non-criminal cases, a vast category that covers everything from commercial disputes between companies, to divorce cases and care proceedings, or claims for medical negligence, personal injury, libel or trespass, and much more. In this chapter we look at how the civil system works in some of the types of case journalists are most likely to come across (two specialist types of civil case, inquests and insolvency proceedings, are dealt with in Chapters 11 and 26).

At the end of this chapter, you will find definitions of some of the most common civil claims; those which specifically affect the media, such as defamation and breach of confidence, are explained in detail in their own chapters.

THE CIVIL COURTS

The main civil courts are the High Court and the county courts; magistrates' courts also hear some types of civil case (e.g. family proceedings, which decide issues such as contact with children and maintenance payments when couples split up). The vast majority of civil cases are decided by judges or magistrates; juries can only be used in cases of defamation, malicious prosecution, false imprisonment and fraud (and are not always used in these cases).

The High Court

People often refer to the Royal Courts of Justice on the Strand in London as the High Court, but in fact the High Court (like the Crown Court) is not a building at all, but a single court which sits at different places. The Royal Courts of Justice are its administrative headquarters, but High Court hearings also take place in some of the larger county courts around the country. High Court cases are usually heard by High Court judges, either in London or when they go 'on circuit' around the country, but in some situations a circuit judge may hear a High Court case.

The High Court is made up of three divisions, which work separately, each with its own judges:

- **The Family Division** hears cases concerning marriage, children and families, such as divorce cases and disputes over wills.
- **The Chancery Division** deals mainly with disputes over money and property, such as tax cases, business disputes and bankruptcy.
- **The Queen's Bench Division** is the biggest division, and has the most varied caseload. It deals with specialist commercial and shipping cases, but the bulk of its work is hearing

breach of contract and tort cases. A tort is the civil law's version of a crime, but whereas a crime is a wrong against society as well as the individual victim, and is punished by the state, a tort is seen as a wrong against a specific person (or company), who can sue the wrongdoer for compensation (see the end of this chapter for definitions of some common torts). The High Court generally hears tort and contract cases involving claims of at least £15,000, or in cases where the claim is for personal injury, at least £50,000. The Queen's Bench Division also includes the Administrative Court, which deals with public law claims (see p. 12).

The county courts

There are 218 county courts spread across the country. They hear the majority of civil cases, comprising claims for debt repayment, some family cases, housing disputes and those tort and contract cases which are not heard in the High Court. Around 170 county courts are designated as divorce county courts and can hear undefended divorce cases and cases concerning adoption and guardianship.

Writing about civil litigation

There are several important things to be aware of when writing about these kinds of cases.

Terminology: The parties in civil litigation are called the claimant (who brings the case), and the defendant. The claimant sues the defendant, and if the claimant wins, the defendant is found liable (do not use 'guilty'). 'Torts' are the name given to civil wrongs for which the victim can claim damages, such as breach of contract, negligence, trespass or defamation (for more on terminology, see p. 12).

Standard of proof: In a criminal case, the prosecution must prove its case beyond reasonable doubt, but the standard of proof in the civil courts is lower. The claimant only has to prove their case 'on a balance of probabilities', which effectively means that they have to prove that there is a more than 50 per cent chance that the defendant committed the civil wrong they are claiming – or to put it another way, that it is more likely than not that the defendant is liable. This is why a person can be acquitted in a criminal case, yet be successfully sued for damages regarding exactly the same event, in the civil court.

Settlements: The vast majority of civil law disputes never actually get as far as the courts. Though the claimant may start legal proceedings, in most cases, the parties will agree a settlement between them before the case actually comes to court. While such settlements are legally binding, they are not the same thing as a decision by the court as to which party was in the right. For this reason, it is not correct to treat a story about a settlement as though it has implications for similar cases, or as an indication of what the law is on a particular issue. If a case is settled, the result of the case is a matter between the parties concerned, and not something which changes or even clarifies the law for future cases.

Costs: If a civil case goes to trial, the parties do not necessarily each pay their own costs. At the end of the case, the judge will make an order stating who should pay what.

Traditionally, the rule is that the loser pays the winner's costs (as well as any compensation ordered), and although some costs are incurred during the pre-trial preparation, costs escalate drastically once a case goes to court. This means that the threat of having to pay costs can be used as a weapon to try to get one side or the other to settle out of court, even if the offered amount is less than they would get if they won their case. This has always been a particular problem where, for example, the claimant is an ordinary individual and the defendant a wealthy company (as is the case in many personal injury cases, where the defendant is an insurance company). However, since 1990, solicitors have been allowed to work under what are called conditional fee agreements (sometimes known as 'no win, no fee'), which mean that if the client loses, they pay no fee (or sometimes a vastly reduced one), and if they win, the lawyer is paid a percentage over what the basic fee would have been. The solicitor arranges insurance to pay the other side's costs if the case is lost. In conditional fee cases, the financial pressure to settle is obviously much less; however, they tend only to be used in cases where the claimant has a very high chance of success.

4

Civil courts and procedure

CIVIL LITIGATION PROCEDURE

Civil litigation is the name given to most of the disputes handled by the civil legal system (others, covered later in this chapter, include family and divorce cases). This category covers all the cases where one individual (or organisation) sues another. These include, for example, businesses suing other businesses for unpaid debts or other breaches of contract; people injured in accidents or through medical negligence suing for compensation; landowners suing for trespass or nuisance; and of course, the media being sued for libel.

The processing of most types of case through the civil courts is laid down in the Civil Procedure Rules 1998 (often referred to as the CPR). Because civil cases are often lengthy and complex, they can also be very expensive. Successive governments have been keen to find ways to control costs, so the CPR give courts a duty to manage the progress of a case so that the parties are treated fairly but resources are allocated sensibly, and neither time nor costs are wasted.

Stage 1: making the claim

The majority of civil cases begin with the claimant filling in a claim form, which will explain the basis of their claim, and the remedy that they want (this is most often damages, but the courts can also issue a range of orders, for example stating that the other party must do something or stop doing something). The court then sends the claim form to the defendant; if the defendant wishes to fight the claim, they have 14 days to send the court details of their defence; if this is not enough time, they can send the court an 'acknowledgement of service', which extends the total time allowed to 28 days.

In some cases, the defendant does not bother to fight the claim, and if they do not file a defence, the claimant can ask the court to pass judgment 'in default', which means that judgment is made in their favour, without the need for a full trial (though there may still have to be a hearing in these cases to decide the amount of damages payable).

■ Stage 2: allocating the case

If a defence is filed, the court will then allocate the case to one of three 'tracks':

- **The small claims track** is the usual route for claims worth less than £5,000, which are dealt with at the county courts, but using a faster, simplified procedure which is designed to allow claimants to represent themselves rather than using lawyers. (Cases brought in this way are often described as being heard in the small claims court, but it is not in fact a separate court.) Cases for possession (e.g. where a tenant has not paid their rent) are not heard on the small claims track even if worth under £5,000.

- **The fast track** is for claims worth £5,000–£15,000 (or for personal injury claims, up to £50,000), which are usually heard by the county courts. Once a case is allocated to this track, the court gives directions for the management of the case, and sets a timetable for the pre-trial process and a date for the trial. Cases should be heard within 30 weeks, and the hearing should not last more than a day.

- **The multi-track** is for cases worth more than £50,000, or which are particularly complex. When a case is allocated to the multi-track, the court will issue case management instructions, and set a timetable for the required steps to to be taken, but because these cases are usually the more complex ones, it does not usually set a trial date at this stage. This is done as early as possible but there may be a case management conference or a pre-trial review to sort out certain matters or promote a negotiated settlement, in the meantime.

■ Stage 3: Pre-trial procedure

Whichever track a case is on, the parties will each put their claim into a statement of case: the claimant details the basis of the claim, and the defendant explains their defence to it. They will also exchange copies of documents and witness statements to be used in the case, so by the time the trial takes place, each side knows what evidence the other intends to put forward. Where a case involves technical or scientific details (e.g. medical evidence in personal injury cases), expert witnesses may be used; this can only be done with the court's permission. Expert witnesses have a legal duty to give evidence impartially, and as part of the court's duty to manage cases so that they do not waste time or money, the court will often insist that a single expert is used for both sides, rather than one each, unless the evidence is likely to be a matter of serious dispute between the parties.

Although this work is done as preparation for an eventual trial, the majority of civil claims never actually make it that far. Typically, the defendant will make an offer of compensation, and the claimant will either accept, or try to negotiate a higher figure. If they eventually agree, this is known as settling out of court, and ends the case (see the box above, *Writing about civil litigation*). It may be done at any time before the trial starts, and it is not unknown for cases to settle on the day planned for trial – this is often described as a case being settled at the door of the court.

■ Step 4: The trial

Fast-track and multi-track trials follow roughly the same procedure, but small claims track procedure is different, and much less formal.

Fast-track and multi-track cases usually involve lawyers for both sides, but this is not obligatory and a small number of people choose to conduct their cases themselves. A claimant who chooses to do this can ask another lay person (known as a Mackenzie friend), to give advice and help them with things like taking notes, but this person is not usually allowed to address the court directly.

Before the trial, the judge will have been given the 'trial bundle', a package of documents which details the legal arguments being put forward by each side, and includes written statements from witnesses and any other relevant documentation. The judge reads this before the case starts, so they are already familiar with the issues and evidence.

The claimant's witnesses are called first, and asked to confirm that the contents of their statements are true; they are not usually required to give the evidence again verbally, though the claimant's lawyer may ask some supplementary questions. Each witness is then cross-examined by the defendant's lawyer, and sometimes the judge will ask questions too. The same process is followed with the defence witnesses, and then the lawyers for each side address the judge, arguing their case on the basis of the evidence given and how they believe the law should be applied. In the few cases where there is a jury, the judge then sums up the case for jurors, and they retire to decide their verdict.

Where there is no jury, the judge may give judgment there and then, or may reserve judgment to a later date. In this case the judgment will be a written one, which can either be read out in court or 'handed down' (issued in writing). Accredited court reporters are usually given a copy of the judgment.

Finally, the judge will make an order dictating who should pay the costs of the trial (see the box, *Writing about civil litigation*).

Small claims track hearings take place before a district judge, often in the judge's office rather than a courtroom (though the hearing is still a public one) and the procedure is less formal than in the other courts, with less strict rules about what can and cannot be put forward in evidence. The idea is that claimants should be able to put their own case, without needing to use a lawyer, which means the procedure is less expensive. If they prefer, the claimant can ask another lay person, such as a friend, to put the case for them. The judge will often ask questions to try to establish the truth of what happened. Judgment is usually given there and then, and the judge must give reasons for their decision.

OTHER TYPES OF CIVIL PROCEEDINGS

■ Family proceedings

Hearings related to the care, custody, maintenance, paternity and adoption of children are known as family proceedings, and are held in the magistrates' courts, the county courts and the High Court (sometimes a court sitting in family proceedings will be referred to as a family court, even though it is not actually a separate court). The law covering these issues is contained in the Children Act 1989, which gives courts wide powers to protect the welfare of children. For the purposes of these hearings, the Civil Procedure Rules are replaced by the Family Proceedings Rules 1991.

In family proceedings, the person bringing the case is called the petitioner or the applicant, and the other side is called the respondent. Most cases are heard by magistrates or district judges (depending on the court), but the most serious or complex cases come before a circuit judge.

Family cases are normally heard in private, but reporters may attend some cases; either way, family proceedings are subject to strict reporting rules, which are explained in Section 2 later. Documents relating to the case are not usually open to inspection, with the exception of decrees or orders made in open court, and cannot be disclosed to anyone except the parties and their lawyers without permission from a judge.

Applications to marry from people aged 16–17 are also treated as family proceedings, though these are rare now because they are only needed where parents refuse permission for a marriage or civil partnership.

Divorce proceedings

Though most people believe that Britain allows divorce on demand, it is still officially the case that a court has to decide whether a couple should be allowed to divorce. Legally, divorce is only allowed if a court accepts that the marriage has irretrievably broken down, which has to be demonstrated in one of the following five ways: adultery, unreasonable behaviour, desertion, the parties having lived apart for two years (if both consent to the divorce) or five years (in which case consent is not necessary). In practice, where both parties consent (as is usually the case), there is little real chance of a court refusing a divorce.

Where the partners in a civil partnership wish to split up, the process is called dissolution, but the procedure is as for divorce.

The procedure

A divorce action begins when one partner (called the petitioner) fills in an official document called a petition, and files it with the court. A copy is sent to the other spouse (called the respondent), who is asked to say whether they will be defending (meaning opposing) the divorce. These days, it is difficult to prevent a divorce if the other spouse wants one, so it is fairly rare for a respondent to defend. If someone does, this is called a contested divorce and the dispute has to be heard and decided by a judge and this would usually take place in a county court.

If (as in the vast majority of cases) the divorce is uncontested, the papers go before a judge, who issues a date when the decree nisi will be made. This is a provisional decree of divorce, issued six weeks before the divorce becomes final, and is read out in court (usually in a list with others). Within 14 days of a decree nisi being issued, anyone can inspect it.

The final step is when the court issues the decree absolute (usually around six weeks later), which makes the divorce final, leaving the ex-partners free to remarry.

Rule 48 of the Matrimonial Causes Rules 1977 (SI 344) provides that within 14 days of a decree nisi being issued, anyone can see the certificate, and any affadavit or other supporting evidence. Copies can be issued, for a fee. The courts should supply any details which are not confidential, and are a matter of public record, such as the date of the marriage, names and addresses of the parties, and the order made by the court.

Other orders concerning marriage breakdown

There are three other orders which may be issued by a court:

- **Decree of nullity:** This is issued when the court rules that a marriage was not valid, usually because it has not been consummated, or because one or other party was forced into the marriage or was unable to give proper consent. A decree of nullity can also be issued where, unknown to the husband, the wife was pregnant by another man at the time of the marriage, or where either partner had a contagious venereal disease at the time of the marriage.
- **Decree of judicial separation:** This is granted on proof of the same facts which are necessary for a divorce, but it does not allow the spouses to marry other people. It is usually sought by people who see divorce as a stigma, or oppose it on religious grounds.

■ **Decree of presumption of death:** This is granted where one spouse has been absent for at least seven years, and reasonable efforts to trace them have been unsuccessful. It makes the remaining partner free to marry, and continues to apply even if the missing spouse later turns out to be alive.

Licensing

Pubs, restaurants and other businesses that sell alcohol, provide public entertainment, or offer late-night food must be licensed. Until recently, these licences were granted by local magistrates, but the Licensing Act 2003 changed this. Licences are now granted by local council committees, who can hear objections to the granting of a particular licence, for example from local residents.

Magistrates still retain a role in the licensing process, however, as the 2003 Act provides for appeals against licensing decisions to be made to the magistrates' courts. An applicant can appeal against refusal of a licence, or against any conditions which are placed on the issue of a licence, while anyone who has brought objections to a particular licence before the licensing committee can appeal if the committee decides to issue that licence.

Other civil proceedings before magistrates

Magistrates' courts also have powers to issue three important types of order.

Anti-social behaviour orders (ASBOs)

ASBOs are civil orders, issued by magistrates (see p. 30). An application for an ASBO can be made by local authorities, the police, British Transport Police, county councils, Registered Social Landlords and Housing Action Trusts, against anyone aged ten or over who has acted in a way that is likely to cause harassment, alarm or distress to someone who does not live in the same household as the person whose behaviour is in question.

Child safety orders

Where a person under ten has committed or risks committing an act which, had they been older, would be a criminal offence, or where they have breached a curfew notice, or behaved in an anti-social manner, the local authority can apply to magistrates for a child safety order, which requires the child to be at home at specified times, or to avoid certain people or places.

Sex offender orders

These orders compel convicted sex offenders to comply with directions from the court, such as obeying a curfew, or staying away from children.

APPEALS IN CIVIL CASES

As with the criminal legal system, there is a system of appeals from decisions made in the country courts and the High Court. All of the appeal routes (see Figure 4.1) can be used by either party in the case (assuming they get any necessary permission).

4

Civil courts and procedure

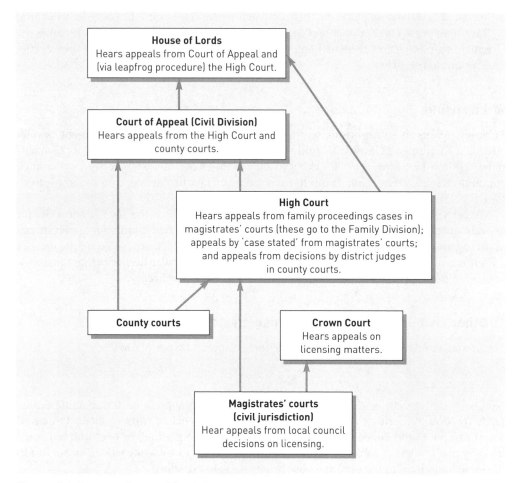

Figure 4.1 **Routes of appeal in civil cases**

▧ From the county courts

If either side believes the county court has wrongly judged the facts of a case or the application of the law, they can appeal to to the Civil Division of the Court of Appeal (unless the decision was made by a district judge; in this case appeals normally go first to a circuit judge and then to the High Court). The appeal hearing does not sit through all the evidence again, but examines the notes made by the trial judge and/or any documentary evidence that was presented. The appeal court can confirm or reverse the judgment, or vary the remedy given (e.g. increasing or decreasing the level of damages awarded).

From the Court of Appeal, either side can make a further appeal to the House of Lords, but only with permission from the Court of Appeal or (more usually) the House of Lords. This is not often granted.

▧ From the High Court

Cases which begin in the High Court can be appealed (by either side) to the Civil Division of the Court of Appeal, and as with appeals from the county court, the case is usually examined on paper rather than being heard again. From there, a further appeal can be made to the House of Lords, with permission from the Court of Appeal or the House of Lords.

There is also an additional appeal route, known as the 'leapfrog' procedure, by which a High Court case can go straight to the House of Lords, bypassing the Court of Appeal, where it concerns a matter on which the Court of Appeal would have to follow an earlier House of Lords precedent (which therefore makes the Court of Appeal stage a waste of time).

■ From the civil jurisdiction of magistrates' courts

Appeals concerning family proceedings go to the Family Division of the High Court, and further appeals from there to the Court of Appeal and then the House of Lords (with permission from the House of Lords). Appeals on licensing matters are heard by the Crown Court. Appeals concerning points of law can also be appealed using the 'case stated' procedure, explained at p. 30.

Law in practice Reporting appeals

It sometimes comes as a surprise to non-lawyers that judges can totally disagree about what a particular legal provision means, and how it should be applied. Interpretations often differ between different levels of the appeal system; it is not at all unusual, for example, for the Court of Appeal to declare that the law means one thing, and then for the House of Lords to state that it means the complete opposite (after all, if this was not the case, there would never be any point in appealing to a higher court).

Such disagreements can also happen between judges sitting in the same court. In the Court of Appeal, cases are usually heard by three judges, and in the House of Lords by at least five (sometimes as many as nine in very important cases). In some cases, one judge will give a fully-explained judgment, while the others will simply record that they agree with it, but there are cases where one judge (or more in a larger panel) may disagree, and produce a full written judgment explaining why. Because each judge will make it sound as though their interpretation is the only possible one, it is important to know which side of the fence a judge is on when you quote them, and point out if the judge you are quoting was in disagreement with the decision of the majority (this is known as 'dissenting'). Otherwise, it is easy to give a completely skewed idea of the verdict, which makes your report appear ill-informed.

■ Judicial review

Judicial review is a procedure which can be used to challenge decisions made or actions taken by most public bodies and officials, including the Government, local councils, the police, and the courts. Cases are heard by the Administrative Court, which is part of the Queen's Bench Division of the High Court.

Essentially, an application for judicial review alleges that the decision was unlawful, and so the focus is on the way in which the decision was made. Judicial review does not consider whether a decision was right or wrong, so it cannot be used as a form of appeal where an applicant simply believes the wrong decision was made. There are three basic ways in which a decision may be considered unlawful:

- **Illegality:** this applies, for example, where an authority has misunderstood the law, has acted in excess of its powers, or has refused to act because it (wrongly) believed it had no power to do so.

- **Irrationality:** a decision may be unlawful if it was 'so unreasonable that no reasonable authority could have made it'. This is often known as 'Wednesbury unreasonableness' after the name of the case which established the principle.

- **Unfairness:** this applies where the way in which the decision was made was unfair, for example if one side failed to get a fair hearing, or there was a possibility of prejudice for or against one side on the part of the decision maker.

If the High Court finds against the decision-making body, it can quash the decision made, and either make the decision itself, or ask the public body to consider the matter again, in the light of the court's views about the fairness of the process.

COMMON CIVIL CLAIMS

There is a vast number of possible claims under civil law, many of which are very specialised. However, there are some which come up more commonly and are often the basis of news stories, and it is worth having a basic idea of how these arise and are defined.

Breach of contract

A contract is a legal agreement between two parties; it need not be in writing. Every contract includes terms, which lay down what each of the parties is obliged to do. Sometimes these terms are agreed by the parties, but in many types of contract, the law provides that certain terms will be included, whether the parties agree to them or not. For example, when you buy something from a shop, you enter into a contract between you and the retailer, and the Sale and Supply of Goods Act 1994 states that it is a term of that contract that the thing you buy must be as described to you, and of satisfactory quality; if not, the seller is in breach of contract. Where one party breaches a contract term, the other party can sue for damages, and breach of contract cases include everything from small consumer disputes to claims worth millions of pounds concerning contracts made between companies.

Negligence

Negligence is the most important tort in modern law. To put it at its simplest, where someone is injured or caused loss by someone else's failure to take reasonable care, negligence law allows the injured person to sue for damages that will put them back in the position they would have enjoyed if this carelessness had not happened. (This is a very much simpler definition than most lawyers would give, and it is important to know that not every instance of carelessness amounts to negligence, and not every kind of loss will be compensated in a negligence action.) Typical claimants include people injured by substandard medical treatment or in accidents that are someone else's fault, but negligence can also, in some circumstances, compensate for psychological injury, financial loss and damage to property, and actions can be brought by companies as well as individuals. A key area of negligence law is personal injury, which covers cases where someone is injured, either physically or mentally, through another's negligence.

One important thing you should know about when reporting negligence cases is the role played by insurance. If, due to your carelessness, you run someone over in your car, it would be your insurance company who had to pay if the claim was successful; equally, if you hurt yourself at work and sue your employer, they would have insurance against this type of claim. In practice, most people or organisations sued in negligence are covered by insurance relating to the activity in question, and this can lead to what seem to be odd cases: for example, in *Hunt* v *Severs* (1994), the claimant was very seriously injured in a car accident caused by her fiancé, and sued him for damages, yet still married him. This seems less strange when you realise that he would have had car insurance, and so she was effectively suing the insurance company, and not her fiancé.

▓ Nuisance

This tort protects against unreasonable interference with a person's use of their land (whether they own or rent it). It covers, for example, cases where noise, dust, fumes or smells spread onto someone's land (or into their house) from neighbouring land; water leaking from one flat down into another; tree roots encroaching across a boundary; and even cricket balls escaping onto land adjacent to a sports ground.

▓ Trespass

Most people think of trespass as meaning entering land where you are not permitted to be, and trespass does include this. However, trespass to land is wider than that, and includes any unreasonable interference with someone else's land (e.g. throwing something on to it). In addition to trespass to land, there are torts of trespass against the person, which can be committed by any unlawful touching of the person; and trespass against property, which is committed by any unlawful touching or movement of someone else's property (though, in practice, most cases involve more than mere touching of either person or goods).

▓ CHAPTER SUMMARY

Civil courts

Civil cases are handled by:

- magistrates' courts,
- county courts,
- the High Court.

Civil procedure

Civil cases go through up to four stages:

- making the claim;
- allocating the case to a track;
- pre-trial procedure (possibly leading to settlement);
- trial.

Other types of civil proceedings

Other important civil proceedings are:

- family proceedings;
- licensing appeals;

- applications for ASBOs, child safety orders and sex offender orders;
- judicial review.

Appeals

- County court cases are appealed to the Court of Appeal.
- High Court cases go to the Court of Appeal, or by 'leapfrog' procedure straight to the House of Lords.
- Family proceedings appeals go to the Family Division of the High Court.
- Licensing appeals go to the Crown Court.

Common civil claims

- Breach of contract applies when someone breaks the terms of a contract.
- Negligence allows someone to sue if they are injured or caused loss by another's failure to take care.
- Nuisance protects against unreasonable interference with a person's use of their land.
- Trespass comprises any unreasonable interference with someone else's land, property or person.

TEST YOUR KNOWLEDGE

1 Which kinds of civil cases are decided by juries?

2 Name the three divisions of the High Court.

3 What are the parties in civil litigation called?

4 Explain the different standards of proof in criminal and civil cases.

5 Explain the terms 'decree nisi' and 'decree absolute'.

6 Who grants licences to pub landlords?

7 What is the 'leapfrog' procedure in the civil appeals system?

8 Where are claims worth less than £5,000 heard?

9 Explain the standard of proof in civil cases.

10 A local hairdresser has sued her employer after she claimed that the hairspray she used at work gave her asthma. She has settled out of court, with her employer agreeing to pay damages of £10,000. Which of these sentences can accurately be used in this story?

　　(a) Hairdressers can no longer be forced to use hairspray, after a local stylist who developed asthma through her work won her case against Curly Top hairdressers.

　　(b) Local stylist Sharon Crimper has won her case against Curly Top hairdressers.

(c) Curly Top hairdressers have been forced to pay a stylist damages of £10,000, after she developed asthma at work.

11 What are:

(a) ASBOs

(b) child safety orders

(c) sex offender orders?

12 What is judicial review?

13 On what grounds can judicial review disturb the decision of a public body?

ONLINE RESOURCES

www

The Courts Service website has information on the civil courts, at:
www.hmcourts-service.gov.uk

The Community Legal Service website has information on personal injury claims, at:
www.clsdirect.org.uk

The Children and Family Court Advisory and Support Service has information about family proceedings, at:
www.cafcass.org.uk

The Public Law Project has information on judicial review, at:
www.publiclawproject.org.uk

For further resources and updates please go to the Companion Website for this book at www.pearsoned.co.uk/practicaljournalism

Human rights and English law

As we saw in Chapter 1, the European Convention on Human Rights was incorporated into English law in the Human Rights Act 1998. Human rights is an important area of law for journalists, for two main reasons. Firstly, more and more legal cases are being brought under the provisions of human rights law, and many of these are will make the news. Secondly, several of the rights protected have a direct impact on laws which govern the work of journalists, the most important being the rights to freedom of expression, privacy and a fair trial.

THE EUROPEAN CONVENTION AND THE HUMAN RIGHTS ACT

The set of human rights which is protected in the UK today was originally laid down in the European Convention for the Protection of Human Rights and Fundamental Freedoms (better known as the European Convention on Human Rights), an international treaty that was drawn up in 1950. It was a reaction to the horrors of the Second World War, and aimed to secure for the people of Europe a set of basic rights, which all countries who signed up to the treaty would respect. A special court, the European Court of Human Rights (ECHR), was set up to deal with claims that countries (or their official organisations) had breached the provisions of the Convention. (The ECHR is not the same thing as the EU court, which is called the European Court of Justice – see p. 8.)

There are now 45 countries which have signed up to the Convention. The UK has been a signatory since 1953, but the protection it offers to people in this country was greatly strengthened when the Human Rights Act 1998 was passed. This incorporated the Convention into UK law, which had several important effects.

Breaches of the Convention: The provisions of the Convention are now applicable in UK courts, so anyone whose rights have been breached can bring their case in the UK courts, instead of going to the court in Strasbourg, as they would have had to do before the Act was passed. Individuals can still takes cases to Strasbourg if they are not satisfied that the UK courts have correctly applied the Convention provision, but they must take any legal action that is available through the UK courts first.

Interpretation of legislation: As we saw in Chapter 1, the courts often have to interpret legislation in order to work out how it should apply in a particular case (see p. 6). The Human Rights Act provides that UK courts should, as far as possible, interpret all UK legislation in a way which is compatible with the rights detailed in the Convention, so if there are two ways of interpreting a particular statutory provision, courts must choose the one that conforms to the Convention. Where a statute is clearly in conflict with the Convention, the courts cannot refuse to apply the statute, but they can make a declaration that there is a conflict, and when that happens, the Government can (but does not have to) use a fast-track procedure to amend the domestic legislation to bring it into line with the Convention.

Effect on public bodies: The Act makes it unlawful for any public body to act in a way that is incompatible with the rights provided by the Convention, and an individual whose Convention rights have been violated by a public body can bring an action against the body concerned. Public bodies definitely include national and local government, the courts, and organisations which are obviously 'public', such as the NHS and the police, but there is still some debate over how far the definition extends beyond these.

Precedent: A UK court deciding questions connected with a Convention right must take into account any decision of the ECHR on that issue. As we saw in Chapter 1, decisions made by the higher courts form precedents that build up into the body of case law. This is equally the case for decisions involving Convention rights, so over time, case law will increasingly come to show the influence of human rights law.

New legislation: When passing new legislation (since 1998), the relevant Minister has to make a statement saying whether or not the new law is compatible with the Convention (so although new law does not have to be compatible, attention will be drawn to any provisions that are not).

■ Protected rights

The original Convention lists 12 basic rights and freedoms which are to be protected, and three more were added in 1952 by an additional document called the First Protocol. The rights protected are:

- right to life (Article 2);
- freedom from torture, inhuman or degrading treatment (Article 3);
- freedom from slavery and forced labour (Article 4);
- right to liberty and security of the person (Article 5);
- right to a fair trial (Article 6);
- freedom from unlawful punishment (Article 7);
- right to respect for private and family life (Article 8);
- freedom of thought, conscience and religion (Article 9);
- freedom of expression (Article 10);
- freedom of assembly and association (Article 11);
- right to marry and found a family (Article 12);
- right to peaceful enjoyment of possessions (Article 1, First Protocol);
- right to education (Article 2, First Protocol);
- right to take part in free elections by secret ballot (Article 3, First Protocol).

The Convention also provides that people are entitled to enjoy these rights without discrimination on any ground such as sex, race, colour, language, religion, political or other opinion, national or social origin, association with a national minority, property, birth or other status.

A few of the rights are protected absolutely, which means that any breach of them, whatever the circumstances, is a breach of the Convention; an example is the right to freedom from torture, protected by Article 3. However, most of the rights are subject to what are called derogations, which means the Convention allows them to be restricted in certain important circumstances. For example, Article 8 provides that the right to respect for private and family life can be subject to such restrictions as are 'necessary in a democratic society in the interests of national security, public safety or the economic well-being of the country, for the prevention of disorder or crime, for the protection of health or morals, or for the protection of the rights and freedoms of others.' Even Article 2, the right to life, can be restricted in certain situations, for example where someone kills in self-defence.

The phrase 'necessary in a democratic society' has been interpreted by the ECHR as meaning that restrictions subject to this requirement are only allowed where there is a 'pressing social need' for them.

◼ Applying the Convention rights

When considering human rights cases, the courts often describe themselves as performing a balancing act. This might be between two conflicting rights: for example, a journalist's right to freedom of expression might conflict with what the subject of a story feels is their right to privacy. Alternatively, the balancing act might be between a Convention right, and one of the circumstances in which restrictions on it are allowed. For example, the right to freedom of expression can be restricted 'where necessary . . . in the interests of national security', so if the Government sought to suppress publication of information in the interests of national security, the courts might be called upon to decide whether the restriction was really 'necessary in a democratic society'.

In performing this balancing act, the courts are required to follow the principle of 'proportionality'. This means that any restriction on a Convention right must be proportionate to the reason for that restriction; in other words, the restriction must not just be necessary in the first place, but must go no further than is necessary. Take, for example, a case where a court issues an order preventing the press from publishing details of a trial so as to avoid prejudice to the defendant's right to a fair trial. The principle of proportionality might allow the press to argue that, although some restriction is justified in the circumstances, the right could be adequately protected by postponing, rather than banning publication.

HUMAN RIGHTS AND MEDIA LAW

The Convention contains three rights that have an important effect on the laws, which in turn could affect the way you do your work as a journalist. They are:

- ◼ the right to freedom of expression;
- ◼ the right to a fair trial;
- ◼ the right to respect for private and family life (often called the right to privacy).

◼ Freedom of expression

Article 10 provides that:

   1 Everyone has the right to freedom of expression. This right shall include freedom to hold opinions and to receive and impart information and ideas without interference by public authority and regardless of frontiers. This Article shall not prevent States from requiring the licensing of broadcasting, television or cinema enterprises.

2 The exercise of these freedoms, since it carries with it duties and responsibilities, may be subject to such formalities, conditions, restrictions or penalties as are prescribed by law and are necessary in a democratic society, in the interests of national security, territorial integrity or public safety, for the prevention of disorder or crime, for the protection of health or morals, for the protection of the reputation or rights of others, for preventing the disclosure of information received in confidence, or for maintaining the authority or impartiality of the judiciary.

Note that the right to freedom of expression includes a right to receive information as well as to impart it. This means that when the term 'freedom of expression' is applied in a case involving the media, what is at stake is not just the journalist's freedom to write, but the ability of the public to find out what he or she has to say.

As explained above, when applying Convention rights, the courts often have to balance competing rights and interests against each other. The ECHR has made it plain that the right to freedom of expression is considered extremely important, and should not easily lose out when this balancing act is performed, and in the earliest cases heard after the Human Rights Act came into force, the English courts confirmed this approach. However, despite being decribed by one judge as 'the trump card that always wins', the right to freedom of expression is not an absolute licence to print anything, and there are clearly cases where other rights will prevail. The major step forward though is that now, whenever the media's activities are threatened with restriction, the courts will bring freedom of expression into the balance.

 In October 2000, orders granted to the Secretary of State preventing publication of details about the role of the security forces in Northern Ireland were overturned, when the *Sunday People* argued that the orders breached the right to freedom of expression. The judge said that the starting point was that the scales were weighted in favour of freedom of expression, and the orders could only be allowed if they were strictly necessary and proportionate to the state's aim; in this case, they were not.

 In the same year, an order preventing the *Mail on Sunday* from reporting a story involving a child removed from her foster parents as a result of the local council's race policy was overturned. Again, the judge pointed out that where freedom of expression was concerned, the scales were weighted in favour of the right.

 In *Venables and Thompson* v *News Group Newspapers and Others* (2001), the courts were asked to consider whether the media could be prevented from publishing the new identities which would be given to the killers of James Bulger, who was murdered at the age of two in 1993, by two ten-year old boys. Weighed against the media's right of freedom of expression were the killers' rights to life and freedom from torture (it was argued they might be attacked or killed if their whereabouts were publicly known), and to privacy. The Family Division of the High Court agreed that the order should be issued.

The courts' obligation to take into account the importance of freedom of expression is likely to have an impact in any case involving the media, and is already becoming important in areas such as defamation and contempt of court, as you will see when you read the chapters on those areas of law.

Protection against injunctions

Section 12 of the Human Rights Act adds some extra provisions concerning the protection of this right, which apply in cases where someone (such as the subject of a newspaper story) is seeking an order which would restrict freedom of expression. The provisions would apply where someone applies to the court for an injunction (a form of court order) to stop publication or broadcast of a story. An injunction can be ordered to stop the media repeating something which has already been published, or can be ordered to prevent it being published in the first place.

Decisions on injunctions: Section 12 provides that in deciding whether to grant an injunction, the courts must take into account the right to freedom of expression. In addition, where the material concerned is journalistic, the court has to take into account how far the information has been, or is about to be, available to the public; to what extent publication would be in the public interest; and the provisions of any relevant privacy code.

Media representation: Section 12(2) states that orders which would restrict freedom of expression should not be granted where the potential recipient of the order is not present, unless all practical steps have been taken to notify them, or the court is satisfied there are 'compelling' reasons why they should not be notified. In the past, injunctions were sometimes granted at the last minute before publication, without the newspaper or broadcaster in question even knowing that an application had been made. This provision is designed to ensure that the media get a chance to argue their case before an injunction is granted, though as we will see, it does not always work (see p. 247).

Injunctions preventing publication: Where someone is asking for an injunction which prevents the material being published in the first place, further provisions apply. For many centuries before the Convention was drawn up, it was a fundamental principle of English law that the press should not, as a rule, be censored before publication. This was known as the 'rule against prior restraint', and meant that although pre-publication injunctions could be allowed in certain circumstances, in general, English law preferred to deal with the consequences of unlawful publication afterwards (e.g. with damages for defamation or fines for contempt of court) rather than prevent publication in advance. Section 12 preserves this approach, and provides that where an interim injunction would restrict freedom of expression, it should only be granted where the court is satisfied that when the issue goes to trial, the party seeking the injunction will be able to prove their case.

In *Cream Holdings Ltd* v *Banerjee* (2004), the House of Lords held that this meant that unless the party seeking the injunction could establish that it was more likely than not that it would win at trial, the courts should be 'exceedingly slow' to grant the order. However, there might be some cases where it was appropriate to grant the order even without such a strong case, such as where the consquences of publication were especially serious, or where time factors meant the court needed to impose a 'holding injunction' in order to consider the appliction for an interim injunction.

Section 12 does not apply to criminal proceedings, so it cannot be used in cases concerning reports of criminal cases.

■ The right to a fair trial

Article 6 provides that:

> In the determination of his civil rights and obligations or of any criminal charge against him, everyone is entitled to a fair and public hearing within a reasonable time by an independent and impartial tribunal established by law. Judgment shall be pronounced publicly but the press and public may be excluded from all or part of the trial in the interest of morals, public order or national security in a democratic society, where the interests of juveniles or the protection of the private life of the parties so require, or to the extent strictly necessary in the opinion of the court in special circumstances where publicity would prejudice the interests of justice.

For journalists, the area where this right has most effect is in covering the courts and police investigations. In a number of cases, lawyers have tried to use Article 6 to restrict court reporting, arguing that reports might otherwise prejudice their clients' right to a fair trial. In response, the media have put forward the right to free expression, and the courts have had to strike a balance between the two. These cases are covered in Section 2 of this book.

The right to respect for private and family life

Article 8 provides that:

1 Everyone has the right to respect for his private and family life, his home and his correspondence.
2 There shall be no interference by a public authority with the exercise of this right except such as in accordance with the law and is necessary in a democratic society in the interests of national security, public safety or the economic well-being of the country, for the prevention of disorder or crime, for the protection of health or morals, for the proctection of the reputation or the rights of others, for preventing the disclosure of information received in confidence, or for maintaining the authority and impartiality of the judiciary.

It is obvious that there are many situations where the media's right to freedom of expression will clash with the right of those they write about to respect for their privacy, and when the Human Rights Act was passed, it was thought that it might mean the creation of a right of privacy that would allow celebrities and other public figures to prevent reporting of their private lives. This has not yet proved to be the case, but there have been developments towards a privacy law, which are covered in Chapter 17.

CHAPTER SUMMARY

The European Convention and the Human Rights Act

The Human Rights Act incorporates the Convention into UK law. As a result:

■ Convention cases can be brought in English courts;

■ legislation should be interpreted compatibly with the Convention;

■ public bodies must act in accordance with Convention rights;

■ UK courts must take into account decisions of the ECHR;

■ Ministers must make a statement on compatibility of new legislation.

The European Convention on Human Rights lays down 15 basic rights, including:

■ absolute rights, which cannot lawfully be breached;

■ rights subject to derogations.

The European Court of Human Rights (ECHR) deals with breaches of these rights.

Human rights and media law

Three Convention rights have particular influence on the media:

■ the right to freedom of expression;

■ the right to a fair trial;

■ the right to privacy.

Section 12 of the Human Rights Act 1998 provides special protection against orders which restrict freedom of expression.

TEST YOUR KNOWLEDGE

1 How does the Human Rights Act 1998 affect the decisions of UK courts?

2 Which of these statements about the incorporation of the Convention into UK law through the Human Rights Act are true?

   (a) Parliament must ensure that all UK laws passed since 1998 protect the rights laid down in the Convention.

   (b) If a law conflicts with the Convention, UK courts do not have to apply it.

   (c) Public authorities can be taken to court if they breach the Convention.

   (d) Cases involving breaches of the Convention rights are brought before the European Court.

3 What is the principle of proportionality?

4 Which three rights have the most important impact on the work of journalists?

5 You have a story on a local politician, which accuses her of embezzling party funds. When you contact her for comment on the allegations, she goes to court to get an injunction preventing you from publishing the story. What issues does s12 of the Human Rights Act require the court to take into account when deciding whether to grant the order?

6 A UK citizen believes his right to privacy has been breached by an NHS Trust. Where can he bring his case?

ONLINE RESOURCES

www

The Human Rights Act 1998 can be read at:
www.opsi.gov.uk/ACTS/acts1998/80042—b.htm#12

The European Court of Human Rights website is at:
www.echr.coe.int/echr

Cream Holdings Ltd v *Banerjee* (2004) can be read at:
www.publications.parliament.uk/pa/ld200304/ldjudgmt/jd041014/jee.pdf

For further resources and updates please go to the Companion Website for this book at www.pearsoned.co.uk/practicaljournalism

WRITING ABOUT THE COURTS

One of the basic standards for a just and fair court system is that the workings and decisions of the courts should be open for the public to see. The idea behind this principle is that in order to do its job, a court system has to command the respect of the society it serves, and it is more likely to do this if the system is open and clear, than if decisions are made behind closed doors and the reasons for them not revealed. As a result, in the UK, there is a basic rule that court proceedings should be held in public, so that anyone who wishes to can go along to a court to watch and listen. Since most members of the public have neither the time nor the inclination to spend hours sitting in court, it is accepted that it is important for the media to have access to the courts, so that we can act as the public's eyes and ears.

However, neither access to the courts, nor the right to report what goes on there, are unrestricted. There are three main types of restriction, which are discussed in this section:

■ **Contempt of court:** The law on contempt of court aims to prevent any publication which could affect the workings of the law. For example, it is contempt to publish anything during a trial which carries a substantial risk of seriously prejudicing the result of that trial, such as details of a defendant's previous convictions. These rules are covered in Chapter 6.

■ **Restrictions on access:** Most court cases are held in public, but some types of case may be held in private, in which case the media can be excluded from them. In some circumstances it is still possible to report on these cases, even though journalists have not been allowed to hear the proceedings. Chapter 7 covers the rules on when journalists may or may not attend court hearings, and whether you can report those you are not allowed to attend.

■ **Reporting restrictions:** The fact that reporters are allowed to be present at a hearing does not always mean that they can report everything they hear. The Contempt of Court Act 1981 gives courts discretionary powers to postpone or ban reporting of a case, or specific details about it, and these powers are the subject of Chapter 8. In addition, particular courts and types of case may be subject to specific restrictions, some of them automatic and some discretionary; these are covered in Chapters 9–12.

The final chapter in this section covers the actions members of the press can take when they believe reporting restrictions have been wrongly imposed. This happens surprisingly often, and there are many cases where the media have been able to get restrictions either lifted or relaxed, so that they can report a case properly.

Chapter

6

Contempt of court

The popular image of contempt of court – largely created by courtroom dramas on TV and film – is of a defendant or lawyer being rude to a judge, or somone shouting abuse from the public gallery, at which point the judge usually tells them to be quiet or 'I'll have you in contempt'. While this kind of behaviour is certainly included within the definition of contempt of court, the phrase also has a wider meaning. Essentially, contempt of court is the court system's means of punishing anyone who interferes, in any way, with the functioning of the court system.

The main way in which a journalist can become liable for contempt is by publishing something which creates a substantial risk of serious prejudice to the outcome of a particular court case (this is usually referred to as prejudicing a fair trial). Examples might include:

- publishing a defendant's previous convictions;
- publishing background information which might sway a jury's view of the defendant or witnesses;
- publishing a photograph of a defendant in a trial where the identity of the culprit is at issue.

There are also other ways in which a journalist can be liable for contempt, including:

- publishing something which puts you in breach of a court order or an undertaking given to a court;
- using a tape recorder or taking photographs in court;
- publishing, or even just asking questions about, the deliberations of a jury.

In this chapter we look first at contempt by prejudicing a fair trial, as that is the most common issue journalists face, and then consider the other forms of contempt afterwards.

However it is committed, contempt of court is an extremely serious issue, because if a publication is judged to be in contempt, the court can order whatever punishment it sees fit. There is no limit on the fines that can be imposed and, in very serious cases, there may even be a sentence of up to two years' imprisonment.

In deciding contempt cases involving the media, the courts must take into account the right to freedom of expression under Article 10 of the European Convention on Human Rights, which has to be balanced against the Article 6 right to a fair trial. Because of the importance of this balance, most cases of contempt are referred to the Attorney-General, and he or she also maintains an overview of the law on contempt, and from time to time issues guidelines to the media on particular aspects of it, and on reporting of high-profile cases (see *Online resources* at the end of the chapter).

PUBLICATIONS PREJUDICIAL TO A FAIR TRIAL

There are two offences of contempt which relate to publications prejudicial to a fair trial:

- 'strict liability' contempt, which was created by the Contempt of Court Act 1981;
- 'intentional contempt', which comes from common law.

In both cases, what the law seeks to prevent is the publication of information or opinion that could sway those deciding the case. This is because it is a principle of English law that cases should be decided on the evidence before the court, and nothing else (this is also the reason why information about a defendant's previous convictions is not usually given in court).

Given this, it is accepted that cases which are to be decided by a jury (and to a lesser extent, by lay magistrates) are more at risk of being prejudiced by media reports than cases being decided by a judge, because judges are trained to put aside other influences and judge on the evidence alone. This means that the media is most likely to be held in contempt when reporting criminal trials in the Crown Court, which are decided by juries. Contempt actions are less of a risk in civil proceedings, which are usually heard by a judge, but it is important to remember that the law on contempt still applies in these cases, and even if it is unlikely that a judge would be swayed by anything they read, it is possible that a court could find that a publication might influence witnesses and perhaps colour the evidence they give. A few civil actions (most libel cases and certain actions against the police) are heard by juries, and these demand the same extreme care as criminal proceedings.

'STRICT LIABILITY' CONTEMPT

Defined in s2(2) of the Contempt of Court Act 1981, this is the form of contempt action which is most often used today. Actions under the Contempt of Court Act can only be brought by the Attorney-General (see p. 15), a provision which was designed to protect the media from frivolous cases being brought by people who have lost their court cases and seek to blame media coverage. If the Attorney-General decides not to bring a case then no one else can do so. (The abbreviation A-G in the names of contempt cases stands for Attorney-General.)

The Act states that strict liability contempt applies to any publication about 'active' proceedings, which 'creates a substantial risk that the course of justice in the proceedings in question will be seriously impeded or prejudiced.'

There are therefore three elements to the rule:

- strict liability,
- 'active' proceedings,
- a substantial risk of serious prejudice.

Strict liability

Strict liability essentially means that if you publish something about active proceedings that carries a substantial risk of prejudice, you can be liable, regardless of whether or not you intended to prejudice the proceedings, or realised you might do so. Nor will you escape liability because you can prove you did all possible checks, took legal advice, or only committed contempt because you made a mistake about something. (The one exception is if you can prove that despite taking all reasonable care, you did not know that proceedings were active; this is the defence of 'innocent publication' – see p. 77.)

A court may take some of these issues into account when deciding on a suitable punishment, but they will make no difference to whether you are found guilty or not. Motive is also irrelevant, and a publication that amounts to contempt will not escape liability just because it might be considered a public service, such as, for example, revealing the past convictions of a suspect still at large, in order to warn the public (but see p. 66 on police appeals).

■ Active proceedings

The Contempt of Court Act lays down the points at which cases will become active, and when they stop being active. When proceedings are not active, as defined by the Act, there is no liability for strict liability contempt (though there may be liability for intentional contempt, which is discussed later). A case that is active is sometimes described as being *sub judice*, a Latin phrase which translates as 'under judicial consideration'. There is a widespread belief that once a matter is *sub judice*, the media cannot mention it at all, but this is categorically not the case. The case can still be reported, so long as what is said does not create a substantial risk of serious prejudice.

Schedule 1 of the Act defines when cases become active and cease to be active, as follows.

Criminal proceedings

Criminal proceedings become active when any of the following apply:

- a suspect is arrested without a warrant;
- a warrant for arrest is issued;
- a summons to appear in court is issued;
- an indictment or other document specifying the charge is issued; or
- a suspect is orally charged.

Often a case will feature more than one of these steps, but it will become active as soon as any one of them happens. It quite often happens that someone is arrested, but later released without being charged. In this case, proceedings cease to be active, unless the person is released on bail. If the suspect is released on bail, the proceedings remain active – even though the suspect may in fact never be charged with the offence.

It is also possible for a warrant to be issued for someone's arrest, and that person not to be arrested for months, if at all – they may, for example, have left the country. If the person is not arrested within a year of the warrant being issued, the proceedings cease to be active – but until then, they are subject to restriction, even if the prospect of a trial seems, in practice, to be small.

Criminal proceedings stop being active when any of the following occur:

- a person arrested is released otherwise than on bail;
- 12 months have passed since the issue of a warrant and no arrest has been made;
- the charge or summons is withdrawn;
- the defendant is found to be unfit to be tried or unfit to plead;
- the defendant is acquitted;
- the defendant is sentenced; or

- any other verdict or decision brings the proceedings to an end (such as, for example, the court deciding that charges should 'lie on file', which means no further action will be taken about them).

Note that if a defendant is found guilty, the proceedings remain active until after they are sentenced. Where magistrates hear a case, they may decide that their sentencing powers are insufficient and refer to the case to the Crown Court; it remains active until the Crown Court has passed sentence. Even where the case has originally been heard in the Crown Court, there is often a longish gap between conviction and sentence, especially if the judge asks for sentencing reports. In practice, however, if the sentence is to be passed by a judge, it is unlikely that anything published about the case at this stage would be considered to create a substantial risk of prejudice, because professional judges are considered to be able to ignore such influences. However, if the sentence is to be passed by magistrates, more care needs to be taken with anything published between conviction and sentencing.

Law in practice Investigation and arrests

Reporting investigations: It is not always clear whether someone who is being interviewed at a police station has been arrested or not, and asking the police will not always help, because if there are other suspects, the police may not want to disclose whether someone has been arrested. If someone is being held at the police station against their will, then in law they are under arrest, even if the formalities of an arrest have not taken place, which therefore makes proceedings active. If they are at the police station voluntarily (or 'helping police with their inquiries' as it is usually described), proceedings are not active, but they could of course become active at any time, so extreme care needs to be used in this situation (especially as there can also be libel risks in naming someone who is 'helping police with their inquiries' – see Chapter 14).

It is not contempt of court to name someone who has been arrested for a particular crime, nor to give general background about the suspect and the crime. However, it is absolutely essential that such stories do not contain details which could be said to link the suspect to the crime (in the sense of suggesting that they did it), even if those details are given out by the police.

Police appeals: In some cases, the police will want to appeal for the public's help in tracing a suspect, after a warrant has been issued for their arrest. Strictly speaking, publishing such an appeal puts the media at risk of committing contempt, since the warrant makes proceedings active, and the appeal would clearly suggest that the police think that person committed the crime. However, during the passing of the Contempt of Court Act, the Attorney-General stated that in helping with such appeals, the media were performing a public service, and should not be discouraged. He said that the press 'has nothing to fear from publishing in reasoned terms anything which may assist in the apprehension of a wanted man'. This has been taken as an assurance that helping with police appeals will not result in a contempt charge, and no such charge has been brought to date.

Bear in mind however that publishing or repeating the same information after the person has been found and arrested would not be covered by this assurance, since to do so would not be helping to apprehend the suspect.

Reporting after an arrest: Once someone has been arrested, it is very important to take care in what you write about the case.

- You can report that 'a man' has been arrested in connection with a particular crime, but not that 'the man' who police have been looking for or suspect has been arrested.

- You can name the person who has been arrested, and give some general background, so long as none of the details given suggest that that person actually committed the crime.

- If an arrest has been made, steer clear of publishing any descriptions given by witnesses to the crime. If you say, for example, that a mugger was tall and blonde with several piercings, and the person arrested fits that description, this could be contempt.

- Never state that a person who has been arrested has previous criminal convictions.

- Be careful reporting anything that an arrested person says. Contempt can be committed by suggesting that someone is innocent as well as suggesting they are guilty, and statements made by the person arrested themselves are no less likely to lead to a contempt action than information from any other source.

- Do not assume that because information about an arrested person (or any other information, for that matter) has been issued by the police, it is safe to publish. In 1995, the BBC was found in contempt for broadcasting details of a suspect's previous convictions, even though the information was provided in a police press conference.

Civil proceedings

Civil proceedings become active when:

- arrangements are made for the case to be heard (this is usually when the case is 'set down for trial', which means it is put on a waiting list, which may be months long); or

- when the trial begins.

It should be possible to find out from the court where the trial is to be held whether or not a date has been fixed, and the Attorney-General has instructed courts to help journalists seeking this information.

Before a civil case is heard, there may sometimes be pre-trial proceedings. For example, in a procedure called a striking-out application, the defendant argues that there is no legal case to answer. Without trying the case fully, the court asks whether, assuming the facts alleged are true, there is a legal cause of action or not; if not, the case can be 'struck out' and not continued. Similarly, in a libel action, for example, the claimant may seek an interim injunction to prevent publication or further publication, and the hearing to decide whether this should be granted takes place before the full trial. Pre-trial proceedings like these become active from the time a date for the hearing is fixed, and stop being active when the hearing is over. In practice reporting them carries a fairly low risk of contempt action, because they are always heard by judges.

Civil proceedings cease to be active when they are:

- settled by the parties;

- decided by the judge;

- discontinued; or

- withdrawn.

Appeals

If either party in a case decides to appeal, the appeal proceedings become active when that party applies for leave to appeal, or when the notice of appeal is lodged. This means that anything published after the initial case is concluded, and before the appeal becomes active is not at risk of strict liability contempt (though intentional contempt can still apply – see p. 79). Often, the announcement that someone intends to appeal comes straight after the verdict, but the proceedings will still not be active until the formalities have started.

In 2000, Ulster Television was taken to court over a programme about two men who had recently been convicted of murder. The programme contained information that had not been put before the jury. The men claimed that they intended to appeal, and that this appeal might result in a re-trial, which could then be prejudiced by the information in the programme. They therefore sought an injuction to prevent the programme being shown. The court refused the injunction, saying that it was by no means certain that there would be a retrial, given that the appeal might not overturn the guilty verdict.

Appeals from summary trials in the magistrates' court and from Crown Court trials to the Court of Appeal are lodged at a Crown Court office, while appeals from Crown Court trials to the Queen's Bench Division of the High Court go to the Royal Courts of Justice in London.

Appeal proceedings cease to be active when the hearing of the appeal is completed, but if a retrial is ordered, that trial becomes active from the date that the order for retrial is made. In practice it is very unlikely that anything written about an appeal would result in a charge of contempt, simply because appeals are heard by the legal system's most experienced judges, who are considered very unlikely to be prejudiced by anything they read in the papers or see on TV. This was specifically stated in *Re Lonhro Plc and Observer Ltd* (1990). However, if a retrial is ordered, much more care is needed, as the retrial will be heard by a jury.

■ Substantial risk of serious prejudice

To fall within the definition of contempt under the Contempt of Court Act, a publication must create a substantial risk of serious prejudice to a particular court case, but what does this actually mean? In *A-G v News Group Newspapers* (1986), the court said that the first question to be asked was:

■ Is there is a real risk that the trial will be affected at all by what has been published?

If the answer was yes, the court should ask a second question:

■ Would the potential effect of the publication amount to serious prejudice?

Summing up the test, the High Court in *A-G v Guardian Newspapers Ltd (No 3)* (1992), stated that 'a substantial risk of serious prejudice' would exist where there was a real prospect that as a result of the publication, the outcome of the case would be different, or the jury would have to be discharged. Having to stop the hearing or move the trial to another area would also be considered serious prejudice.

In assessing this question, the courts are likely to take into account the following factors:

■ who the case is tried by;
■ timing of publication;
■ location of the trial;
■ circulation of the publication;
■ content of the report.

Who the case is tried by

For a publication to prejudice a trial, it must have the potential to influence the person or people who will decide that case. The risk, therefore, varies according to whether a case is being tried by judges, a jury or magistrates.

As explained at the beginning of this chapter, it is generally assumed that professional judges have the training and experience to be able to resist being influenced by anything other than the evidence before them. As a result, it is unlikely that a publication would be considered to create a substantial risk of serious prejudice to cases which are being heard by a judge or group of judges alone (though in theory it could happen). This means that most civil cases and appeals are low-risk with regard to contempt, and in fact no publisher or broadcaster has been punished for contempt of an appeal court in the past 60 years.

Cases tried by juries are the area of highest risk, as juries are considered much more likely to be influenced by outside factors than a professional judge would be. This means that Crown Court trials, and the handful of civil cases in which juries sit, demand the highest standards of care with regard to possible contempt. However, the courts do allow for the fact that juries are told in court to disregard anything but the evidence before them, and several judges have suggested that a publication would have to be quite extreme to make it impossible for them to follow that instruction.

 In *R* v *West* (1996), the murder trial of Rosemary West, wife of the serial killer Fred West, her lawyers argued that the enormous adverse publicity about the couple when the killings were discovered meant that she could not possibly get a fair trial. This argument was roundly rejected by the then Lord Chief Justice, who said that if that were the case, then it would never be possible to try any alleged murderer where the details of the crime were especially horrifying. He stated that juries are reminded to judge on the evidence alone, and that there was no reason to believe they could not do that.

As we saw in Chapter 3, the vast majority of criminal cases are tried by lay magistrates. They have some training, and often considerable experience of hearing cases, and are considered less likely to be unduly influenced than jurors, but more so than professional judges. Some magistrates' court cases are tried by district judges (formerly known as stipendiary magistrates). They are professional judges, and for contempt purposes should be viewed like any other judge.

Timing of publication

The longer the time between the publication and the start of the court proceedings, the less likely it is that a court will find a substantial risk of serious prejudice. However, it is important to note that the factors on the list above are not taken in isolation, but interact with each other: so, for example, a publication that is made six months before a trial but widely seen might be more likely to be in contempt than one made the same length of time before a trial but seen by fewer people. Equally, a story whose content is particularly strong or dramatic may be considered memorable enough to stick in people's minds over several months, as might particular details about a defendant, such as a serious criminal record. In his speech to the 2003 Law for Journalists conference, the Attorney-General commented that stories about cases involving celebrities were also very likely to stay in people's minds for a long time.

This means that although contempt is much more likely to arise from material published close to a trial, it is possible to be in contempt over publications made at a very early stage, if the details are particularly memorable.

 In *A-G* v *News Group Newspapers* (1986), the Attorney-General applied for an injunction to prevent the *News of the World* from publishing allegations that the cricketer Ian Botham had been taking drugs. Similar allegations had been published in the *Mail on Sunday* some time before, and Botham was suing the *Mail on Sunday* for libel. The Attorney-General argued that the *News of the World* story could prejudice the libel case, which was due to come to court in 11 months' time.

The Court of Appeal refused the injunction, saying that it was not satisfied that a publication so far in advance of the trial created a substantial risk of serious prejudice.

 In **A-G v Unger** (1997), the *Daily Mail* was taken to court over a story about a woman who had been charged with theft from an elderly woman who employed her as a home help. The *Mail* had video film of the thefts, and shortly after the arrest, published stills, with the headline 'The home help who helped herself'. The trial judge found this to be a clear case of 'trial by newspaper', comprising exactly the kind of assumption of guilt that the law of contempt is there to prevent. However, at the time of publication, the trial was still nine months away, and the court held that by that time, the story would have faded from potential jurors' minds so that there would be no real risk of serious prejudice to the defendant. This is often referred to as the 'fade factor'.

 In **A-G v BBC and Hat Trick Productions** (1998), the BBC TV programme *Have I Got News for You* referred to Kevin and Ian Maxwell, sons of the newspaper proprietor Robert Maxwell, as 'heartless scheming bastards'. At the time, the Maxwell brothers were awaiting trial for fraud, with the hearing due in six months' time. Despite the time delay between the broadcast and the trial, the court pointed out that the programme was very popular, and the speakers well-known, which could increase the impact of their statements. In addition, the programme had been repeated even though the Maxwell's solicitor requested that it should not be. The BBC and the programme's production company were found to be in contempt and fined £10,000.

 In **A-G v Morgan** (1998), the *News of the World* published an article under the headline 'We smash £100m fake cash ring'. The story concerned an investigation by the paper, which had uncovered a conspiracy to distribute counterfeit money. The paper had passed the details it discovered to the police, who had arrested two men. The story was published the day after the arrests, and clearly assumed the two men's guilt. It also mentioned the men's previous convictions, and was generally written in a very dramatic style. At this stage the trial was about eight months away, but the publishers were held to be in contempt, because the court said that the prominence and effect of the story made it likely that potential jurors would remember it, and in particular the information about previous convictions. This was made even more likely by the fact that the reporter would be called as a witness for the prosecution. The publishers were fined £50,000.

Publications made during the course of a trial carry the greatest risk of being found in contempt, as this is the time when a jury is actively considering the evidence.

 In **A-G v MGN** (2002), the *Sunday Mirror* published an article about a trial for assault, where the defendants included two Leeds United footballers. The piece was an interview with the father of the victim, and it alleged that the attack was racially motivated. The judge in the trial had specifically told the jury that there was no evidence of this. The timing of the article could not have been worse, in terms of the risk of contempt: it was published when the jury had begun considering its verdict, and had been sent home for the weekend. The trial collapsed, and a new one had to be held several months later. MGN was fined £75,000.

 The 1999 case of **A-G v News Group Newspapers** concerned the trial of men charged in connection with a bomb attack in London. One of the accused was convicted of conspiracy to bomb, and then the jury went off overnight to consider the second charge of murder. At this point the *Sun* published a story alleging that one of the defendants was under arrest as an IRA sniper. As a result, the murder charge had to be abandoned. The *Sun* was fined £35,000 for contempt.

Location of the trial

In assessing whether a substantial risk exists, the courts will consider how likely it is that potential jurors would see or hear the publication in question. So, for example, a report published in a local paper in Kent is fairly unlikely to carry a risk of prejudicing a trial to be held in Newcastle. There is a possibility that potential jurors in Newcastle might have come across the report, but a mere possibility is not enough to amount to a substantial risk.

 In *A-G* v *Sunday Newspapers Ltd* (1999), *Sunday Business* was acquitted of contempt after it was proved that there was only a 2000:1 chance of a copy of it being sold to someone in the jury catchment area for a trial it had written about. This factor only applies to local publications, and can be cancelled out if the publication is available on the internet. However, if a local story is picked up and published by national media and thereby prejudices a trial, the local paper would not be held responsible unless it had in some way encouraged exposure to a wider audience (e.g. by selling the story on).

Circulation of the publication

Obviously, the smaller the circulation, the smaller the chance that a potential juror will read the report. Again, this can be cancelled out if the publication is available on the internet. A very high circulation (or viewing figure) will increase the chance of a court finding that there is a substantial risk of serious prejudice – as we saw above, this was a factor in the *Have I Got News for You* case, where it was pointed out that the total audience was 6.1 million people.

Content of the report

There is no set list of the types of content that will be considered seriously prejudicial; anything that a court could consider likely to influence those deciding the case is a risk. However, the following are some of the obvious areas over which care must be taken.

Criticism of the decision to prosecute: The fact that the police believe a crime has been committed and know who is responsible does not necessarily mean that that person will be prosecuted. Both the police and the Crown Prosecution Service have a degree of leeway in deciding which cases should go to court, and in making this decision, they take into account the public interest. Therefore, general criticism of a decision to prosecute (such as stating that the law in question is outdated) can legitimately be published before the trial is over. However, if this spills over into suggesting the likely result of the trial, or criticising the witnesses or the victim, contempt is a risk.

 In 1974, a group of pacifists was being tried for encouraging soldiers in Northern Ireland to desert (meaning to leave the army, without permission). The pacifists' actions were illegal under the Incitement to Disaffection Act 1934, which makes it an offence to encourage soldiers to desert their 'duty or allegiance'. The trial judge asked the Attorney-General to seek an injunction to prevent the broadcasting of a TV programme criticising the incitement to disaffection laws, but the Attorney-General refused.

Previous convictions: In criminal trials, the defendant's previous convictions were traditionally kept from the jury, on the basis that a juror who knows the defendant has a criminal record might be unduly swayed by that knowledge when deciding whether the defendant has committed the crime in question. The Criminal Justice Act 2003 now allows disclosure of previous convictions in some circumstances (see p. 26), but there are still strict rules as to when this is permitted, and the Attorney-General has said that the change does not mean the press can publish details of previous convictions without risking contempt. However, if the previous convictions are already widely known about, it becomes much more difficult to prove a substantial risk of serious prejudice.

 In *A-G* v *Evening Standard* (1998) the *Evening Standard* published a story about defendants who were on trial for attempting to escape from prison. The report was published in the middle of the trial, and mentioned that some of those accused of trying to escape were IRA terrorists. Although the court accepted that by the nature of the charge, jurors would already know that the defendants had been convicted of something serious enough to put them in prison, it said that the revelation that some of them were terrorists posed a substantial risk of serious prejudice, and the *Standard* was fined £40,000.

 In 1996, the *Sun* carried an interview with snooker player Ronnie O'Sullivan, in which he said that he was determined to win the Master's title, in order to celebrate his mother's release from prison, after serving a 12-month sentence for evading VAT. Unfortunately, at the time the interview was published, Mrs O'Sullivan was on trial again, this time for dealing in obscene publications. The *Sun* story made it possible for jurors to find out about her previous convictions, and the jury had to be discharged. The *Sun* was fined £10,000.

 In *A-G v MGN* (1997), several tabloids were taken to court over stories published about Geoff Knights, boyfriend of the actress Gillian Taylforth. Mr Knights had been charged with assault, and the *Mirror, Star, Sun, Today* (now closed) and *Daily Mail* all published articles referring to his violent past and previous convictions. As a result, the criminal proceedings against Knights were dropped, with the court deciding that it was now impossible for him to receive a fair trial. The five newspapers were prosecuted for contempt, but the court held that in the circumstances of the case, it was impossible to single out one particular report that created a substantial risk of serious prejudice, because Knights' background was already public knowledge; it had been widely written about when Ms Taylforth brought a libel action some months earlier (see p. 193). Therefore none of the newspapers was guilty of contempt.

Defendant's background or character: As with previous convictions, publishing details of a defendant's background which puts them in a bad light or makes them sound like the kind of person who would be likely to commit the crime in question could clearly make a juror more likely to convict, and therefore the publisher may be in contempt. But information which makes the defendant look bad is not the only danger – publishing details of a defendant's good character, or any attempt to suggest an honourable motive for the crime, could influence a juror towards an acquittal and is therefore a possible risk. It is not, however, contempt to publish the defendant's own protestations of innocence, so long as the overall publication does not go so far as to amount to a call for an acquittal.

 In 1979 a Scottish newspaper was fined £20,000, after publishing an article about four people arrested for drugs offences. The story stated that three of them imported chemicals, and that a large quantity of drugs had been seized from the house where they were living, which the court believed could have led potential jurors to assume they were guilty.

Circumstances of the offence: The Attorney-General's 2003 speech warned against publishing detailed reports of the circumstances leading up to criminal charges in particular cases, which go into the evidence that will be presented, the defences that may be argued, and other issues which the jury will have to decide. He stated that the jury should decide on the evidence before them and not on what they might have seen or read in the media.

Assertions of fact: Issues which are to be decided in the trial should not be presented as if they are already fact. The Attorney-General has cited the example of reports which describe someone as a murderer or rapist.

 In 2003, the *Sunday Life* in Belfast was fined £5,000 for a report about a man who was about to be tried for drugs offences. The piece, published a month before the trial, described him as a drug dealer who had been on the run from the police, and also linked him to previous articles which said that cocaine had been found at his home, and that he had escaped and travelled back to Belfast to meet his criminal contacts.

Photographs/description: Where the identity of the culprit in a crime is in question (such as, for example, where the suspect denies being anywhere near the scene of the crime, but a witness claims to have seen them there), showing a photograph of someone who has been arrested or is the subject of a warrant can amount to contempt, as can describing their physical appearance. The Attorney-General has explained that if a suspect's photograph is published, they may refuse to take part in an identification parade, which makes the police investigation more difficult, and may weaken the prosecution's case. Even if the suspect does take part in an identification parade, the defence can argue that the result should not be admitted as evidence because the court could not be sure whether the witness identified the defendant from actual memory of the event, or from their recollection of the photograph or report (the situation may be different where the police ask for a photograph to be published – see p. 66). Where identification is not in question, it is permissible to publish a photograph of someone who has been arrested, is the subject of a warrant, or is a defendant, but the Attorney-General warned that publication should not happen unless it is absolutely clear that there is no question, and will be no question, about identification.

 In 1994, the *Sun* was prosecuted for contempt after publishing a photograph of a defendant, six weeks before he was to take part in an identity parade. Two witnesses who picked out the man in the ID parade had seen the picture in the *Sun*, and as a result, the defence lawyers were able to argue that their identification was unreliable, and the prosecution had to be stopped. The *Sun* was fined £80,000 and its editor £20,000.

 In 2005, the *Daily Star* was fined £60,000 for contempt after it identified two suspects in an alleged rape case. The two, who were well-known professional footballers, were among four men questioned by police about allegations of a gang rape at a London hotel. The press had been repeatedly told not to identify the suspects, because identity was an issue in the case, but the *Star* published both their names and a pixellated picture of one of them. It argued that there was a 'real possibility' that the alleged victim knew their identities, but the court said there was no evidence of this, and therefore the publication created a real risk of substantial prejudice. In the event, neither of the men was charged with the offence.

 In 1992, the BBC was held to be in contempt after it showed footage of a man on trial for murder being taken from a police van for his appearance in court. The judge ruled that the defendant was clearly identifiable.

Guilty pleas to other charges: Where a defendant is charged with several different offences, they may plead guilty to some, and not guilty to others. The jury is not in court for this part of the case, and is only brought in afterwards to try the offences to which the defendant has pleaded not guilty. Reporting the guilty pleas clearly has the potential to influence jurors' views of the other charges, so these should not be mentioned until after the trial is over, regardless of whether or not the judge points this out.

Involvement in other proceedings: The Attorney-General has stated that reports containing details of other proceedings in which a defendant or witness has been involved can influence jurors' views of the evidence, or the credibility of witnesses.

 During a 2001 rape trial, a local radio station broadcast a short item, stating that the jury in the case was about to return its verdict, and mentioning that the defendant in the case had also been charged with a second rape, arising from an incident two years later. This was to be the subject of a separate trial, but this was not made clear in the report. At the time, the jury had already begun considering its verdict, but as jurors had not been able to agree, they had been sent home for the weekend. The judge was told about the report, and on the Monday, asked the jury whether it had heard any broadcasts about the case. One juror said she had, and further questions revealed that as a result of what she had heard, she believed that the defendant had committed a rape before. She was discharged from the jury, which went on to return a 10–1 verdict of guilty. The Attorney-General declined to proscecute after finding that the radio station had made an inadvertent mistake and taken steps to prevent it happening again, but the case was quoted by the Attorney-General as an example of the 'serious consequences' that could arise.

Proceedings without the jury: Once the trial has started, the jury is sometimes sent out of the court while the lawyers and the judge discuss certain issues – for example, if there is a question about whether certain evidence is admissible, the jury will be sent out while this is discussed, as clearly it would make no sense to let jurors hear what the evidence is and then declare it inadmissible. It is fine to state that the jury was sent out, and to report anything which was said about the discussions while the jury was still in court, or after it came out, but publishing details of anything not heard by the jury could well be considered to prejudice the trial, even if this material is already in the public domain. A report from the Judicial Studies Board in 2000 suggested that such publications were 'very likely' to lead to a contempt action.

Assuming guilt: In his 2003 speech, the Attorney-General said that a story which 'asserts or assumes, expressly or implicitly' that the defendant is guilty runs a clear risk of contempt. This might be done in a single headline, or in biased commentary about the evidence, either before or during a trial. The Attorney-General made it clear that this applies regardless of how obvious the facts seem to be. Even if a suspect has admitted the crime, whether to journalists, police or anyone else, it is dangerous to assume that they are guilty, or even that they will necessarily plead guilty.

In *A-G* v *Unger* (1998), the case of the home help accused of theft described at p. 70, the defendant had been confronted by a newspaper with the video evidence of her thefts, and had broken down and admitted that she had taken the money. She later admitted the same to police. The papers therefore wrote the story in terms that took it as read that she was guilty, describing her as 'The home help who helped herself'; they had in fact had legal advice which suggested that as the case appeared clear-cut, there was no substantial risk of prejudice. However, they were prosecuted for contempt, and the court severely criticised their approach. It said that the media should not assume that someone was guilty just because they had confessed, or because the evidence seemed clear-cut. In this case, for example, the video evidence showed that the defendant had physically taken the money, but that alone did not make her guilty of theft as defined by the criminal law, which also requires that she had dishonestly intended to deprive the money's owner of it permanently. In addition, it had not been established that the video evidence was admissible, so making potential jurors aware of it could easily be prejudicial. In the end, the papers were acquitted of contempt because of the long period of time between publication and the likely date of the trial, but the remarks in the case still provide useful guidance about the courts' view of assuming a defendant's guilt.

Assuming the outcome of preliminary issues: The Attorney-General has warned that in a case where there are preliminary issues to be decided before the case begins (such as whether the defendant will be mentally fit to stand trial), the press should not publish any assertions about the outcome, or write as though the outcome was already decided.

Speculating about damages: When a jury hears a civil case (such as defamation or malicious prosecution), it decides not only who wins, but the amount of damages. Therefore, it is important not to speculate about how much a jury might award, even after the verdict has been announced. Theoretically, this principle also applies in cases heard by a judge, but as we have seen, in practice it is viewed as very unlikely that any publication would run a substantial risk of influencing a judge.

In 1999, the *Birmingham Post* reported that a jury had decided in favour of a man claiming malicious prosecution against the West Midlands Police, and said that the man was likely to get damages of £30,000. At this stage, although the verdict had been reached, damages had not been decided. As a result of the story, the judge held that the proceedings had been tainted and, rather than go through a retrial, the claimant decided to abandon his case. Contempt proceedings were not brought (though they could have been), but the judge issued a reminder to the press that civil proceedings were still active until after damages had been decided.

Protected documents/information: In civil cases, certain types of communications or documents are protected from being disclosed to the court, and publishing details of them can easily put a publication in contempt. For example, a defendant can make a 'payment into court', which is an offer to settle the case for the sum of money paid in. If the claimants refuse the offer, and go on to win the case but are awarded less than the sum paid in, they can only claim back their legal costs up to the date of the payment into court. Neither juries nor even the judge are allowed to know about a payment into court, so a newspaper revealing that such a payment has been made would run a high risk of contempt.

Interviewing witnesses: Publishing interviews with witnesses, even before a trial starts, can be problematic, as it can be argued that a witness who has seen their words reported in the media might be more likely to stick to their story, regardless of truth. Even interviewing witnesses with a view to publishing material after the trial can be risky, for much the same reason. Paying witnesses, while not illegal, can be a breach of the Press Complaints Commission (PCC) Code of Practice (see p. 84).

Undermining witnesses: The Attorney-General has warned that assessing the reliability of witnesses is a task for the jury to do, based on what it sees and hears in court; it is not something that should be influenced by the media. Stating or suggesting that a witness might not be telling the truth, might have an ulterior motive for what they say, or might be habitually dishonest could clearly sway a juror's view of their evidence, and therefore be contempt.

Interfering in proceedings: Any publication that could have the effect of persuading a witness not to testify, or to change their evidence, or which could intimidate them in any way, may be contempt. The same applies to a publication which could deter the claimant in a civil case from pursuing their claim.

Inaccurate reporting: A report which contains inaccuracies about critical issues in a trial could wrongly influence jurors, and can therefore be contempt.

 In 1992 the BBC was fined £5,000 for broadcasting a report about a trial, while the case was still being heard, that contained misleading comments and factual errors.

■ Balancing the relevant factors

As explained earlier, the factors listed above are not taken in isolation, or in any hierarchy of importance, but interact with each other, making it quite difficult to predict which factors a court will place most importance on. In *A-G v MGN* (1997), the Geoff Knights case referred to at p. 72, the court gave some useful guidelines on the way in which the courts should approach these factors. It said that each case must be decided on its own facts; previous cases may be helpful, but they can only be guides.

In deciding whether there has been a 'substantial risk of serious prejudice', the court will look at:

- the likelihood of the publication being seen by a potential juror, bearing in mind where the publication was in circulation, and how many copies were published;

- the likely effect of the publication on an ordinary reader, given its prominence and and the novelty of the content (i.e. how interesting or attention-grabbing it was);
- the residual impact at the time of the trial.

The judge in the Knights case made it clear that the third factor, 'residual impact' was the most important. It essentially asks how likely it is that a theoretical juror would be influenced by the publication when they came to try to the case. The time period between publication and trial would be relevant in assessing this, but the court should also consider how far the experience of taking part in the trial and listening to all the evidence would increase the juror's ability to set aside any outside influences and concentrate on the evidence. The court should also take into account the fact that the judge would be able to direct the jury to ignore outside influences, and allow for the effect of such directions. Only if the court, after assessing all these factors, was certain that there was a substantial risk that the trial would be, not just prejudiced, but prejudiced to a serious degree, should it convict a publisher of contempt.

 In 1994, ITN, the *Daily Express*, *Today* (now closed), *Daily Mail* and *Northern Echo* were prosecuted for contempt over stories about two men arrested for murdering a special constable. Two days after the arrests, ITN and three of the papers carried stories naming one of the men as an IRA terrorist who had been convicted of murdering an SAS officer. The other paper also published details about the man's background. Lord Justice Leggatt said that those details should not have been published before the trial, which at that stage was likely to be about nine months away. However, having weighed up the factors of time and type of publication against the content of the stories, he concluded that there was only a very remote risk of serious prejudice. The relevant factors leading to this conclusion were that the publication was a long time before the trial, that relatively few papers containing the offending material had been in circulation, and that ITN had only carried the details in one broadcast, which was unlikely to make a sufficient impression on viewers to cause a serious risk of prejudice to a trial nine months later (though the court said this might have been different had the story been repeated in later broadcasts). Although there was a possiblility that a potential juror had seen the stories, it was a very small one, and therefore not sufficient to justify a conviction for contempt.

Multiple publications

Where a particular allegation or information has been published at different times by different publications, the court in *A-G v MGN* (1997) made it clear that each publication will be assessed separately. The fact that an earlier publication has already created a risk of prejudice does not mean that a later one cannot be judged to create a new and further risk.

Contempt on TV

The same rules on contempt of court apply to both print and broadcast journalists, but one pitfall which uniquely affects TV news reporting, is that of using reconstructions to show what is alleged to have happened during the commission of a crime. Judges take a dim view of this, as the vivid portrayal of dramatic events clearly has the potential to influence juries.

In 1983, a judge trying a case at the Old Bailey criticised ITV's *News at Ten* for showing a reconstruction, played by actors, of events which had been described during a court case that day. He suggested that the programme was wrong to put forward its own interpretation of events, which it had not witnessed, and said that he had considered contempt proceedings, though in fact none was brought.

The courts have also acted against reconstructions of trials themselves, even where there is no possibility of a jury being influenced.

In 1987, an injunction was granted preventing Channel 4 from showing a reconstruction of the appeal hearing for the men convicted of the Birmingham pub bombings (who were eventually found to have been wrongly convicted). The broadcast was to have taken place while the proceedings were still going on, but as appeal hearings are heard by judges, not juries, it would not usually be considered that anything broadcast or published could influence the outcome of the case. However, the Lord Chief Justice, who issued the injunction, said that using actors to play witnesses would allow viewers to make judgements based on what seemed to be the real thing, but was not. This might then affect the public's view of the court's eventual judgment.

■ Defences

The Contempt of Court Act 1981 provides for three defences against a charge of strict liability contempt:

- innocent publication;
- fair and accurate contemporary reports;
- discussion of public affairs.

Innocent publication

Although the name of this defence suggests it might cover publication of details by mistake, this is not the case. As explained earlier, strict liability means that you can be liable regardless of whether you intended to prejudice a trial, or simply made a mistake that caused a risk of prejudice. 'Innocent publication' in fact covers only one very specific (and in practice rare) situation, detailed in s3 of the Act. It provides that a publisher is not guilty of strict liability contempt if

at the time of publication (having taken all reasonable care) he does not know and has no reason to suspect that proceedings are active.

A publisher who seeks to put forward this defence must prove that:

- they took all reasonable care; and
- they had no reason to suspect that proceedings were active.

This is not an easy test to pass. Usually, a call to the police, the court or the defendant's lawyer will establish whether proceedings are active, and if the publisher has not done this, it cannot be said to have taken all reasonable care. It is therefore essential that anyone making such calls takes, and keeps, notes of whom they spoke to, date and time, and what was said. Similarly, the requirement that the publisher must have 'no reason to suspect' that proceedings were active is a tough one, when the mere fact of knowing that someone is 'helping police with their enquiries' naturally gives reason to suspect that that person might at some point be arrested.

 In *Solicitor-General* v *Henry and News Group Newspapers Ltd* (1990), the *News of the World* published a news story about the disappearance of a woman called Shirley Banks. They reported that a man had been arrested for armed robbery, and after the arrest, Mrs Banks' car had been found in his garage. He was described as a 'sex beast' and the story gave details about his previous conviction for a sex offence. The man was rearrested, while still in custody, for the murder of

Mrs Banks, which made the proceedings with regard to her murder active. The newspaper said it did not know this, but nevertheless, was found in contempt and fined £15,000.

In practice, the main situation in which this defence is likely to be of use to publishers is where proceedings become active just as the presses are rolling or the programme is being transmitted, but even in this situation, the responsibility is on the publisher to prove that it took all reasonable care to avoid the situation occurring.

The defence is also available to distributors, and for them the rules are slightly less restrictive. A distributor will have a defence if it can prove that, having taken all reasonable care, it had no reason to believe or suspect that a publication it distributed contained material that was in contempt of court. This is why distributors often demand that publisher provide them with a lawyer's view that the publication is free of contempt; the legal advice may turn out to be wrong but the distributor can still claim to have taken all reasonable care.

Fair and accurate contemporary reports

Section 4(1) of the Contempt of Court Act 1981 provides that:

> a person is not guilty of contempt of court under the strict liability rule in respect of a fair and accurate report of legal proceedings held in public, published contemporaneously and in good faith.

To successfully use this defence, therefore, a publisher needs to show that the report was:

- fair and accurate;
- published contemporaneously (both this and the 'fair and accurate' requirement are essentially the same as for the defence of absolute privilege in libel – see p. 202);
- published in good faith (meaning honestly and without any ulterior motive);

and that the legal proceedings in question were held in public (which means that the public must be freely entitled to attend).

Discussion of public affairs

Section 5 of the Contempt of Court Act provides that:

> a publication made as, or as part of, a discussion in good faith of public affairs or other matters of general public interest is not to be treated as contempt of court under the strict liability rule if the risk of impediment or prejudice to particular legal proceedings is merely incidental to the discussion.

Essentially, this defence means that discussion of important public issues does not have to stop merely because a case which raises those issues becomes active.

 In *A-G* v *English* (1983) the case concerned an article in the *Daily Mail*, arguing for a Pro-Life election candidate, and strongly criticising an alleged practice among doctors of allowing severely handicapped babies to die of starvation. At the time the article was published, a doctor was on trial for murder, after allegedly allowing a baby with Down's Syndrome to starve. The article did not specifically mention the case. The *Mail* was prosecuted for contempt, but the prosecution failed. The House of Lords held that although the article was likely to prejudice the trial, it met the requirements of s5 of the Act, and therefore there was no contempt. The point of the article was a serious discussion of a matter of public interest, and the prejudice was merely a side-effect of that discussion.

 In *A-G* v *Associated Newspapers* (*The Times*, 12 February 1983), the *Mail on Sunday* published pre-judicial information about the character of Michael Fagin, who was accused of burglary after breaking in to Buckingham Palace and making his way to the Queen's bedroom. The paper was able to rely on the s5 defence, because the details were part of a report on the security precautions around the Queen, and the court held that the Queen's safety was a matter of public interest.

In *A-G v English* the House of Lords spelt out the test to be applied in judging whether prejudice is 'merely incidental'. It said that the court did not need to ask whether the story could have been written just as effectively without the potentially prejudicial parts, or whether the piece could have been worded differently in order to reduce the risk. Instead, the question to be asked was whether the risk of prejudice actually created by the words was no more than an incidental consequence of the author getting their message across.

The fact that an article discusses a matter of public interest will not, however, always save it from the danger of contempt. Essentially, the closer the subject matter comes to the specific facts of a case, the higher the chances that the prejudice will not be considered merely incidental, and the defence will fail. Actually mentioning the defendant(s) clearly increases the risk.

 In *A-G v TVS Television Ltd* (*The Times*, 7 July 1989), TVS had shown a programme called 'The New Rachmans'. Rachman was a landlord who was infamous during the 1960s for bullying and harassing tenants, and the programme alleged that certain landlords in Reading were behaving in a similar way, and were also obtaining money by deception from the Department of Health and Social Security (DHSS). One of the landlords featured in the programme was on trial for conspiracy to defraud the DHSS, and as a result of the programme his trial had to be stopped, at a cost of £215,000. He had been shown on the programme, and although his face was blacked out, he was still identifiable. When TVS was prosecuted for contempt, it sought to use the s5 defence, arguing that the programme was an examination of the general shortage of rental accommodation in the south-east of England, which was an issue of public interest; the situation with the landlords in Reading was an example of the problem. The details of the Reading situation, it said, were merely incidental to this discussion. The court did not agree; the prejudice was not merely incidental and TVS was guilty of contempt.

 At around the same time as the *Daily Mail* published the article referred to in *A-G v English*, above, the *Express* printed a piece specifically about the murder case involving the doctor and the Down's Syndrome baby. It criticised the fact that the trial was taking five weeks, and stated that if the baby had been allowed to live for that long, he might have found someone other than God to love him. This was judged to amount to contempt. Express Newspapers was fined £10,000 and the editor, who wrote the piece, £1,000.

■ Scope of strict liability contempt

Section 19 of the Contempt of Court Act 1981 provides that strict liability contempt applies to proceedings of 'any tribunal or body exercising the judicial power of the state'.

This clearly includes all cases heard in the criminal and civil courts, and in employment tribunals, coroner's courts, mental health tribunals and courts martial. However, not every kind of tribunal is covered by the statute – for example, in *General Medical Council v British Broadcasting Corporation* (1998), it was held that the General Medical Council was not a body exercising the judicial power of the state.

INTENTIONAL CONTEMPT

Intentional contempt is a common law offence which existed before the Contempt of Court Act 1981 was passed. Although it overlaps with the contempt offence defined by the Act, there are differences, which means there are situations where someone who is not guilty of contempt under the Act may nevertheless face liability under the common law offence. For example, if the proceedings you write about are not active, there is no liability for contempt under the Act, regardless of what you write – but there may be liability at common law. Because the offence requires proof beyond reasonable doubt that the publisher intended to prejudice a trial, common law contempt is harder to prove than strict liability contempt, and prosecutions are rarer, but do still happen.

A person (or company) will be guilty of intentional contempt if they publish material with the intention of prejudicing or interfering with proceedings which are 'imminent or pending'. There are therefore two important differences between intentional contempt and strict liability contempt:

- proceedings must be 'pending or imminent', rather than 'active' (though there is some overlap – see below);
- the publisher must intend to prejudice the trial.

Proceedings pending or imminent

It is generally understood that once someone has been arrested, proceedings can be considered to be 'pending'. The issue of when proceedings are 'imminent' is less clear, but it seems that proceedings can be considered 'imminent' even before someone is arrested, which means that the period in which proceedings are pending or imminent may begin before the period in which they would be 'active' under the Contempt of Court Act.

In *R v Beaverbrook Newspapers and Associated Newspapers* (1962), the *Daily Express* was fined for publishing prejudicial material about a man who had not been arrested at the time of publication, but was obviously about to be.

Intention

The prosecution must prove, beyond reasonable doubt, that the publisher intended to prejudice the trial. In everyday speech, to 'intend' to do something means to act with that purpose in mind, and a publisher who deliberately set out to prejudice a trial would certainly be covered by the offence. However, given the possible punishment for contempt, such cases will clearly be rare, and for the purposes of contempt, intention also has a wider meaning than its everyday one. Intention can be assumed if a publisher was:

- aware that proceedings were imminent; and
- aware of the nature of the material it was publishing.

In other words, someone who publishes material that is obviously likely to cause prejudice can be assumed to have intended such prejudice, even if they say they did not mean for or wish that to happen. It was made clear in *A-G v Sport Newspapers* (below), however, that intention should only be assumed where the probability of prejudicing the trial was 'little short of overwhelming.'

In *A-G v News Group Newspapers* (1988), the *Sun* announced that it was funding a private prosecution against a doctor who was alleged to have raped a little girl. There was medical evidence that the child had been raped, but because she was only nine, the Director of Public Prosecutions decided not to prosecute. The *Sun* expressed its outrage at the decision with the headline 'Rape Case Doc: Sun Acts', and the offer to pay for the private prosecution. It called the doctor 'a beast and a swine', clearly assumed he was guilty, and accused him of other sexual crimes. The prosecution took place, and the doctor was acquitted. The *Sun* was prosecuted for contempt. It maintained that it had not intended to prejudice the trial, but the judge said that, in the circumstances, the editor must have realised that talking about the doctor as a rapist and offering to fund the prosecution were potentially seriously prejudicial. The paper was found guilty and fined £75,000.

 In *A-G* v *Sport Newspapers* (1992), the *Daily Sport* published a story about the rape and murder of a 15-year-old schoolgirl, which said that police suspected a man called David Evans of the crime, and gave details of Evans' considerable criminal record. The story called him a 'vicious, evil rapist' with a 'horrific history of sex attacks'. At the time, Evans was on the run, and five days before the article was published, the police had held a press conference to ask for the public's help to find him, though no warrant had been issued for his arrest at this stage. At the conference, the police spokesman specifically stated that publishing details of Evans' criminal background was likely to prejudice a future trial. The *Sport* did not have a reporter at the conference, but was told about the police's wish to keep Evans' record out of the media at least two days before it published the article. Five days after publication, Evans was arrested, and was tried and convicted of the murder in the following year. The *Sport* was prosecuted for contempt. The editor argued that he had not intended to prejudice the trial, and that his reason for ignoring the police requests not to publish was in order to publicise the fact that the man was a danger to women. The Court of Appeal said the case did not have the necessary intent, because at the time of publication, it was uncertain whether Evans would actually be caught, let alone charged and tried.

 In *Dobson* v *Hastings* (1992), a finance writer from the *Daily Telegraph* was writing a story about some company directors who were facing proceedings for disqualification. She went to the court to look at the relevant file, and was told that she had to have the court's permission to do so. She was given the file to take to the registrar in order to get this permission, and while she waited to do so, she took notes from documents in the report. This was a breach of court rules, but she did not know this, having never dealt with court documents before. When she told the registrar what she had done, he complained to her editor, but her story was still published. The company directors tried to bring an action for contempt, but it was dismissed on the grounds that she had made an honest mistake and there was nothing on which to base an assumption of intention.

OTHER TYPES OF CONTEMPT

So far, we have looked at the issue of publications which are in contempt because they may prejudice the outcome of a particular court case. But these are not the only way that a journalist or publisher can commit contempt of court. Other ways include:

- contempt in the face of the court;
- scandalising the court;
- using a tape recorder or taking photographs in court;
- failing to comply with a court order;
- frustrating court orders addressed to others;
- using documents disclosed during proceedings;
- investigating or publishing jury deliberations;
- interfering with witnesses;
- reporting hearings heard in private;
- breaking embargoes on court judgments.

Contempt in the face of the court

This covers the kind of behaviour so beloved of courtroom dramas: loud demonstrations, insulting the judge to their face, and generally anything done in the courtroom which undermines the authority of the court. A journalist will only be liable in this way if they themselves behave in a way that amounts to contempt; it is not contempt to report that someone else has done so (unless, for example, what is said in the report amounts to contempt in some other way such as by prejudicing the trial).

Scandalising the court

This is committed by making a statement (written or spoken) which is designed to bring the court or a judge into public contempt, or lower their authority. Examples would include accusing a judge of being biased, taking bribes, or falling asleep in court, and the criticism need not refer to particular proceedings.

In *R v New Statesman ex p DPP* (1928), the *New Statesman* was convicted of scandalising the court after it published a story claiming that Maria Stopes, who was well-known for her campaigns to make contraception more easily available, could not get a fair trial in front of a Roman Catholic judge.

In practice, prosecutions for scandalising the court are now extremely rare and attacks on a particular judge are more likely to be met with a request for an apology, or possibly a libel action.

Tape recording and photographs

Section 9 of the Contempt of Court Act 1981 provides that it is contempt to use, or even take into court, a tape recorder (unless permission is given). Section 25 of the Criminal Justice Act 1925 makes it contempt to take any photograph, make or attempt to make any portrait or sketch of a judge or witness in, or a party to, any proceedings before the court, either in the courtroom or its precinct. (In Northern Ireland a similar rule applies under the Criminal Justice (Northern Ireland) Act 1945.) It is however permissable for an artist to sit in on a trial and make notes, from which they produce sketches afterwards, away from the court. This is how the drawings which often accompany reports of a high-profile trial are produced.

Failing to comply with a court order

If a court makes an order, disobeying that order will be contempt. An example would be if a court granted an injunction preventing a paper from publishing a particular story, and the paper went ahead and printed anyway. Such deliberate defiance would obviously be likely to incur serious punishment, and few, if any, publishers would take such a risk.

It is possible to disobey a court order unintentionally, but even here, the courts may be severe.

In 1997, the *Daily Mail* and its columnist Nigel Dempster were fined £25,000 and £10,000 respectively for non-intentional breach of an injunction not to repeat an allegation that the claimant in a libel trial against them was mean. The judge said that if he had thought the disobedience was deliberate, he would have sentenced Dempster to prison.

A publisher can only be liable for this form of contempt if there has been a court order; the fact that a judge has requested the media not to behave in a particular way, or publish certain material, is not enough to create liability if the request is not complied with. There must also be proof that the publisher was given notice of the order. (If it is an order not to publish something and is delivered in court, the fact that someone from the publisher was in court at the time will be sufficient notice.)

▣ Frustrating court orders addressed to others

It is not only court orders directed specifically against them that can cause problems for publishers. It can also be contempt to breach a court order directed against another publication.

 In 1987, a former MI5 officer, Peter Wright, published *Spycatcher*, his memoirs of his time in the Secret Service. The book was banned in the UK, but was published in America. The *Guardian* and *Observer* sought to publish extracts from the book, but were prevented from doing so when the Attorney-General successfully sought an injunction against them. A little later, four other papers printed details from the book, and were then taken to court. None of them had been named in the injunction, and the House of Lords agreed that they could not be said to have disobeyed the court order as it was not addressed to them. However, by publishing the details, they had effectively destroyed the purpose of the injunction, which was to keep the book's contents secret; once they were made public, there was no point in the injunction. The House of Lords held that this was contempt.

▣ Using documents disclosed during proceedings

Care needs to be taken if you get hold of documents from one party to a case which belong to the other party and have been disclosed as part of the court proceedings (disclosure here refers to the pre-trial exchange of information between the two parties, not necessarily disclosure in court). Publishing the information in such a document is a breach of the Civil Procedure Rules (see p. 43), and could easily lead to a contempt charge. The exception is if the document was was read to or by the court, or referred to at a public hearing.

▣ Investigating or publishing jury deliberations

In some countries (notably the USA), it is very common for jurors to be interviewed by the media after a trial about why they reached the decision they did. In this country, however, the law states that jury deliberations should be secret, and jurors are not allowed to tell anyone at all what was said in the jury room.

For this reason, s8 of the Contempt of Court Act 1981 states that it is contempt of court to

> obtain, disclose or solicit any particulars of statements made, opinions expressed, arguments advanced or votes cast by members of a jury in the course of their deliberations in any legal proceedings.

Contempt proceedings under s8 can only be brought by the Attorney-General. Note that it is not only publishing details of jury deliberations that will get you into trouble: it is also an offence to 'solicit' such information, so even just asking a juror questions about how the verdict was reached can be contempt.

Section 8 only applies to jury deliberations, in other words the process of reaching a verdict. It is not contempt under s8 to ask for, or publish, a juror's view of, for example, whether the prosecution should have been brought in the first place, how the trial was conducted, or whether the eventual sentence was appropriate, as long as no questions are asked and no information published about anything said or done during the jury's deliberation on the verdict, or what led it to reach that verdict.

 In *A-G* v *Associated Newspapers* (1994), the *Mail on Sunday* published an article about the 'Blue Arrow' trial, a long-running, high-profile fraud case. The piece contained quotes from several jurors, detailing what they thought of the evidence in the trial, and mentioning that one juror had only agreed on a verdict because he wanted to get home. The paper was prosecuted for contempt, but argued that it could not be said to be disclosing the jurors' deliberations, because they had already been disclosed to an American researcher, and it was the research that the paper had published. The House of Lords rejected this view, saying that publication itself could amount to disclosure, and in this case it did. Publication could only be distinguised from disclosure where it was merely repetition of known facts.

■ Interfering with witnesses

In high-profile cases, the media will sometimes pay a key witness for the exclusive rights to their story (to be published after the trial). Theoretically, this could prejudice the trial, since the witness might be tempted to embellish the story to make it more saleable, or to stick to it even if cross-examination suggested it was wrong. This is even more likely if the amount payable is dependent on the result of the case. In his speech to the 2003 Law for Journalists conference, the Attorney-General said that he regarded it as 'a serious matter', pointing out that it can undermine the credibility of witnesses, and could lead to the acquittal of the guilty, as well as the conviction of the innocent. However, no contempt action has so far been brought for paying a witness, and in the discussion paper published when the Government considered making paying witnesses a specific offence in 2002, it concluded that the current law on contempt probably did not cover witness payments. A new offence was not introduced however, and it appears that the only current rules against paying a witness are in the PCC Code of Practice (see the box below).

Where a newspaper has paid a witness for their story, it may insist that the witness does not speak to other publications, or even hide the witness away so that other publications cannot get to them. According to the media law experts Geoffrey Robertson QC and Andrew Nicol QC, this is not in itself contempt, but a contempt charge could result if the witness's evidence is tampered with, or the witness is concealed from the police or prosecuting authorities.

The PCC Code on paying witnesses

The PCC Code states that once proceedings become active, payment should not be offered to anyone who might reasonably be expected to be called as a witness. This ban lasts until any one of the following happens:

■ the suspect is freed unconditionally or proceedings are otherwise discontinued;

■ the defendant pleads guilty; or

■ the court gives its verdict.

Where proceedings are not yet active, but are likely and foreseeable, payment to potential witnesses should not be offered, unless it can be shown the publication of the information concerned is in the public interest, and there is an overriding need to make or promise payment in order to get access to the information. In that case, all reasonable steps should be taken to make sure the payment does not affect the outcome of the trial; it is never permissible to make payment conditional on the outcome of the trial (e.g. by promising a witness more money if the defendant is convicted).

Any person who has been paid for their story should be warned that they must disclose this to the defence and the prosecution if they are called as a witness.

■ Reporting hearings heard in private

Section 12 of the Administration of Justice Act 1960 provides that it is not automatically a contempt to publish details of a hearing heard in private. However, the Act provides that it is contempt to report 'information relating to the proceedings' of a hearing in private where that hearing concerns any of the following:

- the Children Act 1989;
- wardship of court;
- other matters relating to the maintenance or upbringing of children;
- mental health proceedings (such as a patient applying to a mental health tribunal for discharge from a secure mental hospital);
- national security;
- a secret process, discovery or invention which forms part of the issues in the case.

As with any other hearing, it is also contempt to report information disclosed in a private hearing where the court has made an order prohibiting or postponing such disclosure.

Although it is contempt to publish anything said during a private hearing which falls into one of the above categories, it is not contempt to publish the fact that the hearing was held, when and where, or the fact that it was held in private. It is also permissible to report the verdict, any order made, any comments from the parties or details from documents they hold, so long as the court does not make an order prohibiting such disclosures (and of course anything written about a hearing in private is subject to the normal rules on contempt if it creates a risk of prejudice).

In *Pickering* v *Liverpool Daily Post* (1991), a man who had been detained in a secure mental hospital after being convicted of sexual attacks was applying to a mental health tribunal for discharge from the hospital. He wanted to stop the press from reporting his application, but the House of Lords said that the media were free to report that a named person had applied to a tribunal, and the result, because that was not 'information related to the proceedings.' It was not, however, permissible to report the reasons the tribunal gave for its decision because doing so would reveal the evidence given in the hearing.

Where a private hearing does not fall within any of the categories listed above, and no reporting restrictions are imposed, reporting the hearing will not in itself be contempt, provided the usual rules on contempt are followed.

Breaking embargoes on court judgments

Judgments from the higher courts are routinely supplied to lawyers and their clients before they are officially handed down, subject to an embargo. Publication of the result or any details before the judgment is officially handed down will be contempt.

In 2006, the magazine *The Lawyer* broke a court embargo by publishing details of the judgment in **Baigent v Random House** (2006), the case involving the book *The Da Vinci Code* (see p. 287), on its website, 90 minutes before the judgment was handed down. The judge in the case accepted that the magazine had not known of the embargo rules on judgments, and in view of the fact that it agreed to print a front page apology, there was no prosecution for contempt. However, the magazine was ordered to pay costs, and the judge warned that in future, any other publications which breached a court embargo could face 'severe consequences'.

CONTEMPT PROCEDURE

Some contempt proceedings can still be brought by the affected court but, in practice, most incidents are referred to the Attorney-General, who makes the decision whether to prosecute. As we have seen, this is a legal requirement for offences under the Contempt of Court Act 1981; the Act also states that any alleged contempt by publication relating to a magistrates' court must be referred to the Attorney-General, not dealt with by the magistrates.

Where a reference to the Attorney-General is not required by law, a trial judge can hear a contempt case referring to proceedings in their own court, but the Court of Appeal in *R v Tyne Tees Television* (1997) held that this should only happen in exceptional circumstances. Therefore a reporter who is threatened by a judge with immediate committal for contempt should get legal advice, so that the lawyers can argue for the matter to be referred to the Attorney-General.

If the Attorney-General gives consent, proceedings will usually not be brought until after the case said to be prejudiced is finished; this is to avoid further prejudice arising from publicity about the contempt case, and also to give the Attorney-General the chance to weigh up whether prejudice actually occurred. Usually, the Attorney-General will write to the relevant editor, explaining in detail why their publication is considered to have risked prejudicing the case, and giving them the chance to argue against the charge (in this situation, it would obviously be wise to take legal advice before giving a response).

Contempt is the only serious criminal offence to be tried by judges, rather than juries.

Sanctions for contempt

As explained at the beginning of this chapter, being found in contempt of court can have serious implications for the media. The court may order a fine, and as some of the cases in this chapter show, these can amount to thousands of pounds. In serious cases, an editor can even be sent to prison for contempt.

In addition, regulations made under s93 of the Courts Act 2003 give magistrates' courts, the Crown Court and the Court of Appeal power to order that where a trial is delayed or stopped as a result of 'serious misconduct' by a third party (meaning someone other than the people involved in the case), the third party can be ordered to pay costs. Serious misconduct is not defined in the legislation, but in a press release issued when the change was announced, one of the examples given was of prejudicial reporting of a criminal case, and it seems clear that the provisions could well be applied to the media. When you consider that a case which collapses due to prejudicial reporting can waste a million pounds or more of public money, this is a formidable threat, though when the regulations were introduced, the Lord Chief Justice said they would need to be used 'with discretion'. A further concern is that, unlike a prosecution of contempt, a costs order does not require the consent of the Attorney-General; the decision is made by the magistrates or judge in the relevant case.

Preventing publication

Court actions for contempt are not limited to situations where the contempt has already taken place; where it is known that material about to be published may be in contempt, a injunction can be sought to prevent publication, or even research into a story (as in the HTV case below). However, as with all injunctions preventing initial publication, the standard of proof is very high. The applicant must prove beyond reasonable doubt that there is a real risk of prejudice, and that, without an injunction, the publishers will go ahead and publish the material.

In *Ex Parte HTV Cymru (Wales) Ltd, Crown Court at Cardiff* (2002), the High Court agreed to an injunction against HTV, preventing it from interviewing witnesses in a murder trial for a documentary, even though the programme would not have been shown until after the end of the trial. The judge held that being interviewed for the programme might change the witnesses' views on the evidence they had given, and given that at least one of them was likely to be recalled before the end of the trial, there was a serious risk of substantial prejudice. The injunction was only to last until all the witnesses had given their evidence.

In 2005, Channel Five defeated an attempt to prevent broadcast of a programme just two hours before it was due on air. The programme covered the activities of the Noonan brothers, described as well-known underworld figures in Manchester. Two days before it was due to be shown, one of the brothers, Desmond, was fatally stabbed. The killing was widely covered by the press that weekend, and the stories included details of Desmond's criminal activities. On the day the programme was due to go out, the police applied for an injunction to prevent it, arguing that it would seriously hinder the investigation into Desmond's murder, and stop people coming forward as witnesses because they would be intimidated by the picture given of the Noonans as powerful underworld figures. Channel 5 argued that much of the information had already been reported, and the Noonans were already known to the public, but the injunction was granted. With just two hours to spare, Channel 5 secured a late sitting with the Court of Appeal, which lifted the injunction. It said that there had to be clear and significant evidence of substantial prejudice to the police investigation, and this had not been identified.

Applications for injunctions can be made by the Attorney-General, or if the alleged contempt is intentional contempt under common law, by the person affected by the contemptuous statement, without the consent of the Attorney-General. It is not clear whether persons affected can apply for an injunction in cases where the allegation is one of strict liability contempt under the Contempt of Court Act (this was considered in a 1991 House of Lords case, but no rule was stated).

Injunctions are usually issued by the High Court, but in the *HTV Cymru* case referred to above, the High Court held that injunctions to prevent contempt by publication could be issued by the Crown Court. However, the High Court stated that circumstances in which this would be appropriate would be rare, the court would have to take into account the right to freedom of expression under the European Convention of Human Rights, and that if an injunction was necessary, the restriction it imposed should be as small as possible. The court also advised that the media should be ready to challenge any injunction which seemed to be stricter than necessary or proportionate to the threat.

Law in practice Common problems with contempt

Contempt and privilege: Many media law students get confused about the relationship between contempt of court and the privilege defence. Although they both apply to court reports, they do two completely different things:

- Contempt of court punishes anyone who publishes material which could prejudice a court case.

- Privilege allows the media to report statements which would otherwise be considered defamatory, where those statements are made in court and reported fairly, accurately and (for absolute privilege) contemporaneously.

The Contempt of Court Act provides a defence for fair, accurate and contemporaneous court reports, made in good faith, but this is a defence that is specific to contempt, and should not be referred to (as it often is by students) as 'privilege for contempt'.

Contempt and libel: When reporting anything to do with criminal investigations and court cases, it is easy to focus on contempt of court provisions and forget about libel. It is important always to remember that they are two separate actions, and you can be as careful as possible about one and yet still leave yourself open to the other. For example, take the situation where you write that someone is being investigated for fraud. If the proceedings are not active, you will not be in danger of strict liability contempt, and if you can show that you did not intend to prejudice the trial, you will not be guilty of intentional contempt either. None of this, however, prevents you being sued for libel if your words can be shown to have a defamatory meaning.

Gagging orders: As stated earlier in this chapter, there is a widespread belief that any case which is *sub judice* cannot be reported. This myth is sometimes used to try to stifle criticism, by issuing a writ for libel against one publication, and then threatening the others with contempt if they write about the matters that are the subject of the libel case. This is known as a 'gagging order'.

Such threats can sound very plausible, but in *Thomson v Times Newspapers* (1969), Lord Salmon stated that: 'There is no authority that I know of to support the view that further comment would amount to contempt of court.' As long as what is written about a libel case does not pose a substantial risk of seriously prejudicing that case, nor suggest that the publisher intended to prejudice it, there should be no risk of contempt (though clearly there may be a risk of libel if the defamatory allegations are repeated).

Police information: Prejudicing a trial can, in extreme cases lead to the cost and hassle of a retrial, and even to suspects being allowed to evade justice. For that reason, it is tempting to assume that information provided on the record by the police must be safe to use, since they are unlikely to want this to happen, and, you might assume, they know the rules. This is not a safe assumption, however, and there have been prosecutions for contempt based on publication of information supplied by the police. Regardless of where information comes from, it should only be used within the rules of contempt.

CHAPTER SUMMARY

Publications prejudicial to a fair trial

There are two different contempt offences which can be committed by publishing prejudicial material; both can be punished with fine or imprisonment.

Strict liability contempt

This is committed by publishing any material which

■ concerns 'active' proceedings, and

■ 'creates a substantial risk that the course of justice in the proceedings in question will be seriously impeded or prejudiced'.

Whether there is 'substantial risk of serious prejudice' depends on:

■ who the case is tried by;

■ how close to the hearing the report was published;

■ where the trial is being held;

■ the circulation of the publication;

■ the content of the report.

There are three defences:

■ innocent publication;

■ fair and accurate contemporary reports;

■ discussion of public affairs.

Intentional contempt

This is committed by publishing material with the intention of prejudicing or interfering with proceedings which are 'imminent or pending'.

Intention covers both:

■ material deliberately published with the purpose of interfering with legal proceedings; and

■ material published when the publisher knew proceedings were imminent or pending and knew the nature of the material it was publishing.

Other types of contempt

Journalists can also be found guilty of contempt if they:

■ cause a disturbance in court;

■ use a tape recorder or take photographs in court;

■ fail to comply with a court order;

■ frustrate court orders addressed to others;

■ use documents disclosed during proceedings;

■ investigate or publish details of jury deliberations;

■ interfere with witnesses;

■ report hearings heard in private.

Contempt procedure

Strict liability contempt can only be prosecuted by the Attorney-General.

Injunctions can be ordered to prevent publication of material that poses a real risk of prejudice to a trial.

TEST YOUR KNOWLEDGE

1 When do proceedings become active, and cease to be active, under the Contempt of Court Act 1981?

2 Which of the following statements could leave you open to a charge of contempt?

(a) Jack Smith was arrested yesterday for the murder of Jane Jones.

(b) After a month-long search for the killer of Jane Jones, the man sought by police was arrested yesterday.

(c) After a month-long search, police yesterday arrested a man for the murder of Jane Jones.

(d) A man who spent five years in prison for assault was arrested yesterday in connection with the murder of Jane Jones.

(e) Jack Smith, a convicted rapist, was yesterday arrested for the murder of Jane Jones.

(f) After a nationwide manhunt, police said yesterday that they had arrested the killer of Jane Jones.

3 Police find the body of a young woman at her boyfriend's home. Her boyfriend has disappeared. The police hold a press conference at which they reveal that the boyfriend has previous convictions for violence against women. They describe the boyfriend as 'a very dangerous man' and ask for anyone who knows where he is to come forward. The local TV channels that evening name the boyfriend, and report what was said at the press conference. The following day, the boyfriend is found and arrested. Four days later, the local weekly paper reports the arrest, stating that the suspect was described as 'very dangerous' by the police, and mentioning the previous convictions that the police listed at the press conference. Do the TV stations run the risk of being found in contempt? Does the newspaper?

4 In what circumstances can it be contempt to publish a photograph of someone suspected of a crime?

5 You have been researching a feature about women who steal other people's babies. You have spoken to a number of experts, and the feature puts forward the idea that, rather than punishing such women, society should be sympathetic to them, because they are usually suffering from some kind of trauma or mental problem. A few days before the piece is due to be published, a baby is snatched from the local maternity unit; it is found within 24 hours, and the woman who took it is arrested. Can you safely publish your feature? Would your answer differ (and if so, why) if:

(a) the woman was already on trial;

(b) your feature focused on the trauma that babysnatching causes the victims, rather than being sympathetic to those who take babies.

6 Can you be found in contempt of court for writing about someone suspected of a crime, before the proceedings become active?

7 A fraud trial has just ended at your local Crown Court. It has been going on for almost six months, and there was a huge amount of very convincing evidence against the defendants. However, the jury found them not guilty, by a majority of 10–2. Afterwards, you interview one of the fraudster's victims, who says the whole case has been a miscarriage of justice, and the defendants were clearly guilty. She is willing to give you an on-the-record interview about how the fraud has wrecked her life. Back at the office, you get a call from one of the jurors. He says that ten of his fellow jury members admitted in the jury room that they were scared of the fraudsters, and were not willing to take the risk of finding them guilty. He is willing to give you a full interview so long as you do not name him in print. Can you safely use either or both of these stories?

8 A woman convicted of assault appeals against her sentence. The court quashes her conviction, and orders a retrial. When do the retrial proceedings become active?

9 Information about legal proceedings can come from many different sources. Which of these is it always safe to quote, as far as contempt is concerned?

   (a) details given in police press conferences;

   (b) off-the-record comment from police sources;

   (c) information from the victim;

   (d) comments from the lawyers in the case;

   (e) anything the defendant says.

10 What does it mean to say that particular legal proceedings are *sub judice*?

ONLINE RESOURCES

www The Attorney-General's speech on contempt to the 2003 Law for Journalists conference can be read at:
www.mediawise.org.uk/print.php?id=715

Guidance notes issued by the Attorney-General can be read at:
www.lslo.gov.uk/whatsnew.htm

The Crown Prosecution Service website has information on prosecuting contempt of court, at:
www.cps.gov.uk

For further resources and updates please go to the Companion Website for this book at www.pearsoned.co.uk/practicaljournalism

6

Contempt of court

Access to the courts

As explained in the introduction to this section, as a general rule, the English courts are open to the public, and that means to the media as well. There are circumstances in which both the public and the media can be excluded from a court hearing, but this can only be done where the law specifically allows it; a judge cannot simply decide to hear a case in private, nor can either of the parties simply demand this.

There are, however, situations where a judge or magistrates may try to exclude the press even though they do not have a lawful justification to do so, and in such cases, the press can often get the decision changed if it can show that the law does not allow it. To be able to recognise those situations, and know what action to take, you need to have a firm grasp of the law in this area.

THE GENERAL RULE ON ACCESS

Support for the general principle that courts should be open to the public and the media can be found in case law, in statute, and in the rules and guidelines to which the court system works, all of which can be helpful if you have to challenge exclusion from a court.

Case law: The basic rules about media access to the courts were summed up by the House of Lords in *A-G* v *Leveller Magazine* (1979). There, Lord Diplock said that it was a fundamental principle of justice that proceedings should be held in open court, and that nothing should be done to discourage publication of a fair and accurate report of those proceedings. The courts should only depart from this principle where not doing so would 'frustrate or render impracticable the administration of justice.' Other cases, such as *Scott* v *Scott* (1913), have specifically stated that preventing embarrassment to the parties in the case is not by itself a lawful reason for excluding the press from a court.

Statute: The Human Rights Act 1998, which brings into English law Article 6 of the European Convention on Human Rights, details the right to a fair hearing before the courts, and confirms that a fair hearing should be one held in public. It also lays down certain circumstances in which the media can be excluded from all or part of a trial. These are:

- in the interest of morals, public order, or national security;
- where required in order to protect the interests of juveniles;
- where required in order to protect the private life of the parties;
- where publicity would prejudice the interests of justice.

This does not, however, mean that a court can restrict press access merely because, for example, a case contains details about the parties' private lives. When deciding whether to restrict press access on any of these grounds, the court is required to balance that interest against the right of freedom of expression contained in Article 10 of the Convention.

Court rules and guidelines: The Civil Procedure Rules reiterate the principle that hearings should usually be in open court, as do two sets of guidelines issued by the Judicial Studies Board to magistrates' courts and the Crown Court (see below).

■ Types of hearing

In terms of access, there are three types of hearing:

- in open court,
- in private,
- in chambers.

In open court means that the hearing is in a courtroom, and both the public and the press are admitted. However, the fact that a hearing is in open court does not necessarily mean you can report everything said or done there, and in some circumstances reporting restrictions will apply, either automatically or by order of the court. These restrictions are examined in later chapters of this section.

In private means that the hearing is closed to the press and public (such hearings were traditionally known as 'in camera', and this term is sometimes still used, but the Civil Procedure Rules which came into force in 1999 make it clear that the official term is now 'in private'). Unless reporting restrictions apply, proceedings held in private can be reported, assuming someone present is willing to tell the press what happened, but note that a report based on such information is not considered to be a report of court proceedings for the purposes of the privilege defence in defamation (see p. 202).

In some cases, a judge may not specifically state that a hearing is to be held in private, but may take deliberate steps that effectively ensure the press is excluded. In *R (on the application of Pelling)* v *Bow County Court* (2001), it was held that such measures could amount to holding a hearing in private, and if there is no legal right for that hearing to be held in private, the exclusion of the press (and public) will be unlawful. In the *Bow County Court* case, the court said the test was whether the arrangements, take as a whole, inhibit public access to such an extent that the hearing is in reality a private one.

In *McPherson* v *McPherson* (1936), the case was the divorce hearing of a Government minister. He was keen to avoid publicity, and so the judge held a hearing at lunchtime, in his library, which was accessed by a door marked 'Private'. Although the door was left ajar, and the judge stated before proceedings started that the hearing was open, the Privy Council stated that the openness was a sham and in reality the hearing was held in private. At the time there was no lawful reason for such hearings to be private, and so the order made at the end of the proceedings was invalid.

In *Storer* v *British Gas* (2000), an employment tribunal which held a hearing in a room whose door could only be opened with a key code was held to have sat in private.

In chambers usually refers to a hearing held behind closed doors, usually in a room which is not open to the public in the way that an ordinary courtroom usually is, such as an office (though unfortunately 'in chambers' is also sometimes used, incorrectly, to refer to a secret hearing). Many types of hearing are conducted in chambers, usually for reasons of convenience, rather than secrecy; bail hearings are a common example, while in civil cases, hearings in chambers are often held to discuss technical issues relating to trial procedure.

In most cases, hearings in chambers are of no interest to the press, but there are some types of cases heard this way which the media may want to report. If a hearing is held in chambers, but there is no sign on the door saying that the proceedings are private, the media should be allowed in. However, this can obviously create problems if the hearing is being held in a small office, and this issue was addressed in **Hodgson v Imperial Tobacco** (1998). In that case, Lord Woolf stated that judges should usually make arrangements to ensure that holding a hearing in chambers did not materially interfere with the right of the public, including the media, to know and observe what happens in legal proceedings. If the media want to report a particular hearing in chambers, but there are practical problems (e.g. lack of space), Lord Woolf advised that the judge should use their discretion to make this possible, for example by allowing one representative of the press to attend, or giving judgment and an account of the proceedings in open court.

Even where reporters are not allowed to sit in on a hearing in chambers, the fact that the case was held in chambers does not in itself mean they cannot report what was said, if one of the parties wishes to tell them about it. Whether the hearing can be reported will depend on whether there is a specific legal provision which prevents reports; this was confirmed in **Malik v Central Criminal Court** (2006) (see below).

If you are not sure whether reporters are allowed into a hearing, ask for an enquiry to be sent to the judge.

RESTRICTIONS ON COURT ACCESS

There are three main types of power that the courts can use to exclude the press from a court: common law powers; powers derived from statute; and powers detailed in court rules (which are delegated legislation). The common law powers apply in all courts, but the statutory powers and court rules are specific to particular areas of the court system. The Human Rights Act 1998 also provides for certain circumstances in which the press and/or public can be excluded from court proceedings. Where a lower court was legally entitled to hear a case in private, the Domestic and Appellate Proceedings (Restriction of Publicity) Act 1968 provides that a court hearing an appeal from such a case can also sit in private.

In a few cases, the courts are required to exclude the public from a hearing, but in the majority of cases, the powers are discretionary. This means that, if the required circumstances apply, the court can choose to sit in private, or can choose not to; the existence of powers to exclude does not mean that a court should always do so.

In **Malik v Central Criminal Court** (2006), the Divisional Court considered the Criminal Procedure Rules which allow that bail applications 'may' be dealt with by a judge in chambers. The defendant wanted his application heard in public, but the Crown Prosecution Service (CPS) had argued that it was 'normal practice' for bail applications to be held in chambers, and there was nothing about this case that meant normal practice should not be followed. The court held that 'may' meant only that bail hearings could be dealt with in chambers where it was necessary to do so; it did not mean that there was a presumption that bail hearings should be held in private. While it was fine to hold hearings in private, if there was an application to hold one in public, it should be accepted, unless there was a sound reason for excluding the public. The court stated that such applications could legitimately come from the media, as well as parties to the case.

General powers to restrict access

All courts have a general common law power to control their own proceedings (often referred to as an 'inherent jurisdiction'), and this power can be used to exclude the public and/or press from a trial where it would be impossible or impracticable for justice to be done if the trial (or part of it) were held in open court. An example might be where evidence concerned a secret commercial process (such as the formula for a food or drink), and giving the evidence in public would reveal that secret and therefore make the proceedings pointless.

In practice, magistrates and judges these days are more likely to use the statutory powers which are specific to their courts (and described further on in this chapter). The inherent jurisdiction still exists, but in *A-G v Leveller Magazine* (1979), the House of Lords stressed that this power should only be used in exceptional circumstances, where it is clear that justice would be frustrated if the hearing was in public. Similarly in *R v Malvern Justices, ex parte Evans; R v Evesham Justices, ex parte McDonagh* (1988), the Court of Appeal explained that exclusion was not justified merely to save parties, witnesses or others from embarrassment or to conceal facts which might, on more general grounds, be desirable to keep secret.

In *R v Reigate Justices ex p Argus Newspapers* (1983), the case concerned a criminal trial, where the defendant had helped the police. His lawyer intended to mention this help as part of the pleas in mitigation (see p. 25), but the defendant did not want it to be publicly known that he had helped the police, and persuaded the magistrates to exclude the press and public from the court while the pleas in mitigation were made. Their decision was strongly criticised by the Queen's Bench Divisional Court, because it was not necessary in order to do justice in the case.

In general, if the public are excluded from a hearing using these powers, the press can be too. However, in *R v Crook* (1991), the Court of Appeal stated that there might be cases where the press should be allowed to remain even though the public were excluded. They gave the example of a prosecution for offences related to pornography, where they said the public might have to be excluded while a pornographic film was shown to the jury, because laughing and giggling from the public gallery would make it harder for jurors to do their job. This would not require the removal of the press as well.

Access to the criminal courts

Both the magistrates' courts and the Crown Court come under the general rule that cases should be heard in public, but in both cases there are circumstances where a case can be held in private.

The Magistrates' Court Act 1980 states that magistrates must sit in open court when trying a case, or imposing prison sentences. They are also required to sit in public when they are acting as examining justices (which essentially means during committal proceedings, sending for trial or proceedings which lead up to either of these), except where there are statutory provisions to the contrary, or where a public hearing would not be in the interests of justice. Where the magistrates are sitting as examining justices, written statements, depositions and other documents admitted in evidence should be read aloud unless the court commits the accused for trial without consideration of the evidence under s6(2) of the Magistrates' Courts Act 1980, or unless the the court otherwise directs, in which case an oral summary of the part of the statement not read aloud should be given.

The importance of openness in the magistrates' courts was stressed by guidelines issued to magistrates by the Judicial Studies Board (JSB) in 2001. *Reporting Restrictions in the Magistrates' Courts* confirmed that there were exceptional circumstances in which statute or common law allowed restrictions on access to, or reporting of, the courts, but emphasised that outside these exceptional circumstances:

- court proceedings should be held in public, and a court should not order or allow the exclusion of the press or public from any part of the proceedings;
- evidence should be communicated publicly, and a court should not permit information to be withheld from the open court proceedings;
- the court should not take any action to prevent fair, accurate and contemporaneous reporting of the proceedings, unless strictly necessary in the interests of justice.

The guidelines advised that where magistrates have a legal power to sit in private, or to impose reporting restrictions, they should not automatically choose to do so, but should consider whether there are less restrictive ways to achieve the administration of justice. They should also be prepared to listen to arguments from the media about why restrictions should not be imposed in a particular case. The booklet also points out that the law recognises that, in publishing news, speed is important, and so disputes relating to court access or reporting restrictions should be addressed as quickly as possible.

The JSB reminded magistrates that when deciding on whether to restrict access to the courts or impose reporting restrictions, they should take into account the Human Rights Act 1998, and Articles 6 and 10 of the European Convention on Human Rights, which require the courts to comply with rights to fair and public hearings, public pronouncement of judgments and the right to receive and impart information, subject to strictly limited exceptions.

The JSB has issued similar guidelines to Crown Courts, in 2000, which stress that as a general rule, their hearings should be in open court. Its Preface states that, before restricting press access, the courts should take the utmost care to ensure that such restrictions are necessary, and should be prepared to listen to representations made by the media when there is a feeling that restrictions unnecessarily interfere with open justice or make sensible reporting difficult.

Restrictions on access to the criminal courts

In addition to the common law powers of exclusion explained above, the situations in which criminal courts are permitted to exclude the public and/or the press from the court (subject to the guidelines detailed above) include the following.

Child witnesses in sex offences: Under s37 of the Youth Justice and Criminal Evidence Act 1999, the public can be sent out of court while evidence is given by witnesses under 18 in cases involving offences against decency and morality (which effectively means sex offences). However, bona fide representatives of newspapers, broadcasters and news agencies cannot be excluded under this provision. The law on this point is different, however, in Northern Ireland, where the Criminal Justice (Children) (Northern Ireland) Order 1988 allows a court to exclude anyone not concerned in the case, where a witness who is under 18 is giving evidence likely to be of an indecent or immoral nature.

Special measures directions: Section 25 of the Youth Justice and Criminal Evidence Act 1999 allows magistrates to make what is called a 'special measures' direction to exclude anyone from the court while a child or vulnerable witness gives evidence in a case concerning a sexual offence, or where there are grounds for believing that the witness has been, or could be, intimidated. However, the JSB guidelines (see above), state that this provision is not intended to apply to the press, who should not routinely be excluded along with the public. If there is reason to exclude the press as well – for example, to make the court less intimidating for the witness – one nominated representative must be allowed to stay in court. The Act also bans the media from reporting, before the end of the trial, that a special measures direction has been made, unless the jury is told of it.

Hearings in camera: The Crown Court Rules 1982 (as amended) allow Crown Court trials to be held in camera for reasons of national security, or for the protection of the identity of a witness or someone else. A party who wishes all or part of a trial to be held in private for one of these reasons must give the court written notice, at least seven days before the trial. The media may make representations against such an order, and s159 of the Criminal Justice Act 1988 gives the media a formal right of appeal against restrictions in this kind of case. The JSB guidelines state that courts should not automatically hold such cases in private, and where they do, proceedings should be brought back into open court as soon as exclusion of the public is unnecessary. In *Ex p Guardian Newspapers* [1999], the Court of Appeal said that if the defence applied to have a case heard in private on grounds of national security, the judge should ensure that he or she had evidence from the government as to the national security implications, rather than simply making the decision based on the evidence submitted by the defence.

Youth Court proceedings: Section 47 of the Children and Young Persons Act 1933 states that the public is not entitled to attend Youth Court proceedings, except at the court's discretion. The press, however, may attend.

Applications for further detention: Where the police want to continue keeping a suspect in detention before charging him or her, s45 of the Police and Criminal Evidence Act 1984 requires that the magistrates hearing the application should not sit in open court.

Cases under the Official Secrets Act: Section 8(4) of the Official Secrets Act 1920 and s11(4) of the Official Secrets Act 1989 provide that a court can order the public or a section of it to leave the court during any part of a hearing concerning an offence under the Act, if publication of the evidence to be given would be prejudicial to the safety of the country.

Law in practice **Defendants in multiple trials**

A common reason for excluding the press from the criminal courts is where the defendant is involved in multiple trials, and the court fears that reporting the current trial may prejudice later ones. Tony Jaffa, Head of Media at solicitors Foot Anstey, advises that in these cases, it can be worth challenging the exclusion on the basis that there are less restrictive ways to avoid that prejudice, for example by making a s4(2) order postponing reporting of the current trial until the others are over (see p. 105).

Obtaining information from the criminal courts

Daily Crown Court lists are available online (see *Online resources*, at the end of this chapter). Magistrates' courts cases are listed at too short notice to be published on the site, but magistrates' courts are encouraged by the Home Office to supply court lists to the media in court on the day of hearings. Home Office Circular 80/1989 states that magistrates' clerks should meet reasonable requests by the media for copies of court lists, and the register of decisions in magistrates' courts. Where provisional lists are prepared in advance, copies should also be made available on request. As a minimum, the lists should contain each defendant's name, age, address and, where known, their profession and the alleged offence. The circular also says that the courts should provide their local newspaper with a copy of the court register when it is prepared. Media representatives can be charged a fee for such materials, to cover the costs of staff time and resources.

Section s6(5) of the Magistrates' Courts Act 1980 provides that, following committal proceedings – either on the same day or on the day after – the court should display a public notice detailing the name, address and age of the defendant, the offence with which they were charged, and whether they were discharged or committed for trial. If the person was committed, the notice should include the charges, and the court to which the defendant has been committed. Such notices are subject to s4 of the Sexual Offences (Amendment) Act 1976, and so must not identify complainants of sexual offences (see Chapter 9). The name and address of any person under 17 years old should not be included in the notice, unless the justices have stated that, but for this prohibition, such information would have been included, and the name needs to be mentioned in order to avoid injustice to the person aged under 17.

The JSB guidelines on reporting restrictions make it clear that the identity of magistrates presiding over particular proceedings should be made public, in accordance with the decision in *R v Felixstowe Justices ex p Leigh* 1987 QB 582, *R v Evesham Justices ex p McDonagh* (1988), which stated that a court could not legally withhold the name of a sitting magistrate from the press.

The judgments in criminal appeal cases are available online (see *Online resources*, at the end of the chapter).

Information from the prosecution

In 2005, the Director of Public Prosecution (DPP) announced a new Protocol covering the type and amount of information which the media can generally expect to be provided by the prosecution in criminal cases. It states that the aim is to ensure greater openness in reporting legal proceedings, by making sure that the media has access to as much relevant material as possible, and 'at the earliest appropriate opportunity'. The Protocol divides information into two categories:

1   Information which the prosecution used when making their case in court. This category of information should automatically be released to the media and includes:

   ■ CCTV footage of the defendant (provided that copyright issues do not prevent its release);

   ■ photos or video footage of crime reconstructions;

   ■ maps, photos, diagrams or drawings used in court;

   ■ video footage of the crime scene, or seized property, stolen goods or weapons, recorded by the police;

   ■ transcripts of interviews and/or statements (or part of them) as read out in court.

2   Other material which may be released after consideration by the CPS, in consultation with the police, victims, witnesses and/or relatives. This includes:

   ■ statements made by victims and/or witnesses;

   ■ video and audio recordings of police interviews with defendants, witnesses and victims;

   ■ photos or CCTV footage of the defendant and the victim, or the victim alone, which has been seen in court by the jury and the public (as long as release is not prevented by copyright).

The above rules apply both where the accused pleads not guilty and the matter proceeds to a full trial, and to cases where the accused pleads guilty. However, in the case of not guilty pleas, the Protocol provides that only material which informs the court's decision on sentencing will be released; this must be material which reflects the prosecution case and was read out, shown in court or placed before the sentencing judge.

The Protocol provides that where the criminal justice agencies decide not to release a particular item, the media can make representations to the Crown Prosecution Service Head of Strategic Communications, who will review the decision.

Names and addresses

Home Office Circular 78/1967 makes it clear that courts should ensure that the names and addresses of defendants are read out in open court. This is to help the press ensure that it identifies the right person, and to avoid confusion with other people who may share the same name.

 In *R v Evesham Justices ex p McDonagh* (1988), a newspaper brought an action for judicial review against a decision by magistrates to allow a defendant not to have his address stated in court, because he feared harassment by his ex-wife. The Queen's Bench Divisional Court upheld the newspaper's argument, and confirmed that addresses should, as a rule, be read out in open court.

The names of witnesses, whether for the prosecution or the defence, should usually be stated in open court, but in exceptional cases (such as where a witness may be in danger if they are identified), a court can allow a witness to write down their name, rather than having it stated out loud.

▨ Access to the civil courts

The principle of open justice is equally important in the civil courts, and rule 39.2 of the Civil Procedure Rules, which covers the county courts and the High Court, confirms that as a general rule, proceedings should be held in public. However, the Rules state that a hearing may be held in private if:

- publicity would effectively make the proceedings pointless;
- the case involves information relating to national security;
- the case involves confidential information, which would no longer be confidential if the case was heard in public (this can include personal financial information);
- the case involves uncontentious matters concerning the administration of a trust, or the estate of someone who has died;
- privacy is necessary to protect the interests of a child or a patient;
- the case is an application without notice (which means in the absence of the person against whom the application is sought), and a public hearing would be unjust to the other side;
- the court considers privacy necessary to protect the interests of justice.

The Civil Procedure Rules are delegated legislation (see p. 5), and as such, the courts are obliged to interpret them, as far as possible, in a way compatible with the Human Rights Act 1998, which means they must give due weight to the importance of freedom of expression.

Certain types of civil cases, such as family proceedings, are subject to special rules regarding press and public access; the following are some of the most important to journalists. The rules on access to inquests, tribunals and divorce proceedings, however, are dealt with in the relevant later chapters.

Family proceedings

The rules on press attendance at family proceedings differ according to which court the proceedings are held in.

Magistrates' courts: Although family proceedings are not generally open to the public, s69(2) of the Magistrates' Courts Act 1980 provides that representatives of newspapers and news agencies are entitled to attend hearings. The exception is adoption proceedings: not only does the press have no right to attend these, but the Adoption Act 1976 provides that the court cannot give the press permission to do so. In other family proceedings, the magistrates' court can exclude the press while any evidence concerning indecency is given, if the court considers it necessary in the interests of justice or public decency (s69(4) of the Magistrates' Courts Act 1980).

The Family Proceedings Courts (Children Act 1989) Rules 1991 enable magistrates to sit in private in proceedings in which any powers under the Children Act 1989 may be exercised. However this power can only be exercised if it is the interests of the child concerned; magistrates should not simply sit in private as a matter of course in these cases. Even if the court does sit in private, the press need not be excluded – the court can specify 'other persons' who may attend in addition to the officers of the court, the parties and their lawyers (rule 16).

County Courts and the High Court: Although the Family Proceedings Rules only state that these proceedings should be held in chambers (which, as explained earlier, does not automatically mean that the press are not allowed in), it is usual practice for them to be closed to the press and public, unless the court specifically directs that any part should be open. This approach has been criticised recently, and it is becoming more common for judgments of High Court judges to be given in open court or made available to the press (see below). Wardship cases (see p. 140) must be held in private. However, in *Re P-B (a minor)* (1997), the Court of Appeal said that where there were issues of public interest, judgment could be given in open court, provided that directions were given to avoid identifying the child, where that was necessary to protect their interests.

Court of Appeal and House of Lords: Proceedings are usually open to the press and public, but in many cases one or more of the parties to the case are unidentified.

The issue of increasing press and public access to Family Proceedings has recently been examined by the Department for Constitutional Affairs (DCA), as part of a set of possible reforms aimed at increasing public confidence in this area of the judicial system. Campaign groups such as Fathers4Justice have highlighted the way in which holding proceedings in private allows the family courts to avoid public scrutiny of their decisions, and there have also been cases in which families have alleged that their children were wrongfully taken into care, again on the basis of court hearings held behind closed doors and not reported. The Department of Constitutional Affairs' 2006 consultation document, *Confidence and Confidentiality: Improving Transparency and Privacy in the Family Courts* (see *Online resources*, at the end of the chapter), recommends that there should be a basic right for the press to attend family proceedings, and that powers to order reporting restrictions should be more flexible. It seems likely therefore that things will change in the near future.

Recent cases suggest that the courts themselves are becoming more ready to accept that there is a public interest in press reporting of family proceedings, and that the privacy of the families involved can be protected without completely preventing media reports.

 In *An NHS Trust v MB & Anor* (2006), the High Court considered an application from an NHS Trust to withdraw artificial ventilation from an 18-month-old child with the degenerative disease spinal muscular atrophy. The Trust claimed that this would be in the child's best interests, as his condition was incurable and his quality of life was so poor that it was unethical to keep him alive. His parents opposed the application, arguing that he still had some quality of life, and that, in time, they hoped a cure might be found. The case was initially heard in private, but journalists at the BBC heard about it, and asked for permission to report it, as long as the parents did not object. Mr Justice Holman then agreed to open the court to the press and public for the rest of the hearing, but made an order that nothing could be published which might identify the family. In his eventual judgment (which rejected the Trust's application), he commented that it had been appropriate for a case of this nature to be held in public, and he was glad that the BBC had made the application.

Housing cases

Practice Direction 39, which supplements the Civil Procedure Rules, provides that where a landlord is claiming possession of a house or flat due to non-payment of rent, or where a mortgage lender is repossessing a house, the hearing is normally listed as a private one. However, the judge can decide to hold such hearings in open court, after hearing representations on the matter (this presumably includes arguments from the press, though the Practice Direction is not specific about who can make representations).

Applications for injunctions

In the county courts, applications for injunctions must be held in open court if the person the injunction would be against is represented by a lawyer (this does not apply to injunctions concerning domestic violence). Applications for injunctions in the Queen's Bench Division are usually heard in private, but in the Chancery Division, they usually take place in open court.

■ Obtaining information from the civil courts

Anyone bringing a civil case must fill in a claims form to start the case, and rule 5.4 (2) of the Civil Procedure Rules provides an automatic right, on payment of a fee, for any member of the public or press to search for, look at and/or obtain a copy of:

- any claim form, once an acknowledgement of service or a defence has been filed;
- any judgment or order made in public.

Changes made in October 2006 provide that the statement of claim, which gives full details of the basis of the case, should also be made available. However, this will only apply to claims filed after 2 October following complaints by the Law Society that parties in cases filed earlier would not have known that the details were likely to be made public.

Anyone named in a claim form can apply to the court to have the form's availability to the public and press restricted, or for the form to be edited before being made available to anyone not involved in the case. In family proceedings under the Children Acts, only a record of the order made is available to the press and public; other documents can only be issued with the judge's permission.

County court judgments, some High Court and Court of Appeal judgments, and all House of Lords judgments are available on the internet (see *Online resources*, at the end of the chapter).

If a hearing was held in private, you will need to apply to the judge for leave to obtain a copy of the order or judgment made. The Court of Appeal in *Hodgson* v *Imperial Tobacco* (1998) stated that such documents should usually be made available.

In some cases, the evidence given in a case may include written statements, which are not read out in court, but are given to the jury and referred to by the lawyers. This can make things quite difficult for court reporters, who do not have the relevant statements to refer to. To address this problem, rule 32.13 of the Civil Procedure Rules states that a witness statement which is used as evidence should be open to public inspection, unless the court directs otherwise. Grounds for a court refusing to make a statement available include:

- the interests of justice;
- the public interest;
- the nature of medical evidence contained in the statement.

Information after a case is over

There are many situations where you might want to find out the details of a case after it is over, for example as background to a later story. The issue was addressed in the 2004 case of *Re Guardian Newspapers Ltd* (Court record; Disclosure), where the *Guardian* applied to a court for witness statements concerning payments made by a British arms firms to the daughter of the then President of Indonesia. The material was needed for research into a story about bribery by the arms industry. The documents had been disclosed during a court hearing, but the case had been settled before it could be reported. The judge hearing the paper's application for the documents confirmed that statements referred to in court should usually be made available to the press and public, and said that the fact that the case had ended did not change this.

Records of judgments are held by individual courts, and many can also be accessed online (see *Online resources*, at the end of the chapter).

CHAPTER SUMMARY

The general rule on access

Hearings should be held in public; a court can only exclude the public if it has a legal power to do so.

Restrictions on access

All courts have a common law power to restrict public access where it would frustrate the administration of justice.

Statute and court rules allow exclusion in specific circumstances:

- child witnesses in sex offences;
- special measures directions;
- hearings in camera for reasons of national security, or protection of identity;
- Youth Court proceedings;
- applications for further detention;
- cases under the Official Secrets Act.

Information from the criminal courts

- Daily lists should be available to the press.
- Details of committal proceedings should be displayed within a day.
- Prosecution material should be given to the press where possible.
- Names and addresses of defendants should be read in open court.

Access restrictions in the civil courts

- the Civil Procedure Rules state when hearings can be held in private;
- family proceedings are subject to special rules;
- repossession cases are normally held in private, but can be held in open court;
- applications for injunctions may be public or private, depending on the court.

Information from the civil courts

- claim forms are open to inspection;.
- judgments are published online.
- witness statements should be available for public inspection;
- documents disclosed during a case should be available to the press.

TEST YOUR KNOWLEDGE

1 What is the difference between 'in camera' and 'in chambers'?

2 List the four circumstances in which the Human Rights Act 1998 allows the media to be excluded from all or part of a trial.

3 You arrive at your local court to report a case, only to be told that the judge has decided to exclude the press from the court room. What is the first thing you should do?

4 Name the four situations in which a court could use its common law power to exclude the press from a trial.

5 You are in court to report the trial of a man for the rape of a teenage girl. The judge states that she will exclude the press and the public while the victim gives her evidence. What arguments could you put forward to enable you to stay in court?

6 Can the press attend proceedings of Youth Courts?

7 You are assigned to report a Crown Court trial, but on the first day, the judge announces that the whole of the proceedings will be held in camera, for reasons of national security. What arguments can you use to get access to some or all of the proceedings?

8 You are reporting cases in the magistrates' court. Can you refer to the magistrates hearing the cases by name?

9 What information can a reporter working on criminal cases expect to get from the prosecution side?

10 You are reporting a case involving a well-known local businessman who is charged with shoplifting. He asks the court not to allow his address to be read out, as it would be embarrassing given his high profile in the community. The magistrates agree but can you provide any arguments to change their minds?

11 List the seven circumstances in which a civil hearing may be held in private.

ONLINE RESOURCES

www The Judicial Studies Board guidelines on reporting restrictions are available at:
www.jsboard.co.uk/publications.htm

The Civil Procedure Rules can be read at:
www.dca.gov.uk/civil/procrules_fin/index.htm

Crown Court lists are available at:
www.courtserv2.net

County court judgments and High Court judgments since 2006 are available at:
www.registry-trust.org.uk

(The site only shows the name and address of the defendant, the amount owing, the date of judgment and the name of the court; other information is held by the court itself.)

Court of Appeal judgments are available at:
www.courtservice.gov.uk

House of Lords judgments are available at:
www.publications.parliament.uk

Recent Home Office Circulars (and details of how to obtain older ones) can be found at:
www.homeoffice.gov.uk/about-us/publications/home-office-circulars

The Department of Constitutional Affairs' 2006 consultation document, *Confidence and Confidentiality: Improving Transparency and Privacy in the Family Courts*, is available at:
www.dca.gov.uk/consult/courttransparencey1106/consultation1106_intro.pdf

For further resources and updates please go to the Companion Website for this book at www.pearsoned.co.uk/practicaljournalism

General reporting restrictions under the Contempt of Court Act

In the previous chapter, we looked at the rules on when reporters are allowed to attend court hearings. Being allowed to attend a hearing, however, does not necessarily mean that you can report everything you see and hear. In this chapter, we look at the general reporting restrictions contained in the Contempt of Court Act 1981, which can apply in any type of case, and at the end of the chapter, at some miscellaneous restrictions contained in other statutes.

REPORTING RESTRICTIONS UNDER THE CONTEMPT OF COURT ACT 1981

As we saw in Chapter 6, the laws on contempt of court aim to prevent the publication of anything which could seriously prejudice a trial. In many cases, the press is allowed to make its own decisions on which cases to report, and how, provided that it does not publish material that breaches the law on contempt. However, the Contempt of Court Act 1981 also gives courts a general power to make orders which ban the reporting of particular court hearings, or aspects of them, where it is necessary to avoid a substantial risk of prejudice.

There are two types of reporting restriction allowed under the Act:

- orders under s4(2) allow a court to postpone publication of reports of a trial, or of any specific detail from the trial;
- orders under s11 allow a court to ban publication of a name, or any other information related to a trial.

The main difference between the two is that s4 orders are temporary, and s11 orders are permanent. The media can challenge either type of order, either on the grounds that the judge was wrong to make it at all, or that its terms are too restrictive (see Chapter 13).

Where orders may be used

The Act provides that s4(2) and s11 orders may be made in any court, defined in s19 as 'any tribunal or body exercising the judicial power of the State'. This means that these orders can be made in any of the civil or criminal courts, and also in the coroners' court, and in any tribunal which has been established by statute.

POSTPONING PUBLICATION: THE S4(2) ORDER

Section 4(2) provides that a court may, where it seems necessary to avoid a substantial risk of prejudice in any proceedings (whether already started, pending or imminent), order the postponement of any report of the whole proceedings, or any part of them.

There is no type of case in which a court has to make a s4(2) order; in each case, it should decide whether such an order is necessary. In practice, however, there are three situations in which s4(2) orders are almost always made:

■ **Where matters are discussed in the absence of the jury,** such as when one side asks the judge to exclude a certain piece of evidence on legal grounds. Clearly exclusion would be pointless if the jury heard the discussion about whether the evidence should be allowed or not, so jurors are sent out, but the press and public are usually allowed to remain. However, a s4(2) order is usually made so that the jury cannot find out about the discussion through the media.

■ **Where material arising during the trial carries a substantial risk of prejudice to other pending or imminent trials.** This might be, for example, because the defendant is being tried for several offences in separate trials, or because someone else in the case is facing trial on a separate issue. In these situations, reporting the current trial, or particular details of it, could cause prejudice to those which are due to take place afterwards. Section 4(2) only allows postponement where the trial which could be prejudiced is imminent or pending, which effectively means where the defendant has already been charged, or where it is known that a charge is about to be brought.

■ **Where a defendant has been acquitted, but the court believes there may be a new trial as a result of witness intimidation in the current one.** In this situation, publication is usually postponed until after the new trial.

Under s4(2), a court can also make an order preventing the disclosure of a person's name in open court.

Although these are the most common situations in which a s4(2) order is used, as stated above, the court has discretion to make such orders wherever it believes it is necessary to avoid a substantial risk of prejudice. Unfortunately, this discretion in some cases leads the courts to believe their powers are wider than they actually are. This problem was recognised by the then Lord Chief Justice, Lord Bingham, in the 2002 case of *Ex Parte News Group Newspapers*, where he commented that there was a 'serious problem' in some areas of the country with courts making orders restricting publication 'in situations where they should not be made'. It is important, therefore, to know what a court can and cannot do with s4(2) orders, and from the words of the statute, decided cases and Judicial Studies Board (JSB) Guidelines, the following principles emerge.

▦ The order must be necessary

The Act states that an order can be made where the court deems it 'necessary', and the courts have pointed out, in the cases below and others, that this means an order should not be made purely because someone involved in the case has a good reason to want one. This is an issue which has been examined more often in cases involving s11 orders, where it has been made clear that sparing embarrassment is not a good enough reason for such an order. In several s11 cases, the courts have said or implied that the same reasoning applies to s4(2) orders.

In 2004, Southwark Crown Court refused to issue a s4(2) order postponing publication of the address of Marvin Dawkins, better known as Romeo of the rap group So Solid Crew, who was on trial for wounding with intent to cause GBH and violent disorder. His lawyer had initially won a s11 order banning publication of his client's address, on the grounds that his client already suffered harassment from female fans turning up at his home, and this would increase if the address was published. The Press Association pointed out that s11 orders should not be granted merely to spare the feelings of defendants, referring to the case of *R* v *Evesham Justices ex p McDonagh* (1988) (see p. 110), and the court overturned the order. It then refused to issue a s4(2) order postponing publication of the address until after the hearing was over.

In *R* v *Burrell (2004)*, an official in the Department of Constitutional Affairs (DCA), Michael Burrell, was accused of raping a senior civil servant. As we will see in Chapter 9, the press is banned from publishing the identity of rape complainants, but this does not prevent reporting of the case itself and the evidence given. The complainant asked for a s4(2) order preventing publication of large sections of her evidence, on the grounds that some of her colleagues knew she was the complainant, and that if the evidence was published, she would feel unable to return to her job. She suggested that without such an order, she might not give evidence at all. The judge refused the order, for three reasons. Firstly, Parliament had granted rape victims anonymity under the Sexual Offences (Amendment) Act 1992, and the fact that it had chosen not to provide for reporting restrictions in the same Act must mean it accepted the need for such evidence to be given in public, as a part of the general principle of open justice. Secondly, the defendant wished to exercise his right to a public trial, and the court was obliged to take this into account, and weigh it against the complainant's right to privacy. Thirdly, in several cases involving s11 orders, the courts had refused to grant orders which were requested in order to spare embarrassment or damage to career or business. The same principles applied with regard to s4(2) orders. In the event, the trial collapsed after the complainant became ill, and the judge entered a formal verdict of not guilty.

An order will not be considered necessary where the same effect could have been achieved by less restrictive means.

In *Ex p Central Independent Television Plc* (1991), it was held to be unnecessary to ban reports of a trial while the jury was considering its decision overnight, because risk of prejudice could have been avoided by the court telling jurors not to switch on televisions or radios.

■ The risk must be substantial

This is clearly stated in s4(2), and means that a s4(2) order should not be made merely because some risk of prejudice exists; it must be a substantial risk.

In *MGN Pension Trustees Ltd* v *Bank of America National Trust and Saving Association and Credit Suisse* (1995), the judge was asked to make an order postponing publication of reports of civil trials concerning the pension funds of companies owned by the tycoon Robert Maxwell, to avoid prejudice to future fraud proceedings related to the same funds. The judge stated that in deciding whether postponement orders should be allowed or refused, there were three questions to be asked:

- Was there a substantial risk of prejudice to the administration of justice if publication was not postponed? If yes,
- Did it appear necessary that a postponement order be made in order to avoid that risk? If yes,
- Should the court use its discretion to make the order, and if so, what should its terms be? Even if there was a risk of substantial prejudice, it did not automatically follow that an order should be made.

In this case, he said, the risk of prejudice was not substantial, and the words of the statute made it clear that an insubstantial risk was not enough to displace the importance of a free press.

In *R* v *Horsham Justices, ex P Farquharson* (1982), the Court of Appeal considered whether it was justified to use a s4 order to postpone reports of a trial, on the basis that reading them each night could prejudice the jury in the trial. It held that the risk of a jury being prejudiced, during a trial, by daily reports of it was insubstantial. Lord Denning, the Master of the Rolls, pointed out that jurors are instructed by the trial judge to decide the case only on the evidence before them, and are perfectly capable of ignoring newspaper stories. Therefore the risk of prejudice was not substantial and did not justify a s4 order.

In 2004, the Fathers4Justice campaigner David Chick was tried for causing public nuisance, after dressing up as Spider-Man and climbing a crane near Tower Bridge, where he stayed for six days, causing massive traffic disruption in the local area. Not surprisingly, the protest was widely reported at the time it happened, and when the case came to court, the trial judge imposed a s4(2) order postponing reports of the hearing until it was over, on the grounds that they might remind jurors of the previous publicity and thus prejudice the case. The Press Association was able to get the order lifted, by pointing out to the judge that press reports of the daily proceedings were no more likely to prejudice the jury than hearing the same details in court each day.

■ The order must remove the risk

In *R (on application of Telegraph Group PLC)* v *Sherwood* [2001], the Court of Appeal pointed out that after deciding whether there is a substantial risk of prejudice, a court should ask whether a s4 order would actually remove that risk; in some cases, it would not, and therefore no order should be made. Even if an order would remove the risk, before granting it, the court should consider whether there are other, less restrictive ways of achieving the same result.

■ Proceedings must be current, imminent or pending

Section 4(2) orders can only be made where there is a risk of prejudice to the proceedings before the court, or to other court cases which are already under way. Details of events which do not take place in a court cannot be covered by a s4(2) order.

In *R* v *Rhuddlan Justices ex p HTV Ltd* (1986), magistrates had made a s4 order purporting to prevent HTV from broadcasting a programme which showed a man being arrested. On appeal, it was found that they had acted outside their powers, and the order was invalid.

■ Postponement must be for a specific time

Typically, a postponement order runs until the end of the trial in question, or where it is made to avoid prejudice to later trials, until the end of those. However, it is up to the court to decide the length of the order, and in some cases, courts will try to use s4(2) to impose what really amounts to a permanent ban. In *R* v *Horsham Justices ex p Farquharson* (1982), the court stated that this was not an appropriate use of s4(2), and confirmed that orders should last for no longer than was necessary to avoid the risk of substantial prejudice.

■ The public interest must be considered

The 2001 JSB guidelines for magistrates' courts stress that when deciding whether to make a s4 order, courts should seek to strike a balance between the public interest in open justice, and the right of the defendant(s) to a fair trial; in some cases this may mean that a small risk of prejudice is worth taking in the cause of open justice. This approach was backed up in *R (on application of Telegraph Group PLC)* v *Sherwood* [2001], where the Court of Appeal pointed out that there may be cases where the public interest in open justice means a s4 order should be refused, even if that means a trial could be prejudiced as a result.

In 2006, a determined reporter from the *Plymouth Evening Herald* persuaded a court to lift a s4(2) order, on his third attempt. The case concerned three men involved in supplying cocaine, as part of a supply chain that stretched from the local area to South America. The judge imposed a s4(2) order because the men were also involved in other legal proceedings. However, reporter Matt Fleming argued that the seriousness of the case meant that the public were entitled to know about it, and the s4(2) order meant that it could be as long as a year before it could be reported. His first two attempts to challenge the order were rejected, but finally, with help from the prosecution lawyer, he managed to persuade the judge to lift most of the restrictions, so that the ban only covered reporting of any material which might prejudice the later trial.

The JSB guidelines also state that where a case is already covered by the automatic restrictions contained in s8 of the Magistrates' Courts Act 1980 (see p. 117), a court should be reluctant to impose further restrictions by means of a s4 order.

PREVENTING PUBLICATION: THE S11 ORDER

Section 11 of the Contempt of Court Act 1981 gives a court power to restrict or ban publication of details given in court proceedings. The section provides that:

> In any case where a court (having power to do so) allows a name or other matter to be withheld from the public in proceedings before the court, the court may give such directions prohibiting the publication of that name or matter in connection with the proceedings as appear to the court to be necessary for the purpose for which it was so withheld.

The phrase 'having power to do so' means that this section only applies where the court already has powers to withhold the relevant information from the public (e.g. s12 of the Administration of Justice Act 1960 allows a court to withhold information in certain cases involving children). If there is no legal provision which allows the court to withhold the information in the first place, a s11 order will be invalid.

■ The name or matter must be withheld in court

Section 11 orders can only be made to prevent publication of details which have not already been revealed in open court.

In *R v Arundel Justices ex p Westminster Press* (1985), s11 reporting restrictions banning publication of a person's name were quashed, because the name had already been mentioned in open court. The Divisional Court held that a court had no power to make a s11 order in those circumstances.

In 1999, lawyers for News Group Newspapers were able to persuade a recorder to refuse to make an order banning publication of the name of a defendant accused of stealing from a prostitute. The recorder accepted the argument that the man's name and address had already been given in open court.

In a 2004 case, a s11 order banning publication of the addresses of a couple on trial for sexual offences involving children was lifted after representations from the *Kent Messenger*. The defendants' counsel had argued for the order because his clients' home had been fire-bombed after their address and the charges had appeared in the press. The trial judge delayed considering lifting the order until the end of the trial, but agreed to lift it then, on the grounds that the defendants' address had already been given in public at the magistrates' court hearing, and so could not be covered by a s11 order.

◼ The ban must be necessary in the interests of justice

Section 11 is a severe restriction on the principle of open justice, and both the higher courts and the JSB have made it clear that it should only be used where absolutely necessary, which essentially means where the interests of justice would be seriously harmed by publication. The JSB's 2001 guidelines specifically state that orders should not usually be made simply to spare the blushes of defendants or witnesses, or to protect their business interests or professional reputation.

 In *R v Evesham Justices ex p McDonagh* (1988), an ex-MP was being tried on a motoring offence, and asked for his address to be kept secret because he feared harassment from his ex-wife. The magistrates agreed, but on appeal, the Divisional Court ruled that the order was not necessary in the interests of justice. It pointed out that there were many defendants who, for various reasons, would prefer not to have their addresses published, but s11 orders were not designed to be used to protect 'the comfort and feelings of defendants'.

 In *R v Legal Aid Board, ex p Kaim Todner* (1999), a London solicitors' firm had had its legal aid franchise taken away, and sought judicial review of the Legal Aid Board's decision. It asked for a s11 order banning the press from publishing the name of the firm, but the judge refused. The Court of Appeal upheld the refusal, stating that the principle that justice should be done in public should only be compromised where justice demanded it, and protecting a firm's reputation was not such a situation.

 In *R v Dover Justices, ex p Dover District Council* (1992), a defendant charged with public health offences was granted a s11 order by magistrates, on the grounds that reports of the case would inevitably damage his business reputation, and therefore the business itself. The Divisional Court overturned the order, stating that these were not sufficient grounds for such a severe restriction on reporting.

 In a 2002 case, magistrates agreed, at the request of the defence, to issue a s11 order preventing the naming of two people accused of involvement in a house fire in Huddersfield, on the grounds that publication of their identity might prejudice witnesses who had yet to come forward. The Press Association was able to get the orders overturned, because of the public interest in reporting the case fully.

 In the 2004 case involving rapper Romeo (see p. 106), the Press Association was able to get a s11 order banning publication of the star's address overturned. It had been requested to protect him from the attentions of female fans, but the Press Association pointed out the ruling in *R v Evesham Justices* that s11 orders should not be made for the 'comfort and feelings' of defendants. In addition, it pointed out that as the star already had a problem with fans turning up at his house, his address must already be known. The judge overturned the order.

The courts will, however, allow s11 orders in a situation where sparing someone embarrassment is itself in the interests of justice. In *R v Legal Aid Board, ex P Kaim* (see below), Lord Woolf pointed out that, for example, a witness who was needed for a hearing but had no personal interest in the proceedings might have a good claim to anonymity, because the courts would be dependent on their cooperation. Similarly, s11 orders are commonly used to conceal the identity of victims in blackmail cases, on the grounds that such victims would be much less likely to report the crime if they thought that their secrets would be exposed in court, and clearly the interests of justice would be damaged if, as a result, fewer blackmailers were brought to justice.

 In *R v Socialist Worker Printers and Publishers Ltd ex p Attorney-General* (1975), the *Socialist Worker* was prosecuted for contempt after naming two blackmail victims who had been granted anonymity by a court.

Equally, where the effect of a person's identity being published goes beyond embarrassment and becomes possible mental harm, the courts may allow anonymity under s11, on the grounds that the interests of justice give that person the right of access to a court, and without anonymity, they will be unwilling to take up that right, or be unable to do so, without harming themselves. The courts have therefore allowed s11 orders for very vulnerable defendants, and some who are required to give medical evidence of a very personal nature.

In *Re JCA* (13 November 2003, unreported), a man who had mental problems was appealing against his conviction for manslaughter. The Court of Appeal found that a s11 order granting anonymity was justified because he was particularly vulnerable and might suffer mental harm from publicity. The Court stressed, however, that this was a different situation from cases where s11 orders were sought in order to spare embarrassment or distress, and confirmed that those were not appropriate grounds for an order.

In *H v Ministry of Defence* (1991), the Divisional Court allowed a s11 order granting anonymity to a defendant in a personal injury case, which involved embarrassing medical evidence. The Master of the Rolls, Lord Donaldson, said that in some such cases a s11 order might be necessary to protect defendants, because public knowledge of the evidence given would be more than merely embarrassing, and might cause genuine harm to the defendant. Without such protection, defendants would be put off seeking justice.

■ Risks to the person claiming anonymity

In some cases, a s11 order will be requested in order to protect someone (usually a witness) who fears for their own personal safety if their identity or address is revealed. The approach of the courts to these cases has varied, as the cases below show, but it seems that orders requested for this reason will only be granted in very exceptional cases.

In *A v Inner South London Coroner* (2004), Times 11 November, the Court of Appeal upheld the use of a s11 order to protect a police officer who it found had reasonable grounds for fearing for his life.

In 2004, s4 and s11 orders were made by magistrates in Birmingham, covering a case in which a police officer was charged with careless driving, after knocking down a teenage girl. The police officer's lawyers had argued that as he was due to be a witness in a forthcoming murder trial, publishing his name and address could endanger his life, and might also prejudice that trial. The orders were challenged by the local press, and a district judge overturned them, on the grounds that although it might be true that the officer himself believed he would be in danger, there were no objective grounds to suggest his belief was correct, and there was no connection between the trial for careless driving and the murder case. Similarly, it is clear that the mere fact that someone involved in the case is a police officer or prison officer is not by itself grounds for anonymity, and on several occasions the press has successfully challenged s11 orders made on this basis.

In *Re W (Children) (Care Proceedings: Witness Anonymity)* (2002), a s11 order was used to protect the identity of a social worker in care proceedings. The case involved a woman whose children were under threat of being taken into care, but who had been told she might be allowed to keep them if she broke off contact with her husband, who had a history of extreme violence. She agreed, but before the care proceedings took place, a social worker happened to see her with her husband. The social worker agreed to give evidence in the proceedings, but given the possible risk to her from the husband (who had threatened that if he lost the children he would kill himself and, among others, the social workers), she asked to do so anonymously; the judge agreed and made a s11 order. The woman, however, appealed, and the Court of Appeal upheld her claim, stating that it was generally recognised that social workers were routinely threatened with, and actually experienced, violence in their work, and had to regard this as part of their job. This was not an exceptional case, and so the s11 order could not be said to be necessary in the interests of justice.

In *Re Belfast Telegraph Newspapers Application* (1997), a man charged with indecent assault was granted a s11 order by magistrates, on the grounds that he feared attack if his address was published. The Queen's Bench Divisional Court overturned the order, stating that, while such a risk might well exist, it was not something that could prejudice the trial and therefore a s11 order was not appropriate.

In 2006, the *Oxford Mail* managed to overturn a s11 order banning identification of a man convicted of attempting to have sex with a 12-year-old girl. The order had been put in place at the request of the man's lawyer, because he was said to be a vulnerable individual who would be at risk of bullying in prison, and might even be a suicide risk. The *Oxford Mail* objected, arguing that the man had been sent to a normal prison, and his name was already in the public domain because it had been said in open court, and shown in court listings on the internet. The judge agreed that this was not an appropriate use of s4(2) powers.

■ Notice of s4(2) and s11 orders

Practice Directions issued in 1982 and 1983 make it clear that both types of order should be put into writing, stating the purpose for which the order is being made, precisely what it covers and, if not permanent, when it ceases to apply. Courts should notify the press when such orders are made, and court staff should be willing to answer queries about such orders (Practice Direction (Sup Ct: Contempt: Reporting Restrictions) [1982] and Practice Direction (Contempt of Court Act: Report of Proceedings: Postponement Orders) (1983)).

Law in practice   Is an order in place?

If an order imposing reporting restrictions of any kind is in place, a notice will usually be posted up in the court complex. However, Tony Jaffa, Head of Media at solicitors Foot Anstey, points out that some courts are more careful about doing this than others. The Practice Directions instructing courts to notify the press about orders make it clear that even if this is not done, the responsibility for finding out whether an order exists and following it remains with the press, so the fact that a notice has not been put up will not help you if you break it because you did not know it existed. If you are reporting a case where you would expect that an order might be made, but there is no notice to that effect, always check with the court staff.

OTHER STATUTORY REPORTING RESTRICTIONS

In addition to the restrictions on reporting court cases detailed so far, there are some miscellaneous statutory provisions which apply either generally or to specific types of case.

■ Divorce cases

The Judicial Proceedings (Regulation of Reports) Act 1926 provides that reports of divorce, nullity or judicial separation proceedings must **only** contain:

- the names, addresses and occupations of the parties and any witnesses;

- a concise statement of the charges, the defence, and any counter-charges for which evidence has been given, but not abandoned charges or counter-charges (this provision means that reports cannot be published until all the evidence has been given);

- submissions made on any point of law, and the court's decision on them;

- the court's judgment, and the judge's comments on it. Other remarks made by the judge during the hearing cannot be included.

Maintenance proceedings

When a marriage ends, either party can apply to the court for an order compelling the other party to make periodic payments intended to cover the living expenses of that spouse and/or any children from the marriage (in most cases, the woman applies for maintenance from the man, but the reverse can be true).

Maintenance applications can be reported, but under s1(1)(b) of the Judicial Proceedings (Regulation of Reports) Act 1926, the reports must be limited to the same four categories of information as listed above for divorce hearings.

Medical evidence

Section 1(1)(a) of the Judicial Proceedings (Regulation of Reports) Act 1926 forbids publication in court reports of any indecent medical, surgical or physiological details which would be calculated to injure public morals. In practice, however, it has been many years since a successful prosecution was brought under this provision, and it seems likely that these days, a report would have to be extremely distasteful in order to break the law.

CHAPTER SUMMARY

Reporting restrictions under the Contempt of Court Act 1981

Courts can order reporting restrictions where necessary to avoid a substantial risk of prejudice, in any type of case.

The s4(2) order

This order can be used to postpone publication, under these conditions:

- the order must be necessary;
- the risk of prejudice must be substantial;
- the order must remove the risk;
- proceedings must be current, imminent or pending;
- postponement must be for a specific time;
- the public interest must be considered.

The s11 order

This allows courts to ban publication of any matter that has been withheld from the public during court proceedings.

General reporting restrictions under the Contempt of Court Act

Section 11 orders can only be used where:

- the information has not been given in court;
- an order is necessary in the interests of justice.

Neither order should be given merely to spare defendants embarrassment.

Notice of s4(2) and s11 orders

Both orders must be put into writing, stating the purpose, scope and duration.

Other reporting restrictions

Statutory restrictions also apply to:

- divorce and maintainance proceedings;
- indecent medical evidence.

TEST YOUR KNOWLEDGE

1 Explain the difference between a s4(2) order and a s11 order.

2 In which courts can these orders be made?

3 In what situations will a court be justified in granting a s11 order to spare embarrassment to someone involved in a case?

4 A local restaurant owner is on trial for fraud offences involving customers' credit cards. He asks the court for a s4(2) order banning publication of the name of his restaurant, on the grounds that publicity about the case could damage his business. What argument(s) could you use to persuade the court not to make such an order?

5 A police officer is on trial for fraud. Her lawyer asks for a s11 order, banning publication of her home address, on the grounds that she has previously appeared as a witness in trials of very dangerous criminals, and fears for her safety if her address is made public. What argument(s) could you put forward to convince the court not to grant the order?

6 You have been attending a shoplifting case in the magistrates' court, which has followed standard court procedure. After the defendant is convicted and given a community sentence, his lawyer asks the court for a s11 order, banning the press from mentioning his client's name in reports of the case. He says that his client is unemployed, and the publicity would affect his chances of getting a job. What argument(s) would you use to dissuade the court from making the order?

7 What details can you report about a divorce case?

ONLINE RESOURCES

www   The Judicial Studies Board guidelines on reporting restrictions are available at:
http://www.jsboard.co.uk/publications.htm

Useful reports of cases where reporting restrictions have been imposed or overturned can be found at the Hold the Front Page website:
www.holdthefrontpage.co.uk

The Society of Editors website also reports current cases on reporting restrictions, at:
www.societyofeditors.org

For further resources and updates please go to the Companion Website for this book at www.pearsoned.co.uk/practicaljournalism

8

General reporting restrictions under the Contempt of Court Act

Chapter

9

Reporting restrictions in criminal cases

Of all the work done in the courts, criminal cases probably hold the most interest for journalists, and no local paper would be complete without its coverage of the magistrates and Crown Court. This coverage not only sells papers, but also has a social value, in that the thought of being featured in the press is, in a sense, part of an offender's punishment (as any reporter who has been begged to keep a case out of the paper will know). One result of this, however, is that defence lawyers will often do their very best to persuade magistrates and judges to restrict reporting, so journalists need a good grasp of the reporting restrictions in order to challenge them where this is possible. It is also, of course, essential to know about those reporting restrictions which are mandatory in certain types of cases, particularly those involving sex offences, where publishing certain types of information is a criminal offence.

Most criminal cases involving adults can be freely reported (within the provisions of the law on contempt, explained in Chapter 6), but some types of case, or parts of a case, attract specific reporting restrictions. They fall into three main groups:

- restrictions on hearings which take place before a trial;
- restrictions on cases involving rape and sexual offences;
- restrictions on pleas in mitigation.

There are also reporting restrictions designed to protect witnesses in certain circumstances.

(Criminal cases involving children and young people are subject to separate rules, which are discussed in Chapter 10.)

RESTRICTIONS ON HEARINGS BEFORE TRIAL

As we saw in Chapter 3, before a criminal trial begins, there are one or more hearings, depending on the type of case. Most of these hearings are subject to special restrictions on what can be reported. These restrictions support the general principle that when the trial begins, the jury should be able to judge on what they hear and see during the trial, and not anything that may have happened before it.

Preliminary hearings in the magistrates' court

Where a defendant is charged with an either way offence (see p. xx), a preliminary hearing will be held to determine whether they are to be tried in the magistrates' court or the Crown Court. Cases involving indictable offences also begin in the magistrates' court, with a preliminary hearing called sending for trial. In both these types of hearing, the magistrates are said to be acting as examining justices.

In the past, sending for trial was known as committal proceedings (and is often still referred to in this way, although not technically correct), and entailed an initial examination of the evidence, but now the magistrates merely look at the documents detailing the case. However, a defendant can at this point argue that there is not sufficient evidence against them for the case to go ahead.

Section 8(1) of the Magistrates' Courts Act 1980 imposes restrictions on what can be reported in both types of preliminary hearing. The media can **only** publish:

- the names of the court and of the magistrates;
- the names, addresses and occupations of the parties and the witnesses, and the ages of the defendant(s) and witnesses;
- the offences with which the defendant is charged (if this is only given as a summary, reporters can ask the clerk of the court or the prosecution for details, such as when and where the offence is alleged to have been committed, and the name of the victim if any);
- the names of the barristers and/or solicitors representing the parties;
- if the proceedings are adjourned, the date and court to which they are adjourned;
- whether the case was transferred to the Crown Court;
- any arrangements concerning bail on committal or adjournment;
- whether legal aid was granted to any of the defendants;
- whether reporting restrictions were lifted.

Details which should therefore **not** be mentioned include:

- reasons given by the police for opposing bail;
- reasons given by the magistrates for refusing bail;
- any previous convictions of the defendant.

These restrictions effectively mean that nothing either side alleges can be reported at this stage. You can report details of the alleged offence which have already been published (e.g. where and when the incident is said to have happened), but only where these details do not create a risk of prejudice.

A report which contains details other than those on the list can get a publisher or broadcaster into trouble, even if in the circumstances the extra information revealed would not in fact cause serious prejudice to the trial.

In 1996, the owners and editor of the *Gloucester Citizen* were fined £4,500 for publishing a report of murderer Fred West's first appearance in the magistrates' court. The story was an accurate account of the hearing, but in addition to the permitted details, it included a statement that West had admitted killing his daughter. Even though the case had already been widely discussed in the media before the hearing, the paper was guilty of contempt.

The restrictions only apply to reports of the committal hearing itself, so it is legal to publish, for example, details of who arrived at the court with the defendant, or in high-profile cases, the fact that a crowd has gathered outside the court. As always though, be careful not to include anything likely to prejudice the case.

Lifting the restrictions

The reporting restrictions can only be lifted if the defendant applies to have them lifted and it is in the interests of justice to do so. If there is more than one defendant, and they disagree about whether restrictions should be lifted, the magistrates can lift them where they believe it is in the interests of justice to do so. Bear in mind that even if restrictions are lifted, reports of the hearing should not include details of previous convictions or any other information that carries a substantial risk of serious prejudice to the Crown Court trial, as this would be contempt of court.

When do restrictions end?

The reporting restrictions come to an end when one of the events below occurs:

- **The magistrates accept that there is insufficient evidence and dismiss the case.** In this situation, the Magistrates' Courts Act 1980 (as amended) states that such written statements as were accepted as evidence should be read aloud, unless the court directs otherwise. If the court does direct that the evidence should not be read out, it must be summarised instead.

- **All the defendants have been tried at the Crown Court.** Even though this may be some time after the committal hearing, a fair and accurate report of that hearing will still be treated as a contemporaneous report for the purposes of defamation law.

- **The court decides to try one or more defendants summarily.** In this situation, the press can report the summary trial, even if it takes place before that of the defendants who are going to be tried in the Crown Court.

Once the court has lifted reporting restrictions, it cannot then reinstate them. This was established in *R v Blackpool Justices, ex p Beaverbrook Newspapers Ltd* (1972).

Note that there is a form of committal hearing where reporting restrictions do not apply. Section 70 of the Proceeds of Crime Act 2002 allows magistrates to make an order committing a convicted defendant to the Crown Court, where a hearing will decide whether a confiscation order should be made against the defendant, to deprive them of any property gained by their crimes. In this case, the magistrates are not sitting as examining justices, so reporting restrictions do not apply.

Law in practice Committals for sentencing

As explained in Chapter 3, there are limits on the sentences which magistrates can impose. As a result, magistrates who have found a defendant guilty will often decide that the offence justifies a more serious sentence than they can order, and so will send the defendant to the Crown Court for sentencing. Although this is usually described as 'committing' the defendant to the Crown Court, it is not a preliminary hearing like those described on this page, because the defendant has already been tried, and so restrictions under s8 of the Magistrates Courts Act 1980 do not apply.

Liability under s8(1)

Only the publisher, proprietor or editor of a paper, or those with similar functions in a broadcasting company, can be prosecuted under s8(1). Prosecutions can only be brought with the consent of the Attorney-General.

Bail applications

Section 8 of the Magistrates' Courts Act 1980 limits reporting of bail hearings to 'arrangements as to bail on committal or adjournment'. This means you can report whether bail was granted, and any bail conditions, but should not include arguments about whether bail should be granted, nor any reasons given if bail was refused.

◼ Pre-trial hearings

Where a defendant is to be tried in the Crown Court, the Criminal Procedure and Investigations Act 1996 allows the court to hold a pre-trial hearing to pinpoint the key issues in the case, and deal with any disputes about the admissibility of evidence. The Act defines a pre-trial hearing as one which is held after a defendant has been sent to the Crown Court for trial, but before that trial begins (the beginning of the trial is defined as when the jury is sworn in, or when the court accepts a guilty plea).

Sections 41 and 42 of the Criminal Procedure and Investigations Act 1996 prevent reporting of any rulings made at these hearings, or of any of the rulings requested by either side, for the very obvious reason that there is no point in the court ruling a certain piece of evidence inadmissible if the jury can read of its existence in their daily paper.

A similar type of hearing can be held in the magistrates' court, for cases which are to go to summary trial. The Courts Act 2003 prohibits reporting on any ruling made in such a hearing until the end of the trial (because of the potential that it could prejudice magistrates in the trial itself).

In both cases the restrictions apply until the trial of all defendants in the case has concluded. However, the restrictions can be lifted in whole or in part, provided that the court is satisfied, after hearing the representations of all the accused where any of them object, that it is in the interests of justice to do so.

◼ Preparatory hearings

Preparatory hearings are also defined in the Criminal Procedure and Investigations Act 1996, and are often confused with pre-trial hearings, though they are in fact a separate type of proceedings. They are held in the Crown Court, in cases which are likely to be long and/or complicated, and are designed to help both sides make the issues and evidence in the case as easy to understand as possible for the jury. These hearings are held at the start of the trial, but before the jury has been sworn in.

Sections 37 and 38 of the Criminal Procedure and Investigations Act 1996 provide that reports of such hearings may **only** contain:

- the name of the court and the judge;
- the names, ages, home addresses and occupations of the accused and witnesses;
- the offence or offences charged or a summary of them;
- the names of the lawyers in the proceedings;
- where the proceedings are adjourned, the date and place to which they are adjourned;
- any arrangements as to bail;
- whether legal aid was granted.

The Crown Court, Court of Appeal and House of Lords can lift the restrictions, either completely or partially. If any of the defendants object, the court has to be satisfied that it is in the interests of justice to lift the restrictions, after hearing the representations of each accused. If the restrictions are lifted, the ban continues to apply to the accused's objections to their being lifted, which cannot be reported. Otherwise, the restrictions end on conclusion of the trial of the accused or the last of the accused to be tried.

■ Applications to dismiss

Where a defendant has been committed to the Crown Court for trial on an either way offence (see p. 18), or on a summary offence (this usually happens where they are also charged with a related offence triable in the Crown Court), they can apply to the court to dismiss the case on the grounds of insufficient evidence. Under the Crime and Disorder Act 1998, reports of applications to dismiss can **only** include:

- the names of the court and of the judge;
- the names, addresses and occupations of the parties and the witnesses, and the ages of the defendant(s) and witnesses;
- the offences with which the defendant is charged;
- the names of the barristers and/or solicitors representing the parties;
- if the proceedings are adjourned, the date and court to which they are adjourned;
- any arrangements concerning bail on committal or adjournment;
- whether legal aid was granted to any of the defendants.

If the application to dismiss is successful, the restrictions no longer apply and a full report can be published. If it is not successful, details of the application to dismiss other than those listed can only be published after the trial is over. If there are two or more defendants and they all make an application to dismiss, restrictions only end when all of them have succeeded in their dismissal applications or been tried.

A judge hearing an application to dismiss can lift reporting restrictions if it is in the interests of justice to do so; if one or more of the defendants objects, the judge must hear their arguments and can only lift restrictions if having heard them, they still believe it is in the interests of justice.

Serious fraud cases

Some cases of serious fraud can bypass the usual committal proceedings, and be transferred straight to the Crown Court. This procedure is put into practice where one of a list of designated persons (which includes the Director of Public Prosecutions, the Commissioners of the Inland Revenue and the Director of the Serious Fraud Office) certifies the case as being suitable for direct transfer.

Where this happens, the defendant(s) can apply to the Crown Court for the transfer to be dismissed on the grounds of insufficient evidence. If such an application is made, reporting restrictions apply. The same restrictions also apply if the Crown Court orders a preparatory hearing to go through the issues in the case. The restrictions provide that media reports may **only** contain:

- the name of the court and the judge;
- the names, ages, home addresses and occupations of the defendants and any witnesses;
- any relevant business information (this essentially means only the names and addresses of any relevant business, firm or company);
- the alleged offence(s) or a summary of them;
- if the proceedings are adjourned, the date and court to which they are adjourned;
- any arrangements regarding bail;
- whether legal aid was granted.

These restrictions end if the defendant is successful in their application to have the case dismissed, or if goes to trial, at the end of the trial.

■ Transfer of sexual offence cases involving children

Where a case involves a sexual offence, s53 of the Criminal Justice Act 1991 provides a procedure by which the normal rules on committal for trial can be bypassed, and the case transferred directly to the Crown Court without any examination by magistrates. This procedure is used where the Director of Public Prosecutions is satisfied that that following three conditions apply:

- The nature of the offence makes it suitable for trial in the Crown Court.
- A child who is either the victim or a witness will be called to give evidence.
- The case should be moved to the Crown Court without delay, in order to avoid any prejudice to the welfare of the child.

In such a case, the defendant can apply to the Crown Court to dismiss the transfer on the grounds of insufficient evidence. If a defendant makes such an application, reporting restrictions apply, and reports must be limited to the same details as specified for committal proceedings, above.

Schedule 6 of the Criminal Justice Act 1991 provides that the judge can lift reporting restrictions in such cases, but if the defendant objects, the restrictions can only be lifted where it would be in the interests of justice to do so.

RESTRICTIONS IN RAPE AND SEXUAL OFFENCES

In order to encourage the victims of sexual offences to report them to the police, reporting restrictions usually prevent the media from identifying such victims, not just during the trial but for the whole of their lifetimes. These restrictions have recently been tightened, and are now covered by the Sexual Offences (Amendment) Act 1992, as amended by the Sexual Offences Act 2003, and by Schedule 2 of the Youth Justice and Criminal Evidence Act 1999.

The combined effect of these Acts is that once someone (man or woman) has made an allegation of a sexual offence, then 'no matter relating to that person shall, during the person's lifetime, be included in any publication if it is likely to lead members of the public to identify that person as the person against whom the offence is alleged to have been committed.' The legislation does not define 'allegation'; in practice this has been treated as meaning making a complaint to the police, but some lawyers believe it may apply earlier than this. Once someone has been accused of the sexual offence, a reporting restriction expressed in slightly different words applies, though the effect would appear to be the same: 'no matter likely to lead members of the public to identify a person as the person against whom the offence is alleged to have been committed shall, during the complainant's lifetime, be included in any publication.'

What will amount to 'matter' that could lead to identification? A new sub-section 3(a) in the amended 1992 Act states that this category includes:

- the person's name;
- their address;
- their school or any other educational establishment they attend;

- their place of work;
- any still or moving pictures of them.

However, publishing information which is not on this list can also be an offence, if it is likely to lead to identification of the person concerned. An obvious example would be stating the name of the defendant and saying that he is charged with raping his niece, since that would allow the public to identify the victim.

■ Offences covered by the restrictions

The restrictions described apply not just to rape, but also to most other offences which contain a sexual element (including offences which do not involve any physical contact, such as indecent exposure). These include:

- rape (see p. 35 for the definition of this offence, which is now wider than often believed);
- attempted rape;
- aiding, abetting, counselling and procuring rape;
- incitement to rape;
- conspiracy to rape;
- burglary with intent to rape;
- indecent assault;
- offences involving indecency or sexual activity with children;
- indecent exposure;
- internet 'groooming';
- trafficking for sexual exploitation;
- voyeurism.

(Note that these are examples, and not the complete list; essentially, if there is a sexual element to an offence, it is likely to be covered by the reporting restrictions.)

The same restrictions apply to both female and male complainants, and children as well as adults. Unless lifted by a court, the restrictions last for the whole of the complainant's lifetime, even if the complaint is withdrawn or the defendant is acquitted.

The provisions apply to all proceedings which involve allegations of a sexual offence, and not just those held in the criminal courts. They would also apply, for example, in civil cases where there are allegations of a sexual offence (sex discrimination cases in the employment tribunal, for example, may involve allegations of indecent assault). They also apply to any other kind of story which could identify someone as the victim of a sexual offence, and not just reports of court cases.

In 2005, the editor of *Marie Claire* magazine was fined £2,500 after the magazine named the victim of a sex offence. In a feature reviewing stories that had hit the news over the previous year, the magazine mentioned a teenage girl who had run away from home to be with a 31-year-old former US marine. The piece included her name and a photograph. After the girl came home, the man was charged and convicted of incitement to commit gross indecency. The girl had been widely named during the period while she was missing, but at that stage, no complaint of a sex offence had been made so the ban on identification did not apply; by the time *Marie Claire* published its story, it did. The editor argued that she had no reason to suspect that the girl might be the victim of a sex offence, but the judge found that in the circumstances, this was not a realistic argument.

Lifting the restrictions

A judge can make an order lifting the restrictions, in two circumstances:

- Where, before a trial, the person accused of rape asks for restrictions to be lifted, in order to encourage people who may be needed as witnesses to come forward, and that person's defence is likely to be substantially prejudiced if the reporting restrictions are not lifted.

- At the trial, where the judge is satisfied that retaining the reporting restrictions would impose 'a substantial and unreasonable restraint' on the reporting of proceedings, and that it would be in the public interest to remove the restrictions.

With regard to the second of the above reasons, judges are most likely to lift restrictions in cases where the case being tried includes other, very serious offences.

In *R v Hutchinson* (1986) the case involved the murder of three members of a family, and the rape of a fourth member, who survived the attack. The rape victim was the main witness in the murder trial, and as she had the same surname as the rest of the family, mentioning their names would have identified her. The press pointed out that this made it impossible to report the murder case adequately, and the judge agreed that it was in the public interest to lift the victim's anonymity.

Restrictions can also be lifted at the request of the victim, but only if they are over 16 when consent is given. The victim must give written consent to each publication that will identify them, and the decision must have been made freely, and not under pressure from anyone. Proof of the victim's consent is a defence for a newspaper or broadcaster prosecuted under the Act.

It is also a defence for a publisher to prove that it was not aware, and neither suspected nor had reason to suspect, that the material published was likely to lead to the complainant's identification as an alleged victim of the sexual offence. A further defence, introduced in the Youth Justice and Criminal Evidence Act 1999, applies if the publisher can show that it neither knew nor suspected that an allegation of a sexual offence had been made.

Other restrictions in sexual offence cases

It is important to realise that the above provisions are quite specific and protect only the victim. They do not create a general power to impose restrictions on publication of any other details, such as the defendant's name or any potentially embarrassing details given in evidence. There are, however, clearly cases where naming the defendant would mean identifying the victim (e.g. if you report that John Smith of Anytown raped his daughter, you identify her even though you do not give her name). In those cases, you would commit a criminal offence if you published the name of the defendant, because it would be material that could lead the victim to be identified.

A court can in some cases use its other powers to impose reporting restrictions in a sexual offence case (e.g. a s39 order where the defendant is a juvenile), but it has to follow the rules relating to those powers; the fact that the case involves a sexual offence is not enough in itself to justify restrictions other than those on naming the victim.

In *R v Praiil* (2004), a judge at Maidstone Crown Court lifted an order banning the media from naming the chief executive of a charity, who had been charged with rape and indecent assault. The order had been made on the grounds that mentioning his place of work and other details would identify the complainants, but Mr Justice Aikens found that their identity could be protected without imposing such severe restrictions.

9

Reporting restrictions in criminal cases

In 2004, a district judge in Cardiff refused to grant an order protecting the identity of a teacher charged with sexual offences, which was claimed to be necessary because naming the teacher would effectively identify the girls involved. The judge said that he had no power to make such an order, and deciding whether to publish the defendant's name had to be a matter of judgement for the press; if it did so in such a way as to identify the victims, there were criminal penalties to deal with that.

Law in practice Jigsaw identification

The main danger in reporting sexual offence cases lies in inadvertently identifying the victim through what is known as 'jigsaw' identification, advises Tony Jaffa, Head of Media at solicitors Foot Anstey. This arises where, although the name of the victim is never mentioned, details which are given can be pieced together, perhaps by someone who knows the victim, to work out their identity. 'An example would be a case where a man rapes his stepdaughter, and you report that the offence happened ten years ago, when the victim was 15. If you also mention a stepdaughter who is 25, it doesn't take a genius to work out who the victim probably was. In those cases, if the facts are especially newsworthy and you want to report them, the safest option is not to name the defendant.'

■ Special rules on incest cases

In Northern Ireland, sexual offence cases involving incest may be prosecuted under the Punishment of Incest Act 1908, which no longer applies in England and Wales. The Act allows both press and public to be excluded from court proceedings, and the victim has anonymity, but the court case can be reported unless an order restricting reporting is made.

REPORTING PLEAS IN MITIGATION

When a defendant has pleaded or been found guilty, their lawyers can make pleas of mitigation on their behalf, which essentially means putting forward reasons why the court should deal with the defendant more leniently than it might otherwise do. In some cases, such pleas will involve derogatory accusations against another person. For example, take a case where the defendant has attacked the victim because the victim made a particularly unpleasant racist remark. If the defendant has pleaded guilty, they might wish to use this as part of their pleas in mitigation.

Usually, such matters can be reported, but ss58–61 of the Criminal Procedure and Investigations Act 1996 provide that reporting restrictions may be applied where there are 'substantial grounds' for believing that:

■ something said in the pleas in mitigation is derogatory to someone's character (e.g. because it suggests that their conduct is or has been improper, immoral or criminal); and

■ those allegations are untrue, or that the facts stated are rrelevant to the defendant's sentence.

The court can order that the allegations may not be reported for up to a year after the trial.

It is important to note that the Act requires 'substantial grounds'; restrictions should not be ordered where there is merely a chance that the allegations may be derogatory and untrue or irrelevant.

In 2006, a reporter on the *Scarborough Evening News* was able to get a reporting restriction on pleas in mitigation overturned in an assault case. The defendant was convicted of assaulting another man, and as part of the pleas in mitigation, his lawyer explained that the defendant had believed the victim was having an affair with his wife, and that she was pregnant with the victim's baby. The court was going to impose reporting restrictions on the grounds that this was a derogatory statement about the victim, but the reporter pointed out that it had to have 'substantial grounds' for believing the statement was untrue, and it did not have such grounds. The reporter also pointed out that the claim was not irrelevant to the sentence, as the magistrates had said it was grounds for giving the defendant a lighter sentence. The magistrates agreed not to make the order.

The order can be made at any time before the sentence is decided, or as soon as reasonably practical after that, and can be cancelled at any time. Such an order cannot be made, however, if the allegations concerned have already been made during the trial (because in that case there would have been a chance to challenge them during the trial).

If such an order is made, it is an offence to publish the allegations while it lasts, even if the report does not name the person who the allegations are about, so long as it contains material which would make it likely that a member of the public could identify that person.

PROTECTING VULNERABLE WITNESSES

Section 46 of the Youth Justice and Criminal Evidence Act 1999 gives the courts power to prevent identification of vulnerable adult witnesses where the witness is eligible for protection (see below) and reporting restrictions are likely to improve:

■ the quality of evidence given by the witness; or

■ the level of cooperation the witness gives to any party in the case, during the preparation of their case.

A witness is eligible for protection if the court is satisfied that the quality of their evidence, or the level of their cooperation is likely to be diminished by fear or distress about being identified by members of the public as a witness in the proceedings. The 'quality' of evidence is defined by the Act as relating to completeness, accuracy and coherence.

In assessing this, the court must take into account:

■ the nature and circumstances of the alleged offence;

■ the age of the witness and, if relevant, their social and cultural background, religious and political beliefs, and domestic and employment circumstances;

■ any behaviour towards the witness by the defendant, the defendant's family or associates, or anyone else who is likely to be defendant or witness in the proceedings;

■ the witness's own views on the matter.

This provision only applies to adult witnesses; children are covered by separate rules – see Chapter 10.

If a court decides to make a s46 order, the order bans publication of any material relating to the witness, which could lead to them being identified as a witness in the case. This includes the person's name and address, any educational establishment they have attended, their workplace or any still or moving picture, but the wording suggests the list is not exhaustive and other material which could identify them would also be included.

In 1999, the Home Office issued explanatory notes which made it clear that the provisions are intended to be used in cases of real fear or distress, and not merely embarrassment about possible publicity. The guidelines also pointed out that the fact that a witness exhibits sufficient fear or distress to make use of video evidence or a screen desirable (see below), did not necessarily mean that it was also necessary to ban the press from revealing the witness's identity.

In 2005, the *Sunday Express* successfully challenged a s46 order, covering the trial of a convicted paedophile who had sent sexually explicit letters containing death threats to the family of Milly Dowler, who was murdered in 2002. The man, Paul Hughes, was in prison when he began to send letters to the family; most of them were stopped by the prison's security system, but one slipped through the net, and was opened by Milly's sister, Gemma. Hughes was charged with threatening to kill Mrs Dowler, and the judge in the case made a s46 order prohibiting the press from identifying Gemma Dowler. However, the *Sunday Express* argued that as the defendant had pleaded guilty, no witnesses were called, and if Gemma Dowler was not a witness, she could not be protected by a s46 order. The court lifted the order.

Section 46(8) of the Act provides that in judging whether to grant an order, the court must decide whether an order would be in the interests of justice, and take into account the importance of not putting unreasonable restrictions on the reporting of court proceedings. The Act also gives the courts power to lift or amend an order once made. A witness who is over 16 can waive their rights under a s46 order, in writing, so long as nobody interfered with their 'peace or comfort' in order to obtain that waiver.

Witnesses in adult courts who are under 18 have similar protection provided by s39 of the Children and Young Persons Act 1933. However, these orders come to an end when the young person turns 18, and in the Judicial Studies Board's 2000 guidelines on court reporting, the JSB confirmed that it was not possible for a court to make an order concerning a witness who was under 18 which would last after that person's 18th birthday.

The Youth Justice and Criminal Evidence Act 1999 also gives courts in criminal cases powers to issue a 'special measures direction', under which the public is excluded from the court while a vulnerable or intimidated witness gives evidence (see p. 96). Such a direction can also be used to allow a witness to give evidence by live video link from elsewhere, or from behind a screen. Section 47 of the Act makes it an offence to report before the end of a trial that such an order was made, though the evidence the witness gives can be reported, as can their identity (unless an order concerning identity has been made). The Serious Organised Crime and Police Act 2005 now provides that special measures directions can also be made in hearings concerning ASBO applications, even though these are civil proceedings.

Section 88 of the Serious Organised Crime and Police Act 2005 makes it an offence to publish the new identities of witnesses who are under police protection, or to reveal any other details about their protection.

CHAPTER SUMMARY

Restrictions on hearings before a trial

Special reporting restrictions apply to:

- preliminary hearings in the magistrates' court;
- bail applications;
- pre-trial hearings;

- preparatory hearings at the start of long and/or complex trials;
- applications to dismiss a case for lack of evidence;
- transfer of serious fraud cases;
- transfer of sexual offences involving children.

Restrictions on rape and sexual offence cases

- Once a complaint is made, it is an offence to publish anything relating to the complainant that might identify them as the person making the allegation.
- Once someone has been accused, no material at all which might identify the complainant as the alleged victim can be published.

These restrictions last for the complainant's lifetime, and apply to most sexual offences.

Restrictions on pleas in mitigation

Publication of arguments which are derogatory to someone else can be restricted for up to a year if they are untrue and/or irrelevant, and have not been made in open court during the trial.

Protecting vulnerable witnesses

Courts can prohibit publication of anything which could identify a vulnerable witness, where fear or distress at being identified would otherwise affect:

- the quality of evidence; or
- their cooperation with a party to the proceedings in preparing their case.

TEST YOUR KNOWLEDGE

1 A report of committal proceedings in the Crown Court reads: 'James Jones, 36, appeared before magistrates this morning, charged with burglary. Ms Jane Smith, prosecuting, told the court that the defendant had been caught red-handed leaving a luxury flat in King Street; he later admitted burgling ten other apartments in the same block. The magistrates refused bail, with the Chairman, Jake Pake, explaining that there was a clear risk that the defendant would offend again before the trial.'
   Which bits of the report should be removed before publishing?

2 You are reporting a bail application. The prosecution opposes bail on the grounds that the defendant is likely to try to leave the country before the trial, but the magistrates grant bail, provided the defendant surrenders his passport. What can you put in your report?

3 Explain the difference between a pre-trial hearing and a preparatory hearing.

4 Why is it prohibited to report rulings made in pre-trial hearings?

5 When do reporting restrictions on preparatory hearings end?

6 What details can you include in a report of an application to dismiss?

7 What restrictions apply to rape cases when a complaint is first made? How do they differ once someone has been accused?

8 When can the restrictions on reporting rape cases be lifted?

9 Which of these sentences is permissible in a report of a rape trial?
   (a) John Smith is charged with the rape of his niece.
   (b) John Smith is charged with the rape of his niece, Jane.
   (c) A Birmingham man has been charged with the rape of his niece.
   (d) A plumber of Hope Street, Birmingham, has been charged with raping his niece.
   (e) A care assistant from Birmingham told the court how she was raped by her uncle.

10 John Smith has been charged with assault after punching a man whom he claims made indecent suggestions to his wife. His solicitor's pleas in mitigation include information about the victim's relationships with women. In what circumstances does the Criminal Procedure and Investigations Act 1996 allow the court to prevent the press from reporting these remarks?

11 What powers does the Youth Justice and Criminal Evidence Act 1999 give courts to protect vulnerable witnesses? What must the court consider when deciding whether to use these powers?

ONLINE RESOURCES

www The Youth Justice and Criminal Evidence Act 1999 can be read at:
www.opsi.gov.uk/acts/acts1999/90023--e.htm#46

The Sexual Offences (Amendment) Act 1992 can be read at:
www.opsi.gov.uk/acts/acts1992/ukpga_19920034_en_1.htm

The Criminal Procedure and Investigations Act 1996 can be read at:
www.opsi.gov.uk/acts/acts1996/1996025.htm

The Judicial Studies Board guidelines on reporting restrictions are available at:
www.jsboard.co.uk/publications.htm

Useful reports of cases where reporting restrictions have been imposed or overturned can be found at the Hold the Front Page website:
www.holdthefrontpage.co.uk

The Society of Editors website also reports on the use of reporting restrictions, at:
www.societyofeditors.org

For further resources and updates please go to the Companion Website for this book at www.pearsoned.co.uk/practicaljournalism

Reporting restrictions concerning children

It is often believed – by magistrates as well as journalists – that the law imposes a blanket ban on identifying juveniles involved in criminal proceedings, but this is not the case. However, there are rules which restrict the press from identifying children and young people who are involved in court cases, whether as victims, witnesses or defendants. Some restrictions are automatic, though most of these can be lifted by the courts in certain circumstances; others are applied at the court's discretion.

When considering whether to lift or apply restrictions in cases involving children, the higher courts have made it plain that the courts must give sufficient weight to the Human Rights Act 1998, and in particular, the Article 10 right to freedom of expression on the one hand, and on the other, the rights under Articles 6 and 8 to a fair trial and respect for private and family life respectively.

As far as the law discussed in this chapter is concerned, 'child', 'young person' and 'juvenile' are all used to mean a person under 18. However, under English law, a child who is under ten cannot be charged with a criminal offence; children under ten who have committed acts which would be criminal offences if they were older can however be made the subject of a child safety order (see p. 47).

Until a criminal case comes to court, the media is free to publish the names of any juvenile involved, just as for adults, provided that doing so does not create a risk of prejudicing any trial, under the normal rules on contempt of court (explained in Chapter 6). The one exception is where the offence is a sexual one, in which case the complainant may not be identified (see p. 121).

YOUTH COURT CASES

The first point to note here is that many magistrates, and magistrates' clerks, believe that Youth Courts are closed courts. This is incorrect: although these courts are not open to the public, s47 of the Children and Young Persons Act 1933 provides that bona fide journalists from newspapers and news agencies have a right to attend Youth Court proceedings.

Where a young person is being prosecuted in a Youth Court, the media cannot identify them unless the court or the Home Secretary lifts reporting restrictions. Section 49 of the Children and Young Persons Act 1933, bans the media from publishing or broadcasting:

- the name, address or school of any child or young person who is involved in the proceedings (as well as defendants, this includes witnesses and victims who are under 18);

- any details that are likely to lead to a young person involved in the proceedings being identified;

- any photograph of a young person involved on the proceedings.

(In Northern Ireland, similar provisions apply, but under the Criminal Justice (Children) (Northern Ireland) Order 1998.)

If the ban is breached, the proprietor, editor or publisher of the newspaper (and those who have corresponding functions in a broadcasting company) may be prosecuted for a breach of the Act. They will have a defence if they can prove that they were unaware and did not suspect that the material published breached s49.

The effect of s49

Section 49 makes it clear that the ban goes beyond merely mentioning the name of a Youth Court defendant: you cannot publish anything at all which is likely to identify them. It is not sufficient to make sure that no ordinary member of the public can recognise the young person from the details or images shown; the offence can be committed even if only those who know the young person would be able to identify them from the story. For this reason, merely concealing the face in a photo, for example, may not be enough to avoid prosecution.

In 2003, the *Plymouth Evening Herald* was fined £2,500 for publishing a photo of a 15-year-old boy who had been convicted at a Youth Court after stabbing another child. The paper had partially concealed the boy's face in the photo they used, but his friends and family gave evidence that they could still tell that it was him.

Law in practice Adults in Youth Court proceedings

Take care with naming adults who are involved in Youth Court proceedings (such as witnesses). Although there is no ban on naming anyone aged over 18, naming an adult could accidentally provide information which could identify someone under 18 in the case (e.g. if they are related). Essentially, if someone who did not already know the details of the case could name the child as a result of reading the report, there is a risk of committing an offence under the Act.

Lifting the s49 restrictions

There are three situations in which the Youth Court reporting restrictions can be lifted.

1 **Avoiding injustice:** Section 49(5) of the Children and Young Persons Act 1933 allows the Home Secretary, or the court concerned, to waive the ban on identifying a child involved in Youth Court proceedings, 'if satisfied that it is appropriate to do so for the purpose of avoiding injustice to a child or young person.' An example of the way in which this provision might be used is where a young witness has been publicly confused with a young defendant, and naming the defendant would avoid injustice to the witness. This provision is not designed to be used as a means of 'naming and shaming' defendants.

2 **Tracing suspects:** The Criminal Justice and Public Order Act 1994 provides that the Director of Public Prosecutions can apply to a Youth Court to remove reporting restrictions where this could help trace a juvenile charged with or convicted of a violent or sexual

offence, or any offence for which an adult could receive a sentence of 14 years or more in prison. The court can decide the extent to which restrictions are lifted, so may, for example, put a time limit on the order.

3 **After conviction:** Once a child has been convicted in a Youth Court, the Crime (Sentences) Act 1997 allows the court to waive the ban on identifying them, where it is in the public interest to do so. Before doing so, it should take into account any arguments for or against lifting the ban put forward by either side in the case. In 1998, the Lord Chancellor's Department and the Home Office circulated jointly-produced advice on the kinds of circumstances in which waiving restrictions would be justified in the public interest. These include:

- where the young person was a persistent or very serious offender;
- where the offending had affected a large number of people;
- where publicity could help prevent further criminal activity.

The advice also identified circumstances where it would generally not be in the interests of justice for reporting restrictions to be lifted. These include:

- where publicity might put the young person or their family in danger of harassment or harm;
- where the offender was especially young or particularly vulnerable;
- where the offender was sorry for their actions, and prepared to take responsibility for them;
- where naming the offender would mean identifying the victim, and this would lead to unwelcome publicity about the victim.

Unless the court chooses to exercise one of these three options, the ban applies automatically; the court does not need to make an order imposing it. Where the media feels that the ban should be lifted, they can make representations to the magistrates.

 In *McKerry* v *Teesdale & Wear Valley Justices* (2001), the case concerned a 15-year-old who had pleaded guilty to taking a car without consent. The magistrates sought to lift the reporting ban, on the grounds that the offender had shown a complete disregard for the law and was a danger to the public, and that if he was identified, the public would find it easier to protect themselves from his activities. The Divisional Court of the Queen's Bench stated that the power to lift reporting restrictions on Youth Court cases had to be used with care, and should not, for example, be used as an additional punishment to 'name and shame' the offender. However, the court agreed that this was an example of a situation in which there was a legitimate public interest in identifying the defendant.

Where the young person turns 18 during the proceedings, the s49 restriction is automatically lifted. This was confirmed in *Todd* v *Director of Public Prosecutions* (2003).

Other courts where s49 restrictions apply

The reporting restrictions described above also apply to reports of appeals from the Youth Courts, either to the Crown Court, or to the Divisional Court of the Queen's Bench on a point of law. They also apply where proceedings are held in any court to vary or withdraw a supervision order against someone under 18, as long as the reporting restrictions are stated in open court.

Young people who are accused of very serious crimes may be committed by the Youth Court for trial at the Crown Court. These proceedings are covered by the usual reporting restrictions on committal proceedings, explained at p. 117. The Crown Court trial itself will not be covered by the restrictions applicable to Youth Courts unless a specific order to that effect is made (see *Children in adult courts*, below).

Law in practice Youth Court anonymity after 18

Youth Court anonymity lasts only until the defendant's 18th birthday, so if a defendant is soon to turn 18, you may not need to bother asking the court to lift anonymity, as you will be able to write about the case after their birthday anyway, advises Tony Jaffa of solicitors Foot Anstey. This also means that once an offender turns 18, you are free to write about their Youth Court history, so if they are convicted again as an adult, it is permissible to use this as background.

CHILDREN IN ADULT COURTS

In cases of serious crime, or where there is an adult co-defendant, a person under 18 may be tried in the magistrates' Court or Crown Court. The rule that the court should sit in public still applies, but a Practice Direction issued in 2000 states that in some cases, it may be appropriate to take steps to make the courtroom less intimidating for a very young defendant. Where this would include restricting press access to the courtroom, arrangements should be made to relay the proceedings to another room within the same building, preferably by video but at least via an audio link (Practice Direction (Crown Court: trial of children and young persons) 2001).

Where a juvenile is involved in proceedings before any court except a Youth Court, their age does not automatically create any reporting restrictions. However, s39 of the Children and Young Persons Act 1933 allows the court to order that:

- newspaper or broadcast reports of the proceedings may not reveal the name, address or school of the young person, or include any details designed to lead to the young person being identified; and
- no pictures of the young person can be published or broadcast.

Such orders can cover any person under 18 who is 'concerned in the proceedings', including witnesses and victims as well as defendants (but not victims who are dead; see below). In Northern Ireland, broadly similar provisions apply, but under art. 22 of the Criminal Justice (Children) (Northern Ireland) Order 1998.

The court is not obliged to make a s39 order, but they commonly do. However, guidelines issued to Crown Court judges by the Judicial Studies Board in 2000 warn that the power should not be used 'as a matter of routine'; the courts should balance the need to protect young people against the importance of open justice.

Where a judge is considering making an order, the press can put forward arguments against it. The basis for such arguments would generally be that in the case concerned, the importance of press freedom outweighs the possible effects of publicity on the child. The judge then has to weigh up the competing interests of press freedom and protection of the child.

In *R v Winchester Crown Court, ex p B (A Minor)* [2000], Lord Justice Simon Brown spelt out the issues a court should consider when deciding whether to impose a s39 order:

- where the juvenile in question was a defendant, their age, and the potential damage to them of being identified as a criminal at that age;

- the responsibility placed on the court, under s44 of the Children and Young Person's Act 1933, to have regard to the welfare of the young person;

- the deterrent effect on the defendant themselves, and others, of publicity relating to the case;

- the public interest in open justice, and specifically in knowing the identities of those who have committed crimes.

Clearly some of these principles conflict with others, and the court must try to strike a balance between them in the circumstances of the individual case. The correct balance, Lord Justice Brown said, might be different at different stages of the case: for example, once a defendant had pleaded or been found guilty, it would often be right to give greater weight to the public interest in knowing who had committed the crime.

The following cases indicate some of the ways in which the courts have juggled these issues.

In *R v Central Criminal Court ex p Crook and ex p Goodwin* (1995), the case concerned a s39 order made in the trial of a couple for the manslaughter of their son, and cruelty to their other three children. Not being able to identify the children made it very difficult to report anything meaningful about the case, and the order was challenged by the press. However, the court held that in the circumstances of this case, the importance of protecting the children outweighed the public interest in knowing about the case.

In *R v Central Criminal Court ex p Simpkins* (1998), the Divisional Court upheld a judge's decision to lift an order banning identification of three teenagers accused of indecent assault and rape. In deciding to lift the order, the judge had emphasised the deterrent effect that publicity was likely to have on other young people. In the divisional court, Mr Justice Sullivan upheld this approach, and said that there had to be a good reason for imposing a s39 order; if they were too frequently used, there was a danger of blurring the distinction between Youth Courts, where anonymity was the norm, and the Crown Court. The fact that a defendant was young was not, in itself, a good enough reason for a s39 order.

In *R v Lee* (1993), the Court of Appeal approved the refusal of a judge to issue a s39 order for a 14-year-old boy who had taken part in a robbery, while he was on bail after being charged with rape. The judge had said that identifying the boy would have a strong deterrent effect on others, and the public interest in knowing who he was was greater than any potential risk of harm to the boy himself. The Court of Appeal approved this reasoning.

In 2005, two reporters from Yeovil's *Western Gazette* were able to persuade magistrates to lift a s39 order banning identification of twin boys aged 14, whose mother was charged with failing to send them to school. The order effectively meant that the mother could not be named either, and the journalists were able to argue that this was in breach of the principle of open justice.

In 2006, a s39 order protecting a teenager who killed her mother's boyfriend was lifted after a reporter from the *Lancashire Evening Telegraph* pointed out to the court that the ban made it virtually impossible to report the case at all. The victim had been a well-known figure in the area, and the reporter pointed out that the ban meant that if he was named, his relationship to the defendant, and the place where the murder happened, could not be mentioned, as these details would identify the defendant. The murder had received a lot of publicity and the restrictions would mean that readers would not even realise that it was the event referred to in the court report. In addition, it was pointed out that the ban would make it impossible to report the mitigating circumstances put forward for the defendant, so she would appear to have killed in cold blood. The order was lifted despite opposition from defence lawyers.

In 2006, the *Liverpool Echo* persuaded a court to lift a s39 order covering a teenage boy who ran over and killed a pensioner in the man's own car. A s39 order had covered the trial, but when the boy was convicted of manslaughter, a reporter was able to persuade the judge that any negative impact on him was outweighed by the public interest in finding out who had committed such a serious crime.

In 2006, a judge at Liverpool Crown Court agreed not to make a s39 order banning identification of a victim, after representations from the press. The 13-year-old victim was viciously attacked at school by another teenager, resulting in national press coverage, and the *Liverpool Echo* argued that her name had already been used in reports of the attack, and that her family did not object to her being named.

In 2006, the *Manchester Evening News* was able to get reporting restrictions lifted in a case involving a 15-year-old who punched a man so hard that the victim was left in a coma. In a written application, the paper's reporter stressed the public interest in open reporting of the case, pointing out the seriousness of the attack, and the fact that it took place at a time when anti-social behaviour was a topic of enormous public debate, with the Government putting forward proposals to deal with it. The court agreed to lift the order.

In 2006, a trainee reporter from the *Dorset Echo* persuaded a court not to impose a s39 order banning identification of a 17-year-old who had pleaded guilty to burglary. The reporter pointed out that the youth had already been named in a plea and directions hearing, and also repeated the judge's comments about the distress that burglary causes to its victims, as evidence of the public interest in hearing about the case fully.

As a rule, the courts should not impose s39 orders on the grounds of protecting the defendant's family from publicity. In **Chief Constable of Surrey v JHG and DHG** (2002), the Queen's Bench Division held that the effect of publicity on the family should only be taken into account in very exceptional cases, where the impact on the relatives would affect the rehabilitation of the offender themselves, or where a member of the family might suffer a degree of emotional or psychological trauma that went beyond the normal effects of being connected with someone publicly known to have committed crime.

In 2002, an Old Bailey judge lifted a s39 order which banned publication of the identity of a 17-year-old convicted of murder, and had been issued to protect his younger siblings from the effects of publicity. The judge agreed to lift the order, because of the importance of deterring other young people from similar crimes.

▨ Very young children

The Judicial Studies Board (JSB) guidelines acknowledge that where a child is very young, they are much less likely to be damaged by publicity, and so s39 orders are less likely to be appropriate. The JSB does not specifically define 'very young', but explains that the risk is smaller because the child will not be aware of the publicity, which suggests the principle is confined to children young enough not to be aware. In a number of cases, the press has been able to get restrictions lifted on this basis.

In 2004, a judge at Aylesbury Crown Court removed a s39 order prohibiting the press from naming a six-week-old baby who had been thrown against a wall by his father. The judge agreed with the arguments of a local press reporter that the baby could not be hurt by the publicity, and that the protection was actually covering the defendant, rather than the child.

In 2000, the *Banbury Guardian* convinced local magistrates to lift a s39 order preventing identification of an 18-month-old child, whose father had pleaded guilty to being drunk in charge of a child.

The magistrates agreed that a child of this age could not be affected by any publicity about the case.

In 2004, a reporter on the *Worcester Evening News* successfully challenged a s39 order banning identification of a two-year-old, in a child neglect case. The reporter cited the *Banbury Guardian* case above, and the court agreed that this was a similar case where the child was too young to be affected and the ban would unreasonably restrict reporting.

In 2006, the *Eastern Daily Press* persuaded a court to lift a s39 order which applied to a 11-month-old baby, whose stepfather was accused of child cruelty. The paper pointed out that a ban on identifying the child meant it could not name the defendant either, and the judge agreed that as the child was so young, there was no real chance of it being affected by the proceedings.

Naming dead children

There have been cases where judges have attempted to use s39 orders to ban publication of the names of dead children, even though the names have already been made public, for example in inquest reports or news stories about the deaths. The JSB guidelines for both magistrates' courts and the Crown Court state that the powers under s39 cannot be used in this way. However, it is important to make sure that mentioning a dead child does not mean that other children who are subject to a s39 order (such as siblings) are effectively identified as well.

Children not 'concerned in the proceedings'

As explained earlier, s39 permits orders to be made in respect of children 'concerned in' court proceedings. This clearly covers children who are defendants, victims and witnesses in criminal cases, and s39 orders are also routinely made concerning children who are the subject of family and education cases. However, it is sometimes possible to dissuade a court from issuing, or persuade them to lift, a s39 order on the basis that the child in question is not 'concerned in the proceedings'.

In 1998, the local press in Bingley, West Yorkshire, were able to convince magistrates to lift a s39 order banning identification of a 14-year-old boy whose mother was assaulted by his father's girl-friend, during a row about the boy.

It seems that the child must be concerned in the actual proceedings before the court making the order; a court cannot make a s39 order banning identification of a child because the child is concerned in another court case (though, of course, the court in that case can).

In *R v Lee* (1993), the Court of Appeal held that a s39 order covering a hearing in a magistrates' court could not apply when the same case reached the Crown Court. If anonymity was necessary, the Crown Court judge would have to make their own order.

Protecting adult defendants

There may be cases where to name an adult involved in a trial inevitably means identifying a child who is the subject of a s39 order. Where this is the case, naming the adult will breach the order. However, the JSB's 2001 guidelines state that it is not lawful for a court specifically to ban publication of an adult's identity in a s39 order. This was confirmed in *R v Southwark Crown Court ex p Godwin* (1992), where the Court of Appeal said that there were cases where publishing the name of an adult would breach an order because it would mean the child was identified, and that in these cases, judges could advise on whether publication of certain names or details would breach the order, but they could not use the order to ban publication of those names.

■ Issuing the s39 order

Section 39 orders should be clear and unambiguous. In *R v Central Criminal Court, ex p Godwin and Crook* (1995). Lord Justice Glidewell said that a court issuing a s39 order should:

- make the terms completely clear, and if there is any room for doubt over which child or children the order covers, this should be spelt out clearly;
- draw up a written copy of the order as soon as possible after it has been made orally, and keep a copy in the court office so that journalists can have access to it;
- include in the court lists a reference to the order, so that its existence is clear even to those who were not in court when it was made.

Lord Justice Glidewell confirmed that a court considering making a s39 order can hear representations from anyone with a legitimate interest in opposing the order, which includes the press.

There have been cases where magistrates challenged over a s39 order claim they have no power to lift or relax it, but this is not the case. The power to do so has been recognised in several cases before the Divisional Court of the Queen's Bench, including *R v Central Criminal Court ex p Simpkins* (1998), and *R v Manchester Crown Court, ex p H* (A Juvenile) [2000].

Law in practice   Challenging s39 orders

According to Tony Jaffa, Head of Media at solicitors Foot Anstey, s39 orders are the single most common type of reporting restrictions to be wrongly imposed by the courts:

> We deal with several cases every month of courts trying to impose s39 orders banning identification of adults, or dead children, or children who are not involved in the proceedings. The legislation makes it absolutely clear that it does not cover adults or children who are not involved in the proceedings, so I would advise court reporters always to have a copy of the relevant section with them, so they can quote from it. The legislation itself doesn't specify that dead children are not covered, but that is well-established now, so it may also be useful to be able to refer to the Judicial Studies Board guidelines on this.

■ Child victims of sex offences

Children who are the alleged victims of sexual offences are given the same protection as adults (see p. 121), and nothing which can identify them can be published. However, cases involving children can be particularly vulnerable to the problem of 'jigsaw identification', particularly as so many cases take place within the family, so that anything which identifies the defendant runs the risk of identifying the victim as well.

To address this problem, the Press Complaints Commission Code of Practice contains provisions to prevent such 'jigsaw' identification in sex cases involving children. Paragraph 7 states that:

1 The press must not, even where the law does not prohibit it, identify children under the age of 16 who are involved in cases concerning sexual offences, whether as victims or witnesses.
2 In any press report of a case involving a sexual offence against a child –
(i)   The child must not be identified.
(ii) The adult may be identified.
(iii) The word 'incest' must not be used where a child victim might be identified.
(iv) Care must be taken that nothing in the report implies the relationship between the accused and the child.

Similar provisions covering broadcasters are contained in the ITC Programme Code.

ANTI-SOCIAL BEHAVIOUR ORDERS (ASBOS)

ASBOs (see p. 30) can be ordered against anyone over the age of ten, and around half are issued against people under 18. In this situation, the reporting restrictions that apply depend on how the ASBO is imposed:

- by magistrates in civil proceedings; or
- in a Youth Court, where a juvenile has been convicted of a criminal offence (this is often known as a 'bolt-on' ASBO).

ASBOs in civil proceedings

The Anti-Social Behaviour Act 2003 provides that there is no automatic ban on identifying a young person who has been given an ASBO, but a court can choose to make an order banning their identification, using its powers under s39 of the Children and Young Persons Act 1933 (see below).

Both the JSB and the courts have suggested that there is a strong public interest in the courts not making s39 orders covering people who are the subject of ASBOs. In their 2001 guidelines, the JSB points out that enforcing an ASBO usually depends on the general public being aware the fact that it has been made, and to whom. This was reiterated in *Chief Constable of Surrey* v *JHG and DHG* (2002), where Mr Justice Elias pointed out that people would not be able to report breaches of ASBOs to the authorities if they did not know that the person concerned was the subject of an ASBO. Protecting the public from people who had committed anti-social behaviour was the whole point of ASBOs, and such protection was more likely if the public knew who those people were.

 In *R (on the application of Stanley)* v *Commissioner of Police of the Metropolis* (2004), a group of six youths attempted to claim that publicity about them being the subject of ASBOs infringed their right to privacy under the Human Rights Act 1998. The Queen's Bench Divisional Court dismissed their application for judicial review, saying that publicity in these cases was often intended to reassure those who had been or might be the victims of anti-social behaviour, and to deter others from behaving in similar ways. It could not have this effect unless it included photographs, names and at least partial addresses, and therefore the public interest in conveying this information outweighed the right to privacy.

 In 2006, the *Nottingham Evening Post* persuaded a court to lift a s39 order protecting four youths who had been given ASBOs. The paper argued that for the ASBOs to be properly enforced, the community needed to know who the boys were and what they had done.

Applications for ASBOs are often adjourned if the person who is to be the subject of the order objects, and in such cases, an interim ASBO may be ordered, which stays in place until the full hearing. There seems to be no reason why the same rules should not apply to interim hearings as for proceedings where a full ASBO is ordered.

■ ASBOs in Youth Courts

'Bolt-on' ASBOs given after Youth Court proceedings for a criminal offence pose a more difficult problem. The usual s49 restrictions (see above) apply to the Youth Court proceedings, but the part of the hearing in which the ASBO is imposed counts as civil proceedings. This effectively means that where an ASBO is imposed by a Youth Court, and the court does not choose to lift the Youth Court reporting restrictions, the press has a choice: it can name the person who is the subject of the ASBO, but not write about the crime(s) which led to it being imposed; or it can report the case, including the ASBO, but without naming the defendant. It cannot, however, name the recipient of the ASBO and publish details of the case which led to the ASBO being imposed.

In 2004, a reporter for the *Wakefield Express* used the problem explained above as an argument to persuade a court to lift Youth Court reporting restrictions so that his paper could fully report a case in which a young offender was given an ASBO. The reporter pointed out that the youth was a persistent offender, and that in all previous hearings he had had anonymity, and this clearly had done nothing to deter him from futher offending. He argued that ASBOs needed publicity so that they could be policed by the community, and explained that unless the reporting restrictions were lifted, his paper would not be able to report fully on why the youth had been given the ASBO. The court agreed to lift the s49 restrictions.

If a person under 18 breaches an ASBO, they will normally be brought before a Youth Court. The Serious Organised Crime and Police Act 2005 provides that, in this situation, the normal reporting restrictions on Youth Courts do not apply. The court can however make a s39 order imposing restrictions; if it chooses to do this, the 2005 Act requires it to give reasons.

PROCEEDINGS UNDER THE CHILDREN ACT

The Children Act 1989 was intended to update and bring together provisions covering the care and upbringing of children. Starting from the principle that in any situation involving children, the welfare of the child is the most important consideration, it covers issues of parental responsibility, and the responsibilities of other services children come into contact with, such as education, health and local authority care. It is used in a number of different types of case involving children, including disputes between divorcing parents over care of and contact with their children, and applications to put a child into local authority care. Cases under the Act may be heard in the magistrates' courts, the county courts, or the Family Division of the High Court.

Reporting restrictions for these proceedings are contained in the Children Act itself, and also in the Magistrates' Courts Act 1980, where provisions dealing with the old domestic courts now cover the Family Proceedings Courts (see p. 45). The combined effect of these two Acts is that very few details about these cases can be published, and there is a complete ban on publishing anything that could identify the children involved.

Section 97 of the Children Act 1989 makes it an offence to publish anything which is intended or likely to identify any person under 18 'as being involved' in court proceedings involving the Act before magistrates, or to state that any address or school is that of a child involved in such proceedings. The Access to Justice Act 1999 extends the same protection to under-18s in Children Act cases heard by the county courts or the High Court. The ban on identification can be lifted or relaxed by the court, or by the Home Secretary, if they are satisfied that the welfare of the child requires such an action.

A publisher charged with publishing material that could identify a child in a Children Act case will have a defence if it can prove it did not know, and had no reason to suspect, that the material was likely to make it possible to identify the child.

In addition to this restriction, s71 of the Magistrates' Courts Act 1980 provides that reports of family proceedings may **only** contain:

- the names, addresses and occupations of the parties and any witnesses (other than children, or adults whose names could identify children in the case);
- the grounds for the application, and a brief statement of the charges, defences and counter-charges;
- submissions on any points of law that arise in the proceedings, and the decisions of the court on those points;
- the decision of the court, and any remarks made in connection with the decision.

In effect, this means that the media can only report evidence given in the case if it is referred to by the magistrates when giving their decision. In practice this will often be the case as the Children Act requires magistrates to give reasons for their decisions.

Scope of the restrictions

Until very recently, it was assumed that the anonymity granted to under-18s in the Children Act cases went beyond reports of the hearings themselves, and also covered any later story which could identify the children as having been involved in such proceedings. This made it difficult to report, for example, cases where parents feel their children have been wrongly taken into care, even where the parents themselves wanted to publicise their situation. However, in *Clayton* v *Clayton* (2006), the Court of Appeal said that this was not the case. It stated that the anonymity provided by the Children Act applied only as long as the proceedings were actually taking place. If a court wanted to make sure that children involved in such proceedings were not identified after the proceedings, it had to issue an injunction to that effect, and before doing so, should weigh up the Article 8 right of the child to privacy, against the Article 10 right to freedom of expression, both of the parents and the press. The Court stressed, however, that this decision did not mean that parents could talk to the press about what went on during family proceedings, and nor could the press publish such information if it was given to them.

Hearings in private

Many family proceedings are held in private, and in this situation, restrictions are stricter. In *Re B (A Child) (Disclosure), Re* [2004] it was held that it was both contempt of court and an offence under s97 of the Children Act 1989 to publish, without court permission, anything regarding the proceedings, apart from the court's decision. This applies even where the material does not identify the child. It is important to realise that these restrictions apply regardless of whether or not the parents in the case want it to be made public. Journalists whose jobs do not involve court reporting can easily forget this – or even be unaware of it – when parents come armed with court documents and heart-rending stories which they want told.

Family proceedings not involving children

The above provisions do not apply to family proceedings which do not involve children.

In *Allan* v *Clibbery* (2001), the Court of Appeal was asked to consider the competing claims of privacy and freedom of expression in a case arising from the breakdown of a relationship between a wealthy businessman and his girlfriend. The woman had been living in a flat owned (but not lived in) by the man, and when the relationship broke down and he asked her to move out, she went to court to try to get a legal order allowing her to stay there. When the court found that she had no legal right to do so, she went to the *Daily Mail* and told her story, in part, she said, to warn other women about how few rights they have when an unmarried relationship breaks down. Previously, it had been assumed that family proceedings held in chambers (as this case was) were not to be reported, and the businessman got a court order banning the ex-girlfriend from giving details of the legal proceedings to any other publication. However, the Court of Appeal held that a blanket ban on reporting family proceedings that did not concern children was not 'necessary in a democratic society' (i.e. there was no pressing social need for it), and said the order was not proportionate to the Article 8 aim of protecting the man's privacy.

ADOPTION CASES

All adoption hearings are classified as family proceedings under the Children Act 1989, so s97 provides that children in such proceedings may not be identified in any way. In addition, the Adoption Act 1976 provides that High Court hearings may be held in chambers, and s69 of the Magistrates' Courts Act 1980 states that adoption hearings before magistrates must be in private. The result of these two provisions is that publishing any report of such a hearing is likely to be considered contempt of court under s12 of the Administration of Justice Act 1960.

The Adoption and Children Act 2002 makes it an offence to publish an advertisement or other information stating that a particular child is available for adoption, that a parent or guardian wants a child to be adopted, that a person wants to adopt a child, or that a person other than an adoption agency is willing to receive a child given to it with a view to the child being adopted, or that a person is willing to take a child outside the UK with a view to them being adopted. None of this applies however, where the information is published by or on behalf of an adoption agency.

WARDSHIP CASES

Where a child is at risk of serious danger, the High Court has the power to make them a ward of court, which means that the court becomes responsible for the child. Day-to-day care is provided by a named individual or a local authority, but all important decisions about the child – from change of school to agreement to medical treatment – are taken by the court. Recent examples of wardship cases include a boy who had run away with a religious group, whose grandmother applied to have him made a ward of court so that if he was found, he could be taken away from the cult; and an HIV positive three-year-old whose father would not consent to her having medical treatment.

Wardship hearings may be held in county courts, or in the Family Division of the High Court; in both cases, proceedings are held in chambers, and are held in private. Section 12(1) of the Administration of Justice Act 1960 prevents the press from reporting the proceedings in which a child is made a ward of court, and also prevents publication of certain types of story about the child once they have been made a ward. It does not, however, as commonly believed, mean that nothing can ever be written about a child who is a ward of court.

If no specific injunction has been made regarding the child, the position is as follows:

- If a story or interview states that the child mentioned in the story is a ward of court, the child must not be identified, and details of the wardship proceedings (such as why they were brought) may not be given.
- If a story concerning a child who is a ward of court names the child, the press may not say that the child is a ward of court, or connect them with the wardship proceedings.
- A story which both names the child and says that they are a ward of court can only be published with the court's permission. Once this permission has been given and a child has already been named as a ward of court, this information can continue to be published unless an injunction is ordered.

These restrictions can be lifted by a court, either completely or partially. This tends to happen in cases where a child's whereabouts are not known, and there is a possibility that they may be taken out of the country, clearly in these cases publicity can be helpful.

A publisher who did not know or have reason to suspect that it was publishing information concerning wardship proceedings will have a defence.

Injunctions affecting wards of court

In many cases concerning wards of court, the courts will put in place an injunction concerning publication of information about the child concerned. These injunctions can be very wide, and may, for example, prohibit the press not just from speaking to the child, but also to their parents, carers, social workers or teachers. This can make it impossible to print anything about the child, even if you do not name them, and as penalties for breaking an injunction can be severe, you should always check whether there is an injunction in force before writing anything about a person who is a ward of court. It is safest to confirm this with the relevant court or the child's lawyers, rather than relying on information from the family, who may not necessarily understand the far-reaching nature of some injunctions.

Injunctions which place unreasonable restrictions on reporting cases of public interest can be successfully challenged. In *Re M and N (Minors), Re* [1990], the Court of Appeal laid down guidelines for courts making such injunctions, and reminded them that the public interest in freedom of expression had to be considered in such cases. The court said that an injunction should be no wider than was necessary to achieve the purpose for which they were made, and that its scope should be clear. When deciding this scope, the courts should take account of the public interest in a free press, and recognise the distinction between articles on matters of public interest, and those which were merely satisfying public curiosity.

 The teenager who ran away with a religious group, referred to above, was the subject of *Kelly* v *BBC* (2001), where the BBC challenged an injunction preventing it from broadcasting an interview with the boy. In response to publicity about his grandmother's fears for his welfare with the group, the teenager had telephoned the BBC's *Today* programme, wanting to give his side of the story. The court imposed an injunction preventing the programme from broadcasting the interview, on the grounds that the boy was a ward of court, but the injunction was overturned. Munby J said that it was too wide a restriction on press freedom to require that no interview with a ward of court could be published without permission. He stated that permission would only be required where the media activity represented a major step in the ward's life, or where the media involvement was related directly to, or interfered with, the child's upbringing. The interview in question did not fit into these criteria and therefore could be broadcast.

In *Nottingham Council v October Films* (1999), journalists making a documentary interviewed children who were in care. The court held that these interviews did amount to an interference with their upbringing in local authority care, and so the interviews could not be broadcast.

In a 1989 case, Kensington and Chelsea Borough Council had obtained an injunction which banned a local paper from publishing an interview with a foster mother who had had two foster children taken from her without explanation, after having looked after them almost all their lives. The Court of Appeal held that the story the paper wanted to print covered a matter of public interest, namely the way in which a local authority had exercised its powers, and ordered that the injunction should be altered, so that the interview could be used, as long as the children, their school and the family were not identified.

In *Re R (Wardship: Restrictions on Publication)* (1994), the case concerned a child whose parents had separated; the courts had ordered that she should live with her mother, and gave her father only access. The father then abducted the child, and took her to Israel. She was eventually brought back and her father was extradited to stand trial in the UK. The little girl had been made a ward of court, and so the Family Division issued an injunction banning reports of the criminal proceedings against her father. He challenged the order, because he wanted to publicise his case, which he felt was an example of the unfair treatment of fathers by the family courts. The court agreed to vary the order, to allow reporting of his trial, on the grounds that reporting of criminal trials should only be restricted where necessary to protect 'the proper administration of justice'. The wardship court did not have discretion to make an order prohibiting identification of the child, where such reporting had nothing to do with the exercise of the court's wardship jurisdiction; essentially, it could not give wards of courts rights that other children did not have.

◼ Incidental prevention of identifying adults

In some cases, an injunction made to protect a child's identity may effectively prevent identification of an adult as well, and therefore provide a severe restriction on the ability of the press to report a story. In some cases, the press have been able to challenge such injunctions on these grounds, and have them modified to allow the story to run.

In 2003, an injunction was passed preventing the press from publishing the identities of the children of a woman who had had a relationship with Ian Huntley, the notorious murderer of two schoolgirls in the Cambridgeshire village of Soham. The ban effectively meant that the press could not report the identity of the woman either, since this would clearly make it possible to identify her children. Several newspapers challenged the injunction, and the court agreed to change its terms, allowing publication of the mother's identity but preventing publication of pictures of the children or details of which schools they attended.

◼ PROVISIONS NOT YET IN FORCE

The Youth Justice and Criminal Evidence Act 1999 contains important new provisions on reporting cases involving people under 18. However, these provisions represent a severe restriction on the ability of the press to report such cases, and were opposed by the media. Although no official statement has been made, it is now thought unlikely that they will ever come into force. However, they are worth including here, because there have been cases of judges assuming that they are in force, and trying to impose reporting restrictions which are not yet legal; in one case this was at the suggestion of a QC, who was also unaware that the provisions were not in force. If you know about the provisions that are not in force, you will be in a better position to make a challenge in such circumstances.

The two controversial provisions are contained in s44 and s45 of the Act, and if implemented would replace s39 of the Children and Young Persons Act 1933 (see p. 132) in criminal proceedings, so that s39 orders would only apply to civil cases. Section 44 of the 1999 Act provides that as soon as the police begin a criminal investigation, the media would automatically be banned from identifying any person under 18 who is involved in the case, whether as a suspect, witness or victim. (This would have meant, for example, that in the Soham murder case, the press would have been unable to publish the names of the two girls involved, once the investigation had started.) The ban would prevent publication of the juvenile's name, address, school or workplace, or any picture of them. The ban could be lifted by a court if it was in the interests of justice to do so, and the juvenile's welfare would not be adversely affected.

The automatic s44 ban would come to an end once court proceedings begin, but at this point, the court would have discretion under s45 to ban the media from identifying any juvenile involved in the case, where it is in the interests of justice and will not impose a substantial and unreasonable restriction on reporting of the proceedings.

CHAPTER SUMMARY

Youth court cases

- Section 47 of the Children and Young Persons Act 1933 gives the press a right to attend Youth Court proceedings.
- Unless restrictions are lifted, the press may not publish anything that could identify a defendant, victim or witness under 18.

Children in adult criminal courts

No automatic restrictions apply, but courts can ban publication of anything that would identify a witness, defendant or victim under 18.

Jigsaw identification

The Press Complaints Commission requires precautions against identification via more than one publication.

Anti-social behaviour orders

- No automatic restrictions apply to ASBOs from civil proceedings but a s39 order may be made;
- In Youth Court proceedings, the press cannot name the recipient of the ASBO and publish details of the case which led to the ASBO being imposed.

Family proceedings

- The Children Act 1989 bans identification of any child involved in proceedings brought under the Act, during and after the case.
- The Magistrates Court Act 1980 imposes further limits on reports of family proceedings.
- Reports of adoption proceedings are likely to be in contempt of court.

■ Details of wardship proceedings cannot be published, and children described as wards of court cannot be named.

Provisions not in force

Sections 44 and 45 of the Youth Justice and Criminal Evidence Act 1999 severely restrict reporting of juveniles in criminal cases, but are not in force and may never be.

TEST YOUR KNOWLEDGE

1 You have been sent to report a Youth Court case, but the court clerk refuses to let you in, stating that Youth Courts are closed to the public. Which statute gives you the right to be there?

2 You are reporting a Youth Court case, for which restrictions have not been lifted. Which of these statements can you make in your report?

(a) A 17-year-old from Birmingham has appeared in court, accused of shoplifting.

(b) John Green, 17, of Tower Road, Birmingham has appeared in court, accused of shoplifting.

(c) A 17-year-old from Tower Road, Birmingham has appeared in court, accused of shoplifting.

(d) A boy from Green Gates school has appeared in court, accused of shoplifting.

(e) The Birmingham schoolboy who last year hit the news when he saved a dog from drowning has appeared in court, accused of shoplifting.

(f) Mrs Jane Green, from Birmingham, cried in court as her son was accused of shoplifting this week.

3 You are reporting a Youth Court case, and the magistrates make no order regarding reporting restrictions. Can you safely name the defendant?

4 A Youth Court case you have been following is appealed to the Crown Court. The defendant is still under 18. What reporting restrictions apply?

5 You are reporting a case where a 16-year-old girl has been given an ASBO in civil proceedings. What reporting restrictions apply?

6 A teenager known as a local tearaway has been convicted of criminal damage in the youth court, and has been given an ASBO in the same proceedings. Which of these statements can you make?

(a) John Brown, 14, has been convicted of criminal damage and given an ASBO, banning him from going near the Roundish Estate.

(b) A teenager who was convicted of eight counts of criminal damage has been given an ASBO, banning him from going near the Roundish Estate.

(c) John Brown, 14, of Oxford Road, has been given an ASBO, banning him from going near the Roundish Estate.

7 You are reporting a case where a man is accused of murdering his 18-month-old daughter. The judge imposes a s39 order, banning the press from identifying the little

girl. What arguments could you use to get the order lifted? What arguments would you use if the charge was not murder but assault?

8   What is jigsaw identification?

9   What precautions does the Press Complaints Commission Code of Practice require the media to take in order to prevent 'jigsaw identification' of children in sex cases?

10   You are contacted by a couple whose children have been taken away from them and put into care, because social workers believe they have been abused. The parents deny this and want to put their side of the story. The court case was a year ago. Do any reporting restrictions apply?

11   You are contacted by a teenager who you know is a ward of court. She wants to give an interview about the situation which led to her being made a ward of court. Can you use her name in the story?

12   A local teenager saves a dog from drowning, and you are sent to interview her. At the end of the interview, she mentions that she is a ward of court. Can you run the story? What checks should you make?

13   You are reporting a case involving a defendant who is under 18. The magistrates announce that they are making an order under s46 of the Youth Justice and Criminal Evidence Act 1999, banning publication of the defendant's name. What argument could you use to get this restriction lifted?

 ONLINE RESOURCES

www   The Children Act 1989 can be read at:
www.opsi.gov.uk/acts/acts1989/ukpga_19890041_en_1.htm

Clayton v *Clayton* can be read at:
www.lexisnexis.co.uk/lawcampus/dataitem.asp?ID=62712&tid=7

The Judicial Studies Board guidelines on reporting restrictions are available at:
www.jsboard.co.uk/publications.htm

Useful reports of cases where reporting restrictions have been imposed or overturned can be found at the Hold the Front Page website
www.holdthefrontpage.co.uk

The Society of Editors website also reports on the use of reporting restrictions, at:
www.societyofeditors.org

Practice Direction (Crown Court: trial of children and young persons) 2001 can be viewed at:
www.hmcourts-service.gov.uk/cms/926.htm

For further resources and updates please go to the Companion Website for this book at www.pearsoned.co.uk/practicaljournalism

10

Reporting restrictions concerning children

Reporting inquests

An inquest is a special type of court hearing, which is held to look into sudden or suspicious deaths. Unlike a criminal hearing or a civil claim concerning a death, an inquest is not about attributing blame for the death: instead, its aim is to find out who the dead person is (if not known), and how and why the death occurred. The nature of the deaths investigated by inquests mean that there is often press interest in the proceedings, both local and sometimes national.

INQUEST PROCEDURE

An inquest is held when a death:

- is sudden and unexpected (though where a death is sudden but a post-mortem examination shows it was due to natural causes, a coroner may rule that there is no need for an inquest); and/or
- is suspected to be unnatural or violent; and/or
- occurred in certain types of custody.

A coroner must hold an inquest where a person has died a violent and unnatural death abroad, and the body has been brought back to that coroner's district. In practice, around one in 20 deaths is investigated by an inquest.

The hearing

Some cities have specific coroner's courts, but most inquests are held in the local magistrates' courts. Hearings are held in public, and most are presided over by a coroner, who must be a barrister, solicitor or doctor, with at least five years' professional experience. Currently, acting as a coroner tends to be done in addition to being a doctor or solicitor, but planned new legislation will provide for full-time, legally qualified coroners (see below).

Most inquests are decided by a coroner alone, but the Coroners Act 1988 states that there are three circumstances where a jury must decide the verdict. These are where the death:

- raises issues of public health or safety;
- occurs in prison or police custody;
- may have been caused by a police or prison officer.

A coroner can also summon a jury to hear any other inquest where they feel the death is of significant public interest, but the three circumstances above would cover most of these situations.

Where there is a jury, it decides on the verdict; otherwise, it is the coroner who decides. A jury is usually described as having 'returned a verdict' at the end of an inquest, but if a coroner decides the case, they are usually said to have 'recorded a verdict'.

Whether heard by a coroner alone, or with a jury, most inquests take place in two stages:

- The first hearing is held as soon as possible after the death, when the coroner opens the inquest. It is then usually adjourned while the coroner conducts investigations, and draws up a list of witnesses to be called.

- At the second hearing, the coroner questions each witness, and leads them through their evidence; the style of questioning is aimed at finding out the truth, and is often quite different from that used in a criminal trial, where the opposing barristers are trying to prove or defend a case. Close relatives and anyone potentially implicated in the death (or their lawyers) are entitled to ask questions and make statements, and the coroner has discretion to allow others to do so. This does not, however, usually extend to reporters.

Inquest verdicts

There is no set list of the verdicts that an inquest can return (it is technically up to the coroner to decide the the most accurate way of describing the death), but in practice, there are standard terms, of which these are the most common:

- natural causes,
- lawful killing,
- unlawful killing,
- dependence on drugs,
- want of attention at birth,
- suicide,
- accident or misadventure,
- industrial disease,
- open verdict (this is the verdict given when there is not enough evidence to produce any other verdict).

Alternatively, a jury or coroner can return what is called a 'narrative verdict', which rather than attaching a one-word label to the death, is a short statement detailing the circumstances in which, on the evidence, they believe the person died.

It is not the job of an inquest to find out (or even suggest) who is to blame for a death. The inquest can reach a verdict which states that the death was caused by someone else (such as unlawful killing) but by law it is prohibited from suggesting who that person might be, and in 1994 the Court of Appeal found that it should not even express an opinion as to blame. However, in the landmark House of Lords case of *R (on the application of Middleton) v HM Coroner for Western Somerset* (2004), it was held that a jury deciding an inquest into prisoners who had committed suicide could include as part of its findings that the way the prison system was run had contributed to the deaths, though it could not blame a named person. This was to conform with Article 2 of the European Convention on Human Rights 1998, which requires a thorough investigation of deaths in state custody, so is unlikely to be applied to inquests into other types of deaths.

Criminal proceedings and public inquiries

Where a death is already known to be the subject of criminal proceedings, an inquest is usually opened just to take evidence of identity and cause of death, and then adjourned until

11

Reporting inquests

after the criminal proceedings are finished. If the criminal proceedings answer all questions about the death, the coroner can formally close the inquest, but if there are good reasons to continue with the inquest (if, for example, the criminal proceedings were unsuccessful), it can be reopened.

Where several people have died in a major disaster – such as a fire on public transport or a boat sinking – the government will often put in place a public inquiry, headed by a judge. In this situation, the Access to Justice Act 1999 allows the Lord Chancellor to direct that any inquest into one of the deaths should be adjourned, and where this happens, the inquest is not usually reopened unless there are special reasons to do so.

Appeals from inquests

There are cases where relatives or friends of the dead person disagree with the verdict, most often where an inquest finds that the person took their own life, or where the family believe the death is unlawful but the inquest finds it to be an accident. There is, however, no direct right of appeal over an inquest verdict. The only way to challenge a verdict is via judicial review (see p. 49).

Treasure trove

Inquests also have a second, completely different role, of investigating valuable archeological finds. Although this role is centuries old, it is now regulated by the Treasure Act 1996, which provides that if an object found in the ground is at least 200 years old, and fits certain other criteria, it is 'treasure'. Anyone who finds an item that might be treasure is required by law to report the find to the local coroner within 14 days; the find is then notified to a local museum, which, if it believes the find may be treasure, informs the British Museum or the National Museum of Wales. If, as a result, a museum wishes to acquire the find, an inquest will be held to decide whether the item does in fact fit within the legal classification of treasure. If it does, the finder and/or the landowner may be entitled to a financial reward.

REPORTING INQUESTS

Inquests must be held in open court, unless the coroner orders that the public be excluded on grounds of national security (rule 17 of the Coroners Rules 1984 (SI 1984/552). Such an order can be challenged by means of judicial review (see p. 49).

The media has no statutory right to be informed that an inquest is to be held, but a Home Office circular published in 1980 states the coroners are encouraged to make suitable arrangements to ensure that the media, and especially local papers, are given the date, time and place of forthcoming inquests, and the resumption of any inquests which have been adjourned (Circular No. 53/1980).

Reporting restrictions

There are no reporting restrictions specific to inquests. However, rule 37 of the Coroners Rules 1984 allows a coroner to take evidence in written form, rather than orally, where the evidence is unlikely to be disputed. The rule provides that where this is done, the coroner must announce publicly the name of the person who the evidence has come from, and should read it aloud; however, they can direct that the evidence should not be read aloud, and this can be used as a way of preventing the press from reporting that evidence. Usually, suicide notes and psychiatric reports are not read out, though there is no legal provision to prevent this.

■ Inquests and contempt of court

The Contempt of Court Act 1981 applies to inquests, and for the purposes of this Act (see Chapter 6), an inquest is deemed to be 'active' from the time it is opened, even if the opening is only a formality and the inquest is then adjourned indefinitely. The active period ends only when the proceedings are formally closed, and so continues during any adjournment.

Where a death is suspected to be the result of a crime, and the inquest takes place before the criminal proceedings, it is not contempt of court to report the inquest, regardless of the impact the report might have on the criminal proceedings (unless the coroner makes an order restricting reporting and the report breaches this order). However, if an inquest has an important effect on the trial (e.g. if it has to be moved to another area), it is possible that the publisher responsible could be ordered to pay the wasted costs (see p. 86).

■ Inquests and defamation

For the purposes of defamation, inquests are covered by absolute privilege, which means you cannot be sued for reporting anything said during the proceedings (see Chapter 14), so long as your report is fair, accurate and contemporaneous.

Law in practice Getting to know the coroner's officer

Despite the fact that the Home Office encourages coroners to keep the press informed about forthcoming inquests, this does not always happen automatically, even where a case is of obvious interest to the press. In 2003, for example, the inquest into the sudden death of Laura Sadler, a popular actress in the hospital soap *Holby City*, was not attended by any members of the press, because no one in the media had known it was taking place. With this in mind, it is worth calling the coroner's office from time to time, to check what is coming up. Information for the media about when and where inquests are to be held or reopened usually comes via the coroner's officer, who is a police officer attached to the coroner's office (sometimes only part-time). Getting to know the coroner's officer can be very useful if you want information about inquests that might be of interest to your readers.

■ Reform of the law on inquests

The Coroners Bill, which was going through Parliament when this book went to press, will, if passed, introduce changes to the way inquests work, and could severely restrict the ability of the press to report them. The Bill gives coroners powers to exclude the press and public from proceedings, and to ban identification of the person who has died, and any of their friends and family. There is no provision for the media to challenge orders made using these powers.

The Bill also gives coroners wide powers to search for and seize journalistic material, including material concerning confidential sources, which is related to a death they are investigating. The use of these powers is not restricted by the kind of safeguards which apply to journalistic material under other legislation (such as the Police and Criminal Evidence Act 1984 – see p. 263). The Newspaper Society and other media organisations have presented arguments against these proposals and it remains to be seen whether they will survive the legislative process unchanged.

Other changes proposed in the Bill are that:

- the post of coroner will become a full-time one;
- a new Chief Coroner will be appointed;
- bereaved families will have more opportunity to contribute to coroners' investigations;
- a national treasure coroner will be appointed to investigate all treasure finds, which will no longer involve local coroners.

CHAPTER SUMMARY

Inquest procedure

Inquests are held into deaths which:

- are sudden and unexpected;
- are suspicious;
- occurred in certain types of custody.

Inquests seek to find out the facts of death; they do not attribute blame.

Juries are used in cases of public interest.

Reporting inquests

Inquests must be in open court, unless there are issues of national security.

The Contempt of Court Act 1981 applies to inquests.

Absolute privilege in defamation covers fair, accurate and contemporaneous reports.

Reform of the law on inquests

The Coroners Bill proposes legal changes which could severely restrict reporting of inquests.

TEST YOUR KNOWLEDGE

1 What types of death are likely to be the subject of an inquest?

2 When are juries used to decide inquests?

3 In what circumstances can reporters be excluded from an inquest?

4 When does an inquest become active for the purposes of the Contempt of Court Act 1981? When does it stop being active?

5 A teenager has died at a pop concert, after being squashed against barriers at the front of the crowd. An inquest into her death has been opened and adjourned. A security guard at the concert venue comes to you with evidence that his boss has been ignoring safety rules in order to save money. Can you report this evidence?

6 During an inquest, a witness alleges that the dead person was killed by his sister. Can you report this?

7 What reporting restrictions apply to inquests?

ONLINE RESOURCES

www

The draft Coroners Bill can be read at:
www.dca.gov.uk/legist/coroners_draft.pdf

The Department of Constitutional Affairs website has background information on the Bill, at:
www.dca.gov.uk/legist/coronersreform.htm#b

The Newspaper Society response to the Bill can be read at:
www.newspapersociety.org.uk/files/Coroner-Reform.doc

The pressure group Inquest campaigns for improvements in the inquest system. Its website has useful background information on the inquest process and problems with the system:
www.inquest.org.uk

11

For further resources and updates please go to the Companion Website for this book at www.pearsoned.co.uk/practicaljournalism

Reporting inquests

Chapter
12

Reporting tribunals and inquiries

Around half a million cases each year are decided not by the court system, but by tribunals. These are similar to courts, but tend to have more informal procedures. Each tribunal specialises in a particular area of law: the best-known is the Employment Tribunal, which hears cases concerning employees' treatment at work, but there around 80 others, covering areas including access to welfare benefits, housing, school admissions and complaints against professionals such as lawyers and doctors. Which tribunals are of interest to journalists depends on what kind of publication they work for. Trade and professional magazines will often have an interest in the more specialist tribunals which deal with their particular subject area, whereas tribunals dealing with subjects such as housing, welfare or education can be a source of stories for the local and sometimes national press. The most commonly reported tribunal proceedings however tend to be those of the Employment Tribunal, and for that reason, this chapter gives a detailed explanation of its proceedings, after looking at tribunals in general.

This chapter also looks at public inquiries, which may be required under statute (e.g. planning inquiries) or may be one-off tribunals set up to look into an issue of public concern.

REPORTING TRIBUNALS

Because there are so many different types of tribunal, their personnel and procedures vary, but most tribunals are presided over by a panel, rather than a single judge. The panel is usually chosen to represent the different interests associated with that area of law – employment tribunal panels, for example, will usually include members from organisations representing employers, and those representing employees. Most, though not all, tribunal panels also have a legally-qualified chairperson.

Tribunals are designed to decide disputes more quickly and inexpensively than the court system, so procedures are less rule-bound and more informal, and often the parties will make their own case, rather than using a lawyer. However, tribunals are still expected to behave like courts in that they have to give a fair hearing to both sides, and make an open and impartial decision on the case. Under the Tribunals and Inquiries Act 1992, tribunals must, if requested, state their reasons for a particular decision. Some tribunals, notably the Employment Tribunal, have in fact become more formal over the years, and now operate very much like a normal court, with both sides often represented by lawyers.

The decisions made by tribunals can usually be challenged by some form of appeals procedure, and for the most important tribunals, appeals on points of law can be made to the

High Court, and ultimately to the House of Lords. Tribunal decisions can also be challenged under the judicial review procedure (see below).

As the box shows, access to tribunal proceedings varies according to the rules of the tribunal. In the majority of cases, hearings are held in public unless the parties or the court choose otherwise, but the law on when and why they can do this differs. If you need to find out the situation for a particular tribunal which is not covered here, the detailed information will be contained either in the legislation under which the tribunal was set up, or its rules of procedure (in many cases these rules are published on tribunal websites).

Types of tribunal

Which tribunals you come across will depend on the area of journalism you work in – those considered below are the ones journalists are most likely to come across, in addition to the Employment Tribunal, which is examined in detail at the end of this chapter. If you are working for a trade or specialist publication, it is well worth making yourself familiar with the rules of any specialist tribunals in that area.

The Asylum and Immigration Tribunal hears and decides appeals against decisions made by the Home Office in matters of asylum, immigration and nationality. It usually sits in public.

The Criminal Injuries Compensation Appeals Panel determines appeals relating to decisions made by the Criminal Injuries Compensation Authority, relating to compensation for victims of crime. It usually sits in private.

The Special Commissioners Tribunal hears appeals concerning decisions of the Inland Revenue relating to all direct taxes, including income tax, corporation tax, capital gains tax and inheritance tax. Hearings are normally in public, but either of the parties can apply to the tribunal to have them held in private. However, the tribunal has discretion to allow anyone other than the parties to attend, even if proceedings are to be held in private, if the parties agree.

Mental Health Review Tribunals hear applications from patients detained under the Mental Health Act 1983, who wish to be discharged. Hearings are held in private, unless the patient requests a public hearing and the tribunal agrees, and proceedings (including the name of the patient and the decision) may not be reported.

The Social Security and Child Support Appeals Tribunal deals with disputes about a range of welfare benefits, including Income Support; Jobseeker's Allowance; Incapacity Benefit; Disability Living Allowance; Attendance Allowance; and Retirement Pensions. It also deals with disputes about child support maintenance, Tax Credits, Statutory Sick Pay / Statutory Maternity Pay, vaccine damage and decisions on Housing Benefit and Council Tax Benefit. Hearings are public, but the public can be excluded in order to protect privacy.

The Financial Services and Markets Tribunal hears appeals from decisions made by the Financial Services Authority, which regulates the financial services industry. It sits in public, but has discretion to sit in private at the request of one or both of the parties, as long as the interests of justice are not prejudiced by doing so.

Rent Assessment Committees deal with disputes over rents between private landlords and their tenants, for certain types of tenancies which are subject to legal rules about the rents that can be charged. They sit in public.

Valuation Tribunals hear appeals against council tax and business rate valuations. They usually sit in public, but have discretion sit in private at the request of one of the parties.

The General Medical Council Professional Conduct Committee determines complaints against doctors. It sits in public, but has discretion to sit in private where that would be in the interest of justice, or desirable in view of the nature of the case, or the type of evidence to be given.

Bar Council Disciplinary Tribunal and Solicitor's Disciplinary Tribunals hear claims of serious professional misconduct by lawyers (barristers and solicitors respectively). Both usually sit in public, but have discretion to hold all or part of a hearing in private.

Contempt of court

As we saw in Chapter 6, the Contempt of Court Act 1981 lays down rules about what can and cannot be published about court cases. The Act defines 'court' as 'any tribunal or body exercising the judicial power of the state', which means that its provisions apply to reports of some types of tribunal proceedings. However, the Act does not define 'the judicial power of the state', so the courts have had to decide in individual cases which tribunals fit this definition. For example, in *Pickering v Liverpool Daily Post* (1991), the Mental Health Review Tribunal was said to 'exercise the power of the state' because it has the power to restore a person's liberty, and in *Peach Grey & Co v Sommers* (1995), Employment Tribunals were also deemed to 'exercise the power of the state' because they exercise a 'judicial function'. These two, therefore, are defined as courts for the purposes of the Contempt of Court Act, and covered by its provisions. On the other hand, in *General Medical Council v BBC* (1998), the professional conduct committee of the General Medical Council was deemed not to be a court for the purposes of the Act, because it does not exercise a power of the state, and in *A-G v BBC* (1981), the local valuation court was held not to be covered by the Contempt of Court Act because its functions were essentially administrative, rather than judicial.

Unfortunately, with many other tribunals, it is difficult to know whether they are covered by the law on contempt. If your company has an in-house or retained lawyer, they will be able to tell you whether the type of tribunal you want to write about has already been recognised as 'exercising the judicial power of the state' or not, but there are some tribunals for which the question has never been addressed by a court, so the answer is not known. The safest option, if in doubt, is to make sure you do not publish anything likely to prejudice a hearing.

Defamation

The rules of defamation, explained in Chapter 14, must always be borne in mind when reporting tribunal proceedings. Because most tribunals are relatively informal, and the parties will often represent themselves rather than using lawyers, things are often said that would not be allowed in a court, and some of these comments will be potentially defamatory. However, the law does offer some protection for tribunal reports:

- The Defamation Act 1996 provides that fair, accurate and contemporaneous reports of tribunals 'exercising the judicial power of the state' are covered by absolute privilege (see p. 202), so you cannot be sued for a fair, accurate and contemporaneous report of anything said during those proceedings. However, as we saw above, it is not always clear which tribunals this covers.

- Schedule II of the Act provides that fair and accurate reports of any public meeting of a 'tribunal . . . constituted by or under, or exercising functions under, any statutory provision' are covered by qualified privilege, 'subject to explanation or contradiction' (see p. 205). This covers any tribunal which has been set up by an Act of Parliament or delegated legislation (which is most of them). Remember though that statutory qualified privilege only applies to material which is of public concern and published 'for the public benefit'.

Reporting restrictions

A few tribunals (such as the Employment Tribunal – see below) have powers to make specific reporting restrictions relating to their proceedings; again, these powers will be contained in the legislation or procedural rules. Orders under s4(2) and s11 of the Contempt of Court Act 1981 can also be made in any tribunal 'exercising the power of the state' (see above). Remember that the ban on identifying witnesses of sexual offences will also cover any tribunal case where material used in a report could identify someone as the victim of a sexual offence.

EMPLOYMENT TRIBUNALS

Probably the best-known tribunals, these deal with cases involving unfair dismissal, sexual or racial discrimination in employment, redundancy and disputes over employment contracts. They are presided over by a legally-qualified chairman, and two other members, one of whom is drawn from organizations representing employers, the other employers (though naturally they are all required to judge the case independently, rather than as a representative of the relevant organisation). The person bringing a claim is called the claimant, and the other side, the respondant.

Procedure

Employment Tribunals usually sit in public, but some cases may be heard privately (see below). Before the hearing, both sides will have received notice of any documents that the other side intends to use in evidence, and there will often be a pre-hearing to clarify the issues. Just as with a court, witnesses can be compelled to attend an Employment Tribunal, and give their evidence on oath (which means that lying to the tribunal can be prosecuted as perjury).

In most cases, the employer will be represented by a lawyer. Employees may also use a lawyer, and where their case is supported by their union, they will usually be represented by the union lawyer or a union official. Unlike in a court case, there are no set rules for who gives evidence first; usually, in a discrimination case, the person claiming discrimination gives their evidence first, while in unfair dismissal cases, the respondent's evidence is taken first, but this can vary. After a witness has given evidence, they can be cross-examined by the other side, and then may give further evidence to clarify any issues that were raised during cross-examination. The chairperson and/or the other members of the panel may also put direct questions to witnesses.

After all the evidence has been given, both sides will sum up their case, and then the panel retires to consider a judgment. The decision may be given in full at the end of the hearing, but often employment tribunals either give their basic decision and publish the full reasons later, or postpone the decision completely and publish it later. If the decision is given at the end of the hearing, and the claimant wins, compensation will be decided there and then.

In most cases, each side pays its own legal costs, but in a handful of cases (less than 1 per cent), the tribunal may order one side to pay the other's costs. This is only done where either the party concerned is thought to have behaved very unreasonably, or where their case was so weak the tribunal does not believe it should have been brought at all. So if costs are awarded in a tribunal decision you report on, that is a story in itself.

Appeals

Either side in an employment case can appeal to the Employment Appeal Tribunal (EAT), if they believe the decision reflects a legal error. The EAT sits in London, presided over by a High Court judge and two lay members, again from both sides of industry. Appeals can only be made on the grounds that there was an error of law, or the decision was completely unreasonable.

Reporting Employment Tribunals

Employment Tribunals must usually sit in public and admit the press, but there are a few situations in which they can sit in private. The Employment Tribunals (Constitution and Rules of Procedure) Regulations provide that employment tribunals (and the EAT) may hold hearings in private where the evidence is likely to:

- include information which a witness could not reveal without breaching a prohibition imposed by an Act of Parliament;
- include information communicated to a witness in confidence, or obtained as a result of the confidence placed in the witness by someone else;
- be such that disclosure would cause substantial injury to any undertaking of the relevant witness, or any undertaking in which they work, for reasons other than its effect on negotiations over pay and conditions;
- be such that being heard in public would be against the interests of national security.

Aside from these reasons, employment tribunals should sit in public.

 In *Xxx* v *Yyy* [2004] a nanny bringing an unfair dismissal case alleged that the father of the family she worked for had made sexual advances to her. She secretly filmed this one morning, and wanted to use the tape (on which the child could also be seen) in evidence. The Employment Tribunal agreed that it should played during the hearing. The case was appealed to the EAT, which ruled that playing the tape was a breach of the child's right to privacy under the Human Rights Act 1998 because its contents could be described in newspapers and the images circulated. This would be severely damaging to the child as he grew older. The EAT therefore held that the tribunal could have sat in private, because the video could be categorised as evidence which could not be disclosed without breaching a prohibition imposed by an Act of Parliament. (At the time of the case, the 2000 version of the Rules applied, but contained a similar provision to that in the 2004 rules.) The actual decision in the case was later overturned by the Court of Appeal, but the Court of Appeal stated that this did not affect the decision on the child's privacy.

 In *Storer* v *British Gas* (2000), a tribunal hearing was held in an office, which was inside an area that could only be entered by a door marked 'Private.' The Court of Appeal held that this could not be considered a public hearing, because a member of the public would not have been able to enter if they had wanted to, and the chairman had acted wrongly in not holding the hearing in public.

In *R v Southampton Industrial Tribunal, ex P INS News Group* (1995), a tribunal had sat in private because it was hearing sensitive evidence in a sexual harassment case, but the Divisional Court of the Queen's Bench held that this was unlawful, and a tribunal could only sit in private in the situations listed in the Regulations.

Witnesses will usually be asked to give their names and addresses before giving evidence, but the full names, ages and addresses of the parties may not always be read out as a matter of course; they should, however, be available from tribunal officials.

Reporting restrictions

Rule 50 of the Employment Tribunals (Constitution and Rules of Procedure) Regulations 2004 allows employment tribunals to impose restricted reporting orders where:

- a case involves sexual misconduct; or
- a claim is being brought under s17A or s25(8) of the Disability Discrimination Act 1995, and some of the evidence is of a personal nature.

'Sexual misconduct' is defined by s11(6) of the Employment Tribunals Act 1996 as 'the commission of a sexual offence, sexual harassment or other adverse conduct (of whatever nature) related to sex, and conduct is related to sex whether the relationship with sex lies in the character of the conduct or in its having reference to the sex or sexual orientation of the person at whom the conduct is directed.' In effect this means that any case involving allegations of sexual harassment can be made the subject of a restricted reporting order, as well as any case involving allegations of a sexual offence.

The order can be requested by the claimant, or in cases of alleged sexual misconduct (but not disability discrimination), by the respondent. Alternatively, the tribunal itself can choose to make an order. It is not, however, obliged to make an order just because the case fits one of the two categories listed above, and one or both of the parties wants an order. The tribunal must take into account the public interest in the case being reported when deciding whether to issue an order, and in *Kearney v Smith New Court Securities* (1997), the Court of Appeal stressed that full consideration should be given to this question, and tribunals should not merely accede to requests for orders 'on the nod'.

The restricted reporting order prevents the press from naming anyone specified in the order, which may include the victim, or anyone else affected by the allegations (including the person alleged to be the perpetrator). However, in *Leicester University v A* [1999], it was established that for these purposes, a company is a not a person, so such an order cannot state that a company should not be named. A notice that a restricted reporting order is in force will be put on the tribunal notice board and on the door of the hearing room.

Restricted reporting orders can only be made at a pre-hearing review, or the hearing itself, and rule 50(7) of the Employment Tribunal Rules 2004 provides that any person can make an application to the tribunal to put forward arguments about why an order should or should not be made (though whether the application is accepted is up to the tribunal). This provision has been used successfully by the press in preventing such orders.

In some cases, a tribunal may make a temporary order, which it can do without holding a hearing. The parties then have 14 days to apply for the temporary order to be converted into a full one, or revoked, otherwise it lapses. If either side applies for it to be revoked or converted to a full order, both sides must be given a chance to argue for or against this, and the press can also apply to make representations.

A full restricted reporting order usually remains in force until the tribunal has made its decision, including determining any compensation to be paid, and issued written judgments to the parties (which may be months afterwards). In some cases, though an order may state that it only remains in force until the court has decided which party wins. Tribunals can also revoke an order before a case is decided. Where a case to which an order applies is settled before the full hearing (as often happens), the order remains in force unless the tribunal revokes it. Representations from the press can sometimes get an order revoked in this situation.

 In 2004, the NUJ applied for an order to be revoked in a case where a woman was claiming sexual harassment, and the case was settled. The tribunal agreed to revoke the order.

Breaching a restricted reporting order is a criminal offence, punishable with a fine of up to £5,000.

Rule 49 of the Employment Tribunals (Constitution and Rules of Procedure) Regulations 2004 state that in cases involving allegations of a sexual offence (not just sexual misconduct) a tribunal must remove from any documents available to the public (including the judgment), anything which could lead the public to identify the victim or anyone else affected by the allegations. This includes the alleged perpetrator.

In addition to the Employment Tribunal Rules, the Sexual Offences (Amendment) Act 1992 applies to employment tribunal proceedings and prevents identification of the victim of a sexual offence during their lifetime, unless the victim gives written consent to being named (see Chapter 9). This means that even once a restricted reporting order has lapsed, it will still not always be possible to name the claimant.

PUBLIC INQUIRIES

Some Acts of Parliament require that a public inquiry be held before a decision is made on any action affecting the rights of individuals or other public authorities. Such inquiries are often held, for example, in connection with major building projects such as airports or roads, which may require compulsory purchase of land, and will also have a significant effect on life in the area. The idea of the inquiry is to allow people who might be affected to put forward arguments for or against a proposal.

The inquiry is conducted by an inspector, on behalf of the relevant minister. Depending on the requirements of the statute, the final decision may be made by the inspector, or they may report to the minister, who then takes the decision.

Reporting inquiries

Some inquiries have to be held in public, and where this is the case, it will be stated in the statute under which the inquiry has been set up. In other cases, it is up to the person hearing the inquiry whether the proceedings are open to the public or not. There are also instances where proceedings that would normally be public can be heard in private; for example, one of the most commonly reported types of hearing, the planning inquiry, is usually open to the public but the Secretary of State can direct that certain evidence is heard in private, if it relates to national security and measures taken to ensure the security of property, and if disclosing this information would be against the national interest. The findings of these kinds of public inquiries are usually made available to the public.

■ One-off inquiries

In addition to statutory inquiries, governments sometimes order one-off public enquiries to investigate high-profile events which have caused public concern (such as those into Bloody Sunday or the murder of Stephen Lawrence). Most of these are now governed by the Inquiries Act 2005. Section 18 of the Act provides that an inquiry chairman must take reasonable steps to ensure that reporters can attend or see a simultaneous transmission of proceedings, and see the evidence and documents given. Restrictions on this access can only be imposed by the relevant minister or the inquiry chairman when they are required by law, are in the public interest or are conducive to the inquiry fulfilling its terms of reference. Even if enquiries are held in private, their reports must be published, but material can be withheld where it is in the public interest or required by law. However, the Department of Constitutional Affairs website states that powers to withhold information will not be used to prevent disclosure under the Freedom of Information Act (see Chapter 25).

CHAPTER SUMMARY

Reporting tribunals

Tribunals decide cases in specialist areas such as mental health, employment and social security.

Rules on press access are found in the statute under which a tribunal was set up, or its rules of procedure.

Contempt of court

Tribunals which exercise 'the judicial functions of the state' are subject to the Contempt of Court Act 1981.

Defamation

- Tribunals which exercise 'the judicial functions of the state' are covered by absolute privilege in defamation.
- Tribunals set up by statute are covered by qualified privilege subject to explanation or contradiction.

Public inquiries

Some statutes require public inquiries on decisions which affect a large number of people.

Press access to these inquires varies; conclusions are usually made public.

One-off inquiries look into issues of public concern.

The press can attend these unless restrictions are needed because they:
- are required by law;
- are in the public interest; or
- are conducive to the inquiry fulfilling its terms of reference.

12

Reporting tribunals and inquiries

TEST YOUR KNOWLEDGE

1 What are the main differences between courts and tribunals?

2 On what grounds can an Employment Appeal Tribunal sit in private?

3 What does a Family Health Service Committee do?

4 Name two tribunals which are definitely subject to the Contempt of Court Act 1981.

5 What legal protection is there against defamation actions for reports of tribunal proceedings?

ONLINE RESOURCES

www

The Tribunals Service website has links to the websites of 17 key tribunals, which details their functions and procedure:
www.tribunals.gov.uk

The Employment Tribunal website explains the work and procedure of the tribunal:
www.employmenttribunals.gov.uk

The Planning Inspectorate website lists forthcoming planning inquiries, at:
www.planning-inspectorate.gov.uk/pins/inquiries/index.htm

The Inquiries Act 2005 can be read at:
www.opsi.gov.uk/acts/acts2005/50012--a.htm#18

For further resources and updates please go to the Companion Website for this book at www.pearsoned.co.uk/practicaljournalism

Challenging reporting restrictions

There are two reasons why journalists need to know about the restrictions on reporting the courts. The first is, obviously, so that you do not break the law when publishing details about a court case. The second is so that you can spot when a court has ordered restrictions that can be challenged.

As we saw in previous chapters, a court can only impose reporting restrictions where there is a specific legal provision that allows it to do so, and where such a provision exists, it may only order such restrictions as the provision allows. For example, as we saw in Chapter 8, s4(2) of the Contempt of Court Act 1981 allows a court to impose restrictions where is it is necessary to avoid a risk of prejudice, so the restrictions ordered under this provision should only go so far as is necessary to avoid that risk. Yet courts will surprisingly often impose restrictions that are wider than the law allows, or that the law does not allow at all, particularly if defence lawyers press for this. Where this happens, the press can challenge those restrictions and may be able to get them lifted (or even prevent them being applied in the first place). This chapter explains how to do that.

PREVENTING RESTRICTIONS

In some cases, it may be possible for the media to persuade a court not to impose restrictions in the first place. The senior judiciary accepts that the media often have a good knowledge of the law on reporting restrictions, and where a court is considering making a discretionary order imposing reporting restrictions, the higher courts have encouraged lower courts to listen to, or even ask for, the views of the press.

 In *McKerry* v *Teasdale and Wear Valley Justices* (2000) the Lord Chief Justice, Lord Bingham, commented that where a Youth Court was considering whether to lift anonymity from a defendant, it would be approppriate for the magistrates to ask the reporter present in court whether they wanted to argue against restrictions, and that in such cases, members of the press might well have arguments to make which could stop the court from making a mistake.

 In *R* v *Clerkenwell Metropolitan Stipendiary Magistrates, ex p Telegraph plc* (1993), the Queen's Bench Divisional Court confirmed that all courts have discretion to hear arguments from the media about whether or not a s4 order (see p. xxx) should be made. The court commented that the decision involves balancing the risk of prejudice against the public interest in open justice, and it made sense to consult the media, as they were in the best position to represent that public interest.

This view is backed up by the Judicial Studies Board's 2001 guidelines to Crown Court judges, which specifically confirm the Court's discretion to hear representations from the press when considering making, changing or removing a s11 order (see *Online Resources*, at the end of the chapter).

In *R v Beck ex p Daily Telegraph* (1993), Lord Justice Farquharson stated that the media's ability to put forward arguments against discretionary restrictions was compromised if a judge announced such restrictions without warning. Where the need for restrictions suddenly became apparent, he advised, judges should ideally make an order covering just a couple of days, giving the press time to make representations before, if necessary, extending it.

CHALLENGING ORDERS

If you are not able to convince a court not to impose restrictions in the first place, there are three ways of challenging an order:

- application to the original court;
- judicial review;
- appeals under s159 of the Criminal Justice Act 1988.

Applying to the original court

If you think that a court may have made an order which it is not legally entitled to make, or which may be wider than it needs to be, the first step is to make sure you know the legal basis on which the court believes it is acting (e.g. whether it is making a s4(2) order or a s11 one). If this is not stated at the time the restrictions are imposed, you can ask the clerk of the court, or the judge's clerk, for the information. In some cases, this alone will be enough to prompt the court to reconsider the case for restrictions, and as a result, to lift or relax them.

If not, once you know the legal provision being used, you can draw the court's attention to the reason why you believe the restrictions imposed are outside those provisions – for example, if a court has made a s11 order banning identification of a witness, but that person's name has already been stated in open court (see p. 109). The usual way to do this is by asking the clerk to pass a note to the magistrates or judge. Again, this simple (and, unlike all the other options, free) approach will often prompt a re-examination of the relevant law, which, if you are right, should see the restrictions lifted or relaxed accordingly.

If this strategy fails, your publisher can instruct its lawyers to make representations to the court, usually within 24 hours if necessary. The court does not have to hear these representations, but is unlikely to refuse. Of course, a drawback to this option is that unless you have an in-house lawyer who can make the case, it will involve a cost, which means the publisher may have to weigh up the importance of the story against the expense.

Judicial review

If a court refuses to change its decision on reporting restrictions, and the press is convinced that the restrictions are not legally justified, judicial review is a way of challenging the decision in court. Essentially, the procedure asks a higher court to look at the decision of the lower court, and judge whether it was properly made; if the lower court acted outside its powers, or if the decision was clearly irrational, it can be quashed, or the lower court may be asked to look at the question again.

Judicial review has two major drawbacks. Firstly, the process can be slow, which means that by the time the court comes to a decision, the original story may no longer have much news value. Secondly, it is usually expensive, and publishers may not get their costs paid, even if they win. In a 1995 case, for example, Express Newspapers and the INS news agency had to pay estimated costs of £10,000, after successfully challenging the right of an Industrial Tribunal (the old name for Employment Tribunals) to exclude journalists from a case involving sexual harassment.

As a result, judicial review tends only to be used by big publishers in important cases. Judicial review is not available to challenge orders made by the Crown Court with regard to trials on indictment.

Section 159 appeals

Section 159 of the Criminal Justice Act 1988 creates a right of appeal against decisions on access or reporting restrictions in the Crown Court (but not in any other court). Appeals go to the Court of Appeal and can be brought by 'any person aggrieved' by the decision, which can include the press, as well as anyone involved in the case. They may relate to:

- orders made under s4 or s11 of the Contempt of Court Act 1981 (see p. 105), with reference to a criminal trial in the Crown Court;
- any order restricting public access to a Crown Court trial, or part of one, or to any proceedings ancillary to such a trial;
- any order restricting the publication of reports on a Crown Court trial, or part of one, or any ancillary proceedings to that trial;
- an order from the Crown Court restricting reporting of derogatory statements made as part of pleas in mitigation.

However, there are some procedural issues which mean that these provisions are not as useful in practice as they may sound. Firstly, the right of appeal is not automatic; publishers have to apply to the Court of Appeal for permission to appeal. Notice also has to be given to the trial judge, their clerk, both parties in the case to which restrictions apply, and 'any other interested person'. Secondly, the case must be made in writing, and the press has no right to appear before the court and state its case. Perhaps the most significant drawback though is that the appeal can take time. The Court of Appeal does have the power to stop the original case while the appeal is decided, but if it chooses not to do this, and, by the time the appeal is decided, the original court case is finished, the news value of being able to report it fully may be much lower. During the appeal itself, the Court of Appeal can rule that witnesses, or anyone else in the case, may not be identified. If the appeal is successful, the Court of Appeal can lift or alter the order.

Law in practice **Challenging restrictions**

Tony Jaffa, Head of Media at solicitors Foot Anstey, represents newspapers throughout the country in challenges to exclusions from court and reporting restrictions. He has this advice for reporters faced with exclusion from a court hearing, or restrictions that they believe may be unlawful.

- If possible, make your challenge as soon as the order is made, or if that is not possible, make it known that you want to challenge. If you want time to speak to your news editor and/or your legal advisors, you can say that you would like to make representations in writing, or ask if you can come back and discuss the order later. Quick action is especially important where the case is likely to finish on the same day, as once it is over, the magistrates or judge may refuse to lift the order on the grounds that they no longer have jurisdiction over the case.

- Always be polite, and show respect for the judge or magistrates, and the court. It helps to know the correct terminology to use, but your challenge will not fail because you call the judge My Lord instead of Your Honour, so long as you are respectful. Show that you know what you are talking about, for example by quoting the relevant section of the legislation, but do not be tempted to act like Rumpole of the Bailey. You can be persuasive, and even forceful in your arguments, but do not try to make your case sound stronger than it is – and know when to shut up!

- If you are reporting a particular court regularly, it makes sense to develop a good relationship with the clerks there. Once they know and trust you, and the judges begin to do the same, you are more likely to be listened to when you make a challenge.

- Do not challenge orders as a matter of routine – go for the ones where you know you have a good case. If you challenge every order a court makes, human nature means that eventually you will become irritating, and the court is less likely to listen sympathetically. You are more likely to get results if the court recognises you usually have a good reason to challenge.

The risk of incurring costs

One thing to be aware of when considering a challenge to reporting restrictions is that in some circumstances, such a challenge could result in your publication being asked to pay costs. In *A v Times Newspapers* (2002), the Family Division of the High Court said that where the press knew that restrictions were likely to be imposed on a particular hearing, but did not apply to have them lifted until after the proceedings had begun, the publishers concerned risked having an order for costs made against them, even if the application to lift the restrictions was successful. By contrast, if the publishers made the application in good time, the courts were unlikely to impose costs, even if the challenge was unsuccessful, provided that the media at least had an arguable case. Costs are not routinely ordered against the media however, and if such an order is made, the press can put forward arguments against it.

In 2006, a reporter from *The Argus* in Brighton persuaded a court not to impose a costs order which the defence lawyers in the case had asked for. The paper had challenged a s39 order banning the press from naming some children who had had ASBOs imposed on them. When the challenge was unsuccessful, the children's lawyers asked the court for an order requiring the newspaper to pay the costs involved in the challenge, which ran to thousands of pounds. The Argus reporter argued that it was in the public interest for newspapers to be able to challenge orders, and that imposing costs would make this impossible for most papers; she used the Human Rights Act 1998 and Judicial Studies Board Guidelines to back up her arguments. The court agreed not to impose the costs order.

Must invalid orders be followed?

The short answer is yes: no matter how sure you are that an order is invalid, simply ignoring it is not a sensible option. This was made plain in *Lakah Group v Al Jazeera Satallite Channel*

[2002], where Mr Justice Eady stated that while an order exists, everyone who it applies to, and who knows it exists, is under an obligation to obey it, even if they believe it to be invalid, and even if that belief is actually correct. In such circumstances, he said, the answer is to put the issue before a court, not to decide it yourself. Similarly, in **Independent Publishing Co Ltd v Attorney General of Trinidad and Tobago** (2004), the Judicial Committee of the Privy Council stated that publishing material that was likely to prejudice the administration of justice could still be contempt, even if the order banning such publication was itself illegal.

CHAPTER SUMMARY

Preventing restrictions

The higher courts and Judicial Studies Board guidelines encourage courts to listen to press arguments before ordering reporting restrictions.

Challenging restrictions

There are three ways to challenge a court order which is too wide, or unlawful:

- applying to the original court;
- judicial review;
- appeal under s159 of the Criminal Justice Act 1988, for cases heard in the Crown Court.

Costs

Challenging restrictions could result in a costs order against the press.

Invalid orders

Orders imposing reporting restrictions should be followed, even if apparently invalid.

TEST YOUR KNOWLEDGE

1 You are reporting a case in which the defence solicitor has asked for reporting restrictions to be imposed. You think there are good reasons for not imposing restrictions, but the magistrates say that they are not allowed to take your views into account. What arguments could you use to try to change their minds?

2 What do you need to find out before you can argue that an order imposing reporting restrictions is invalid?

3 Name the three ways in which reporting restrictions can be challenged.

4 To which courts does the s159 appeal against reporting restrictions apply?

5 Why is it risky to delay asking a court to lift reporting restrictions?

ONLINE RESOURCES

The Judicial Studies Board guidelines on reporting restrictions are available at:
www.jsboard.co.uk/publications.htm

Useful reports of cases where reporting restrictions have been imposed or overturned can be found at the Hold the Front Page website:
www.holdthefrontpage.co.uk

The Society of Editors website also reports on the use of, and challenges to, reporting restrictions:
www.societyofeditors.org

> **For further resources and updates please go to the Companion Website for this book at** www.pearsoned.co.uk/practicaljournalism

DEFAMATION AND MALICIOUS FALSEHOOD

As far back as the 11th century, English law has provided a legal claim for people whose reputations have been damaged by lies told about them. Over the centuries, this action developed into the modern law of defamation, and its main (though not only) use is now in cases where damaging statements are published by the media. Most legal systems have a form of defamation law, but the rules vary widely throughout the world, and England's are considered to make life more difficult for the media than the laws in many other countries.

Defamation is one of the most important areas of law for a journalist to know about and, for that reason, it is considered in more depth than most other subjects in this book. To keep chapters at a readable length, the coverage of defamation has been split into two. Chapter 14 explains how defamation is committed and thus how to avoid committing it. Chapter 15 explains the defences which can be used in defamation, and also details the remedies which may be ordered against publishers and broadcasters if found liable for defamation.

The final chapter in this section covers a related, but different action, called malicious falsehood. Like defamation, it is concerned with protecting people from lies published about them, but it applies to statements which cause financial damage, rather than damage to reputation.

Chapter 14

Defamation

The law of defamation protects people against untrue statements that could damage their reputation, and is probably the single most important area of law for any journalist to know about. One of the reasons for this is that defamation can affect journalists in any field of work. If you work, for example, for a trade magazine or in the women's press, it's quite possible that you will never need to think about court reporting or official secrets after you've passed your law exams. But almost every kind of journalist, on almost every kind of publication, has the potential to defame someone, and some of the most high-profile defamation cases have involved quite small publications.

The second reason why defamation is such an important part of the law for journalists is that being successfully sued for it can be very expensive. Damages in defamation cases are usually decided by juries; as a result, they are very unpredictable, and can be extremely high. One careless piece of research or unchecked statement could end up costing a publisher tens of thousands of pounds in damages – sometimes even hundreds of thousands – and as much again, sometimes more, in legal fees. Big national papers can absorb such losses (though decreasing circulations mean even they find it difficult), but for smaller magazines, losing a libel case can be disastrous. The magazine *Living Marxism* was actually forced into liquidation after being order to pay damages of £375,000 in a libel case in 2000.

Because of this, most publishers are very nervous of libel actions. One result of this is that, faced with a threat of libel, even where the journalist believes that the story is legally sound, many publishers will choose not to run it, or to water it down. In this way the threat of a libel action can be used to prevent publication of stories that really ought to be brought to the public's attention. Similarly, many publishers, faced with a complaint about a story that has already been published, will back down, print an apology and if necessary, agree to pay some compensation, rather than allow the case to go to court and risk the cost of losing. In fact, the majority of libel claims are now settled out of court, and court hearings are rare.

None of this means that journalists should be so scared of being sued that we never write anything that upsets anyone, but it does mean that every journalist needs to understand thoroughly the basic rules of this area of the law – not just so that you know what not to write or say, but because defamation law does give some protection to press freedom, and by knowing the rules, you can often safely say more than you might imagine. Many newspapers and magazines publish potentially defamatory material every day, but by making sure that what they print is covered by one of several defences to defamation, they can do so safely.

As explained in the introduction, the law of defamation protects people against damage to their reputations. To succeed in an action for defamation, the claimant must prove three things:

- the statement complained of was defamatory;

- the statement referred to the claimant;

- the statement was published.

Even if all these things are proved, a case may fail if the defendant can establish one of a number of possible defences.

As explained at the start of this section, defences for defamation are covered in the next chapter, but one thing worth knowing at this stage (because it will help explain some of the cases in this chapter), is that if you can prove that what you say is true, you will have a complete defence in defamation. This is known as justification.

Forms of defamation

There are two forms of defamation: libel and slander. Libel is committed by publishing a defamatory statement in permanent form, while slander covers defamatory statements in transient forms, such as unrecorded speech. Defamation actions against the media almost always concern libel, which covers defamatory statements which are made in any of the following ways:

- printed;

- broadcast on TV or radio (Broadcasting Act 1990);

- in films and videos;

- on the internet;

- made during public performances of a play (Theatres Act 1968).

For this reason, the terms 'libel' and 'defamation' can be viewed as interchangeable for the purposes of this chapter. There are rare circumstances in which members of the media can face a slander claim through their work; these are covered on p. 188.

THE MEANING OF 'DEFAMATORY'

Most of the original law on defamation comes from case law (see p. 6), rather than statute, so there is no single definition of what defamatory means. Old cases have suggested that a statement will be defamatory if it 'tends to lower the person in the estimation of right-thinking members of society', or exposes the person to 'hatred, contempt or ridicule'. Both of these are still accurate, but a more comprehensive definition, in line with modern legal thinking, is given by the legal academics McBride and Bagshaw in their text book *Tort Law* (Longman, 2005). They say that a statement is defamatory if reading or hearing it would make an ordinary, reasonable person tend to:

- think less well as a person of the individual referred to;

- think that the person referred to lacked the ability to do their job effectively;

- shun or avoid the person referred to; or

- treat the person referred to as a figure of fun or an object of ridicule.

Their definition makes it clear that the important issue is not how the defamatory statement makes the person referred to feel, but the impression it is likely to make on those reading it. The person defamed does not have to prove that the words actually had any of these effects on any particular people or the public in general, only that the statement could *tend* to have that effect on an ordinary, reasonable listener or reader. Nor does the claimant need to prove that they have lost money, or suffered any other kind of loss or damage. As the following cases indicate, a wide range of allegations have been found to be defamatory by the courts, or led to out of court settlements.

In *Byrne* v *Deane* (1937), the claimant was a member of a golf club, whose owners illegally kept gambling machines on the premises. Someone reported them to the police and afterwards a poem was posted up in the club, implying that the claimant had been the informant. He sued, and won the original case, but on appeal the courts held that the suggestion was not defamatory, because a right-thinking member of society (or as it might be expressed today, an ordinary, reasonable person) would not think less well of someone for telling the police about a crime.

In *Mitchell* v *Faber & Faber* (1998), the claimant was a musician who had worked with the rock star Jimi Hendrix during the 1960s. The defendants were the publishers of a book about Hendrix, in which the author said that the claimant had a 'strange contempt' for Hendrix and routinely used words like 'nigger' and 'coon' in everyday conversation. However, he said that the claimant had no idea that what he said might offend anyone, and did not intend any harm. The claimant sued on the basis that the book made him appear to be racist. The defendant argued that the book was not defamatory, in that it made clear that the claimant had not intended to offend Hendrix, and that his attitude was simply typical of many people in the UK 30 years ago. The Court of Appeal said that although it was true that those attitudes were widely held at that time, it was necessary to consider what impression the book would have on people reading it now, and therefore the words could be defamatory.

In *Jason Donovan* v *The Face* (1992), the singer Jason Donovan successfully sued *The Face* magazine for saying he was gay. He based his argument on the fact that he had always presented himself as being heterosexual, and that *The Face* was therefore defaming him by suggested he had deceived the public about his sexuality. The case did not, therefore, test whether it is defamatory merely to say someone is gay.

In *Berkoff* v *Burchill* (1996), the journalist Julie Burchill described actor Steven Berkoff as 'hideous-looking' and compared him with Frankenstein's monster. The court argued that although the kind of remarks made would not usually be defamatory, they become so because the claimant earned his living as an actor, and therefore the words made him an object of ridicule. The result of this case surprised many people, because, as stated above, a statement usually has to go further than being simply unpleasant and rude before it will be considered defamatory. It suggests that if rude personal remarks are judged to be excessively offensive, they may be considered to have crossed the line into defamation.

In 1997, a columnist on the *Express on Sunday's* magazine mentioned a newspaper story which had stated that the film star Nicole Kidman has insisted that builders working on her house should face the wall whenever she walked past. A judge initially found that the story, though unpleasant, was not capable of being defamatory, but Ms Kidman appealed. The Court of Appeal agreed with her that the statement was capable of being defamatory. In the event the case was settled out of court.

In *Cruise* v *Express Newspapers* (1998) Ms Kidman and her then husband Tom Cruise won damages, said to be a six-figure sum, from the *Express*, after the paper falsely claimed that their marriage was a sham, designed to cover up the fact that they were both gay.

In *Parker* v *News Group Newspapers Ltd* (2005), the former Eastenders actor Chris Parker won £50,000 damages from the *Sun*, after a story falsely claimed that he had been sacked from the soap after refusing to see a psychiatrist.

 In 2005, actress Lisa Maxwell accepted an out-of-court settlement with the *Daily Star Sunday*, over a story which falsely claimed that, many years earlier, she had had a one-night stand with a man she had only just met.

 In 2006, Elton John accepted damages and an apology from the *Sunday Times*, over false allegations that he had behaving rudely and arrogantly at his own party, by telling guests that they were not to speak to him unless he addressed them first.

 In 2006, TV presenter Noel Edmonds accepted 'substantial' damages from the *Mail on Sunday*, after it falsely claimed that he had seduced a woman in order to make her leave her husband.

 In *Hudson* v *American News Media* (2006), actress Kate Hudson won damages and an apology from the *National Enquirer* magazine, after it suggested she had an eating disorder, describing her as 'painfully thin' and falsely claiming that her mother had begged her to 'eat something'. Although the magazine is based in the USA, the action could be brought in the UK because it is also published here.

▨ Defamation and truth

As explained above, if you make a statement that is defamatory, but you can prove it to be true, you will be covered by the defence of justification (see p. 193). Equally, if you publish a statement that is not true, but is not defamatory either, you cannot be sued for defamation. For example, if you were to write that two single film stars were dating, when in fact they were not, the celebrities would not be able to sue for libel unless there was something in the story which would have a bad effect on their reputation. If one of them were married, or known to be in a serious relationship, they might have a case in defamation, because the story would be implying that they had been unfaithful, but if they were both single and the story was merely untrue but not libellous, they would not.

Obviously, the fact that there is no legal obligation to be truthful does not mean there is no moral obligation. The Codes of Practice of the Press Complaints Commission (PCC), the National Union of Journalists (NUJ) and Ofcom all recognise that journalists have a duty to ensure that the information they publish is accurate.

▨ Changes over time

In deciding whether a statement could lower its subject in the eyes of others, the jury is asked to consider how an ordinary, reasonable person (referred to in some cases as a 'right-thinking person') would read and understand it. This person is often referred to by judges as 'the reasonable man', and one of the things that makes defamation claims so unpredictable is that clearly, the views of the 'reasonable man' will change over time. At one time, for example, it would certainly have been defamatory to say of an unmarried woman that she spent the night with her boyfriend; this would not be the case today, unless, for example, that particular woman had presented herself as being against extra-marital sex, in which case she might be able to argue that the claim made her appear to be a liar and a hypocrite. In fact things have changed so much that it can now be defamatory to say a woman did not have sex with a man, as the following case shows.

In 2004, the celebrity magazine *Heat* agreed to publish an apology to a woman called Amy Barker, for saying that she had not had sex with pop star Bryan McFadden on his stag night. Ms Barker had originally sold the story of the incident to the *Sunday People*, but in an interview with *Heat*, Mr McFadden suggested that she had made the story up. Ms Barker's legal advisor sought an apology on the grounds that the *Heat* article called Ms Barker's integrity into question; neither side would say whether any damages were paid.

■ Effect of the claimant's existing reputation

What if the person you write about already has a bad reputation? Journalists often assume that if someone already has a low standing in the eyes of the public, then nothing they write about that person could be said to lower them further in the estimation of right-thinking people. This is not the case. For example, if someone was a convicted bank robber, and you wrote, wrongly, that he had been involved in the kidnap of a child, or of a sexual offence, he might well be able to sue successfully for libel. Despite his already bad reputation, it could be argued that your words have lowered his reputation even further.

However, if a person has an extremely bad reputation in one particular respect, and your false allegation is in the same vein and does not make that reputation worse, that person might well have difficulty proving that you have lowered them in the estimation of right-thinking people. For example, if an actor had serious drug problems, and this was well known to the public, he would have difficulties successfully suing for libel if you falsely claimed that he had taken drugs on a particular occasion, even if this was not true (see the Kate Moss case, p. 195).

The law, however, restricts the use which libel defendants can make of background information on a claimant. Evidence can be given to establish the fact that the claimant already has a bad reputation, but the old case of *Scott* **v** *Sampson* (1882) establishes that a defendant cannot put forward in evidence examples of the claimant's previous misconduct, unless the jury has already been told about these as part of a defence of justification. For example, take the case where a newspaper is sued over a story that claimed an actor had had an affair with his co-star, and cannot prove that particular story, but does have evidence of previous affairs. You might assume that if someone can be proved to have had serial affairs, their reputation cannot be lowered by suggesting that they had one with a particular person, but the effect of *Scott* **v** *Sampson* is that the evidence of the previous affairs could not be put before the jury. However, the situation is different where it is established that a libel has been committed, and the court has only to decide what damages should be awarded. In that situation, the case of *Burstein* **v** *Times Newspapers* (2000) establishes that background evidence which is relevant to the publication of the defamatory statement can be used to argue that the damages should be reduced.

■ Innuendoes

A statement does need not make a direct criticism in order to be defamatory – a defamatory implication or innuendo can be just as dangerous. This is fairly obvious when it comes to deliberate hints: if you want to say that John Jones MP has taken bribes, you cannot escape the risk of being defamatory by saying something like 'John Jones MP said he had not taken bribes, and we all know that politicians never lie, don't we?'

In 1986 the *Star* published a gossip column story about Lord Gowrie, an ex-Cabinet Minister, who had stepped down from his post the year before. Questioning why he had resigned, the story referred to 'expensive habits', and said that Lord Gowrie would 'snort' at the idea that he had been 'born with a silver spoon round his neck'. Lord Gowrie sued, arguing that references to expensive habits, snorting and a silver spoon implied that he habitually took cocaine. He won his case.

In *Liberace* v *Daily Mirror Newspapers Ltd* (1959), the American pianist Liberace, who at the time was very famous for his glittering costumes and effeminate manner, sued the *Mirror* over an article which described him as a 'deadly, winking, sniggering, chromium-plated, scent-impregnated, luminous, quivering, giggling, fruit-flavoured, mincing, ice-covered heap of mother-love'. Liberace claimed that the article implied he was homosexual, which he denied. At the time, to be said to be gay was seen as a slur, though it probably would not be today, and his libel claim was successful. (Many years later, he came out as a homosexual.)

In these types of case, the courts will look at what the ordinary, reasonable reader would think the words implied.

A second type of innuendo is where words seem innocent on the surface (and may actually have been meant quite innocently) but can be read as defamatory in the particular circumstances, or because of special knowledge possessed by some readers. For example, take a situation where you interview a celebrity over lunch. To add colour to the feature, you want to describe the meal, but you are unable to remember precisely what the celebrity ate. Assuming that it is unlikely to matter, you write that she 'tucked into a juicy steak'. In most cases, though untrue, this would not be defamatory, but if the celebrity in question was actually an ardent vegetarian, the situation would be different. Your words could then, arguably, be defamatory, since they would suggest to those who know she is a vegetarian that she has betrayed her principles, or that she was a hypocrite in only pretending to be a vegetarian. If that seems extreme, consider the following real-life cases.

In *Tolley* v *JS Fry & Sons Ltd* (1931), the claimant was an amateur golfer, whose picture was used, without his consent, to advertise Fry's chocolate. He argued that anyone seeing the advert would assume he had both consented to and been paid for it, and that this would suggest that he had compromised his amateur status. He won his case.

In *Cassidy* v *Daily Mirror Newspapers* (1929), the *Mirror* published a picture of a man described as Mr Corrigan, with a lady who it said was his fiancée. The man had given these details to the paper, but in fact his name was Mr Cassidy, and he was married to someone else, though they lived apart. Mrs Cassidy sued on the basis that anyone reading the article, who knew her, would assume that if Mr Cassidy had a fiancée, he must be free to marry, and therefore could not have been married to her when they were living together (remember that this case took place at a time when both living together and divorce were uncommon). She won her case, and her victory was upheld on appeal.

A claimant who argues that they have been defamed by innuendo must not only show that the facts or circumstances giving rise to the innuendo exist, but that the statement was published to people who knew of those facts. So, in the example of the vegetarian celebrity above, the claimant would not only have to be a vegetarian, but would have to show that at least one of the readers of your publication would know this. Clearly this is easier in some cases than others.

Pictures

Defamation is not necessarily committed by words alone. It is possible to use quite harmless words, but still defame someone in print, thanks to the pictures used with those words.

In *Dwek* v *Macmillan Publishers Ltd* (2000), a book published by Macmillan included a picture, taken 20 years earlier, which showed the claimant sitting next to a woman who was (correctly)

described as a prostitute. The claimant himself was not the subject of the book, and was not mentioned anywhere in it. He sued, arguing that readers would assume from the picture and caption that he was a client of the prostitute. The Court of Appeal stated that this could be defamatory.

Watts v Times Newspapers (1997) concerned a *Times* article accusing an author, Nigel Watts, of plagiarism. It was mistakenly illustrated with a picture of a completely different person who was also called Nigel Watts. The Nigel Watts shown in the photo successfully sued, claiming that people reading the article would have thought it referred to him.

The now-defunct magazine *Titbits* illustrated a feature on stealing at Christmas with a photograph of a meat porter winning a meat-carrying race at London's Smithfield market. The porter sued, on the basis that the use of the picture suggested he was a thief, and won his case.

In 2005, footballer Andy Johnson forced an apology and damages from Express Newspapers, after they used a picture of him alongside a feature on footballers with drink and drug problems. Although not named in the article, he claimed it implied he took drugs, which was untrue.

In *Capehorn v Independent News and Media* (2006), the *Independent on Sunday* paid undisclosed damages to actor Harry Capehorn, after it used his photo to illustrate a feature on ASBOs – anti-social behaviour orders. The photo was taken six years earlier for a publicity campaign by a charity, and Mr Capehorn, who was then 16, was the model for it. It was originally supplied on the condition that it would be captioned 'posed by models', but the *Independent* failed to do this. Mr Caphorn, who has since appeared in several TV series, said readers could recognise him from the photo and might assume he had been the subject of an ASBO.

In 2006, several national newspapers had to apologise and pay damages to a London woman whose picture they had shown alongside reports about a female suspect arrested as part of the investigations into the alleged plot to blow up planes flying from the UK to the USA. The woman shown in the pictures was not the woman arrested, and the mistake appeared to have arisen from the fact that she had a slightly similar name and was said to have worked at the same school as the suspect.

Juxtaposition

A statement that by itself might be quite innocent can become defamatory as a result of the material it is placed next to.

In 1988 the business magazine *Stationery Trade News* carried an article about counterfeit stationery products which were being imported into the UK. Towards the end of the story, they mentioned a different problem, involving envelopes which were not made in the UK being marketed under a brand name which sounded British. The makers of these envelopes sued the magazine, claiming that the story implied that they were selling counterfeit envelopes. They won their case.

Law in practice Subbing errors

It's important to be aware that libel can creep it at almost any stage of a story, not just in the initial writing. Rod Dadak, Head of Defamation at solicitors Lewis Silkin, advises that all journalists should keep a copy of the unsubbed version of their story:

> Mistakes can be introduced during the subbing process, and a headline or caption can make a piece defamatory even if the original text was not. In practice it is unusual for a journalist to be sued personally, as most claimants sue publishers because they are more likely to have the money to pay damages, but if you were sued personally, you would be able to mitigate your liability by showing that you did not write the offending caption or headline, or that your original words were altered during subbing.

The importance of context

Words alleged to be defamatory must be read in their full context, rather than taken in isolation, and context can potentially include everything else on the page. As a result, an article taken as a whole may be judged to carry a defamatory implication which is not specifically stated anywhere in it. On the other hand, the context may rescue particular words from being defamatory.

Norman v *Future Publishing Ltd* (1999) concerned an article on the opera singer Jessie Norman, in which the interviewer referred to her 'statuesque' size, and quoted an anecdote in which Ms Norman got trapped in a revolving door and, on being advised to get out sideways, responded, 'Honey, I ain't got no sideways.' She sued, claiming that the quote suggested she had spoken in a vulgar, indignified way, which conformed to a degrading racist stereotype. The Court of Appeal, however, looked at the whole of the article, which it found portrayed Ms Norman as a respected professional and a person of high standing. In that context, it held, the words could not be read as defamatory.

In *Charleston* v *News Group Newspapers* (1995), the *News of the World* carried a story about a computer game which superimposed the faces of well-known actors onto other people's bodies, so that they appeared to be engaged in sexual acts. The piece was illustrated with a picture showing a man and woman having sex, with the faces of the actors Ian Smith and Ann Charleston, who played Harold and Madge in the TV soap 'Neighbours', superimposed on their bodies. The headline was 'Strewth! What's Harold up to with our Madge?' Although the article made it clear that the people in the picture were not Smith and Charleston, they sued on the basis that anyone who just read the headline and looked at the pictures might think that they had been involved in pornography. The House of Lords said that using defamatory headlines could be 'playing with fire', but the defamatory effect had to be judged against the article as a whole. In this case, although the headline looked defamatory, a reader only had to glance through the first paragraph to see that in fact the paper was not making any defamatory allegation. The situation might, they said, be different if, for example, the headline was potentially defamatory and the words which explained it and removed the defamatory meaning were not found until well into the article, so that casual readers might not see them.

Cases like *Charleston* are often referred to in terms of 'bane and antidote', the bane being the potentially defamatory allegation, and the antidote those words which show the reader that it is untrue, or take away the defamatory meaning. A jury will be told to take the two together and decide whether the antidote does actually take away the bane.

Broadcast libels

Part of the context of a defamatory remark is of course the medium it is presented in; someone reading a newspaper may well give more attention to that than they would to a TV or radio programme on in the background. Unlike a TV viewer, a reader can also easily go back over parts of the newspaper if a meaning seems unclear. The courts have therefore suggested that words which might not be defamatory in print, where a reader could be expected to see them in the context of a whole article, may be defamatory if they are part of a TV programme, where viewers might not be giving their whole attention and therefore might be more likely to pick up on the defamatory meaning without taking in other material that could have removed the 'sting'.

In *Gillick* v *BBC* (1996), a live TV progamme was broadcast to mark the 25th anniversary of the Brook Advisory Centres, set up to give young people advice about contraception. A guest on the programme was Victoria Gillick, well-known at the time for her campaigns against under-age sex. She had won a court case in which she sought to restrict access to contraceptives for teenage girls, and the programme's presenter said to her, 'But after you won that battle . . . there were at least two reported cases of suicide by girls who were pregnant.' Mrs Gillick sued the BBC for libel, claiming that the words meant she was morally responsible for the deaths of at least two girls. The Court of Appeal held that the words should be judged on the meaning that they would imply to an ordinary person who had watched the programme once, and was neither unusually suspicious or unusually naïve. On this basis the words could carry the meaning Mrs Gillick alleged.

Defamatory remarks made during a broadcast may also be the subject of complaints to Ofcom (see Chapter 29). There is however nothing to stop a person who goes to Ofcom from suing for defamation as well.

Reporting rumours

Can you report defamatory rumours if you make it clear that that is all they are, or even state that you do not believe them? Many journalists believe that if they report rumours in this way, they can argue that the story is true, because they are reporting that there are rumours, and they can prove that the rumours did exist. This is not the case. The law takes the view that readers will assume there is no smoke without fire, and if you cannot prove the rumour to be true (or cover yourself with another defence), you will be taking the risk of liability for defamation.

In 1999 Belfast's *Sunday Life* was successfully sued by the actors Natasha Richardson and her husband Liam Neeson over a story about rumours that their marriage was in trouble. The story focused on the fact that people who knew the couple well had said the rumours were untrue, but the court held that this would not necessarily convince readers, and therefore the 'antidote' did not cure the 'bane'.

In *Major* v *New Statesman* (1993), the *New Statesman* was sued by the then Prime Minister John Major, for an article which repeated rumours that he was having an affair. The magazine said that it was merely reporting that the rumours were in circulation, and had not intended to imply that they were true, but this did not protect them. Ironically, years later it was revealed that Mr Major had been having an affair at the time, but not with the person the rumours alleged.

Implying habitual conduct

Even if you are sure you can prove that a specific allegation of bad behaviour is true, you must be careful that your description of that behaviour does not imply that the defendant behaved that way habitually (unless you can prove that as well). For example, if you were to describe someone convicted of shoplifting as 'a thief', that might be strictly true, since they would have a conviction for theft, and it would be unlikely to be a problem if the person concerned had a string of similar convictions. However, if you use the term 'thief' of someone who has just been convicted for shoplifting a packet of chewing gum, but otherwise has a completely clean record, they could argue that you were implying they were a habitual criminal who could not be trusted, and clearly you would not be able to prove that implication was true. It is not always clear where the line between these two extremes lie, so you should always be careful about using terms or making allegations that could imply habitual conduct, unless you can prove that implication.

In *David and Carol Johnson* v *Radio City* (1988), the radio station was sued by a couple who ran a company offering caravan holidays. The station had featured complaints about the company's holidays, and Mr Johnson was interviewed on air to give the couple's side of the story. However, during the interview, the presenter referred to Mr Johnson as a 'con man'. He sued, claiming that this implied that he was habitually dishonest. The radio station produced 20 former customers who were unhappy with the holidays they had bought, but the company produced an equal number who said they were satisfied. The judge instructed the jury that it had to decide whether the broadcast was only suggesting that some customers had been mistreated, or whether it was implying 'habitual' conduct. The jury found that the latter meaning was implied, and the Johnsons won damages of £350,000.

Reporting investigations

Obviously, saying that someone is guilty of an offence when they are not is defamatory, whether you say it yourself or report someone's else allegation (with the exception of reporting allegations made in court, which are covered by privilege – see p. 202). But what about saying that someone is being investigated in connection with a crime or other wrongdoing, or is under suspicion? Such allegations can easily lead to a claim for libel, if the story is written in such a way as to suggest that they have done something that gives grounds for the suspicion. In the 1964 case of *Lewis* v *Daily Telegraph* (see below), the Court of Appeal stated that, depending on the way it was phrased, a claim that someone was being investigated for a crime could potentially mean any one of three different things:

1 that the person mentioned was guilty of the crime; or
2 that there were reasonable grounds for suspecting the person was guilty of the crime; or
3 that there were reasonable grounds for an investigation into whether the person had committed the crime.

Clearly, meaning (1) is more seriously defamatory (and more difficult to prove) than (2), and (2) is more serious and difficult to prove than (3). As a result, a publisher who means and can prove meaning (3), may still be in trouble if the court decides that the words as written are capable of carrying meaning (2) or even (1), and the publisher cannot prove that meaning to be true.

 In *Chase* v *News Group Newspapers Ltd* (2002) the *Sun* was sued by a nurse, over a story which implied she was involved in the deaths of a number of terminally ill children. The nurse had worked with the children, and the newspaper based its story on the fact that allegations had been made against her to the hospital and the police. The headline ran 'Nurse is probed over 18 deaths' and the story made reference to the GP Harold Shipman, and a nurse called Beverly Allitt, both of whom had been convicted of murdering patients in high-profile cases. After the story was published, the police said that they had no grounds to suspect Ms Chase. When the nurse sued, the paper tried to justify its story by claiming that there were reasonable grounds for suspicion, but the Court of Appeal held that such grounds had to be based on evidence of the claimant's behaviour, not just allegations against her. The *Sun* paid Ms Chase £100,000 damages.

 In *Lewis* v *Daily Telegraph* (1964), the *Telegraph* reported that a company was being investigated by the Fraud Squad, which was true. However, Mr Lewis, who ran the company, said the story implied that he and the company had committed fraud, or at least were suspected of it. The House of Lords said that the story could not be taken to mean that Mr Lewis and his company were guilty of fraud, but it could mean that they were under suspicion, and a jury should be allowed to consider the case on the basis of this meaning. In the event, the case was settled out of court.

The case of *Hayward* v *Thompson* (1981) took place against the background of the 'Scott affair', a very high-profile case in which a man called Norman Scott alleged he was the subject of a murder plot, because of an affair he had had with the former Liberal Party leader Jeremy Thorpe. Mr Thorpe and his alleged conspirators were eventually all acquitted, but while the allegations were still being investigated, the *Telegraph* published a story headed 'Two more in Scott affair'. It said: 'The names of two more people connected with the Norman Scott affair have been given to police. One is a wealthy benefactor of the Liberal Party . . . Both men, police have been told, arranged for a leading liberal supporter to be "reimbursed" £5,000, the same amount Mr Andrew Newton alleges he was paid to murder Scott.' Since the Liberal Party had few wealthy benefactors at the time, it was not difficult to spot that the man meant was a Mr Jack Hayward, and he sued. The *Telegraph* argued that its story meant only that Mr Hayward might be able to help with the investigation, but Mr Hayward claimed that it implied he was guilty of taking part in, or at least condoning, the alleged murder plot. The jury agreed, and the Court of Appeal upheld its verdict, saying that the headline placed Mr Hayward 'in' the Scott affair, and this was backed up by the words 'connected with' in the first sentence. Nothing else in the story counteracted the impression these words gave.

In *Jameel* v *Times Newspapers* (2004), a wealthy Saudi Arabian businessman sued the *Sunday Times* after it published a story headlined 'Car tycoon linked to Bin Laden'. The story stated that Mr Jameel had been named as a defendant in a case brought by the relatives of victims of the September 11 bombings in the USA against over 200 defendants accused of helping to fund terrorist activity. The paper claimed that it was merely reporting the fact of Mr Jameel being named as one of the defendants, which amounted to the level (3) meaning in the list above. It pleaded justification for this meaning. Mr Jameel however said the story implied that there were reasonable grounds for suspecting him of being associated with Osama Bin Laden (the level (2) meaning), an allegation which the *Sunday Times* could not justify (and said it did not seek to make). He pointed particularly to the phrase 'linked with Bin Laden' in the headline, and the fact that a picture of the burning towers of the World Trade Centre was used to illustrate the story. The Court of Appeal agreed with Mr Jameel that the story could be read as meaning that there were grounds for suspicion, and said that the case could be tried on this basis. Mr Jameel then applied to have the *Sunday Times'* justification defence for the level (3) meaning struck out, on the grounds that there was not enough evidence for the paper to plead justification; he was successful. The case was then settled out of court, with the *Sunday Times* publishing a statement that it had not intended to suggest, and did not believe, that Mr Jameel had any connection with terrorism.

■ Previous convictions

Clearly, saying falsely that someone has been convicted of a criminal offence will be defamatory. But if it is true that they have been convicted, the journalist will be protected by the defence of justification. This protection also applies if a person has been convicted of an offence, and you say that they did it. Under the Civil Evidence Act 1968, the fact that someone has been convicted of a criminal offence can be taken as conclusive proof of the fact that they committed that offence, so a convicted burglar, for example, who maintains they are innocent cannot successfully sue a newspaper which says otherwise (though this would change if the burglar appealed and had the conviction quashed).

However, there is an exception to the above rules: the idea of the 'spent conviction'. This comes from the Rehabilitation of Offenders Act 1974, which was designed to help offenders reintegrate into society. Under the Act, convictions which have resulted in a sentence of no more than 30 months' imprisonment become 'spent' after a certain period of time (the time depends on the actual sentence given; see *Online resources* at the end of the chapter). The effect of this is that the offender can, to an extent, wipe the slate clean. Once an offence is spent they do not have to, for example, mention it in most job applications, it should not be mentioned in civil court proceedings, and in criminal proceedings only if absolutely necessary.

You might expect then that the media would be forbidden to mention spent convictions, but this is not the case. Most publishers do respect the provisions of the Act and avoid mentioning spent convictions, but in strict legal terms, if you publish details of someone's spent convictions, and they sue you for libel, in most cases you will be covered by the defences of qualified privilege, justification or fair comment (see Chapter 15). However, the Act provides that if the claimant can show that the publication of a spent conviction was motivated by malice (see p. 211), any of these defences should fail. In addition, if a journalist claims the defence of privilege (see Chapter 14) for reporting a reference to a spent conviction that was made in court, that defence will fail if the conviction is held to be inadmissible in evidence.

Product testing

Product tests are an important feature of many consumer magazines and newspapers, because readers like them and – in many cases – they are cheap and easy to put together. It is often assumed that these features are as safe as they are simple, but that is not necessarily the case. If you look back at the definition of defamatory on p. 170, you'll see that one of the factors which can make a statement defamatory is an allegation that a person is no good at their job or business. If, in criticising a product, you imply that the person or firm producing the product is at fault, you may be at risk of a defamation action.

That does not, of course, mean that every criticism of a product is defamatory of the manufacturer. Simply saying that a particular lipstick did not last well in your tests, or you did not like the way a car handled, are unlikely in themselves to be defamatory. Where they can become so is if they imply that the manufacturer (or possibly the seller) has acted discreditably, or is in some way unfit or unqualified to carry on their business.

In 1985, the manufacturers of Bovril successfully sued the publishers of a book which claimed (wrongly) that the product contained sugar. They were able to base their case on the claim that the book had libelled them by suggesting they lied about the product's ingredients.

In *Walker Wingsail Systems v Sheahan Bray and IPC Magazines* (1994), a case which sent shivers around the magazine publishing world, a jury awarded £1.4 million to the maker of a yacht who claimed he had been libelled in a product test by *Yachting World*. The manufacturers, Walker Wingsail, had made dramatic claims about the performance of their yacht, but when tested by the magazine, it failed to live up to those promises. There was some dispute about whether the statements made in the magazine could be justified or not, because even the claimant's own expert witness found that the yacht did not perform as well as the manufacturers had claimed. However, the main thrust of the claim was that the article had implied that Walker Wingsail was deliberately misleading potential buyers. The firm was owned and run by a husband and wife team, and in court, the wife claimed that the magazine had effectively called her and her husband liars. The magazine denied this, arguing that they had not suggested dishonesty, only that the firm had made its promises carelessly and irresponsibly, which the magazine still claimed was true. The jury, however, found for Walker Wingsail.

Frightening as the *Yachting World* case may appear, it is not a reason to be scared of criticising products. Recent developments in the law on the defence of fair comment (see p. 198) mean that as long as you test fairly (e.g. treating all the products in the same way, and presenting a balanced picture of the results), make sure that any facts in the piece are accurate and state your views honestly, you should be covered by that defence, no matter how rude you are about the products.

REFERRING TO THE CLAIMANT

As well as proving that the statement in question is defamatory, the claimant has to show that an ordinary, reasonable reader or listener, including acquaintances of the claimant, would take the statement as referring to him or her (or it, in the case of companies). That means that if people who know the claimant would assume that the statement referred to him or her, the statement can be said to refer to the claimant; it does not matter that the public at large might not make the same assumption.

In many cases, identification is not in question, since the claimant will be named or pictured (and of course, leaving out the name but using a clearly identifiable title, such as 'the MP for Dover' or 'the head of the Timber Trades Association' is usually equivalent of mentioning that person by name). However, there are numerous situations where a statement can be taken to refer to a claimant even where that person is not expressly identified, and the courts have in some cases been quite relaxed about what they will accept as identification.

In *Morgan* v *Odhams Press* (1971), the case arose from a story about a dog-doping gang. The journalist writing the story was being helped by a kennel girl, and during the investigation, she stayed with the claimant for a few days. The dog doping story was then published, with a photo of the kennel girl, and the following day, the *Sun* published another story, saying that she had been kidnapped by the dog-doping gang. The claimant argued that while she was staying with him, they had been seen out together, and anyone who had seen him with her would assume that he was a member of the gang. The article did not mention his name, and several of the details it mentioned about the gang members did not apply to him. The court said that ordinary readers often skim-read articles and would not necessarily notice the inconsistent details; if, on reading the article they came to the conclusion that the claimant was the person meant, then identification was proved. The jury found for the claimant.

■ Dropping hints

Journalists often assume that if they have a potentially libellous allegation to make, it is safest to avoid naming the person, but this is not necessarily the case. You are unlikely to describe the subject of your story merely as 'a man' or 'a woman'; instead, you will hope you can drop hints that will enable readers – or at least some of them – to spot who you mean, but which will still be sufficiently vague to prevent the story forming the basis of a libel action. This is potentially dangerous, because as soon as you provide enough detail to give any meaning to the story, you give the claimant grounds to say that some readers would know who you were referring to.

The *Burton Mail* was sued by the Police Federation (the equivalent of a trade union for police officers) for a story about a complaint against a woman police officer. She was not named, but gave evidence that people she knew had taken the story to refer to her. The paper paid £17,500 compensation. The case was one of 95 similar actions brought by the Police Federation on behalf of its members during the late 1980s and 1990s, all of which it won.

In *Hayward* v *Thompson* (1981), the case concerning the Norman Scott affair (see p. 179), the *Daily Telegraph* had not referred to Mr Hayward by name, but only as 'a wealthy benefactor of the Liberal Party'. They argued that this description was not sufficient to allow readers to identify him. However, the Liberal Party had very few wealthy benefactors, and there was clear evidence that both Mr Hayward's friends, and the rest of the national media, had realised immediately who was meant.

In *Lloyd v David Syme & Co Ltd* (1986), a newspaper falsely alleged that the Australian media tycoon Kerry Packer had fixed the result of a cricket match involving the West Indian team. The team captain, Clive Lloyd, was not mentioned in the story, and had not played in the match referred to, but he successfully sued for libel on the grounds that the allegation of match fixing necessarily implied that the team had been involved, and that as captain, he must have taken part.

A publication which carries a defamatory story without naming the individual concerned can also be caught out if another publication runs the same story, but does include the name; this clearly makes it possible for readers of the first paper to identify the person meant. The first paper will not be able to evade liability on the grounds that such identification was not its fault.

In fact, not naming your subject may not only fail to protect you from being sued by them, but could expose you to claims from other people. If, for example, you were to write that one of the directors of a particular firm was embezzling the company's money, not only could the person you meant drum up friends or relatives to say that they thought he was the person referred to, but the other directors might do so as well.

▓ Pixellated pictures

As explained above, showing a picture of someone alongside a story means it can be taken to refer to them. Pixellating photographs will not make this strategy safe, if it is still possible to people to identify the person shown.

In 2006, radio DJ Ian Thompson accepted what were said to be 'substantial' damages from the *News of the World*, after it published a story claiming that a 'well-known DJ' and two Premiership footballers took part in same-sex orgies. None of the subjects was named, but the story was accompanied by a picture of Mr Thompson, and footballer Ashley Cole, which had been pixellated to conceal their identities. However, thanks to the pictures and hints in the story, many readers recognised whom the piece referred to, and they were named on internet sites. The allegations were untrue, and the paper made an offer of amends to both of them. It was reported that Mr Cole had also been paid damages of £100,000.

▓ Implied references

Be careful too of statements that imply blame on individuals even though you do not name them. For example, saying that a school is badly-run is effectively the same as saying the head-teacher is running it badly, and several newspapers have had to pay damages to headteachers as a result of similar stories. That is not to say that you should never publish stories about badly-run schools, but if you are aware of the risk of libel, you can take steps to make sure you are covered by a defence, usually justification or fair comment.

▓ Unintended references

It is quite possible to be liable for defamation if you write a story that is true about the person you intended it to refer to, but untrue of someone else who could be identified as its subject, even if you did not know the latter existed. So, for example, if you write that 'Blonde Susan Briggs, 42, of Tunbridge Wells robbed a bank', and this is true of the Susan Briggs you mean, you may still be sued by another blonde 42-year-old Susan Briggs from Tunbridge Wells, if she can make out a case that readers would taken the article to have referred to her. The same could apply if, for example, you report that the Managing Director of Bloggs Ltd has been embezzling, and though this is true of the man you mean, he has since stepped down and the new MD is someone else.

Clearly, without an encyclopaedic knowledge of every person on the planet, this is quite difficult to guard against with certainty, and recent cases suggest that the courts will take into account the practicality of protecting against unintentional references. They are not likely to be so understanding if the mix-up is obviously the result of careless research, or failure to check facts which would be easy to confirm.

 In *Newstead* v *London Express Newspapers* (1940), the *Daily Express* reported that a Harold Newstead, described as a 30-year-old Camberwell man, had been convicted of bigamy. This was true of the Harold Newstead that the paper had intended to refer to, but unknown to them, there was another Harold Newstead living in Camberwell, who was not a bigamist. He sued, claiming that the article could be taken to refer to him, and won his case. In fact the newspaper had known the occupation and exact address of the bigamous Mr Newstead, but had left these out, a fact that was made much of in court and may have influenced the decision. Had the paper published those extra details they might well have avoided being sued, and it is worth remembering that the more details you include, the less likely it is that someone else out there will fit the same description.

 In *O'Shea* v *MGN Ltd*, MGN published an advert for a pornographic website, containing a picture of a woman who looked very like the claimant. There were also certain details in the advert which the claimant said might lead those who knew her to think that she was the woman in the picture. She claimed the advert was defamatory because it suggested that she had allowed her picture to be used. The court agreed that the 'reasonable person' might take her to be the person in the picture, and they said that if a 'lookalike' had been used deliberately, the claimant could have a case in malicious falsehood (see Chapter 16). In this case, however, where the resemblance was totally innocent, it would be an unreasonable restriction on freedom of expression to expect a publisher to check whether every picture it published happened to resemble someone else. The claimant therefore lost her case.

 The BBC was successfully sued by a London police officer, who happened to be walking out of a police station just as it was being filmed for a programme on police corruption. The programme featured general allegations and did not name anyone, but the officer was obviously identifiable from the film and could therefore make out a case that viewers might think he was one of the people to whom the corruption allegations referred.

 In *Gazley* v *Wade* (2004) the *Sun* ran a picture of Great Yarmouth man David Gazley, wrongly identifying him as a convicted paedophile. It took out advertisements in local papers to apologise for its error but still ended up paying £50,000 damages plus costs in an out-of-court settlement.

In 2005, the *Sunday Mirror* paid £100,000 in an out-of-court settlement with a man they had mistakenly labelled as a rapist. The paper ran a story about the convicted rapist Iorworth Hoare, who won £7 million on the National Lottery while serving a prison sentence, but the man whose photograph they showed was someone completely different. The story quoted a woman who was said to have seen him coming out of a bail hostel, who said he looked 'evil' and had a 'distinctive swagger'; in fact the man shown had not come out of the hostel and walked the way he did owing to hip surgery. The paper recalled its first edition and pulped 140,000 copies after it realised the mistake, but the man's lawyer was able to show that at least one copy was on sale near where he lived.

Because the courts have always recognised that it is very difficult to guard completely against the danger of unintentionally referring to someone, the offer of amends defence provides publishers with a way of minimising the harm done, both to the claimant and to their own pockets (see p. 215).

14

Defamation

▉ Defaming a group

Where a defamatory statement refers to a class or group of people (such as 'All footballers are greedy' or 'British politician are corrupt'), it is not usually possible for that group of people to sue for defamation as a group, nor for one member of a group to sue on the grounds that the remark libels them personally. So, for example, if you were to say that plumber John Bloggs was useless at his job, he might be able to sue, but if you were to say that all plumbers are useless, neither John Bloggs alone nor the whole plumbing trade could sue.

In *Knupffer* v *London Express Newspapers Ltd* (1944), the defendants published an article describing the Young Russia party, a group of Russian émigrés, as a Fascist organisation. The group had approximately 2,000 members, 24 of whom were based in the UK. The claimant, a Russian emigrant living in London, sued on the basis that, as a member of the group, the statement defamed him personally. The House of Lords refused his claim, on the grounds that the statement was aimed at a large class of people and nothing in it singled him out.

However, where the group referred to is so small that the statement could be taken to refer to each and every one of them, one or all of them may be able to sue successfully. So while it is not dangerous to say 'All lawyers are useless', it may be a different story if you say 'All lawyers employed at Bodgit, Snatch and Run are useless'. Unfortunately there is no set number above which a class of people will be considered too big for one of the members to be able to sue for a remark aimed at all of them. Each case will depend on the facts and, in particular, how large the potential group is, and how closely the individuals in that group were associated with the defamatory statement.

In *Riches* v *News Group* (1986), the *News of the World* published a letter from a man who was holding his own children hostage at gunpoint, which made serious allegations against the 'Banbury CID', though without mentioning specific officers by name. Ten members of the Banbury CID successfully sued the paper for damages.

In *Aiken* v *Police Review Publishing Co Ltd* (1995), the *Police Review* magazine published a story headlined 'Nazi "humour" forces Jewish PC to quit', alleging that a police dog handler had been forced to leave his job because of the anti-semitic behaviour of some of his colleagues. There were 60 police officers working at the same station, 35 of them dog handlers. Ten of the dog handlers sued for libel, claiming that readers might think the allegations referred to them. The magazine applied to have the action struck out on the basis that readers would not be able to identify the claimants as the individuals whose behaviour was covered in the story. The judge refused the striking out action, saying that it was at least possible that readers might understand the story to be referring to each or any of the claimants.

Certain types of group, such as political parties, are also unable to sue for defamation whatever their size (see p. 187).

▉ PUBLICATION

The final element of defamation is that the statement must be published, which simply means that it is communicated to a person other than the claimant or their spouse. In media cases, of course, publication is usually in print, broadcast or online. Every repetition of a libel – by the same publisher or someone else – is considered a fresh publication, and creates a separate claim.

■ Repeating someone else's words

If someone makes a defamatory statement, and you report it, you are publishing the defamation, even though the words belong to the other person (they may be liable for defamation too, but that will not prevent your publication being sued). Journalists often assume that if they write 'John Bloggs says that Joe Scroggs is corrupt', they only have to prove that John Bloggs said what they say he said, but this is absolutely not the case: unless you can prove what he said is true (or cover yourself with another defence), you should not print his allegation. Repeating statements made by interviewees without being able to prove they are true is in fact one of the most common causes of libel actions.

In 1993 and 1994 the *Sunday Telegraph* and the *Sun* both paid damages to the Birmingham Six, who were falsely accused and later cleared of terrorism offences. Former police officers were accused of fabricating evidence, but a prosecution against them was dropped. Afterwards, the *Telegraph* reported one of the officers as saying, 'In our eyes, their guilt is beyond doubt.' The matter was settled out of court, with the claimants reported to have received £25,000 from the *Telegraph* and £1 million from the *Sun*, which had published an article based on the *Telegraph*'s interviews.

In *Slipper v BBC* (1991), the BBC made a drama programme about the search for Ronald Biggs, who famously escaped from prison after being convicted for his part in a high-profile train robbery. The former Scotland Yard detective Jack Slipper, who led the unsuccessful hunt for Biggs, sued for libel, claiming that the documentary portrayed him as incompetent. He was able to get damages from the BBC, not just for the original libel in the drama, but also for the fact that it was repeated in newspaper reviews of the programme.

Law in practice Readers' letters

A newspaper or magazine that publishes a defamatory statement in a reader's letter can be liable in just the same way as if the same statement appeared in a news story. 'Letters which make potentially defamatory allegations should always be checked,' advises Rod Dadak, Head of Defamation at solicitors Lewis Silkin. 'People often use letters pages to further their own grudges, so check who the writer is, and check whether any defamatory allegations are true, or covered by another defence, before publishing. It is also sensible to check whether the person or organisation criticised in the letter is known to be likely to sue for libel.' The defence of fair comment will often apply to letters (see p. 198).

■ Repetition and the internet

The rule about each repetition forming a fresh libel is especially important for publications which also have website archives. In law, every time an archive article is read it is a new publication. This means that although a libel action cannot normally be brought more than a year after publication, someone who accesses a five-year-old article on the internet could bring a claim, because accessing it is a fresh publication that starts the one-year time limit running again.

In *Loutchansky v Times Newspapers Ltd (No. 2)* (2001) the *Times* published articles claiming that Grigori Loutchansky, a businessman, was involved in crime. He sued for both the paper publication, and the use of the stories on the newspaper's website. The paper argued that, regarding online stories, publication should be deemed to take place just once, when the story was placed on the

14

Defamation

website. The Court of Appeal disagreed, and confirmed that each time the story was accessed it was a fresh publication.

Stories not originally challenged

The fact that a story was not the result of a libel claim when it was first published does not mean it is safe to use it later, even well outside the one-year time limit. If, for example, you are researching a story using cuttings, and you repeat an allegation made in one of them, that is the equivalent of repeating someone else's words, as described above, and if the allegation is defamatory, you may be liable. Even though it may be too late to sue the person or publication who originally made the statement, your publication is a fresh libel and can be the subject of a claim.

In 1981, the *Evening Star* in Ipswich paid damages to a doctor over statements made in its 'Looking Back' column, featuring a news story published 25 years earlier. Although the doctor had not sued then, repeating the story was a fresh libel and gave him a new claim.

Who is the publisher?

In law, a statement published in print can be said to be published by the writer, the sub-editor, the editor, the publisher and the distributor; in online journalism, the internet service provider may also be sued, while in broadcasting, the publisher is usually the broadcasting company. Any or all of these people can be sued, though in practice claimants usually target those with the deepest pockets, namely the company, which is, in legal terms, said to have 'vicarious liability' for what their employees do.

If you are freelance, you may find that the terms and conditions you work under include an indemnity clause, under which you agree to repay the publishers any damages they have to pay as a result of libels in your work. In practice these are rarely enforced, but legally they could be.

Libels in more than one publication

If a defamatory statement appears in more than one publication, the subject of the statement can sue all or any of them, and not necessarily at the same time (though there are restrictions on the overall amount of damages that can be awarded when this happens). This means that the fact that a claimant has not chosen to sue over defamatory allegations in another publication does not mean they are prevented from suing you if you repeat them. It is therefore not safe to assume that because an allegation or rumour has been widely reported, it becomes safe to repeat it.

WHO CAN SUE FOR DEFAMATION?

Individuals: Any living person can sue for defamation. However, there is no action for libelling the dead, so it is not possible to sue for damage to the reputation of a dead relative, for example, unless a claimant can establish that defamation of the dead relative affects the claimant's own reputation as well.

Corporations: 'Corporation' is a legal term, which covers not only commercial companies, but also, for example, organisations such as schools and universities which have a legal existence separate from that of the individuals who manage them. Corporations can sue for libels that damage their business reputations, but not for the kind of libels that might be described as causing hurt feelings in a person. In addition, individual members of a corporation may sue on the grounds that allegations about the company damage their personal reputations. For example, in 1993, the Body Shop as a corporation, and its two founders, Anita and Gordon Roddick, sued Channel 4 over claims that questioned the company's policies on animal testing. In 1999, two environmental campaigners who were being sued by McDonalds for libel tried to argue that it was against the interests of free speech for large corporations such as McDonalds to be allowed to sue for libel, but the courts refused to accept this argument.

Associations: Some associations, such as clubs, are legally incorporated and can sue like any other corporation. If not, an association cannot itself bring a claim, but often defamatory allegations about a club will reflect sufficiently clearly on its officials to allow them to bring a claim on their own behalf.

Trade unions: Although trade unions have sued in the past, the Trade Union and Labour Relations (Consolidation) Act 1992 states that unions are not incorporated bodies. According to the leading academic lawyers McBride and Bagshaw, this means that unions can no longer sue for libel. However, suggestions that, for example, a union is badly run would clearly reflect on the leaders, and they could sue in their own right.

Local authorities and central government: Elected authorities cannot sue for defamation. This was established in the landmark case of **_Derbyshire County Council v Times Newspapers_** (1993), where the House of Lords held that it was important for freedom of speech that there should be free and open discussion of the work of elected authorities, and therefore they should not be able to sue for defamation regarding their 'governmental and admistrative functions'. (They can still sue for defamatory statements regarding their property, and also, in some circumstances, for malicious falsehood – see Chapter 16.) However, once again, individual officers of, for example, a local council, could sue if criticism of the council reflects sufficiently on their personal reputations.

Political parties: In **_Goldsmith v Bhoyrul_** (1998), it was stated that political parties cannot sue for defamation, for similar reasons to those advanced in _Derbyshire County Council_, above. However, it is possible for individuals who are members of or work for a political party to sue for libel over defamatory statements about the party which reflect on their personal reputations.

 In 2005, the _Times_ ran a story suggesting that the Conservative Party could not win the forthcoming election, and quoting remarks to that effect which it said were made by Lynton Crosby, an election advisor to the party. While the party could not sue for damage to its own reputation, a writ was issued against the _Times_ for defamation of Mr Crosby.

Six dangerous myths about libel

Even among experienced journalists, the subject of defamation is often badly understood. The following are some of the beliefs about libel that are commonly and **wrongly** held.

1 The claimant has to prove your statement is untrue.
A defamation claimant has to prove that the relevant statement is defamatory, but they do not have to prove that it was a lie. If a statement is defamatory, the court will

simply assume that it was untrue. If a statement can be proved to be true, you will have the defence of justification, but it is up to you to prove that; the claimant does not have to prove it was false.

2   'I didn't mean it that way' is a defence.
    In general, in defamation the important issue is not what you meant to say, but what a jury believes a reader would think you meant. So it is no defence to say that you did not mean to defame the claimant, or did not realise what your words implied.

3   If you report someone else's words, you only have to prove they said them.
    If you write that 'Joe Circle said Mary Square was a thief', you cannot protect yourself from liability because it was Joe who made the defamatory allegation, and not you, even if you can prove that he said it. If you want to be covered by justification, you have to prove that what he said was true.

4   You can't be sued for publishing something the public has a right to know.
    The fact that publication is in the public interest is not by itself a defence. It is a factor in defences such as fair comment, qualified privilege, and most importantly, in the *Reynolds* defence (see the next chapter) but is not enough on its own.

5   You should always apologise as quickly as possible.
    A too-hasty apology can easily make things worse – see p. 189.

6   You can say what you like about ordinary people, because they can't afford to sue.
    Until recently, this was close to the truth; libel actions are extremely expensive, requiring specialist knowledge beyond most high street solicitors, and with no legal aid available for libel claims, very few ordinary people would have been able to sue, unless they were backed by a wealthy organisation such as a trade union. This has changed with the advent of conditional fee agreements (often known as 'no win, no fee' actions). These allow solicitors to take on cases on the basis that they receive nothing if the claimant loses, but up to a 100 per cent increase in their fees if they win. This means that someone who seems to have a good case can now sue, at no financial risk to themselves.

SLANDER

As explained at the beginning of this chapter, there is a second type of defamation, in addition to libel, called slander. It covers defamatory words that are published in transient forms, such as speech. Obviously, in most cases, journalists are concerned with libel, and cases against the media for slander are rare. Even so, it is worth being conscious of the risk of making a slanderous statement, especially for those involved in investigative journalism. If, for example, you were to confront an alleged wrongdoer and put the allegations to them in the hearing of a third party, or to repeat those allegations to someone else in the process of checking them, you could potentially be liable for slander.

People attempting to sue for slander are subject to a restriction that does not apply to libel cases. You can only be successfully sued for damages for slander if the claimant can prove that your making the slanderous statement caused them some loss (such as loss of business, for example), or if the statement you made contained or implied any of the following allegations:

- that the claimant had committed a crime that potentially carries a prison sentence;
- that the claimant has a contagious disease;
- that the claimant is no good at their job or business;
- if the claimant is a woman, that she is not chaste or has committed adultery.

Law in practice Handling complaints

If you are threatened with a libel action, or receive a complaint that could possibly lead to legal action, handling it correctly could save your publication from a nasty legal bill – while handling it badly can turn what would have been a simple complaint into an expensive court case, or, as the *Campbell-James* and *Turner* cases (see p. 213) show, increase the damages your publication has to pay. Rod Dadak, of solicitors Lewis Silkin, offers this advice:

- If you get a telephone call complaining about a story, it is always safer to say less than more; remember that you may be being taped. Be polite, make a detailed note of what the complaint is, and tell the caller that you need to refer the matter to your editor. Do not get involved in a debate about the story, and never offer an off-the-cuff apology. In most cases, journalists are indemnified by their employers if there is a claim for libel, which means you do not have to pay damages yourself, but if you go out on a limb and make an apology which exposes them to liability, you may lose this protection.

- Never ignore a letter of complaint; reply promptly, acknowledging the letter. Say that you will investigate the complaint, and give a date when you expect to be able to reply.

- Always tell your editor about a complaint, whether or not it seems serious, even if that means bringing to their attention a mistake they might not otherwise have noticed. Ignoring a request for a correction, or trying to hide one in a follow-up story, can very easily result in a complainant who would have accepted a proper apology suing instead. If your publication has insurance against defamation claims (as, for example, most local papers do), it is also essential that the insurers are informed at an early stage if a complaint appears to be serious.

- The Civil Procedure Rules 1999 contain a Pre-Action Protocol for dealing with complaints of defamation, which sets out a code of good practice and aims to promote early resolution of complaints, where possible without going to court. All journalists need to be aware of this procedure, and to follow it. (In 2006, the *Sun* was ordered to pay extra costs to the actor Chris Parker, because it ignored the Protocol – see p. 172). The complete Protocol can be read online (see *Online Resources* at the end of the chapter), but in summary, the steps are:

  - The complainant should notify the defendant of the claim, in writing, as soon as possible. The Protocol details the information which should be provided, and if a letter of complaint does not contain the information required by the Protocol, you should mention the Protocol to the complainant and ask for them to follow it.

  - The defendant should provide a full written response as soon as possible, and if this cannot be done within 14 days, should notify the claimant of the date they intend to respond.

  - Throughout the Protocol process, both parties should act reasonably to keep costs proportionate to the nature and seriousness of the case.

  - The parties should consider whether they can use an alternative to court action to settle the dispute, such as reference to the PCC, or discussion and negotiation between them.

14

Defamation

CHAPTER SUMMARY

The meaning of 'defamatory'

Defamation is the publication of an untrue statement which tends to lower the person it refers to in the eyes of reasonable people.

Defamation can occur in:

- direct criticism,
- hints and innuendoes,
- the effect of words and pictures together,
- the effect of context and juxtaposition,
- reporting of rumours,
- untrue implications drawn from true facts.

Referring to the claimant

It must be clear to an ordinary, reasonable reader that the statement refers to the claimant, but a hint or implication may be enough.

Publication

Every repetition of a libel creates a new cause of action.

Who can sue?

Individuals and corporations can sue for libel; elected authorities and political parties cannot.

Slander

Publication of defamatory words in transient form is slander.

TEST YOUR KNOWLEDGE

1 Which of these statements is potentially defamatory?

(a) Jake Black is a cowboy builder.

(b) Jake Black claims to be an honest builder, and we all know builders never do anything dodgy, don't we?

(c) Customer Mrs Smith said, 'I'm disgusted with the mess Jake Black left behind when he converted my loft. He is a complete cowboy.'

2 A well-known businessman has recently died. In his obituary, a newspaper states that he was a well-known womaniser, who was thought to have links with the mafia. Is the newspaper at risk of a libel action from his family?

3 You are a reporter on the business magazine *Wood and Timber*. At an industry function, you hear a rumour that the finance director of a major timber company, who recently took early retirement, was forced to do so after being discovered stealing company

funds. You are sure that your source is reliable, but the company refuses to confirm the story. Which of these is safe to write?

(a) According to a reliable source, ex-Bloggs Timber Finance Director John White was forced to leave the company after being discovered stealing.

(b) Bloggs Timber have denied that their ex-Finance Director John White was sacked for stealing company funds.

(c) Bloggs Timber have denied that a senior member of staff has been sacked for stealing company funds.

(d) A well-known timber company this week refused to confirm that a recently-retired director was in fact sacked for dishonest conduct.

4 Which of these could sue for libel if you published a defamatory statement about them?

(a) Thomson Holidays.

(b) The Conservative Party.

(c) The mayor of Tunbridge Wells.

(d) The managing director of Marks and Spencer.

(e) Tony Blair.

(f) Bromley Borough Council.

(g) The National Union of Teachers.

5 You work for a woman's magazine, and write a feature about women who have set up their own companies. One of them mentions in passing that she had to start her own business because her husband left her penniless with three small children to bring up. You then get a letter from the husband, who is very angry, because, he says, he did not leave her penniless but in fact signed the family home over to her. His letter goes on to say that the marriage only broke up because she had an affair with his best friend. He says he doesn't want to sue, as long as you publish the letter and an apology. Should you publish it?

ONLINE RESOURCES

www

The Civil Procedure Rules Pre-Action Protocol for Defamation is available at:
www.dca.gov.uk/civil/procrules_fin/contents/protocols/prot_def.htm

The Defamation Act 1996 can be read in full at:
www.opsi.gov.uk/acts/acts1996/1996031.htm

Time periods for spent convictions are detailed at the National Association for the Care and Resettlement of Offenders' website:
www.nacro.org.uk/data/resources/nacro-2005020106.pdf

For further resources and updates please go to the Companion Website for this book at www.pearsoned.co.uk/practicaljournalism

14

Defamation

Chapter

15

Defences and remedies for defamation

In the previous chapter, we saw that publishing a statement which lowers someone in the eyes of reasonable people can make a publisher or broadcaster liable for defamation. However, there are some circumstances in which the law will allow the publication of a defamatory statement, and a publication which falls within one of these circumstances is described as having a defence. There are seven potential defences for defamation, which are discussed in this chapter. Having a good knowledge of them will help you to get stories published and still remain on the right side of the law.

This chapter also looks at the remedies available if a claimant in defamation wins their case.

DEFENCES

A defence can help you in two ways. Firstly, if it is obvious that what you publish would be covered by a defence, you (or your employer) are less likely to be sued in the first place. Secondly, if you are sued, but you can prove you have a defence, you will win the case.

The seven defences which apply to defamation are:

- Consent
- Justification
- Fair comment
- Absolute privilege
- Qualified privilege
- Offer of amends
- Innocent dissemination.

A defendant can also avoid liability if the claimant does not bring their action within a specified time (see p. 216).

Consent

If the subject of a story consents to it being published, they cannot successfully sue for libel. However, in order to plead this defence successfully, the publisher would have to show that consent was given to the content of the article, including any potentially defamatory allegations, and not just consent to be interviewed for or featured in the publication. A refusal to deny something will not amount to consent, so you cannot obtain consent by telling some-one that if they do not confirm or deny your story, you will publish it. In most cases the defence will be used where someone has granted and perhaps even been paid for an interview.

Consent is also known as 'leave and licence'.

■ Justification

If you can prove that what you have written is substantially true, you have a complete defence against a claim of defamation. This defence is called justification, but do not be misled by the name: it is not about proving that you were morally justified in writing what you did, but simply that what you said was factually true.

In *Taylforth* v *News Group Newspapers* (1994), the *Sun* successfully used the defence of justi-fication in its 1994 case against actress Gillian Taylforth. The paper had claimed that Ms Taylforth and her boyfriend had been caught by police having oral sex in a parked car. The claim was undoubtedly defamatory, but the *Sun* presented evidence that it was true, including a police wit-ness. The couple denied it, claiming that Ms Taylforth had merely been massaging her boyfriend's stomach because he felt ill, which led to a bizarre reconstruction in court, where *Sun* journalists played the parts of the couple in the position they said they had been discovered in, in order to demonstrate to the jury how unlikely the massage claim was. The jury found for the newspaper.

The case of *Miller* v *Associated Newspapers Ltd (No. 3)* (2005) concerned the fallout from false allegations of sexual assault made against the ex-MP Neil Hamilton and his wife Christine. The allegations had been concocted by the alleged victim with a view to selling her story to the press, and the investigation into them wasted an enormous amount of time and public money, as well as causing distress to Mr and Mrs Hamilton. At the time, Mr Miller was Detective Chief Inspector of the relevant area, and the *Daily Mail* and the *Evening Standard* both ran stories blaming him for what they called the 'shambles'. Mr Miller had in fact not been the investigating officer in the Hamilton case, and had been opposed to any action being taken against them, and the judge emphasised that he had 'acted in good faith throughout'. He also pointed out that the story had been based on leaked information that was not entirely accurate. Nevertheless, it had been shown that Mr Miller was amongst those responsible for important failures that led to the Hamiltons being arrested when they should not have been, and though 'by no means solely to blame', Mr Miller did bear a share of the responsibility. The newspaper might, the judge pointed out, have 'got it right more by luck than judgement', but even so, they had proved that their allegations were substantially true, and so won the case.

It is important to remember that it is not enough simply for you to know that your story is true; you also have to be able to prove it in court. Journalists should always make sure that they have the evidence to support a story, but as the following cases show, this can be extremely difficult.

In 1992, Scottish Television (STV) was sued over a programme about war crimes. It accused Antony Gecas, a Lithuanian man who ran a bed and breakfast in Edinburgh, of being involved in the murder of thousands of Jews in Lithuania and Belarus, during the Second World War, when he was head of a special police battalion. He sued, and STV pleaded justification, which meant finding witnesses to events that had taken place over 50 years earlier, many of whom had since moved to other countries. Not surprisingly, the case cost around £1.5 million. Had they lost, STV would have had to pay this, as well as damages, but the research paid off and they won their case.

The *Guardian* famously won its 1997 case against the former Conservative Cabinet Minister Jonathan Aitken when vital evidence was found at the very last minute. The paper had claimed, among other things, that Mr Aitken had breached ministerial guidelines by accepting a stay at the Paris Ritz, paid for by a business associate. He sued, and despite four years of research, it was only the last-minute discovery of a hotel bill, during the trial, that proved the *Guardian*'s case. Mr Aitken dropped his claim, and was later jailed for perjury. The complexity of the case meant that costs had by then spiralled to £2 million, a bill that the paper would have had to pay if it had lost.

A further complication with the use of the justification defence is that if you attempt to use it, and then fail to prove your case, that can look to judges and juries as though you are persisting in a lie, and they could look less favourably on you than they would if you had never sought to use the defence at all. When Jeffrey Archer sued the *Star* over allegations that he had paid a prostitute (see p. 195), the *Star* pleaded justification, but failed to convince the jury. The judge commented on the fact that the newspaper had persisted in claiming the allegations were true, and advised the jury that if it found for Archer, it should order damages that would be high enough to 'send a message to the world that the accusations were false'. The jury clearly agreed and awarded damages of £500,000. In fact, Archer was later found to have fabricated evidence, and was jailed for perjury.

Proving justification

The defence of justification can only be applied to statements of fact, not opinion (for opinions, the usual defence is fair comment, see p. 198). The statement must be proved to be substantially true, on a balance of probabilities. 'Balance of probabilities' is simply the term used for the standard of proof that applies in civil cases, and means that you have to convince the jury that the statement is more likely to be true than not to be true (as opposed to the criminal standard of proof, which is proof beyond reasonable doubt).

Substantially true

It is not necessary to prove that every single aspect of a statement is absolutely true, so long as, taken as a whole, it is accurate. Under s5 of the Defamation Act 1952, where a statement includes two or more charges against the claimant, you do not have to prove that each one is true, so long as the words not proved to be true do not materially injure the claimant's reputation, taken together with the fact that the other words are true (this is often referred to as 'the section 5 defence').

Defamation judgments often refer to the 'sting' of a libel. This is essentially the main part of a libel, the allegation that damages the claimant's reputation, in contrast to minor details of the story which do not 'materially injure' the person's reputation. For example, if you were to write that a man hit his wife last Thursday, and he had in fact done so not on Thursday but on Wednesday, the 'sting' would be the allegation that he had hit his wife, and if you could prove that, you would have a defence even if the incidental matter of when the incident happened was untrue.

 In *Alexander v North Eastern Railway Co* (1865), the defendants had said that the claimant had been convicted of a crime and given three weeks' imprisonment. In fact, he had been given two weeks, but the defendants successfully pleaded justification.

 In the case concerning STV and the Lithuanian police commander Antony Gecas (see p. 193), the programme's allegations about Mr Gecas' involvement in the killing of Jews included a claim that he personally 'finished off' Jews who had been thrown into burial pits but were still alive. Though STV were able to prove Mr Gecas' overall involvement in the murders, they could not prove this particular claim, but successfully relied on the section 5 defence. The judge said that this claim did not itself materially injure Mr Gecas' reputation, given the crimes that he had been proved to have committed.

In *Turcu v News Group Newspapers* (2005), the *News of the World* was sued over a story about an alleged plot to kidnap Victoria Beckham. The story claimed that, following an undercover investigation, the paper had discovered that an international gang was 'on the brink' of putting into action the planned kidnap. The claimant, Alin Turcu, was said to be part of this gang, and to have a major role in surveillance. He was arrested the day after the story was published, but when the Crown Prosecution Service decided not to prosecute him, he sued the paper for libel. The court found that there was no gang in the sense that the story suggested, just a loose group of people who were willing to get involved in criminal activity, and the claimant did not have the alleged surveillance role. There was no specific plan to kidnap Mrs Beckham either. However, it was true that the claimant was a petty criminal with a long list of charges and convictions in four different countries, and it was true that he was willing to take part in criminal activities with the others, and that he had taken part in discussions about the possibility of kidnapping Victoria Beckham. Therefore, the judge said, the paper was able to back up the 'sting' of the libel, and prove that the allegations were 'substantially, if not wholly, accurate'. Mr Turcu has been given leave to appeal.

 In 2001 Channel 5 broadcast a programme about the model Kate Moss, which alleged that, at a charity fashion event in Barcelona, she had taken so much cocaine, she had fallen into a coma. Ms Moss sued, but in the period between the programme being shown and the case coming to a pre-trial hearing, a national newspaper published photographs of Ms Moss taking cocaine, and she later made a public apology for 'letting people down'. In a pre-trial hearing for the libel case, her lawyers tried to prevent Channel 5 from using the allegations and her apology as evidence for its claim of justification. Channel 5 lawyers however claimed that the point the programme had made was that she was 'a serious cocaine abuser' and that was the issue, not where and when she did it. The High Court agreed to admit the evidence, but shortly before the trial was due to start, Ms Moss dropped her claim.

 In 2005, the film director Roman Polanski sued over a story in *Vanity Fair* magazine, which alleged that he had tried to seduce a woman on the way back from his wife's funeral. In court, the magazine argued that the incident they had described did happen, but it accepted that it was not on the way back from the funeral, but two weeks later. Mr Polanski said that it had not happened at all. He won damages of £50,000. His evidence was given by video link from France, where he lives, as he is wanted by the USA on charges of having sex with an under-age girl, and feared extradition if he came to the UK.

Proving implications

A defendant who pleads justification must not only prove the factual truth of their statements, but also that any reasonable interpretation of those words, or any innuendo implied by them, is also true. In many cases, there will be dispute over what a statement means, and in this situation, a defendant may plead justification for a meaning which is different (and less serious) than that which the claimant alleges. (This is often referred to as the lesser or lower meaning.)

 In *Marks & Spencer Plc v Granada Television Ltd, CA* (1988), Granada was sued over a 'World in Action' programme which said that M&S clothing marked 'Made in England' was in fact being made by child workers in factories in Morocco. M&S claimed that the programme implied that it was 'knowingly and deliberately' exploiting child labour to increase profits. This, they said, was not true: it had not known about the child labour and had stopped using the supplier as soon as it discovered what the supplier was doing. Granada pleaded a lesser meaning, arguing that its implication went no further than suggesting that M&S was not making adequate checks on its suppliers. There was no problem with proving that this allegation was true, as Granada had film of the factories concerned. The jury found for M&S.

 In *Archer v News of the World* (1987), the newspaper was successfully sued by Jeffrey Archer after it claimed that he paid £2,000 to a prostitute. While it was true – and could be proved – that the payment was made, Jeffrey Archer claimed that the article implied that he had had sex with her, which he said was not true. The paper could not prove this implication and ended up paying £500,000 damages.

Where an article links the claimant with some kind of wrongdoing, the claimant will often argue that the article implies they are guilty of that wrongdoing. If the publisher cannot prove this, it may claim that the piece does not suggest guilt, but merely states that there are grounds for suspicion. It can then seek to justify this lower meaning, rather than the one alleged by the claimant, and it is for the judge or the jury to decide which is the natural meaning of the piece, and whether that meaning has been justified.

In *Armstrong* v *Times Newspapers Ltd* (2006) the champion cyclist Lance Armstrong sued *The Times* over a story which said that his performance in the Tour de France suggested that he must have taken drugs. He claimed that the story implied that he had taken drugs, but *The Times* said that it was merely repeating questions that had been raised in a book, and that the meaning of the article was no more than that there were grounds to suspect that he had taken drugs. *The Times* sought to justify that lesser meaning. In a preliminary hearing, the judge decided that the words bore the meaning that Mr Armstrong claimed; an ordinary reader, looking at the headline and the text, would have understood the article to mean that he had taken drugs to improve his performance. The case was settled shortly afterwards.

Identifying sources

When pleading justification, and most of the other defences, you may need evidence from sources to prove your case. As we will see in Chapter 19, it is a fundamental principle of journalistic ethics that a source who has been promised confidentiality should not be identified, and this principle is – to an extent – upheld by the law. This means that the fact that you cannot identify your source will not necessarily mean you cannot prove your defence.

In *Gaddafi* v *Telegraph Group* (2000), the *Telegraph* was sued by the eldest son of the Libyan dictator Colonel Gaddafi, over an article which claimed he was involved in attempts to break the economic sanctions that had been imposed on Libya after the Lockerbie bombing. The *Telegraph* pleaded qualified privilege (see p. 204), but said it could not identify its sources because they were members of a 'western government security agency', and might be put in serious danger if their names were revealed. The court upheld the paper's right to protect its sources, and said it could still successfully plead qualified privilege, as long as it disclosed enough information to allow the court to judge the reliability of the information provided.

New evidence

A claim of justification need not only be based on such facts as were known at the time of publication; if other facts come to light during the (sometimes very long) period between a claim and the case coming to court, they can be used to back up the defence. This happened rather spectacularly when Jonathan Aitken sued the *Guardian* in 1997, and the final piece of evidence that caused Mr Aitken's claim to fall apart was found, almost literally, at the last minute (see p. 193).

Journalists are often unaware of a procedural factor which can help libel defendants who plead justification: court rules state that claimants must make available to the defence any documents that are relevant to the issues in the case. This is called disclosure, and can mean that the defendants themselves have to hand over the memo, contract or email that contains proof of the story. Not surprisingly perhaps, some claimants decide to discontinue their claim when the order for disclosure is made.

Law in practice Using justification

If you are working on a story that could lead to a defamation claim, and you want to make sure you can plead justification, you need to ensure not just that the story is true, but that you can prove it. Rod Dadak, Head of Defamation at solicitors Lewis Silkin, has this advice:

- Make sure that you have clear, admissible evidence for your allegations before you publish them. It is very much harder to find witnesses, for example, after you have published, and when a court case may already be threatened, than before you go to press.

- If you can, tape your interviews. If you prefer to take notes, always date them, use the pages of your notebook in sequence, and number the pages; this means you can prove that you have not tampered with or added to your notes. If for some reason you can't take a contemporaneous note (i.e. one while the subject is speaking), do it as soon as possible afterwards.

- If you use shorthand (or your handwriting is illegible), transcribe your notes as soon as possible; with shorthand, what you write may be susceptible to two or more different meanings, and that can make it difficult to rely on shorthand notes in court. Ideally, transcribe onto a computer, as this allows you to prove the date on which you did the transcription.

- Keep all your notes for as long as possible, and for a minimum of a year after publication, if your work is published in print. If your work is going onto the internet, you need to keep notes for longer, as every time the article is downloaded it is in law a fresh publication, and a claim can be brought for a year after that.

- Do not rely on just one source. There is always the possibility that you may be dealing with someone who has a grudge, so try to get corroborating evidence from other sources.

- If your story contains allegations made by someone else, consider whether that person would give evidence for you in court, and how they would be viewed by a jury. How old are they? Do they speak English? Is there anything about them that might make a jury mistrust them? If you think there are reasons why your source might not be believed, it becomes even more important to find corroborating evidence or other witnesses.

- If you are going to publish serious allegations, for which you have a witness, ask them to sign a written statement; this means that if you are sued, and your source decides that they do not want to back you up by giving evidence, the court can issue a subpoena, which is a legal demand for them to attend court and be questioned. You can also use a signed statement as evidence if the source dies or goes abroad before the trial. In some cases, it may be worth asking your witness for an affadavit, which is a statement sworn on oath, and therefore carries considerable legal weight.

- If you haven't got enough material to prove your story is true, don't take the risk. If it's a really good story, it's better to wait, get more evidence and publish it when you can stand it up properly.

- Don't assume that because another paper is publishing a story, it would be safe for you to do it too. If you lift a story from another publication, make sure that you check for yourself whether any defamatory allegations are true.

- The level of precautions you need to take will depend on the story; not every story, for example, would require you to get an affadavit. In deciding how far you need to go, the two key things to consider are the subject of the story and the gravity of the allegations. The more high-profile the person you are writing about, the more likely it is that they will have the means to sue, though bear in mind that the availability of conditional fee agreements (see p. 188) has made it possible for people of modest means to sue for defamation. The more serious the allegations, the stronger the precautions you need to take, regardless of who the subject is.

15

Defences and remedies for defamation

Fair comment

Fair comment is a defence which applies to opinions and comments. To be covered by the defence, the defendant must prove all the following:

- the words complained of were a comment or opinion, not a statement of fact;
- the words were about a matter of public interest;
- any facts which the comment was based on are true, or subject to privilege (see p. 202); and
- the comment was made without malice, which in this context essentially means that it was made honestly.

Despite the name of the defence, the comment does not have to be 'fair' in any general sense, and the jury need not necessarily agree with it, nor believe that the ordinary reader would agree with it. The view offered may be exaggerated, extreme or even prejudiced, and still be covered by the defence, so long as the jury believe it is a view that the writer honestly holds.

Comment and fact

This is not always as simple a distinction as it seems. Obviously if a statement includes words like 'I think' or 'It seems to me that', they are more likely to be viewed as a comment (though this should not be relied on). But take the situation where, for example, there has been debate about whether a particular public figure has misled the public, and you express your opinion on the question using the words 'The Chief Constable is a liar'. This might look like an opinion, and might have been intended to be an opinion, but in law it could be taken as an expression of fact, in which case you will not be able to use the defence of fair comment.

 In 1985 the actress Charlotte Cornwell sued the *News of the World* over an article written by its television critic Nina Myskow. The article said that Ms Cornwell could not sing or act, and had 'the kind of stage presence that jams lavatories'. The *News of the World* argued that this was comment on Ms Cornwell's performance, rather than assertions of fact, but the jury disagreed and found for Ms Cornwell.

 In 1995, Jonathan Aitken was sued over a story he wrote in a Kent newspaper, about a wealthy local couple of Conservative supporters called the Pinder-Whites. He described them as being 'dreadful enough' to play JR and Sue-Ellen Ewing in the American soap 'Dallas'. For those too young to remember, JR was a ruthless womaniser, and Sue-Ellen an alcoholic with a number of lovers. Mr Aitken said the story was meant to be ironic and was not intended to be taken literally. In court, evidence was given about the Pinder-Whites' glitzy lifestyle, including riding around in a white Rolls-Royce during a recent election campaign. The jury found that the story could be considered fair comment.

 In **Keays v Guardian Newspapers** (2003), the *Guardian* published a story about Sarah Keays, who was known as the former mistress of a Cabinet Minister and mother of his child. After long refusing to talk to the press, Ms Keays had recently decided to publish her story, and the *Guardian* article speculated about her motives. The judge held that the article could only be read as comment, since the writer could not know as a fact what was in Ms Keays' mind.

 In **Branson v Bower (No. 1)** (2001), Richard Branson sued the writer of a book for saying, about Mr Branson's bid to run the National Lottery, that some people might think he was doing it for 'self-glorification'. The writer claimed that this was fair comment, but Mr Branson argued that it was a statement of fact, the statement meaning that he had less than noble reasons for wanting to run the Lottery. The Court of Appeal disagreed. It said that while a suggestion about someone's motives could in some cases be an assertion of fact, in this case it was clear that the phrase was an opinion held by the writer on the basis of facts referred to in the article.

In *Galloway* v *Telegraph Group Ltd* (2006), the Court of Appeal upheld Labour MP George Galloway's victory over the *Daily Telegraph*, regarding a story which claimed that he had received money from Saddam Hussein's regime. The *Telegraph* pleaded fair comment, but the court said that the stories were allegations of fact, not comment. A headline, for example, stated 'damning new evidence', and the court said that the use of the word 'damning' was not a comment, but a statement that the evidence suggested Mr Galloway was guilty.

To be considered a comment for the purposes of this defence, it must be clear what facts the opinion is based on. For example, if you say 'MP Jessica Onion promotes vegetarianism, yet is happy to wear fur: what a hypocrite!' then your allegation of hypocrisy would be an opinion, based on Ms Onion's conduct, and assuming it was true that she promoted vegetarianism and wore fur, you may be covered by the defence of fair comment. If, however, you simply said 'Jessica Onion is a hypocrite', you appear to be stating a fact, and if the court agrees, the defence will not be available. The opinion and the facts on which they are based do not have to be in the same sentence (and possibly not even within the same article) but it should be clear what facts that opinion is referring to.

 In **Lowe** v **Associated Newspapers** (2006), the *Evening Standard* published a story containing allegations about the Chairman of Southampton Football Club, concerning his acquisition of the club, and his sacking of the then manager. These events had happened some years earlier. The facts on which the comments were based (which the paper said were true) were not stated in the article, but in a preliminary hearing, Mr Justice Eady said that those facts were known to the public and football fans would certainly be aware of them, and so it was not necessary that they were stated in the article itself.

Letters from readers pose particular problems concerning the fact/comment distinction, since they may be commenting on something that was published some time previously, and will not necessarily state the facts that the comment is based on. This was the case in *Telnikoff* v *Matusevitch* (1991), which concerned a letter written in response to an article in the *Daily Telegraph*. The letter stated that the views of the article's author were racist and anti-Semitic, and the author sued the writer of the letter. If the letter writer could have established that his words were comment, he would have been covered by fair comment, but if not, he would lose, as the words were untrue and clearly defamatory. Read alone, the words looked like a statement of fact, but if they were read alongside the article they were responding to, it was clear they were a comment on it: in other words, on their own, the words said 'this person is anti-Semitic', but read with the letter, they were saying 'the fact that this person has said this makes me think he is anti-Semitic'. The question therefore hinged on whether the words should be judged alone, or with the article. The House of Lords said that the jury should only be allowed to look at the letter as it was published.

Telnikoff essentially makes it quite difficult for readers' letters to be covered by the fair comment defence. However, such a case might be decided differently now, given the decision in **Bladet Tromso** v **Norway** (1999), a case brought before the European Court of Human Rights. It stated that allegedly defamatory words in a newspaper should be considered in the light of previous articles on the same subject.

Public interest

The defence of fair comment only applies to stories about matters of public interest. This was defined in **London Artists** v **Littler** (1969) as matters which are 'such as to affect people at large, so that they may be legitimately interested in, or concerned at, what is going on; or what may happen to them or to others'. This covers issues such as the behaviour of public officials and authorities (at least as far as it reflects on their work), all forms of art, entertainment and literature, and court cases.

A more difficult area is whether the private lives of public figures and celebrities can be considered matters of public interest. In general, they are not, but where a celebrity has put certain aspects of their life into the public domain, or where they are viewed as a role models, relevant behaviour may be considered a matter of public interest for the purposes of the fair comment defence. Equally, people who voluntarily attract public attention, for example by running campaigns, can expect their conduct and views to be considered matters of public interest.

True facts

The facts that the comment is based on must be true. So, if you say 'Millionaire actor Joe Dollars has abandoned his sick old father in a seedy nursing home. He is cold, hard and unfeeling', and the claim about abandoning his father is true, then your view that he is 'hard, cold and unfeeling' should be covered by the defence of fair comment. However, if in fact Mr Dollars is paying to have his father looked after in the lap of luxury (regardless of whether or not you knew that), you will not be covered. It is no defence to say that your comment would have been fair if the facts had been true.

 In 2006, chef Gordon Ramsey sued the *Evening Standard* over a TV review which criticised his television programme, 'Ramsey's Kitchen Nightmares'. On the programme, the chef works with the owners of failing restaurants to help them turn their businesses around, and the review alleged that some of the scenes were faked to give a misleading impression of the state of the business. Reviews will usually be covered by fair comment, but because in this case the allegations were untrue, the newspaper lost the case and had to pay £75,000 in damages.

There are, however, two qualifications to the rule that the facts must be true. First, the Defamation Act 1952 provides that where only some of the facts on which a comment is based are proved to be true, the defence does not necessarily fail. It can still succeed if the opinion expressed is fair comment taking into consideration the truth of the facts. To illustrate this, we can adapt the example above. Say that you wrote 'Joe Dollars has abandoned his sick old father in a nursing home, and never even sends him a Christmas card. He is cold, hard and unfeeling.' In fact, it is true that the father is languishing in the seedy old folks home, but Joe does make sure to send a Christmas card each year. In that case, you could be covered by the defence of fair comment for your description of Joe as 'cold, hard and unfeeling', if you could convince the jury that even if you had known that only one of those allegations was true, you would genuinely have been of the opinion that that fact made him 'cold, hard and unfeeling'.

The second exception to the rule is if the facts you based your opinion on were expressed on a privileged occasion (see p. 202). For example, anything said in Parliament is privileged. If an MP, in Parliament, alleges that, say, the head of a large company has been taking bribes for contracts, and you then write that taking bribes makes the company director unfit for his job, you can be covered by fair comment even if it turns out that it was not true that he took bribes.

The defence can only be based on facts that were known at the time of publication (unlike justification, which can take into account facts which come to light later).

Without malice

In everyday language, if you say something maliciously, you say it spitefully, or out of dislike for or revenge on the person you are speaking about. In law, malice has a different meaning. For the purpose of fair comment, to say something with malice means to say it without honestly believing it to be true, or being reckless as to whether it was true or not. Essentially, as the media law specialists Robertson and Nicol put it, malice amounts to turning a blind eye to the truth, rather than, for example being inaccurate through carelessness, or failing to make proper checks.

For a journalist's words to be covered by fair comment, then, the jury must believe that the journalist honestly held the opinion expressed. The jury does not have to agree with the opinion or believe it to be accurate. Nor, despite the defence being called fair comment, does the jury have to believe that what was said was fair. As Lord Diplock put it in a libel case against the *Sunday Express*: 'The basis of our public life is that the crank and the enthusiast can say what he honestly believes just as much as a reasonable man or woman.'

 In the Charlotte Cornwell case (see p. 198), where the actress was described as ugly and having a big bottom, the fact that she was in fact of perfectly normal weight and appearance was evidence that the insulting opinions expressed could not have been honestly held.

Malice and personal spite

What if you actually do feel malice (in the everyday sense) towards the person you are writing about? Take, for example, a situation where you were once ripped off by a restaurant, and you are later asked to write a review about it. Until recently, 'malice' also included the everyday meaning, so that if you wrote an unpleasant review out of spite, you would not have been covered by the defence of fair comment, even if you honestly believed what you said. However, in the 2001 case of *Tse Wai Chun Paul* v *Albert Cheng*, the courts held that even if a writer is motivated by 'spite, animosity, intent to injure, intent to arouse controversy or other motivation', they can be covered by fair comment, so long as they honestly believe in the opinion they express, and the other requirements of the defence are satisfied. The leading judge in the case stated that 'critics need no longer be mealy-mouthed in denouncing what they disagree with'.

This means that, in the restaurant example above, you may very well take great pleasure in writing an unpleasant report, but if the views expressed are your genuine opinion of the meal and the venue, you can still be covered by fair comment. If, on the other hand, you think the meal you eat for the review is fine but you decide to be rude about it anyway, out of spite, your review would not, in law, be covered by fair comment because you do not genuinely hold the opinion you have expressed.

You might well ask at this stage how the jury would know what you honestly believed, and the answer is of course that unless any of them are psychic, they will not know. What they will do is judge on the evidence before them what they think your state of mind was. If, therefore, there is evidence that you might have acted out of malice towards the person you wrote about (if, for example, the claimant gives evidence of a history of animosity between you), the jury is obviously likely to take this into account when it decides whether it thinks you genuinely believed what you wrote. In these circumstances it would be useful to have evidence that shows you did believe what you wrote, regardless of the bad feeling between you.

Whose belief?

What happens if, for example, you publish a reader's letter attacking a local councillor for their incompetent handling of a local problem, and although the writer genuinely believes what she writes, you do not? (Let's assume for the sake of argument that it is obvious you do not agree because you have written leaders saying so.) The letter writer is covered by fair comment – but could you be said to have published the statement maliciously, given that you do not honestly believe it? According to Robertson and Nicol (see *Further reading* at the end of the book), the answer is no: the publisher can rely on the defence of fair comment to the same extent that the writer can.

Where an interviewee, for example, makes statements with malice, and you publish them without malice, their malice will not prevent you being covered by the defence of fair comment.

■ Absolute privilege

The defence of absolute privilege exists because there are some circumstances where freedom of speech is considered more important than protection of reputation. Where absolute privilege applies to the occasion on which words were spoken, no claim for defamation can be made against the person who says them, no matter how defamatory the words, whether they were true or false, or what motivated the speaker to say what they did. For example, proceedings in Parliament are subject to absolute privilege, so during a Parliamentary session, an MP can say anything at all, about anyone (not just other MPs), and even if it is completely untrue, they cannot be sued for defamation. The remarks can also be repeated in the official daily reports of Parliament, known as *Hansard*, and in reports published by order of Parliament (such as White Papers). However, that does not mean that you have quite the same freedom in reporting what MPs say in Parliament, as reports of Parliamentary proceedings are only covered by qualified privilege, which is subject to certain conditions (see p. 204).

There is, however, one circumstance where journalist's reports are covered by absolute privilege, and that is court reports. The reason for this is fairly obvious: by their nature, court proceedings tend to involve people making serious allegations against others, some of which may be untrue. It would not be possible for papers to report court proceedings if they could be sued for repeating those allegations, and since there is clearly a public interest in people knowing what goes on in the courts, absolute privilege makes this possible. It means that the media can, within the rules of the defence, safely publish defamatory statements made in:

- any English court;
- the European Court of Justice and any court attached to it;
- the European Court of Human Rights;
- any international criminal tribunal established by the Security Council of the United Nations or by an international agreement to which the UK is a party.

Not every report of a case in these courts is covered by absolute privilege. To qualify for absolute privilege, reports must be:

- fair,
- accurate, and
- contemporaneous.

Fairness

To be considered fair, a court report must present both sides of the case, and avoid appearing to endorse or give extra weight to the arguments of one party or the other. A court case can last for days, or even months, so separate reports of each day may be carried during the progress of the case. This can mean that if, for example, a whole day (or longer) is spent by the prosecution examining its key witness, the report of that day is likely to reflect largely the prosecution's case. This is not a problem, so long as what you write fairly reflects what is said in court that day. Equally, an evening paper may report what was said in court that day up until the paper went to press, and report evidence given later in the following day's edition.

What you should not do is give a one-sided presentation of what was said in court, for example by leaving out sections of the evidence presented. Such a report will not be considered fair, so the newspaper carrying it risks losing the protection of privilege, and in many cases, no other defence will be available. Equally, if you have previously reported potentially defamatory allegations, and later in the trial those allegations are rebutted, you should report the evidence rebutting the allegations.

Accuracy

Court reports need not be word-for-word accounts of what was said in court, and you will usually need to summarise evidence, but it is essential that your summary accurately reflects what was said. For key or controversial points, it is often better to quote the witness directly.

There are certain areas of court reporting which can be a minefield for the unwary:

- **Allegations**: Make sure you do not report allegations as facts – in other words, if a witness, Jeannie Brown, says she saw the defendant, Joe Bloggs, running from the scene, you should write 'Jeannie Brown said she saw Bloggs running away', rather than 'Jeannie Brown saw Bloggs running away'. This is especially important in headlines, where it it tempting to choose the shorter, snappier version.

- **Names**: Unless you are reporting a high-profile case where everyone knows who the characters involved are, it is surprisingly easy to slip up and call the defendant by the name of one of the witnesses, or someone else involved in the case, especially if the names are similar. Doing this could put you at serious risk of being sued by the person you name. The same could apply if, in a civil case, you mix up the names of the claimant and the defendant, so always double-check you have used the right names. Addresses are also important – give the wrong one and you could face a claim from the person living there.

- **Verdicts**: Reporting that someone has been convicted when they have been acquitted, or that a defendant has lost a civil case when in fact they have won it obviously lays you open to a defamation claim. As well as guarding against this simple but dangerous factual mistake, you should also avoid any statement that tends to suggest that a person should have been convicted, or was guilty and got away with it.

- **Offences**: It can be defamatory to suggest that someone was convicted of a more serious offence than they actually were. In some cases a defendant will be charged with more than one offence, and convicted of some but acquitted of others; it is essential to get the details right.

- **Sentences**: It can be defamatory to suggest someone has received a more severe sentence than they actually have.

Contemporaneous

The requirement that reports must be contemporaneous essentially means that they should be published in the first issue or broadcast following the proceedings, so the exact time scale will depend on the frequency of publication. Broadcasters would be expected to cover court proceedings the same evening, and daily papers the following day, while an evening paper might start reporting a case in its first edition and add to the story in later ones, carrying the remainder of the events in court the following day. What about court reports which are published on the internet, and may therefore remain accessible for a long time after a trial is over? In *Arthur Bennett* v *Newsquest* (2006), it was stated that although absolute privilege could not apply, qualified privilege would, as long as the initial publication was contemporaneous.

In some cases the court may place restrictions on reporting a particular trial. The Defamation Act 1996 provides that once these restrictions are lifted, court reports should be published as soon as practically possible, in order to be viewed as contemporaneous.

Limits of the defence

Privilege only covers reports of the court proceedings themselves. If someone from the public gallery shouts out a defamatory remark, or if someone involved makes comments on the way into or out of court, these are not part of the court proceedings and you will not be protected by privilege if you report them. Nor does privilege cover reports of the contents of documents seen by the judge or magistrate but not read in open court.

The Defamation Act 1996 extends qualified privilege to fair and accurate copies of or extracts from documents 'made available by a court'.

■ Qualified privilege

Like absolute privilege, qualified privilege protects statements made in certain circumstances where free speech is considered to be in the public interest. It applies to a broader range of situations than absolute privilege does, but is subject to one important restriction: it will only cover statements made without malice. (For the meaning of malice as regards qualified privilege, see p. 211.) As with absolute privilege, it also requires that reports are fair and accurate.

The occasions to which qualified privilege applies are:

- a set list of official and public proceedings, decisions and documents, detailed in Schedule 1 of the Defamation Act 1996;
- judicial proceedings in the UK;
- the proceedings of Parliament;
- occasions where someone is defending themselves against a previous attack on their character or conduct;
- occasions where someone who makes a statement has a legal, moral or social duty to make that statement, and the person to whom it is made has a duty to receive it;
- occasions where the media has reported a matter of public interest and has acted responsibly in doing so, taking into account all the circumstances (this is known as the *Reynolds* defence from the case in which it originated – see p. 207).

The first of the above occasions is often called statutory qualified privilege, while the rest are qualified privilege under common law (because the rules were made through cases decided in the courts, not by Parliament – see p. 6).

Qualified privilege under the Defamation Act 1996

Schedule 1 of the Defamation Act 1996 lists the types of statement which are covered by statutory qualified privilege. These fall into two groups, one of which has slightly more restrictions on its protection than the other. The first group, listed in Part 1 of Schedule 1 to the Act, are statements which have qualified privilege without explanation or contradiction. These include, for example, fair and accurate reports of proceedings in public of legislatures anywhere in the world, and fair and accurate copies or extracts from reports published by any government (for the full Schedule, see Appendix II).

The second group, listed in Part II of Schedule 1, are described as 'privileged subject to explanation or contradiction'. This means that statements in the categories on this list are covered by qualified privilege, but that privilege can be lost if a person defamed by a statement supplies a reasonable explanation or contradiction of the statement, and requests its publication, and that request is refused. The list includes, for example, fair and accurate reports of public meetings and meetings of public companies and certain types of organisation (see Appendix 2 for the full list).

Contradictions and explanation: If you publish a story covered by absolute privilege 'subject to contradiction or explanation', and someone asks you to publish a contradiction or explanation, it must be published 'in a suitable manner'. The Act defines this as either in the same manner as the original story or in a manner that is 'adequate and reasonable in the circumstances.' In other words, if you splash a story over the front page, and then carry the denial or explanation in a tiny para tucked away at the bottom of page 8, you are unlikely to keep the protection of the defence.

Watch out, however, for any possibility of defamation in the explanation or contradiction itself. Take, for example, a situation where, in a general meeting of a public company, one of the directors, John Green, makes a defamatory comment about the boss of a rival company, Sarah Black. Provided that you act without malice and publish a fair and accurate report of the meeting, you are covered by qualified privilege for repeating his statement. Sarah Black then demands to have a letter published, refuting the allegations made, and making a defamatory allegation of her own about John Green. If you do not publish her contradiction of John Green's statement, you will lose the protection of qualified privilege, but if you publish her statement and include the defamatory allegation, John Greeen may be able to sue you for libel. In some cases like this you may be covered by qualified privilege at common law, but if you find yourself in this situation, it is worth taking legal advice to make sure you cover yourself either way.

Official information: The first item on the list of publications covered by qualified privilege subject to explanation or contradiction refers to fair and accurate copies of or extracts from 'matter' issued for the information of the public by a series of different types of official body. Note that this list is quite precise and specific; it specifies that privilege attaches to extracts and copies, but it does not mention reports or summaries of official information. Nor does it provide privilege for absolutely any type of official information, or statement made by an authority. It does not cover, for example, statements made by spokespersons, no matter how high up in the organisation, of NHS Trusts, or organisations such as the British Transport Authority, even though these might be considered government organisations, since they cannot be said to exercise 'government functions'. The police, however, are covered by this provision, which means that qualified privilege covers, for example, notices issued by the police about individuals suspected of crime (though such notices must be 'issued', not leaked). Note too that the provision applies to matter 'issued' for the information of the public; leaked documents are unlikely to be covered.

What counts as 'matter'? Clearly published documents, consultation papers, speeches and press releases will count, but what about answers to questions you put to government officials? In *Blackshaw* v *Lord* (1984), the courts said these could in some circumstances be considered to be 'matter issued for the information of the public', but would not always be so. You may therefore want to seek advice before relying on this defence when publishing defamatory statements made by government officials (including the police) which are not published in writing.

Reporting proceedings: A number of the statutory provisions relate to reports of 'proceedings' of various types of official and public organisations. When reporting these, it is important to remember that (as with court reporting) only the proceedings themselves are covered by privilege. Anything said before or after proceedings by anyone involved in them, even if this is merely to expand on or explain what is said during the proceedings, or said during proceedings by anyone not officially involved (such as protestors or spectators) is not covered by the provisions of the Defamation Act (though of course there may be another defence available, including qualified privilege from common law). Similarly, if reporting on an official document, bear in mind that qualified privilege will only cover the actual words of the document and not, for example, anything said about it, even by someone involved in producing it.

Public meetings: Note that the definition of a public meeting is quite wide, and in practice includes most of the kinds of public meeting that a journalist could expect to attend. In **McCartan Turkington Breen v Times Newspapers** (2001), the House of Lords held that it includes press conferences, and press releases issued at press conferences can be considered part of the proceedings, even if not read out at the time.

Findings: Where the statutory provisions provide protection for reports of the 'findings and decisions' of certain types of body, it is important to note that privilege only extends to the findings and decisions themselves, and not reports of the proceedings in which those findings were arrived at, or announced (unless these can be considered public meetings).

Judicial proceedings

As we have seen, fair, accurate and contemporaneuous court reports carry absolute privilege. Qualified privilege applies to fair and accurate court reports which do not have absolute privilege because they are not published contemporaneously.

Proceedings of Parliament

As explained earlier, MPs have absolute privilege for anything they say during Parliamentary sessions. Under common law, there is qualified privilege for fair and accurate reports of those statements.

Reply to character attacks

If someone has been the subject of allegations which attack their character or conduct, and in response to that attack, they make a defamatory statement, they will be covered by qualified privilege, and so will a publication or broadcast which carries their reply. However, privilege only applies to such words as are necessary to address the specific allegations that have been made against them.

 In **Adam v Ward** (1917), the claimant was an MP who, in Parliament, made a vindictive statement about a general in his former regiment. Although the statement was defamatory, the general could not sue, because the statement was covered by absolute privilege. The Secretary to the Army Council issued a statement defending the general against the attack, which was published by several newspapers. The statement was defamatory of the MP, and he sued. The House of Lords held that the secretary was protected by qualified privilege, because he had a duty to defend the general's reputation.

Social, moral or legal duty

The fifth way in which information could traditionally be covered by qualified privilege is if it is passed on by someone who had a duty to pass it on, to someone who had a duty to receive it. This has never been of much use to the media, because the privilege only covers the person who has the duty to make the statement, and not someone else who repeats it. So, for example, it is settled by law that someone who has information about a crime has a duty to report it to the police, and the police have a duty to receive it, so the person giving the information can make a defamatory allegation and the person who is the subject of it cannot sue for defamation. That is not, however, the case if a newspaper publishes the allegation, since neither the informant nor the police have a duty to communicate it to the press.

In the past therefore, this defence could only cover the media where someone had a legal, moral or social duty to tell the media something defamatory, and the media had a legal, moral or social duty to publish it, and this very specific situation was hard to apply. However, this aspect of qualified privilege was adapted to create a new type of qualified privilege known as the *Reynolds* defence, which gives the media a considerable degree of protection.

The *Reynolds* defence

The *Reynolds* defence originated in the case of **Reynolds v Times Newspapers** (1999). The case arose from a news story published by *The Times* about the former Taoiseach (Irish Prime Minister), Albert Reynolds, and the circumstances leading up to his resignation. Mr Reynolds claimed that the article suggested that he had deliberately misled the Irish parliament. *The Times* put forward the defence of qualified privilege, arguing that it should apply to all discussion of matters of serious public interest, because the media had a duty to report such matters and the public a duty to inform itself about them.

While refusing to go quite this far, the House of Lords accepted that it was important that information on matters of public interest should be freely available, so that people could make informed choices about, for example, who they voted for. However, the Law Lords pointed out that it was also in the public interest for individuals such as politicians to be able to defend their reputations against false allegations, because to make an informed choice, voters needed to know who was good as well as who was bad.

A new form of the qualified privilege defence, which essentially seeks to protect information published fairly and responsibly, in the public interest, was therefore developed. This is done by balancing a number of factors, covering the importance to the public of the information revealed, and the behaviour of the media in the process of revealing it. In a subsequent case, **Loutchansky v Times Newspapers Ltd (No. 2)** (2001), the Court of Appeal accepted that the *Reynolds* defence had become a specific new defence, separate from traditional qualified privilege.

When judging whether a publication is covered by the *Reynolds* defence, the court will look at the following ten factors:

1 **The seriousness of the allegation.** This issue can be a double-edged sword: the more serious the allegation, the greater the care the press must show in handling it but, on the other hand, if an allegation is not especially serious, it may be of insufficient public interest to be covered by the defence.

2 **The nature of the information, and the extent to which it is the subject of public concern.**

3 **The source of the information.** Important issues here will include whether the informants had direct knowledge of the events or not, whether they were being paid for their stories, and whether they had their own 'axes to grind'. Of course, many sources do divulge information out of personal spite or to get revenge, and this alone will not mean the defence cannot apply, but it does mean that the journalist has to work harder to check the information through other channels. Similarly, if a source has been paid, they cannot be seen as entirely unbiased, and it would be sensible not to use them as a sole source if you want to claim the *Reynolds* defence.

4 **The steps taken by the journalist to check the information.**

5 **The status of the information.** This factor concerns how authoritative the source of the information is. If an allegation has already been the subject of an authoritative investigation, for example, there would seem to be good reason why the public should be told

about it. The Court of Appeal also mentioned government press releases, reports by the chairmen of public companies and the speeches of university vice-chancellors as examples of sources with authority. In effect, if someone in some kind of authority puts about a defamatory allegation, there is likely to be a public interest in it being published, so that it can be either acted on, or refuted if it is not true.

6 **The urgency of the matter.** This factor takes account of the fact that, as the Court of Appeal puts it, 'news is a perishable commodity'. Although the need to publish quickly will not excuse publishers from failing to make basic checks or attempt to get the other side of the story, the courts should take into account the fact that waiting too long can make it pointless to publish at all.

7 **Whether the claimant was asked to comment on the story.** To have any weight in supporting the defence, the claimant must have been given a fair chance to give a reasoned answer to the allegations. Pouncing on them in public and demanding an instant reply, or doorstepping them, may not be considered to qualify as a fair chance. On the other hand, a claimant who makes themselves unavailable for comment, or who genuinely could not be contacted in time will not be able to argue that the defence does not apply for this reason. The fact that comment was refused or unattainable should be mentioned in the story.

8 **Whether the article included the claimant's side of the story, at least in general terms.** Again, the press will not be disadvantaged by this factor if the reason for not putting the other side of the story is that the claimant refused to give it. The way in which the claimant's side of the story is presented will be important; there is obviously a big difference in the protection the press can expect to get for stating the claimant's view and allowing claimants to speak for themselves and, for example, quoting the view in a context which suggests it is not to be believed.

9 **The tone of the article.** A story raising queries or suggesting an investigation may, the House of Lords implied, be more likely to be protected than one which presented all the allegations as a matter of fact, or sensationalised them.

10 **The circumstances of publication, including the timing.** This last factor allows the court to take into account other factors which seem relevant to the issue of whether the publisher has behaved responsibly.

The court said in *Reynolds* that this list was not necessarily exclusive and other factors might also be taken into account; the weight given to different factors would also vary from case to case. It also stated that in weighing up these factors, the courts should have regard to the importance of freedom of expression, and should be slow to conclude that a publication was not in the public interest, especially where information was already in the field of public discussion. This potentially gives the media a high degree of protection for important stories which are fairly handled.

 In the *Reynolds* case itself, the House of Lords agreed that the subject was one of legitimate public concern. On the other hand, the allegation made was a serious one yet the paper had not mentioned Mr Reynolds' explanation for the events concerned, even though this was available to it. As a result, the Lords found that the story was not covered by qualified privilege.

 In *Bonnick v Morris* (2002), a newspaper published a story about a state-owned Jamaican company, JCTC, entering into two contracts with another company, Prolacto. The claimant was employed by JCTC, but had left just after the second contract was agreed. The newspaper reported that the contracts were unusually advantageous to Prolacto, and that the claimant had left JCTC just after making the second contract. The claimant argued that this was defamatory, because it implied that he had acted improperly in arranging the contract, and that was why he had had to leave. The newspaper pointed out that it had approached JCTC for comments, but it had refused to say anything, and it had also spoken to the claimant, who had explained that there was nothing suspicious about the contracts and that they had no connection with his leaving the company. The court agreed that the article was defamatory, but said it was covered by qualified privilege because the subject was a matter of public interest, and the paper had acted responsibly, particularly given that the story was not one which was obviously defamatory.

In *Grobbelaar* v *News Group Newspapers* (2001), the footballer Bruce Grobbelaar sued the *Sun* over reports that he had been paid to fix the results of matches he played in. The paper had been given a tip-off that Mr Grobbelaar had been involved in match-fixing, and had arranged for the source to tape a conversation in which he accepted money to fix a match, and admitted to doing so in the past. The resulting story took up several pages, with headlines screaming 'World exclusive – Grobbelaar took bribes to fix games' and 'I saved goal by mistake and lost £125,000'. Before the case came to court, Mr Grobbelaar was charged with two criminal offences related to match fixing, but was acquitted. The *Sun* pleaded qualified privilege, but the Court of Appeal held that qualified privilege did not apply. Among the factors which the Court said led to this decision included the facts that the main witness against the claimant was thoroughly unreliable, the newspaper had evidence from a world-class goalkeeper that suggested Mr Grobbelaar's performance on the pitch showed no signs of match-fixing, and that there was no real urgency for the paper to publish when it did. But the main factor was the tone and weight of the story, which appeared over several pages, for seven days, and asserted Mr Grobbelaar's guilt as a fact, rather than, for example, raising questions or asking for an investigation. (However, the result of the case was less of a disappointment for the paper; although Mr Grobbelaar won, the House of Lords reduced the £85,000 damages ordered by the jury to £1, in recognition of the fact that although it could not proved that he fixed matches, he had admitted that he took bribes.)

In *Loutchansky* v *Times Newspapers Ltd (No. 2)* (2001), where the *Times* accused Russian businessman Grigori Loutchansky of being involved in serious crime, the paper claimed qualified privilege because, it said, the subject was one of public concern, and the story was based on authoritative sources, including reports by the CIA and British intelligence services. *The Times* initially lost and appealed, and the resulting series of appeals culminated in the Court of Appeal sending the case back to the original judge to reconsider in the light of the clarifications of the *Reynolds* defence. Second time round, the judge still found against the newspaper. Summarising the *Reynolds* defence, he said the question was whether the paper had behaved responsibly in publishing the articles. He agreed that the matter was one of public concern, but said that that the allegations made were very serious and potentially very damaging to Mr Loutchansky's reputation, and therefore demanded a high degree of care on the paper's part before publishing them. This standard had not been met: some of the sources were unsafe, while the allegations were vague and the paper had not made enough effort to check them. The paper had tried to contact Mr Loutchansky, but, the judge said, it should have tried harder, and although the story stated that Mr Loutchansky had repeatedly denied the allegations, this bare statement did not amount to giving his side of the story.

In *GKR Karate (UK) Ltd* v *Yorkshire Post Newspapers* (2000), the free paper *Leeds Weekly News* was sued for a story which warned readers about doorstep salesmen pushing karate lessons. The story alleged that the firm used unqualified instructors, overcharged and, according to one of the people quoted, 'They just take people's money and then disappear.' Despite the seriousness of the allegations, the reporter's only attempt to get the company's side of the story was to leave a message with its answering service, and when it did not reply, the story was published without a company comment. In addition, she had contacted the local Trading Standards Office and been told that it had not had any complaints against the firm; she did not report this fact in the story. The judge said that there were legitimate concerns about the way the story was investigated, but overall, the subject was one of public concern in the area which the paper served, and that the reporter had based her story on what she honestly believed was reliable evidence. Therefore the defence could apply.

 In *Jameel* v *Wall Street Journal* (2006), the claimant sued over a story which claimed that the Saudi Arabian authorities were monitoring the bank accounts of prominent businesses (including his) for evidence of links to terrorism. The paper claimed the Reynolds defence, but although they had checked the information thoroughly, they had not sought comment from the claimant. The House of Lords held that this did not mean the defence failed; the Reynolds criteria were pointers, not a series of hurdles which all had to be jumped. The key question was whether the subject was one of public interest, and the defendant had acted fairly and responsibly in gathering and publishing the information, and in this case they had.

Note that when assessing whether a newspaper behaved responsibly in publishing a story, the courts will only consider the information that was available up to the point of publication. In *Loutchansky*, new evidence came to light after publication which *The Times* said helped its case, but the courts said this evidence could not be taken into account. This means that the courts are not looking at whether publication was reasonable in the light of all the facts about the story, but whether, on the information it had at the time, the newspaper acted responsibly.

Neutral reportage

In recent cases, the courts have developed a new version of the *Reynolds* defence, known as neutral reportage. It can apply to reports of defamatory allegations on a matter of public interest, where the allegations are presented in a completely neutral manner, without any suggestion that they are or may be true. In these cases, the courts have said that it is not necessary to fulfil the ten Reynolds criteria (see p. xx).

 In *Al-Fagih* v *HH Saudi Research Marketing (UK) Ltd* (2001), a Saudi Arabian politician, Saad Al-Fagih, sued an Arabic newspaper over a story in which it reported a defamatory allegation that one of his political opponents had made about him. The newspaper had made no attempt to check whether the allegation was true, but had simply reported neutrally what the other man said; it had not suggested that the words were true. The Court of Appeal said that although the media would normally have to make efforts to verify information reported if they wanted to claim qualified privilege, there were cases where the public interest in publication outweighed that requirement. In this case it was in the public interest that disputes between politicians were made public and, in addition, the newspaper had acted responsibly in making it clear where the allegation came from, and in presenting it as neutral 'reportage' rather than allegations of fact.

 In *Christopher Roberts and Barry Roberts* v *Searchlight Magazine* (2006), the anti-fascist magazine *Searchlight* published a story about a dispute between factions within the British National Party (BNP). It reported that the BNP newsletter had alleged that three members stole money from a BNP organiser, and that an open letter published by a faction within the BNP newsletter had claimed that one of the claimants had returned this money, and both claimants, who were BNP candidates, had threatened violence against various other BNP members. The claimants were not given a chance to comment on the story, and no steps were taken to verify the allegations, and so they applied for a ruling that the magazine could not plead qualified privilege. Mr Justice Eady rejected the application, pointing out that the story had not reported the allegations as fact, but was reporting on the state of affairs within the BNP, where various factions were making serious accusations against each other; *Searchlight* readers were unlikely to place much faith in what either side had to say. Given that the subject of the story was a political party which was active in the UK, there was a strong public interest in knowing about its inner workings.

 In *Galloway* v *Telegraph Group Ltd* (see p. xx), the paper claimed that, as in the *Al-Fagih* case, it was presenting a neutral report of allegations against a public figure, which the public had a right to know about. This argument was rejected by the judge, who said that the newspaper had not merely reported the content of the documents which formed the basis of the allegations, but had gone further and 'embraced the allegations with relish and fervour'. It had made no attempt to check the allegations, and though it had spoken to Mr Galloway, it had not told him that the forthcoming story would suggest he had acted for personal gain, and so he had not had the chance to reply to those allegations.

In *Charman* v *Orion Publishing Group* (2006), the claimant was a former detective constable who had been required to resign from the Metropolitan Police after a disciplinary panel found that he had acted in a manner which was likely to bring discredit on the force. The defendants published a book, *Bent Coppers*, which Mr Charman claimed suggested there were grounds to suspect that he had colluded with an informant, which he denied. The publishers claimed that the book was neutral reportage, but Mr Justice Gray rejected this defence. He explained that the defence required the relevant facts to be presented in a full, fair and disinterested manner, and this was not the case in the book, which described itself as an 'inside story' and suggested that at least some of the allegations were true.

Law in practice Using the *Reynolds* defence

If you want to make sure that your story is covered by the *Reynolds* defence, Rod Dadak, Head of Defamation at solicitors Lewis Silkin, has this advice:

- Work through all ten of the Reynolds requirements, and make sure you have addressed them all – it's not enough just to satisfy some of them. If you cannot do this, you may still be able to plead the neutral reportage defence, but this will only apply to stories which report defamatory allegations in a completely neutral way, and not where you have suggested or implied that they may be true.

- For the full *Reynolds* defence (as opposed to neutral reportage), you will almost always need to give the subject a chance to put their side of the story. Judges look very critically at any failure to do this, and although there are cases where particular circumstances make it acceptable not to approach the subject of a story, you are taking a very big risk if you do not give a fair chance to comment.

- Bear in mind that the process of satisfying the Reynolds requirements doesn't end with the journalist assembling their material for the story. Editorial decisions, such as the overall slant, and the headline, are important too. To succeed with *Reynolds*, you have to be sure that you have presented a balanced picture, so ensure that the overall slant doesn't assume guilt, and if the subject has put their side of the story forward, make sure their points are presented adequately, and not just mentioned in passing.

Malice and qualified privilege

Qualified privilege, whether statutory or common law, will only be available if the publication is made without malice. For the purposes of qualified privilege, malice has a slightly different meaning to the one it carries with regard to the defence of fair comment. Here, a journalist will be said to have acted with malice if they were motivated to write what they did by spite or ill feeling towards their subject, or with any other improper motive. Evidence that the journalist did not believe what they were writing was true may be evidence of malice, but equally, a journalist who writes a defamatory statement for improper motives may be judged to have acted with malice even if they believed that what they wrote was true. This is because the purpose of the defence of qualified privilege is to help the media do its traditional duty of informing the public about important issues. A journalist who says something defamatory for reasons other than doing that duty cannot be covered by the defence.

Offer of amends

The Defamation Act 1996 provides a special defence of 'offer of amends', which is available only where the publisher of defamatory words:

- did not know or have reason to believe that the words could be taken to refer to the claimant; and
- did not know that the words were false and defamatory of that person.

In other words, the defence is intended to be used in cases where the publisher has simply made a mistake. However, the court will assume that the above conditions apply, unless the claimant proves that they do not (which is why some of the cases below do not seem to fit into this category; if a claimant is happy to accept an offer of amends, they will not seek to prove that the above circumstances do not apply). However, if a claimant does choose to challenge use of the defence, and can prove that you did know or have reason to believe the words referred to them, and you did know the words were false and defamatory, the defence is unavailable.

An offer of amends can be in relation to a statement generally, or to a specific defamatory meaning, in which case it is called a qualified offer. A qualified offer might be used, for example, where the statement made is true, but it carries an implication that is not true and is defamatory.

This defence is particularly useful for cases like *Newstead v London Express Newspapers and O'Shea v MGN Ltd* (see p. 183), where stories have been published that are true of the person the publication intends them to refer to, but could be taken to refer to someone else (and are not true of that person).

 In 2001, Channel 4 used the offer of amends defence in a case involving the comedy programme 'Phoenix Nights'. It contained a character called Keith Lard, a Bolton fire safety officer, with a bushy moustache, who habitually wore a bright yellow safety jacket. Unknown to the writers of the programme, there was a real-life fire safety officer living in Bolton, called Keith Laird, who also had a bushy moustache and wore a yellow jacket. In itself this might not have been a problem, but the programme character also had a sexual interest in dogs, and so Mr Laird sued on the grounds that the programme referred to him and was defamatory. Channel 4 broadcast an apology and paid Mr Laird £10,000.

Using the defence

To use the defence of offer of amends, the publisher must offer to publish a suitable correction and apology, and to pay compensation. If a publisher wishes to choose this defence, it must make the offer before officially putting forward any other defence – it is not possible, for example, to enter another defence and then decide to make an offer of amends later if you think that your original defence might not succeed after all. The offer of amends procedure is designed to be a way for defendants to put right the damage they have done at an early stage, rather than a 'get out of jail card' to have up their sleeves if the case starts to look shaky.

The parties can either come to an agreement on a suitable amount of compensation, or the court can decide it for them. As a recognition of the publisher offering to make amends (rather than being forced to), the court will considerably reduce the amount of damages it would have ordered had the claimant sued and won.

If the offer is accepted, the defamation proceedings come to an end. If a publisher makes an offer of amends, but the claimant refuses it and continues with their claim, the publisher can use the offer of amends as a defence, provided the court accepts that it did not know or have reason to believe that the words published were untrue and defamatory of the claimant. If the publisher does this, it cannot put forward any other defence in addition. However, if it chooses to put forward a different defence, and loses the case, the offer of amends may still reduce the amount of damages awarded.

 In *Nail* v *News Group Newspapers Ltd* (2004). Harper Collins had published an unauthorised biography of the actor Jimmy Nail, which made lurid allegations about his sexual behaviour. Mr Nail claimed damages of £70,000–£100,000, and rejected an offer of amends, which included damages of £37,500. Although he won his case, the judge awarded only £30,000, and said that defendants who tried to make amends were entitled to expect that the court would acknowledge that gesture by reducing the damages payable.

Importance of good conduct

Because the principle of the offer of amends is to allow publishers voluntarily to put right the damage done by defamatory remarks, the courts expect publishers who want to use this defence to behave courteously towards claimants, and to take action swiftly to put matters right, in a way which reflects the seriousness of the allegations. They do not look kindly on publishers whose behaviour suggests they are not actually sorry, and they may well show their displeasure in the damages ordered.

 In *Campbell-James* v *Guardian Media* (2005), the claimant was a distinguished soldier who had spent many years serving in the Intelligence Corps. An article published in the *Guardian* falsely linked him to the much-publicised abuse of prisoners in Iraq's Abu Ghraib prison, even though he was not in Iraq at the time. In addition to the obvious damage to his personal reputation, the allegations put the claimant and his family at serious risk of harm. When his lawyers contacted the *Guardian*, the paper initially claimed that its story was covered by fair comment and qualified privilege. It only made an offer of amends over two months after the article was published, and the published apology was less than generous. When the case went before the court to decide on suitable compensation, the judge was clearly disgusted by the paper's behaviour, saying that this was clearly a case where the allegations should have been corrected immediately, not just as a matter of good journalistic practice, but of 'elementary human decency'. Although there is no set 'discount' for using the offer of amends procedure, previous cases have suggested that around 50 per cent is normal. In this case, in view of the circumstances, the judge allowed only 35 per cent off. This meant that the *Guardian* had to pay £58,500 instead of the £45,000 it might have expected if it had behaved more quickly and considerately.

 In *Turner* v *News Group Newspapers* (2005), the claimant was featured in a *News of the World* story about wife-swapping, in which his ex-wife alleged that he had put pressure on her to have sex with other men. He twice wrote and complained to the editor, but received no reply, and an offer of amends was not offered until six months after the article was published; even then, the brief apology was, as the judge put it, 'tucked away' on page 36. The court held that in view of the dismissive way in which the complaint had been treated, the damages should only be discounted by 40 per cent. (The claimant however still believed this was unfair, as the damages ordered were only £9,000, but on appeal, the award was allowed to stand.)

 In *John Cleese* v *Evening Standard* (2004), the *Evening Standard* had published an apology to the actor and comedian John Cleese, over a story which claimed his career was in decline. They also offered £10,000 in damages. However, when the apology was printed, it was, Mr Cleese claimed, deliberately positioned in such a way that few readers would notice it, and out of proportion to the prominence given to the original story. In addition, the terms of the apology did not, he claimed, make it clear what had been wrong with the story. He went to court and was awarded £13,500.

 In *Veliu* v *Mazrekaj* (2006), Mr Veliu was the subject of a story in an Albanian-language newspaper called *Bota Sot*, which is published from Switzerland but widely read in the UK. The article claimed he was involved in the bomb attacks in London on 7 July 2005 and was a friend of one of the bombers. In fact he did not know the bomber and had no connection with the attacks. The paper initially ignored Mr Veliu's complaints, and when an apology was finally published, it was brief and somewhat flippant, stating that the article 'does not have anything to do with the reality, but it's a pure fantasy'. The publisher made an offer of amends, and the case went to court to decide the issue of damages. The judge commented on the paper's mishandling of the complaint, and the misleading nature of the apology, especially in view of the fact that the allegations made were so serious and caused the claimant great distress. As a result, he allowed a discount of just 30 per cent and awarded damages of £175,000.

▨ Accord and satisfaction

It is of course possible to print an apology even if the case is outside the rules of an offer of amends. Printing an apology or correction is not by itself a defence, but it can become one if the claimant accepts it and, in return, agrees not to sue. This is known as 'accord and satisfaction' or waiver of claim. It will only provide a defence if the person defamed expressly or by implication accepts it as putting an end to their claim.

Although written evidence of this acceptance is not required by law, clearly if someone tries to sue after they have accepted an apology, the publisher is on stronger ground if it can present a written statement by the claimant that they are accepting the apology in full and final settlement and waiving their rights to sue. However, if the complaint comes from the person who is the subject of the story, and not through a lawyer, it may well be the case that they had not considered suing and did not even realise that they could. In that situation, if you ask them to sign a waiver, they may well realise the potential seriousness of the case and consult a lawyer.

If you print a prompt and adequate apology and the claimant does not accept it as accord and satisfaction, but goes on to sue you and wins, the court may reduce the damages it orders in recognition of the apology, typically by as much as 50 per cent. It is important to know however, that a badly-handled apology can actually end up making things worse, so it is often worth getting legal advice at this stage.

Problems with apologies and corrections

An inappropriate or carelessly worded apology can make things much worse. The following are some of the problems that you need to watch out for when printing apologies.

Defamatory apologies: It is very easy to defame someone else in the course of making an apology. Take, for example, a situation where you have quoted defamatory remarks made by someone else. If the subject of the remarks complains, and you print an apology saying that the words were untrue, you may be calling the source a liar, and if the original words are in fact true, that could be defamatory of them.

Making things worse: Be careful that the wording of your apology does not repeat the libel, or even worsen the impression given by the original article.

In the *Stationery Trade* case referred to on p. 175, where the magazine was accused of suggesting that a company was selling counterfeit envelopes, the publication ran an apology which, the court said, made things worse. It repeated the previous headline 'Counterfeits – retailers warned' and said that the claimant company had told them their envelopes were 'now origin marked' so there was no chance of customers being misled. The court said this gave the impression that the company were not selling counterfeit envelopes now, but had been previously.

Damaging admissions: If you make an apology without the claimant agreeing to waive their claim as a result, you take the risk that, if you are sued for libel, the apology will be seen as an admission that what you published was untrue and/or defamatory.

Court report corrections: If an inaccurate remark is made in court proceedings and reported by the media, the publisher may be asked to correct it in print. However, the correction will not carry the same privilege as the original report, so if it is defamatory, the publication can be sued. In this situation the safest option is to ask the complainant to arrange to make a statement of correction in open court (their solicitor can arrange this), which the newspaper can then report.

Your own reputation: If you do write a story which results in a libel claim, and your publishers decide to apologise, keep a close eye on the wording of it, since it could very easily damage your professional reputation. In such cases you may want to take legal advice yourself, and your union should be able to help with this.

■ Innocent dissemination

As we saw earlier, a claimant in defamation can sue not only the writer of the defamatory words, but almost anyone involved in the process of publishing them, right down to the distributors. The Defamation Act 1996, however, provides a defence for many of the parties in the publishing chain. Section 1 of the Act provides a defence for anyone who:

■ was not the author, editor or publisher of the defamatory statement; and

■ took reasonable care in relation to its publication; and

■ did not know or have reason to know that whatever part they played in the publication caused or contributed to the publication of a defamatory statement.

The Act lists people who, for the purposes of this defence, are not considered to be the publisher of a defamatory statement, including printers, distributors, sellers and internet service providers (the last only applies to the services that host websites, and not those who post content online).

The category also includes broadcasters of live programmes in circumstances where they have no effective control over the maker of a defamatory statement. Such circumstances might include, for example, a live phone-in, or a chat show. However, the simple fact that a programme includes contributions from people whose words the broadcaster has no control over will not by itself avoid liability, because of the requirement for reasonable care. This may mean that if there is an obvious risk that contributors to a particular programme might make defamatory remarks, it may be necessary to use a 'delay button', which provides a few seconds delay between words being said and being broadcast, so that defamatory statements can be blocked.

In 1999 the market research organisation MORI sued the BBC, over a live radio interview by politician Sir James Goldsmith, in which he claimed MORI was 'inefficient or dishonest', used out-of-date polls, and used its work to pursue a political agenda. It was argued in court that Sir James had a reputation for plain speaking that should have made the BBC realise he might well say something defamatory, and therefore it should have used a delay button. The case was settled out of court.

■ Time limits and repeat actions

Under the Defamation Act 1996, defamation claims must be brought within a year of publication; a claim brought after this limitation period is said to be out of time, which gives the publisher a complete defence. However, the courts have discretion to extend the limitation period, and have proved to be more ready to do this for defamation claims than in many other types of case. If a claimant applies for an extension of the limitation period, the court will balance the reasons for their delay, against any disadvantage the delay will cause the defendant (e.g. difficulties in finding witnesses).

Remember that each repetition of a libel (including accessing a story in an online archive) is considered a new publication, with its own limitation period running from the date it is published (or accessed). A claimant who has successfully sued for libel can sue the same publication again if that publication later repeats the libel, or leaves it on its website.

 In 2006, the father of comedian Jimmy Carr won a second set of damages from the *Sunday Telegraph*, after the original case was settled out of court, but the paper left the story on its website.

REMEDIES FOR DEFAMATION

There are two main remedies for defamation:

- damages;
- injunctions.

■ Damages

As we have seen, the most common remedy for libel is damages. In cases which are heard by juries, they decide the damages as well as the verdict (in contrast to criminal cases, where juries decide the verdict but not the sentence).

Damages for libel fall into five categories; a single award may include damages from more than one of these.

1 Compensatory damages

These are supposed to be calculated to repair the damage done by the defamatory statement. In practice, it is very difficult to put a price on damage to someone's reputation, and the Court of Appeal has suggested that judges should guide juries by making them aware of the levels of damages typically ordered in cases involving physical injury, and inviting them to compare such injuries with the damage suffered by the claimant. They might point out, for example, that losing an eye would usually mean compensation of around £20,000, and losing a limb around £45,000, while awards of over £100,000 tend to be limited to cases of very serious injury, such as paralysis or severe brain damage.

2 Aggravated damages

These are awarded, in addition to compensatory damages, in cases where the defendant has behaved particularly badly, so that the claimant has suffered more than would normally be expected in such a case. Typical cases might be where a paper has conducted a campaign against a particular person, or where it has repeated a libel even after being told it was untrue.

In *Kiam* v *MGN* (2002), businessman Victor Kiam was awarded £105,000 after a story questioned his business judgement. Part of the award comprised aggravated damages because the article was completely untrue, there was ample evidence that the writer had made no real effort to check it, and further defamatory articles were printed just before the trial, again without checking the facts with Mr Kiam.

3 Exemplary damages

These are reserved for cases where a publisher's behaviour is seen as so bad as to be deserving of punishment (like aggravated damages, they are awarded in addition to compensatory damages). They are generally used in cases where it appears defamatory material has been published deliberately, for example to increase profits.

In *John* v *Mirror Group Newspapers* (1996), Elton John was awarded £350,000 for a story which suggested he had an eating disorder. The award included exemplary damages, because it was clear that the defamatory story was published deliberately, with an eye to its effect on sales. The overall amount was later reduced by the Court of Appeal (see below), but still included an amount for exemplary damages.

4 Nominal damages

These are ordered where the claimant's rights have technically been infringed, but the court feels no real damage has been done. They are usually less than £20.

In *Grobbelaar* v *News Group* (see p. 209), the case involving goalkeeper Bruce Grobbelaar, the House of Lords substituted an award of £1 for the £85,000 originally awarded by the jury, in recognition of the fact that he had admitted taking bribes.

5 Contemptuous damages

These are ordered where a jury (or judge) recognises that the claimant has been defamed, but in the circumstances, considers that the action should not have been brought. The damages (which are instead of compensatory damages) amount to the value of the least valuable coin in circulation (currently 1p). A claimant who is awarded contemptuous damages often has to pay their own costs as well.

In *Pamplin* v *Express Newspapers (No.2)* (1988), the claimant registered his car and television set in the name of his five-year-old son, who because of his age could not be prosecuted for non-payment of licence fees and parking fines. The *Express* published a story describing him as a 'slippery, unscrupulous spiv' and a jury found that he had been defamed, but awarded him only ½p in damages. He appealed, but unsuccessfully.

The Courts and Legal Services Act 1990 gives the Court of Appeal the power to overturn a jury decision on the level of damages if the amount is excessive in the circumstances, and to order instead 'such sum as appears to the court to be proper'. This happened in the Elton John case, where the damages were reduced to £75,000, but in the Victor Kiam case the Court of Appeal held that the award was not excessive in the circumstances of the case.

Injunctions

An injunction is an order preventing publication. If a claimant wins their case, they will often ask for an injunction against the libel being repeated in future, and such injunctions are commonly awarded along with damages. However, a more controversial remedy is the interim injunction, which is ordered before publication. Typically, the claimant finds out that a story they claim is defamatory is about to be published, and goes to court for an order preventing publication. The order can be granted without a trial. Although this is technically a temporary measure, designed to 'hold the ring' until a full trial can be held, in practice a story published months or even years later is really no story at all, so by securing an interim injunction, the claimant can effectively silence the media.

Fortunately, the courts accept that injunctions which prevent initial publication can be a serious restriction on free speech, and will only grant them in exceptional cases. This is known as the rule against prior restraint. This traditional principle has been further strengthened by s12 of the Human Rights Act 1998, which provides that interim injunctions in cases affecting freedom of expression should not be granted unless the court is satisfied that, if the case does go to trial, the claimant is likely to be able to establish that publication should not be allowed. The Human Rights Act further provides that when considering requests for injunctions on journalistic material, the courts must take into account:

- the importance of freedom of expression;
- the extent to which the material is already, or is about to be, available to the public;
- the extent to which publication would be in the public interest;
- any relevant privacy code.

The result is that interim injunctions in libel cases are only likely to be granted where the claimant can convince the court that the defendant is planning to publish defamatory stories which are obviously untrue, and there is no arguable defence, or a defence put forward is certain to fail.

 In *Khashoggi v IPC Magazines* (1986), *Woman's Own* published a feature which claimed that Soraya Kashoggi, who was a famous 'society beauty', was having an extra-marital affair with a Head of State. Mrs Khashoggi sought an injunction to prevent the article being published. The magazine could not prove this particular allegation was true, but said that it could prove justification for the 'sting' of the libel, which it argued was the suggestion that she was a person who was happy to engage in affairs. A number of other affairs had been mentioned in the article, without any complaint from Mrs Kashoggi. The Court of Appeal said that the rule against prior restraint had to apply in such a case; it was possible that the defence could succeed at trial, and if it did not, in the circumstances, the claimant could be adequately compensated by damages.

 In 2003, the *Mail on Sunday* was hit with an injunction to stop it publishing untrue allegations about the sexual conduct of the Prince of Wales. The newspaper admitted in court that it had no corroboration for the story.

 In 2005, London restaurateur Martha Greene attempted to get an injunction preventing the *Mail on Sunday* from publishing allegations that she was a business contact of Peter Foster, a convicted fraudster who has become well-known in the press over a number of years, most recently for his relationship with Carole Caplin, a friend of Tony and Cherie Blair. The *Mail on Sunday* had already printed a story linking Ms Greene to Mr Foster, which she claimed was 'littered with inaccuracies'. Ms Greene then sought an injunction to prevent publication of a further story, based on the content of emails which the paper said she had sent to Mr Foster. Ms Greene stated that the emails were faked, and the judge admitted that expert computer evidence suggested that she was more likely than not to be able to prove this at trial. Even so, he said, there was no absolute, unquestionable 'knockout' evidence that the emails were forgeries. Unless it was obvious that no defence could succeed at trial, the rule against prior restraint meant no injunction should be ordered.

A further limit on the use of interim injunctions is that a claimant applying for one may be asked to promise to pay the cost to the defendant of complying with the injunction, if the matter goes to trial and it is found that the injunction was wrongly granted (e.g. if the allegations are proved to be true). Failure to agree to such an undertaking, or doubts about the claimant's ability to pay, makes it even less likely that an injunction will be granted.

Law in practice Protecting against libel claims

Having read this far, you will have seen that libel can be a complex and unpredictable area of law. Because there is no set definition of a libellous statement, it is often very difficult to forecast with any kind of certainty whether a jury would find for or against a claimant. Even judges can, and do, disagree on whether a statement has the potential to be libellous. An example is the case involving Nicole Kidman, reported on p. 171. The case was brought before a judge as a striking out application, which meant that the judge was essentially being asked whether, in law, the words published could amount to defamation. He said that while the story was unpleasant, it could not be considered defamatory. The Court of Appeal, however, disagreed; it said it was not clear that there was no defamation, and the issue should be put before a jury. Similarly, in *Jameel* v *Times Newspapers*, the case about the Saudi businessman (see p. 179), the High Court said that the article in question was not capable of carrying the meaning that the claimant alleged, and the Court of Appeal then ruled that it was.

Since judges cannot always predict what will and will not be deemed defamatory, clearly no one expects a reporter to be able to do that with absolute certainty either. But while you are not expected to know all the answers, you are expected to know when there is a question to be asked. You should be able to spot when you are making a statement that could be considered defamatory, you should know what you need to do to make sure you are covered by a defence if you decide to go ahead and publish that statement – and most importantly, you should know when to take further advice, whether from your editor or a lawyer.

If you are lucky enough to have an in-house lawyer, use them. On some publications, the whole of each issue is 'legalled' (read by a lawyer) as a matter of course, but if you're working in an area such as women's or trade magazines, where libel problems crop up less frequently, it may be up to individual staff to flag up when a feature needs legalling. If you have got a good story, but you are not certain you can back it up and you think the lawyer might advise against running it, it can be tempting just to 'forget' or 'not realise' that you should get it legalled. But if you do not think you can stand it up to the in-house lawyer's satisfaction, imagine how you are going to feel being questioned in court – or possibly worse, by your publishing director after the company has had to pay to settle out of court. The best resource in these circumstances is not to ignore the risk, but get advice on what you would need to do in order to run the story safely.

Rod Dadak, Head of Media at solicitors Lewis Silkin advises that the best protection is to research your stories on the basis that, if the subject sued, you would have to defend your words in court:

> Although in practice very few libel cases now go to court, if you make sure that you have enough evidence to defend your story if it did go to trial, you will always be in a stronger position. If a potential claimant knows that you have your house in order, they will be less likely to sue in the first place, and more likely to settle if they do make a claim.

DEFAMATION AND THE HUMAN RIGHTS ACT

Defamation law essentially rules over conflicts between one party's right to free speech and another's right not to have their reputation damaged and, traditionally, the English courts have treated this as a simple balancing act (and often seemed to lean in favour of reputation). Now, however, the Human Rights Act 1998 has enshrined into English law a right to freedom of expression. This should mean that the scales have shifted: the Human Rights Act requires the courts to see freedom of expression as a fundamental right, and to allow limitations on it only where they can be justified by a pressing social need.

The effects of this shift are already being seen – most notably in the *Reynolds* defence, and the restrictions on use of injunctions – and it may well be that in future, some of the more restrictive parts of defamation law will be challenged under the Human Rights Act.

CHAPTER SUMMARY

There are seven defences regarding defamation.

1 Consent

Applies where the subject of a statement agreed to its publication.

2 Justification

Applies where the statement can be proved to be substantially true.

3 Fair comment

Applies to comments on issues of public interest, which are based on true facts and made without malice.

4 Absolute privilege

Applies to fair, accurate and contemporaneous court reports.

5 Qualified privilege

Applies to statements made without malice, regarding the following:

- proceedings, decisions and documents listed in Schedule 1 of the Defamation Act 1996;
- judicial proceedings in the UK;
- the proceedings of Parliament;
- replies to attacks on someone's character or conduct;
- statements made from a legal, moral or social duty, to someone with a duty to receive them;
- balanced, responsibly researched reports on matters of public interest.

6 Offer of amends

Applies where a publisher did not realise that a defamatory statement could apply to the claimant, and is willing to apologise and pay compensation.

7 Innocent dissemination

Applies to distributors, printers and so on who have taken reasonable care and did not know of the defamatory statement.

Time limits

Claims must usually be brought within a year of publication; there is some discretion to extend the limitation period.

Remedies

Remedies for defamation are damages and/or injunctions.

TEST YOUR KNOWLEDGE

1 What does it mean to say that, in order to successfully plead justification, you have to prove your statement was true 'on the balance of probabilities'?

2 What is the meaning of 'malice', as used in the defence of fair comment? How does it differ from malice as regards qualified privilege?

3 Benny, Agnetha and Frida are trainee journalists on the *Waterloo Gazette*. Their editor sends them to review three plays which are on locally.

■ Benny goes to see a production of 'Les Miserables', and reports (accurately) that the leading actor, a famous TV star called Terry Lovey, collapsed halfway through the first act, and that the theatre says he is suffering from food poisoning. He goes on to say, 'The *Sun* recently claimed that Terry had sought help for drug problems, but I saw no evidence that Saturday's collapse was anything more suspect than a dodgy curry.'

■ Agnetha goes to see an amateur production of 'Macbeth', and is surprised to discover that the lead role is taken by an ex-boyfriend of hers, from whom she parted on very bad terms some years before. She writes: 'The actor playing Macbeth forgot his lines nine times. He was so pathetically bad that he was an embarrassment to watch. A donkey would have played the part better.'

■ Frida is sent to review a production of 'My Fair Lady', and writes: 'What a fantastic show: wonderful singing, fabulous dancing, and even the youngest performers remembered every line. What a shame that the second act was spoilt for me – and most of the audience – by the unruly behaviour of pupils from St Cedric's School. They showed the complete lack of discipline that people in this town have come to expect from this appalling comprehensive, where it is clear that no one takes the slightest interest in standards of behaviour.'

Could any of the three be liable for defamation? What defences might they be able to use, and what factors will decide whether they are covered or not?

ONLINE RESOURCES

The Defamation Act 1996 can be read in full at:
www.opsi.gov.uk/acts/acts1996/1996031.htm

Reynolds v *Times Newspapers* (2001) can be read at:
www.parliament.the-stationery-office.co.uk/pa/ld199899/ldjudgmt/jd991028/rey01.htm

Armstrong v *Times Newspapers* can be read at:
www.bailii.org/ew/cases/EWHC/QB/2006/1614.html

A useful examination of liability for online defamation can be found in the Law Commission report, Defamation and the Internet, at:
www.lawcom.gov.uk/docs/defamation2.pdf#search=%22defamation%22

For further resources and updates please go to the Companion Website for this book at www.pearsoned.co.uk/practicaljournalism

Malicious falsehood

As we saw in Chapter 14, false statements only give rise to a libel action where they lead to a lowering of the claimant in the eyes of right-thinking people. However, some untrue statements which do not fit the definition of libel can give rise to a different legal action, called malicious falsehood (and potentially, some untrue statements could give rise to both actions).

WHAT IS MALICIOUS FALSEHOOD?

Malicious falsehood is not concerned with protecting reputation, but protecting against financial damage caused by the publication of false statements. A statement may be a malicious falsehood if it satisfies all the following:

- it is untrue;
- it is published maliciously; and
- as a direct and natural result of publication, the subject of the statement was caused financial loss, or was likely to be caused financial loss related to their business or job, or (but only where the words complained of are published in some permanent form) they were likely to cause financial damage in any other way.

The difference between this action and libel can be seen if we take the example of a local paper writing that a builder in the town is retiring. This would clearly not be defamatory, since no one would think less of the builder for retiring. However, it could (if untrue and published maliciously) be a malicious publication, because clearly if local people believe the builder is no longer taking on work, they will be unlikely to contact him when they need work done, and he is likely to suffer financially.

An untrue statement

In libel actions, the courts assume that the statement complained of is untrue, and it is for the defendant to give themselves a defence by proving it true, if they can. However, in an action for malicious prosecution, the claimant must prove that the statement is untrue. The statement need not be a direct one; as with libel, an implication can be enough.

 In *Kaye* v *Robertson* (1991), the claimant was the actor Gorden Kaye, who at the time was starring in a very popular TV comedy called 'Allo, Allo'. He was seriously injured in an accident, and while he lay semi-conscious in hospital, a reporter from the *Sunday Sport* got into his room, and 'interviewed' and photographed him. Mr Kaye sought a injunction to prevent publication of the resulting story and pictures, arguing that by publishing the story, the paper would be implying that he had consented to the interview, which he had not. The judge agreed that this amounted to a false statement.

Malicious publication

For the purposes of malicious falsehood, to publish a statement maliciously means to publish it without reasonable cause or excuse, and with some kind of indirect, dishonest or improper motive. It is not necessary that the defendant was motivated by what we would understand as malice in the normal sense of the word, meaning spite or nastiness.

 In *Kaye* v *Robertson* (1991) malice was found in the fact that the reporter must, in the circumstances, have realised that Mr Kaye was in no fit state to consent to giving an interview.

 In *Joyce* v *Sengupta* (1993), the (now defunct) *Today* newspaper published a front page story about a woman called Linda Joyce, who worked as a maid to Princess Anne. The story, which was based on police suspicions, claimed that Ms Joyce had stolen personal letters from the Princess and given them to a national newspaper. Ms Joyce sued for malicious falsehood and, in an interim hearing, the Court of Appeal held that the publication was malicious because the paper went ahead and published the story on the basis of what the police had told them they suspected, without making any checks as to whether the suspicions were true. Malice, the court said, could be inferred from 'the grossness and falseness of the allegations and the cavalier way they were published'. The case was later settled out of court.

Law in practice Malicious falsehood claims

The requirement for malice means that honest mistakes should not result in a successful claim for malicious publication, as long as the publisher concerned puts things right as soon as possible. If a publication is threatened with a claim for malicious prosecution, the first thing to do is check whether the facts are wrong. If they are, and the mistake was an honest one (and the statement is not defamatory), printing a correction and apology quickly will make it difficult for a court to find malice.

Financial loss

In most cases, the claimant has to prove that publication of the false statement caused (or has the potential to cause) 'special damage', which means actual financial loss.

 In *Graphelli* v *Derek Block (Holdings) Ltd* (1981) the claimant was the famous jazz musician Stephane Grapelli. The defendants were his managing agents, who had arranged a series of concerts by him in the UK. These had to be cancelled and the defendants falsely claimed that the reason for the cancellation was that Mr Grapelli was seriously ill; so ill, in fact, that he might never be able to tour again. Mr Grapelli sued for both defamation and malicious falsehood. The first claim failed because it was not defamatory to say that someone was ill, but the second succeeded, as clearly the statement could damage his career and therefore his income.

 In *Kaye* v *Robertson* (1991) the potential financial damage was held to arise from the fact that, if he chose to, Mr Kaye could have sold his story to a paper of his choice, for a large amount of money. If the story had already been published by the *Sunday Sport*, this right would be much less valuable because the story would no longer be exclusive.

It is usually quite clear if a claimant has suffered financial loss, but there have been cases where claimants have tried to stretch a case further on this point than the courts are prepared to go.

 In *Stewart-Brady* v *Express Newspapers plc* (1997), the convicted serial killer Ian Brady sued the newspaper group over a story which claimed that he had assaulted a female visitor to the mental hospital where he was detained. He claimed that the story would cause him financial loss because it would lead to the withdrawal of privileges which he was currently allowed, such as receiving visits and gifts and making and receiving phone calls, and to the withdrawal or reduction of a discretionary weekly allowance which he received from the hospital. The court held that withdrawal of the privileges was not 'by any stretch of the imagination' a financial loss, and the possibility of losing some or all of the allowance could not be the basis for a claim because there was no reason to believe that it would actually be withdrawn.

 In *Caron* v *BBC* (2002), the case concerned a radio programme about the singer Alma Cogan, who was very famous in the 1950s. The programme portrayed her as a drunk and her mother as domineering, and her sister wanted to stop it being broadcast. As both Ms Cogan and her mother were dead, an action in defamation was impossible, so Ms Cogan's sister (Ms Caron) sued for malicious falsehood, claiming that the programme would damage the assets of Ms Cogan's estate (the money and property left after she died, which would include the continuing income from her records). The court rejected the claim, stating that there was no proof that the programme could do such financial damage.

■ Legal aid for malicious falsehood cases

In the past, legal aid was available for malicious falsehood claims, but not for defamation, so in some cases, claimants who have been the subject of a statement which could be a libel or a malicious falsehood have preferred to sue for malicious falsehood. This distinction no longer applies, as legal aid was removed from actions for malicious falsehood by the Access to Justice Act 1999.

Libel and malicious falsehood: know the differences

	Libel	Malicious falsehood
Statement must be false	Yes	Yes
Must cause financial loss	No	Yes
Must damage reputation	Yes	No
Subject must be alive	Yes	No
Publication must be malicious	No	Yes

CHAPTER SUMMARY

What is malicious falsehood?

A malicious falsehood is a statement that is:

■ false;

■ published maliciously; and

■ causes or is likely to cause financial loss.

'Malicious'

- Malicious means published without good reason, for an improper or dishonest motive.
- Malicious falsehoods can apply to people who are dead.
- Legal aid is no longer available for malicious falsehood.

TEST YOUR KNOWLEDGE

1 What are the three elements of malicious falsehood?

2 What are the main differences between malicious falsehood and libel?

3 Which of these statements, if untrue and published maliciously, could amount to malicious falsehoods:

(a) Popular dentist Joe Brown is to retire after 30 years in practice.

(b) Health inspectors found hundreds of cockroaches in the Happy Loaf bakery.

(c) Local vet Alan Williams has seriously damaged his hand in a tragic accident; doctors say he may never work again.

(d) Careless builder Jack Black set a 300-year-old cottage on fire.

4 What does 'maliciously' mean in the context of malicious falsehood?

For further resources and updates please go to the Companion Website for this book at www.pearsoned.co.uk/practicaljournalism

Section 4

PRIVACY, CONFIDENTIALITY AND COPYRIGHT

This section brings together several different areas of law, but what the chapters have in common is that they largely concern laws which regulate the ways in which the media can use information about others or material owned by others.

The first chapter deals with confidentiality and privacy, a fast-developing area of the law which covers a wide range of information that people may want to keep out of the press, from business secrets, to embarrassing photographs of celebrities. It is concerned with the ways in which confidentiality can be breached by publication, while the following chapter deals with the ways in which journalists may invade people's privacy in the course of putting together a story.

There are many situations in which people who give information to the media may want to keep their identities secret, and it is a basic principle of journalistic ethics that a promise to keep a source confidential should be kept. Chapter 19 details the legal protection which the law provides for this principle, and the situations in which journalists can be ordered to reveal sources or hand over research material.

Chapter 20 deals with a relatively recent addition to the law, in the form of the Data Protection Act. The chapter explains both the media's responsibilities under the Act, and the ways in which journalists can deal with attempts to use the Act to keep information from the press.

The final chapter, on copyright, is about the rules which govern who owns the rights to words, pictures and other forms of expression, and how far the media can make use of such material.

Chapter

17

Confidentiality and privacy

This chapter deals with the way in which the law allows people (or organisations) to prevent publication of information which they would prefer to keep secret. Of all the areas of law covered in this book, it is the one which has changed most in the past few years, but remains one where many of the rules are unclear and the results of cases hard to predict. This is largely because, as we will see, the law as it now stands is an uncomfortable blend of two previously separate strands: confidentiality (or breach of confidence) and privacy.

Many of the cases in this chapter concern celebrities, but the law is not only relevant to this kind of journalism. The law of confidentiality is also used in cases dealing with trade secrets, government information and information about ordinary people, so whatever area of journalism you work in, it is something that you need to know about.

Before we look at the elements of confidentiality though, one important thing to note (because it will help you understand the cases) is that claimants for breach of confidence will usually be looking to prevent information or pictures being published, rather than seeking to get damages after publication. This is because, in many of these cases, once confidential information is published, the damage is done: whereas with defamation, a trial can be used to clear a defendant's name, a trial for breach of confidence obviously cannot make the information secret again. For this reason, the courts are generally more willing to grant such injunctions in confidentiality cases than they would be in defamation actions.

An interim injunction is designed to be temporary and merely to 'hold the ring' until the issue can go to a full trial. However, it can take months for the trial to come on and, in many cases, by that time the information would be too old to make a decent news story or the story would have been overtaken by events. As a result, where an interim injunction is served, the media often does not bother taking the issue to trial, which means that in practice, the interim injunction actually has the same effect as a permanent one (there are, however, still limits on when the courts should give an interim injunction, which are covered on p. 246). On the other hand, if an interim injunction is not ordered, the claimant will often not bother going to a full trial, since the secret is out and a court case would only give it more publicity. The interim stage is therefore a very important one in this area.

BACKGROUND TO THE LAW

To understand the position of the law on confidentiality and privacy today, it will help to look back at how this position was reached. The law of confidentiality was born in the case of *Prince Albert* v *Strange* (1849), when Prince Albert obtained an injunction preventing publication of drawings made by himself and Queen Victoria, after unauthorised copies of them were made by someone on the staff of a printer, from whom the Royal couple had ordered some prints. From there, the law developed over the years, until by the 1990s, an action for breach of confidence was a recognised way to prevent disclosure or publication of confidential material. There were, however, distinct rules about when information would be considered confidential, and there was no general protection for privacy or information which people would prefer to keep private, unless it fell within the rules on confidentiality.

When the Human Rights Act (HRA) was passed in 1998, it was widely thought that a new legal action for invasion of privacy would be created, in order to put into effect the Article 8 right to respect for a person's private and family life. However, the Government has declined to create a new privacy law, so instead it has been up to the courts to apply Article 8 when relevant cases come before them. The courts have repeatedly stated that the HRA does not create a new, separate action for invasion of privacy, so instead they have developed and extended the law of confidentiality to take account of Article 8. However, over a series of cases brought by celebrities, this has led to the development of a new, broader form of breach of confidence action, which is in reality different from traditional breach of confidence and which many lawyers believe is in fact a privacy law in all but name. This new action is still officially part of the law of confidence and does not yet have an 'official' separate name, but was described in the key case of *Campbell* v *MGN* (2004) (see below) as 'misuse of private information', so that is the name used in this chapter. In both the new and the old forms of the action, the courts are taking account of the Human Rights Act, and seeking to strike a delicate balance between the Article 10 right to freedom of expression and the Article 8 right to respect for private and family life.

In this chapter, we look first at traditional breach of confidence claims – which are still very much part of the law – and then at the new 'misuse of private information' action. It is worth noting that many of the cases discussed under the heading of traditional breach of confidence, particularly those involving celebrities, would now be considered as cases of misuse of private information, and so the results might will be different if they were heard today.

BREACH OF CONFIDENCE

The classic definition of breach of confidence comes from the case of *Coco* v *A.N. Clark (Engineers) Ltd* (1969). The facts of the case are not relevant here, but in it, the court defined breach of confidence as arising where:

- the information disclosed or about to be disclosed 'has the necessary quality of confidence' (or in other words, is information that would be considered private rather than public);

- the information was obtained in circumstances which imposed 'an obligation of confidence'; and

- the defendant has made or intends to make unauthorised use of the information.

If all three elements are satisfied, there will be a breach of confidence, unless the defendant can claim a defence. The available defences are discussed later in this chapter but essentially there are three, which arise where the defendant can show that the information was published with the claimant's consent, or was already known to the public or there was a public interest reason for the publication.

■ Confidential information

What type of information will be considered confidential? The latest test for this was defined by the House of Lords in *Campbell* v *MGN* (2004), the case where model Naomi Campbell sued the *Mirror* over stories about her attending meetings of Narcotics Anonymous (see p. 238). Although this case was actually treated as an example of misuse of private information, rather than traditional breach of confidence, Lord Hope was talking about breach of confidence generally when he said that:

> The underlying question in all cases where it is alleged that there has been a breach of the duty of confidence is whether the information that was disclosed was private and not public . . . If the information is obviously private, the situation will be one where the person to whom it relates can reasonably expect his privacy to be respected.

In other words, if a reasonable person would think the information was confidential or private, then for the purposes of the law, it probably is. It was also stated in *Coco* v *A.N. Clark* that the information must have some degree of importance; the law will not protect the confidentiality of trivial material.

Examples of information which the courts have held to be 'obviously private' include ideas for commercial products, trade secrets, people's sex lives, health and medical treatment, diaries, company finances and personal photographs.

 In 2005, author J.K. Rowling won an injunction preventing publication of details of the plot of her forthcoming book, *Harry Potter and the Half-Blood Prince*. The injunction was extremely wide, preventing anyone who came into possession of the book or part of it from disclosing any information about it to anyone.

 In *Fraser* v *Thames TV* (1984), the claimant had developed a proposal for a TV drama series, based on the experiences of a pop group he had managed, comprising three female singers. The idea was discussed with the Thames' management, producers and writers, but was ultimately rejected. A little later, however, the company made a series, called 'Rock Follies', which was clearly based on the characters and stories in Fraser's proposal. He sued for breach of confidence, and evidence was given in court that the discussions he had had with the company, in which both sides were aiming to use the idea commercially, would be regarded in the industry as creating an obligation of confidentiality. His action was successful.

 In *X (HA)* v *Y* (1988), the *News of the World* discovered that two doctors working for the same health authority had been diagnosed with AIDS. The paper got its information from an employee at the hospital where they were being treated. They published the facts of the story and intended to do a follow-up naming the doctors, but the health authority was granted a permanent injunction preventing publication of the doctors' names or the places where they worked.

 In *X Ltd* v *Morgan Grampian* (1991), an unidentified source leaked information about a company called Tetra to the trade magazine *The Engineer*. The source said that the company was having financial problems and had prepared a business plan in order to seek a large bank loan. Tetra said that the information could only have come from the business plan, a copy of which had gone missing. It was granted an injunction preventing publication of the information.

Information about celebrities

The courts have made it clear that the mere fact that someone is a celebrity, and encourages publicity when it is to their benefit, does not mean that no information about them can ever be considered confidential. However, the law acknowledges that celebrities can reasonably be expected to accept that they will be more closely scrutinised by the media than ordinary people might expect to be. In addition, if a celebrity has willingly used particular aspects of their private life to gain publicity, they cannot expect the courts to give that area of their life the full protection of confidentiality.

In *Theakston v Mirror Group Newspapers* (2002), TV presenter Jamie Theakston tried, unsuccessfully, to suppress newspaper coverage of his visit to a brothel. The Court of Appeal pointed out that Mr Theakston had previously been quite happy to talk about his love life in interviews, presumably to enhance his image as a sex symbol and so advance his career. That being the case, the court would not restrict the freedom of the press to comment on related areas of his private life that he was less keen to publicise. (They did, however, impose an order preventing publication of photos of his visit; see below.)

Old information

In some cases the courts have found that information that would once have been considered confidential can stop being so after time has passed.

In *A-G v Jonathan Cape* (1976) the then Government requested an injunction to prevent publication of diaries written by a former Cabinet minister, Richard Crossman. Cabinet discussions are usually considered confidential, but the court refused an injunction, because the information related to discussions that had taken place at least ten years before and could no longer be considered confidential.

Photographs

The courts have always accepted that pictures can count as confidential information for the purposes of breach of confidence (after all, the action for breach of confidence was created to protect Queen Victoria's sketches). In recent cases, they have suggested that photographs may actually be more likely to be considered confidential material than information conveying exactly the same facts would be, and have shown themselves very ready to use the law of confidence to prevent the use of unauthorised photographs.

In *Creation Records v News Group Newspapers* (1997), a photo shoot was arranged for the cover of an Oasis album, involving a white Rolls-Royce in an empty swimming pool. There was heavy security around the set, but a photographer for the *Sun* managed to get unauthorised access to the area, and took some shots which were similar to the one eventually chosen for the album cover. The *Sun* published the picture and offered glossy posters of the shot to readers for £1.99. It was taken to court by the record company and the court found that publication was a breach of confidence.

In *Theakston* (see above), the Court of Appeal refused to suppress revelations of the TV presenter's visit to a brothel, but granted an injunction preventing publication of photos of him there. It said that photos were much more intrusive than merely reporting a story.

In *Douglas And Others v Hello! Ltd And Others* (2003) the film stars Catherine Zeta-Jones and Michael Douglas sued *Hello!* magazine for publishing photographs of their wedding, taken secretly by a photographer who had sneaked in. The couple had sold exclusive rights to pictures of the wedding to *OK!* magazine, and so banned all their guests from taking photographs at the wedding, and put security provisions in place to prevent the press from getting in. Bearing this in mind, as well as the fact that it was a wedding, the Court of Appeal held that the photographs were plainly taken on a private occasion and disclosed information that was private, and 'the intrusion [by the photographer] into the private domain was itself objectionable'. *Hello!* argued that the pictures could not be considered confidential material since, rather than keeping them private, the couple had sold the rights to *OK!* However, the Court of Appeal said that the right of celebrities to sell pictures of themselves was comparable to a trade secret (such as the formula for a drink or the design of a machine), and was therefore protected by the law of confidentiality in the same way. The same protection might well not have been given to an unauthorised report of the wedding, even if it described exactly what would have been seen in the photos. (The court also refused to give the same protection to *OK!* magazine, who had lost sales as a result of the *Hello!* feature, because, the court said, the right of celebrities to sell pictures of themselves was not one which could be transferred to another party).

■ The obligation of confidence

As we have seen, the information concerned must be of a kind that might reasonably be thought of as private or confidential. In addition, it must have been obtained in circumstances where the person obtaining it realised that it was intended to be kept confidential. Classic examples of these kinds of circumstances would be where confidential information is passed between lawyer and client, doctor and patient, priest and parishioner, and the following are some of the other situations where the courts have held that an obligation of confidentiality may arise. However, the list is not closed and new situations may be found as relevant cases arise.

Personal relationships

The law of confidentiality was first used to protect revelations about private relationships in *Argyll (Duchess)* v *Argyll, Duke of Argyll* [1967], where the Duke of Argyll was prevented from publishing details of his stormy marriage, on the grounds that married couples owed each other a duty of confidentiality. In more recent cases, the courts have agreed that this protection can be extended to personal relationships outside marriage, but they have made it clear that the more short-lived or casual the relationship, the less likely it is that revelations about it will be protected.

In *A* v *B* (2002), the footballer Gary Flitcroft tried unsuccessfully to prevent publication of a story about his extra-marital affairs. The Court of Appeal overturned an injunction which had been previously granted, saying that 'transient' relationships could not contain the same element of confidentiality as those between spouses or long-term, committed partners. It declined to define exactly what would make a relationship sufficiently committed to imply confidentiality, but in this case, one of the relationships had lasted for three months, the other for a year; the court made the point that neither of them was serious enough for Mr Flitcroft to consider leaving his wife. The court also pointed out that, as a Premiership footballer, Mr Flitcroft was something of a role model, which meant that it could be argued there was a slight degree of public interest in the truth about his behaviour being revealed. In addition, the mistress in the case had a right to freedom of expression, so her wish to tell her story had to be weighed against Mr Flitcroft's wish for the story to be suppressed (however, this may no longer be a sound argument; see p. 240).

In *Theakston* (see above), the Court of Appeal said part of its reasoning for not allowing an injunction against reports of the TV presenter's visit to a brothel was that the relationship between prostitute and client was too transitory to be protected by confidentiality.

In 2004, Lord Coe, the former athlete who was at the time leading Britain's bid for the 2012 Olympics, tried unsuccessfully to get an injunction preventing revelations about an extra-marital affair he had had. The High Court said that the woman involved wanted to tell the story, and her right to freedom of expression outweighed his to privacy (in the later, 'misuse of private information' cases, this approach seems to have shifted – see *McKennit* v *Ash* [2005], p. 240).

Even where the relationship is a relatively casual one, however, the courts may step in to prevent disclosure of intimate details, which are considered to be confidential even if the basic facts of the relationship are not.

In *Barrymore* v *News Group* (1997), the comedian Michael Barrymore was granted an injunction preventing publication of details divulged by a man whom he had had a sexual relationship with, while he was married. The court said that merely divulging the fact that the relationship existed might not be breach of confidence, especially as Mr Barrymore had already said publicly that he was homosexual. However, going into details about what Mr Barrymore had said about private matters, such as his relationship with his wife, as the defendant had, 'crossed the line'.

Sexual relationships are not the only personal relationships in which an obligation of confidence can arise. The courts have also found that where information is obtained as a result of a friendship, there may be an obligation of confidence which should prevent its disclosure.

In *Stephens* v *Avery* (1988), the claimant and defendant were friends. The claimant, who was married, had a sexual relationship with a woman who was later killed by her husband. The murder case was much written about by the press, and during this time, the defendant told the *Mail on Sunday* about her friend's relationship with the victim and details were published. The claimant successfully sued her friend (or perhaps by then ex-friend) for damages.

Employer–employee relationships

Some employment contracts contain a specific provision, banning the employee from revealing information obtained as a result of their work. Most celebrities, for example, would include such a clause in the contracts of anyone working closely with them, such as nannies or personal assistants, and such clauses are also common in industries where trade secrets are important. In these cases, divulging information gained through work would be a breach of confidence.

In *Archer* v *Williams* (2003), Lady Archer, wife of the novelist Lord Archer, obtained an injunction against her former PA, who had attempted to sell stories about her to the national papers. There was a confidentiality clause in her contract.

In *A-G* v *Barker* (1990), a former servant of the royal family wrote a book, *Courting Disaster*, about his work. His employment contract contained a confidentiality clause, and because of this, the Court of Appeal granted an injunction preventing publication anywhere in the world, at any time.

However, the fact that an employment contract does not contain a confidentiality clause does not mean there will be no breach of confidence if information is disclosed. By accepting an employment contract, all employees take on an implied duty of 'fidelity' to their employer, which means they have an obligation not to do anything which would damage the employer's interest. This duty means that information gained through work is usually obtained in circumstances where an obligation of confidence exists. Leaking it can therefore be a breach of confidence, even after the person has left the job.

In one recent case, the High Court has held that information obtained through employment is not necessarily obtained under an obligation of confidence, although the situation was quite unusual.

In *Tillery Valley Foods* v *Channel 4* (2004), an investigative journalist took a job at a Tillery factory where food was prepared for hospitals and other public organisations. She secretly filmed various procedures which suggested that the company's hygiene standards were in doubt, for a Channel 4 programme. Allegations based on the film were put to Tillery for its comment, and it responded by seeking an injunction, on the grounds that the information was obtained in breach of confidence. Tillery's lawyer agreed that the disclosure of the information might be in the public interest, but said that the court would need to balance that against the company's interest in not having it made public, and part of that balancing act would involve giving the company an effective right to reply, for which it would need both time and access to the material in the film.

The court refused to entertain this idea at all. Mr Justice Mann said this was not a case of breach of confidence, but of potential defamation. The claimants had tried to 'squash' it into the law of confidence, because they were unlikely to get an injunction for defamation owing to the fact that the defendants believed they could prove justification (see p. xx). He said that the fact that the information was obtained through an employment relationship did not necessarily mean it was confidential.

In 1998, the Public Interest Disclosure Act was passed to protect 'whistleblowers', employees who disclose their employer's secrets in order to expose wrongdoing (examples would be an employee who reveals that safety procedures are not being followed or one who discloses information about insider dealing). However, the protection of the Act only applies to the employee and not to the media who report their disclosures. The media's role in publishing such reports would be covered by the usual law on breach of confidence (though in many such cases the public interest defence would apply).

Government employees

Civil servants and members of the armed forces and secret services do not have written employment contracts, but the courts have accepted that they have a duty of confidence with regard to information obtained through their work. The Official Secrets Act 1989 provides for government employees who leak information to be prosecuted, but over the years, juries have proved to be rather reluctant to convict, unless the leaks concerned real threats to national security. As a result, successive governments have turned to the law of confidence to protect their secrets instead, and the courts have been, on the whole, very willing to help them do so.

 In 1986, Peter Wright, a former senior MI5 officer, wrote a book, *Spycatcher*, about his work, which contained allegations of misconduct by the service, and even treason (though the allegations were actually a small part of the book). The book was published in Australia, but the *Guardian* published details of the allegations. The Government was able to get an injunction against further publication, by the *Guardian* or any other UK media, on the grounds that members of the security services owed a lifelong duty of confidentiality. It took two years, during which the book was published in several other countries and read by many people in the UK, before the injunction against the press was eventually lifted because the information had become public knowledge (see below). Even then, the House of Lords reiterated its view that Mr Wright owed a duty of confidentiality, which he had breached.

 In *A-G v BBC* (1987), the Government secured an injunction preventing broadcast of a series of radio programmes called 'My Country, Right or Wrong', because they featured interviews with ex-members of the security services, even though no secrets were revealed. The injunction was only lifted when the Attorney-General read transcripts of the programmes and realised that they were a completely harmless discussion of the moral issues associated with the work of a security service.

In some cases, the Government has successfully used the law of confidence to help them 'manage' news, even where the information concerned was always going to be made public at a later date (though this may now become more difficult as the Human Rights Act requires courts to take into account the extent to which information is about to be made public – see p. 246).

 In 1999, the *Sunday Telegraph* obtained leaked information from a report on a public inquiry examining the unsuccessful police investigation into the racist murder of a black teenager, Stephen Lawrence. The report was due to be published a few days later, but the then Home Secretary successfully obtained an injunction preventing publication of any information from it.

In addition to the general obligations of confidence on government employees, discussions between Cabinet Ministers are protected by confidentiality.

Documents relating to court cases

During a court case, the two sides exchange documents which are to be used in evidence. Disclosure of these documents to anyone else is a breach of confidence (and may be contempt of court as well). The same applies to statements made by suspects to prosecuting authorities.

 In *Distillers Co* v *Times Newspapers* (1975), the *Sunday Times* was researching a story about a drug called Thalidomide, which was later revealed to cause serious birth defects. The paper bought documents which had been disclosed by Distillers to an expert witness. Although there was a clear public interest in the issue, the court granted an injunction against publication of details from the documents, because there was an even greater public interest in protecting confidentiality during the exchange of documents before a trial.

 In *Bunn* v *BBC* (1998), the BBC made a documentary about the Serious Fraud Office (SFO), which the SFO cooperated with. The SFO gave the programme makers a statement by Robert Bunn, a defendant in a fraud trial. The court held that disclosure of such statements could be a breach of confidence (though in this case, there was no breach because the judge in the case had read the statement in open court and therefore it was in the public domain – see below).

Confidential circumstances

An obligation of confidentiality can also be created by the circumstances in which the information is obtained, regardless of whether there is a relationship between the person the information is from or about, and the person obtaining it. In *A-G* v *Guardian Newspapers (No 2)* (1990), Lord Goff said that a duty of confidence could arise when confidential information comes to someone's attention 'in circumstances where he has notice . . . that the information is confidential, with the effect that it would be just in all the circumstances that he should be precluded from disclosing the information to others.'

Lord Goff cited the examples of an obviously confidential document being wafted by an electric fan out of an office window into the street, or a private diary being dropped in a public place. In both cases, anyone picking up the item would be under an obligation of confidence with regard to its contents, because it would be obvious that the information is private.

 In *Creation Records* v *News Group Newspapers* (1997), the case involving a photo shoot for the cover of an Oasis album (see above), the court pointed out that the fact that the record company had taken security precautions to keep people away from the shoot clearly indicated that the way the scene had been set up for the pictures was confidential.

Exceptional circumstances

In a handful of cases, the courts have used the law of confidentiality to protect the identities of people involved in particularly notorious crimes. The cases do not fit very comfortably within the rules of the law on confidentiality, but it appears that the courts have used that law, in combination with the right to life under s2 of the Human Rights Act, to fill a loophole, where there is evidence that publishing the identity or whereabouts of the individuals could put them at real risk, and there is no other way to prevent such publication.

 In *Venables and Thompson* v *News Group Newspapers and Others* (2001), a permanent injunction was granted, preventing publication of any information which might lead to the identification of the two young men who, ten years earlier, had killed a toddler, James Bulger. The two were about to be released from prison, and were being given new identities. The injunction lasts for the whole of their lives.

In *X (formerly known as Mary Bell)* v *SO* (2003), the court considered the case of Mary Bell, who in 1968, when she was 11, was convicted of murdering two younger children. She was released from prison in 1980 and given a new identity, but over the years the press had tracked her down, and she had had to change identities several more times. During that time she had also cooperated with a book about herself. When her daughter was born, the child was made a ward of court, which meant that the press could be prevented from identifying her but, even so, when parents where they lived found out who her mother was, the child was hounded out of school. The wardship ended when she was 18, so her mother applied for an injunction guaranteeing both her and her daughter lifelong anonymity. It was granted, on the grounds that she was in a fragile mental state and press intrusion could have serious consequences for both herself and her daughter.

In 2004, the High Court issued an order banning the media from publishing any information about Maxine Carr, who was the girlfriend of Ian Huntley, who murdered two schoolgirls in the Cambridgeshire village of Soham in 2002. Carr gave him a false alibi for the time of the murder and was sent to prison for 42 months. She received death threats and after her release from prison was given a new identity in a different area. Reporters tracked her down nevertheless and she went to court to get an injunction; the hearing was held within hours of her being found by the press. The injunction forbids the press not only from publishing any information about her new identity, appearance or whereabouts, but also from even trying to find out such information.

The position of the media

In many cases, the media will be a third party in breach of confidence cases. For example, if the nanny to a famous singer's children decides to reveal secrets of the family's life to a newspaper, it is the relationship between the nanny and the singer which creates the obligation of confidence. However, once that obligation exists, it covers not only the nanny, but also anyone else who makes unauthorised use of the information, if they know it was obtained as a result of a breach of confidence.

Therefore, if the media publish confidential information obtained under an obligation of confidence, they can be liable, unless they did not know it was obtained in breach of confidence. Usually this will be obvious from the nature of the information and its source, but where the media are genuinely unaware of the obligation of confidence, there is no breach.

In *British Steel Corp* v *Granada TV* (1981), Granada journalists obtained secret documents from an employee at British Steel. It was pointed out in court that as they were labelled 'confidential' and 'restricted', the journalists must have known they were not intended to be seen by anyone other than top management at the company. They were ordered to return them.

In *PCR Ltd* v *Dow Jones* (1998), PCR published a newsletter which was circulated to a small number of its clients, and contained confidential information about the international cocoa market. A journalist, researching this market, talked to a number of people who happened to have seen this newsletter, and who gave her information they had obtained from it, even though they were under an obligation not to disclose the information. The journalist used some of the information in her report, and PCR sued for breach of confidence. The court found that as the journalist did not know the information she was given was confidential, neither she nor her employer could be in breach of confidence.

■ Unauthorised use

In media cases, this element is usually straightforward: publishing confidential information without consent is clearly unauthorised use of it. A more unusual situation is where a defendant has authorisation to use information for one purpose, but uses it for another; the courts have held that this can be considered unauthorised use.

In *Schering Chemicals* v *Falkman* (1982), the chemical company employed David Elstein, a TV programme-maker, to give media training to some of its employees. As part of this relationship with the company, he obtained information about its work, and decided that there was a TV programme to be made about allegations that the company's drugs could cause birth defects. Mr Elstein did not use any material he had gained as a result of his work with the company, gathering material instead from publicly available sources but, even so, the Court of Appeal held that he had acted in breach of confidence. The main argument for this result was that Mr Elstein had unfairly exploited his confidential relationship with Schering: he had been paid to help improve its image and, as a result of that job, had gone on to make a programme (for which he had also been paid) which did exactly the opposite. The court issued an injunction preventing the programme from being broadcast. The decision has been criticised, given that there was a clear public interest in the subject of the programme.

MISUSE OF PRIVATE INFORMATION

As explained at the beginning of this chapter, in the past few years the courts appear to have developed a new form of breach of confidence, which protects information in situations that would not have been covered by the traditional form of the action, and involves the courts in a balancing act between two rights, both drawn from the Human Rights Act 1998: the Article 10 right to freedom of expression, and the Article 8 right to respect for a person's private life.

The new variant of confidentiality is accepted to have been created in *Campbell* v *MGN* [2004], the case where model Naomi Campbell sued over the *Mirror*'s publication of photos and stories relating to her treatment for drug addiction. It was in that case that the claim was described by one judge as 'misuse of private information'. It has since been used in other cases involving information (or pictures) which can more sensibly be described as 'private' than as 'confidential', even though the claims were technically brought under the law of confidence.

In *Campbell*, the House of Lords held that in cases involving 'misuse of private information', a two-stage test should be applied (in place of the three-stage test in *Coco* v *Clark* – see p. 230). The court should ask:

- did the claimant have a reasonable expectation of privacy with respect to the information disclosed? and if so,

- is the person's right to privacy more important, in the circumstances, than someone's else's right to freedom of expression (usually, though not always, the media's right)?

Reasonable expectation of privacy

In deciding whether the information was of a kind to create a reasonable expectation of privacy, the court in *Campbell* said the question would be a simple one: was the information obviously private? Where the answer was not obvious, Lord Hope suggested that the courts ask:

> whether disclosure of the information about the individual ('A') would give substantial offence to A, assuming that A was placed in similar circumstances and was a person of ordinary sensibilities . . . The mind that has to be examined is that, not of the reader in general, but of the person who is affected by the publicity.'

In effect, this requires judges to make a value judgement about the kind of information which should be protected and the following cases give some examples of their conclusions.

In *Campbell*, the case concerned a story and pictures published in the *Mirror*. The photographs showed Naomi Campbell arriving at a hall in London, which the story (correctly) said was the venue for a meeting of the support group for drug abusers, Narcotics Anonymous. It went on to detail how often she went to meetings and what was likely to happen there. Ms Campbell had previously, on several occasions, denied having a drug problem; in fact she had specifically stated that drug abuse was a big problem in the modelling industry, but she was not one of those involved. The court said that publication of the basic facts of Ms Campbell's drug problem, and the fact that she was attending Narcotics Anonymous, was permissible as it corrected a false image she had previously presented (see below). However, the precise details of her treatment should be protected (as details of someone's medical treatment have always been in the law of confidentiality).

As for the photographs, Lord Hope said that the pictures were not obviously private, because they were taken on a public street and did not show her in an embarrassing light. Therefore, it was necessary to ask what their effect would be on someone in her position; as a recovering drug addict, he said, she would be vulnerable and the publication might well adversely affect her treatment. This suggested there was a legitimate expectation of privacy and the pictures should not have been used.

In *McKennitt v Ash* (2005), the case involved a book written by Ms Ash, about her travels with Ms McKennitt, who is a very successful Canadian folk singer. The two had been friends, and Ms Ash had toured with Ms McKennitt, but they had fallen out before the book was written. The book discussed, among other things, Ms McKennitt's personal and sexual relationships; her personal feelings, including her reaction to the death of her fiancé some years earlier; her health and diet; her emotional vulnerability; and details of a dispute between her, Ms Ash and Ms Ash's business partner concerning a property purchase. In the initial High Court hearing the judge pointed out that Ms Ash herself, in her book, had referred to the fact that it would contain revelations that were only available because of their close friendship. In the circumstances of such a close friendship, the court said, it was not surprising that Ms McKennitt had a 'reasonable expectation' that conversations between them, about personal matters, would stay private. The court granted an injunction banning further publication, along with £5,000 damages. The decision was upheld by the Court of Appeal, which said that the initial judgment had struck the correct balance between Articles 8 and 10.

In 2005, model Elizabeth Jagger was awarded an injunction against further publication of CCTV images which showed her and her boyfriend, as the court put it, 'engaging in sexual activities' just inside the closed door of a nightclub. The court said that this was a situation in which she had a legitimate expectation of privacy, and there was no public interest in the images being published.

In *HRH Prince of Wales v Associated Newspapers Ltd* (2006), Prince Charles sued the *Mail on Sunday* for publishing extracts from diaries he had kept on overseas trips. After such trips, copies of the diaries were routinely sent to a number of the Prince's friends and contacts, and anyone else who he thought might be interested or amused by them. They contained no personal details, but descriptions of his experiences and impressions, such as his view of Chinese officials as 'appalling old waxworks'. The court held that the Prince had a reasonable expectation of privacy, because he had only made the journals available to a selected group, rather than to the public generally; when sent out, the diaries were always in envelopes marked 'Private and confidential'.

In traditional confidentiality cases, it was held that information could only be the subject of a breach of confidence if it was true. This appears not to be the case with the 'misuse of private information' variant of the action.

In *McKennitt v Ash* (see above), the claimant said that many of the 'revelations' about her were inaccurate, distorted or misleading. It was suggested that if that was the case, those revelations could not be considered confidential, but the High Court disagreed: 'the protection of the law would be illusory if a claimant, in relation to a long and garbled story, was obliged to spell out which of the revelations are accepted as true, and which are said to be false.' The Court of Appeal agreed.

■ Privacy v freedom of expression

If the court finds that the information (or photographs) create an expectation of privacy, the next stage is to weigh the claimant's right to privacy against the right to freedom of expression. In *Campbell*, the House of Lords said that as part of this process, the courts should take into account the justifications put forward for interfering with each right, and apply a test of proportionality: would the benefit of suppressing the information outweigh the benefit of publishing it?

In weighing up these issues, the English courts also have to take into account a key decision of the European Court of Human Rights, which was decided two months after *Campbell*. In **Von Hannover v Germany** (2004), Princess Caroline of Monaco went to the European Court over press pictures taken of her going about her daily life. Although she is not frequently featured in the UK press, the papers in some other European countries have a fascination with the princess, and she complained that she was constantly being followed and photographed by paparazzi when she was going about normal daily activities like shopping or taking her children to school. The German courts had found against her, on the grounds that as a public figure, she had to accept that the public had a legitimate interest in knowing about even her ordinary daily life. The European Court of Human Rights, however, disagreed, and said that the key question when balancing the rights of privacy and freedom of expression was how far the material published contributed to 'a debate of general interest'. In this case, it said, the pictures made no real contribution to such debate. There was no legitimate public interest in seeing pictures of Princess Caroline when she was not performing her official role, and she had a legitimate expectation of privacy for her private life, even when she was in public places.

In *Campbell*, the House of Lords said that balancing the two rights meant that part of the publication was justified and part of it not. Ms Campbell had, in the past, gone out of her way to deny that she had a drug problem, and it was in the public interest to know that she had been lying about this. Therefore, with regard to the information that she was a drug addict, and was receiving treatment, the paper's freedom of expression outweighed her right to privacy and it was within the law to publish that information. However, there was not such a strong public interest in knowing the details of her treatment (such as where and how often she attended meetings, and what happened at them). In addition, the photos were particularly intrusive, given that they were taken secretly, when Ms Campbell was at the door of a Narcotics Anonymous meeting. Therefore, with regard to the photos and the detailed information about treatment, Ms Campbell's right to privacy outweighed the paper's right to freedom of expression.

In the case of Prince Charles' diaries, the *Mail on Sunday* had pointed out that the comments in the diaries showed that he was expressing opinions on political matters, something which the royal family are traditionally not expected to do, and this was something that the public had a right to know about and debate. The court said that this factor did not mean that the paper's freedom of expression outweighed the right to privacy, because the comments made only a minimal contribution to public debate.

In *McKennitt*, the court made it clear that the approach in the Princess Caroline case was not limited to cases involving photographs, but created a general principle that people have a legitimate expectation to be protected from intrusion, even when they are in public places. In this case, the court had to weigh Ms Ash's right to freedom of expression with regard to telling the story of her friendship with Ms McKennitt, against Ms McKennitt's right to privacy. The court found that if a person wants to publish information about their relationship with someone else, and that information is of a kind that would normally create an expectation of privacy, the material published has to be shaped in such a way as to protect the other person's privacy. In the High Court, Mr Justice Eady commented that: 'It does not follow that, because one can reveal one's own private life, that one can also expose confidential matters in respect of which others are entitled to protection if their consent is not forthcoming.' In *CC* v *AB* (2006), the claimant, a well-known sports figure, successfully applied for a temporary injunction to stop his affair with a married woman being revealed by the woman's husband. Assessing the competing rights of freedom of expression and privacy, the judge was influenced by the fact that the defendant clearly wanted revenge on the claimant, and had behaved threateningly, and that the claimant's wife and children had rights to privacy which deserved protection, even if it was the claimant who had put that privacy at risk. He agreed to issue an injunction preventing the claimant from talking to the media about the affair, or publishing details on the internet.

 In 2006, the limits of the Princess Caroline case were discussed again – with different results – when Elton John applied for an injunction to stop the *Daily Mail* publishing a picture of him in the street. The picture was taken shortly after he had arrived home and showed him walking from his car with his driver. Mr Justice Eady rejected the application, on the grounds that the photograph did not convey any kind of private information, and was the equivalent to a shot of someone 'popping to the shops for a pint of milk'. There was no harassment, as in the Princess Caroline case.

As we can see from the cases discussed in this chapter, this is a fast-developing area of the law, and important principles have shifted even in the past three years, as shown by the contrast between the Sebastian Coe case and *McKennitt* v *Ash* and *CC* v *AB*, and between the judgment in the Princess Caroline case and those of Theakston, Flitcroft and Elton John. With this in mind, you should be aware that the cases in this chapter are very much a guideline, and if cases with similar facts come to court today, they could be decided differently.

DEFENCES

There are three defences to a claim for breach of confidence:

- consent;
- information in the public domain;
- public interest.

Consent is self-explanatory; if the person who confidential information belongs to, or is about, agrees to its publication, there can be no breach of confidence. The other two defences are explained below.

The defences all apply to both traditional breach of confidence and the misuse of private information type of action, but the recent misuse of private information cases (especially *McKennitt*, see below), suggest there are some differences in the way they apply.

Defendants can also escape liability if a case is brought too late: claims for either type of breach of confidence must be brought within six years from the date of the breach.

■ Information in the public domain

If information is already known to the public – regardless of whether or not it was divulged by the claimant – it cannot be considered confidential, and so there can be no breach of confidence. In a number of cases, the courts have discussed the issue of how widely known information has to be before it can be considered to be in the public domain. In *Lennon* v *News Group Newspapers* (1978) (see below) and other cases, the courts have asked the question of whether information is known to 'a substantial number of people' which suggests that if it is only known, for example, to a handful of people, it will not be in the public domain. However, as these cases show, the courts have not always been consistent in their approach.

In *Lennon* v *News Group Newspapers* (1978), John Lennon tried to prevent his ex-wife Cynthia from selling stories about their marriage to the *News of the World*. He was refused an injunction, because both of them had already talked to the press about their relationship in the past, so the information could not be considered confidential.

In *A-G* v *Guardian Newspapers Ltd (No 2)* (1990), the House of Lords reconsidered the interim injunction forbidding publication of information contained in the book *Spycatcher* (see p. 235). The interim injunction had been imposed in 1986, but in the intervening months, the book had been published in the USA, and the allegations in it reported worldwide. The House of Lords found that the information was in the public domain, and refused to impose a permanent injunction.

In 1982, the *Watford Observer* put together a story about a local company, Sun Printers. It was based on a document which had been leaked to the paper, which said that the company was losing money and its owner, the media magnate Robert Maxwell, wanted to cut staff. Mr Maxwell was able to get an interim injunction preventing publication, but the paper challenged the order. It pointed out that although the document had originally been distributed only to a small number of company managers, it was later circulated to many more people, including officials of the relevant trade unions and, as a result, the paper argued, could no longer be considered confidential. The Court of Appeal agreed, and for this and other reasons (see below) discharged the injunction.

In 2000, Prime Minister Tony Blair and his wife applied for an injunction against publication of details of their family life, disclosed by their former nanny. By the time the application was heard, over a million copies of the *Mail on Sunday*, containing the story, were already in the process of being distributed. Nevertheless, the court allowed an injunction preventing further publication.

The issue of of whether partial revelations mean information is in the public domain is a particularly sensitive one where the information is personal. With information such as a trade secret, once the secret is out, no further damage can be done. However, with personal information, the courts have found that further revelations after an initial publication can still cause distress, and so information needs to be very widely available before the courts will consider it in the public domain.

In *Loreena McKennitt* v *Niema Ash and Purple Ink Press* (see above), one of the private revelations which Ms McKennitt complained about was her reaction to her fiance's death in a sailing accident some years earlier. Ms Ash claimed that as the singer had previously given interviews about her fiance's death, as part of her campaign to prevent similar accidents, the matter was in the public domain. The court said that where a case involved personal information, the fact that the information had been revealed to one group of readers did not mean that fresh revelations to different groups could not cause grief or distress. For such information, protection should only be lost where the information is so generally accessible that it can no longer be considered confidential.

In addition, where information is personal, there may be a difference between revelation of particular facts, and disclosure of intimate details surrounding those facts.

In *McKennitt*, the court was influenced by the fact that the defendant said she disliked personal publicity, and would only give interviews on restricted subjects; with regard to her fiance's death, she had only said enough in interviews as was necessary to get across the message about safety at sea. The court found that there was a clear difference between what was in the public domain as the result of a carefully-measured interview, and the eight pages in which the book author described her friend's 'pitifully grief-stricken reaction' to the death in close-up detail.

It is possible for information that is clearly in the public domain to begin with to then become confidential due to the way it is combined with other information. The main example here is addresses: most addresses in the UK can be found on various public lists, such as the electoral roll or the Land Registry lists. In this sense, they are clearly in the public domain. However, combining an address with other information (such as the name of the person who lives there) could give it the quality of confidentiality which the law would protect. As the cases show, however, this is another area where the approach of the courts can vary.

In 2001, model and campaigner Heather Mills applied for an injunction to stop the *Sun* publishing the address of a new home she had bought near Hove. The injunction was refused, on the grounds that it was already widely known that she lived in the area, and in a busy town like Hove it would be impossible to keep the exact address secret.

In *Green Corns Ltd* v *Claverley* (2005), the claimants were a company which provides residential care for childen referred to it by local authorities. They had chosen four houses in the Wolverhampton area to use as homes, and the *Wolverhampton Express and Star* reported this, publishing the addresses of the homes and describing the children who were likely to be sent there as 'yobs' and 'sex offenders'. After demonstrations were held outside the houses, Green Corns sought an injunction against further publication of addresses. The paper argued that the addresses were in the public domain: neighbours would know which houses were being used and anyone could find out the information by searching through the Land Registry. The court disagreed: by combining the addresses with comments on the disabilities and characteristics of the children, the paper would essentially be creating new information beyond that which was in the public domain.

▥ Public interest

To succeed in this defence, the media must prove that the public interest in receiving the confidential information is greater than the public interest in protection for confidential material. In cases where this arises, the courts have been very clear that there is a distinction between 'the public interest' and 'things the public are interested in'. In general, there will be a public interest in stories which, for example, expose serious wrongdoing, reveal information which affects people's daily lives, health or safety, or which relate to important issues of public debate. There will not, as a rule, be a public interest in stories about the sex lives, eating habits or other activities of celebrities, except in very limited circumstances.

In *Initial Services* v *Putterill* (1968), an ex-employee of a laundry company gave a newspaper company documents which suggested that it had been evading tax. The Court of Appeal refused the company an injunction, on the grounds that this was the kind of misconduct which it was in the public interest to know about.

In *X* v *Y*, the case concerning two doctors with AIDS (see p. 231), the paper argued that there was a public interest in publishing the information. The court agreed that if there was any danger to patients, it would be in the public interest for the general issue to be discussed, but revealing the doctors' names might have the effect of dissuading people who might have AIDS from seeking help, because of concern that their condition might be made public, and that would be against the public interest.

In the case involving the *Watford Observer* and Sun Printers (see p. 242), the judge accepted that it was in the public interest for people in the Watford area to know that a major local employer was considering cutting staff.

 In *Green Corns* v *Claverley* (see p. 241), the case involving publication of the addresses of homes for children in local authority care, the paper argued that it was in the public interest for there to be public debate over how such children were cared for. The court agreed that these were issues of public interest, but said that preventing publication of the addresses did not prevent the debate.

 In *Hubbard* v *Vosper* (1972), a court refused to suppress a book which detailed various courses run by Scientologists, on the grounds that there was 'good ground for thinking that these courses contain such dangerous material that it is in the public interest that it should be made known.'

 In *Times Newspapers Ltd* v *MGN* (1993), the *Mirror* obtained an early copy of the former Prime Minister Margaret Thatcher's autobiography. The book was not yet published, and the publishers had arranged an exclusive serialisation deal with the *Sunday Times*. Both the publishers and the *Sunday Times* tried to prevent the *Mirror* from publishing extracts, which revealed Baroness Thatcher's not very complimentary opinions of her successor, John Major, and his colleagues. The newspaper said that these matters were of public interest, given that at the time the story was published, the Conservative Party was holding its annual conference, at which they were trying to put across the impression that the party was harmonious and united. The Court of Appeal agreed and no injunction was granted.

 In 2000, the Labour fundraiser Lord Levy was refused an injunction against *The Times*, which had a story about his tax affairs, obtained via confidential information. The court said that Lord Levy was known as a high-profile supporter of the Labour Party and the party's manifesto contained a promise to close loopholes in the tax system. It was therefore in the public interest to find out whether Lord Levy's attitude to his own taxes was in line with the aims the party had expressed.

 In *Lion Laboratories* v *Evans* (1985), an employee of a company which made breathalysers used by the police leaked information to the press which showed that the devices were not as accurate as claimed. Even though there was no suggestion that the company had done anything wrong, it was refused an injunction, because this was clearly information that the public had a right to know, given that an inaccurate reading could lead to a wrongful conviction.

 In *Cork* v *McVicar* (1984), a journalist interviewed a former police officer about allegations of police corruption. Parts of the interview were stated by the officer to be 'off the record', but the journalist was secretly taping the whole conversation and used the 'off the record' parts in the story. A court refused to issue an injunction suppressing publication, because the information clearly revealed matters that were of great public interest.

Where a story is claimed to be in the public interest because it exposes wrongdoing, the courts have held that it is not necessary to prove that wrongdoing actually took place before a public interest defence can succeed. In *A-G* v *Guardian Newspapers (No 2)* (1988) (part of the *Spycatcher* litigation – see earlier), the Court of Appeal said that before using confidential information alleging wrongdoing, the media should assess the reliability of the source, do their own investigations into the allegations, and give due weight to the findings of any investigations that had already taken place, but they did not need to be able to prove the allegations true. In other words, as long as the media have acted responsibly, publication of allegations of serious wrongdoing will usually be in the public interest.

However, there is a situation where the courts have found that, although media investigations into wrongdoing are justified, the evidence found should be handed to the appropriate authorities, rather than being published.

In *Francome* v *Mirror Group* (1984), the *Mirror* was given transcripts of telephone conversations, which it believed indicated that the jockey speaking on the phone was involved in serious misconduct and possibly even a criminal conspiracy. The court said that, given that there might be a trial as a result of the findings, it could not find any public interest in publication which would not be equally well served by handing the material to the police or the Jockey Club, and therefore publication was not covered by the public interest defence. The case is, however, quite an unusual one in that the court was influenced by the fact that the tapes had been obtained through a telephone tap, which was an offence under the Wireless Telegraphy Act 1949. No similar ruling has been made in any other case involving the public interest defence.

The public interest and celebrities

As stated above, stories about celebrities' private lives are not, as a rule, subjects of public interest, no matter how interesting the public finds them. However, there has traditionally been an exception to this principle, where the celebrity has presented a particular image to the public, and the confidential information shows this image to be false. However, given the recent recognition that celebrities have a legitimate expectation of privacy in their daily lives, particularly in *Hannover* and *McKennitt*, it may be that this only applies where stories reveal serious misbehaviour.

In *Campbell*, the House of Lords held that there was public interest in the *Mirror* revealing that Naomi Campbell was a drug addict, given that, during her career, she had frequently said that many models had problems with drugs, but that she did not.

In 2005, David and Victoria Beckham failed to get an injunction preventing their nanny from revealing details of their relationship, even though her employment contract contained a confidentiality clause. The nanny, who had lived with the couple for two years, told the *News of the World* she had witnessed a number of rows between them, and alleged that she had heard David Beckham say he wanted them to split up. The couple went to court, claiming that the confidentiality clause meant the revelations were a breach of confidence. However, Mr Justice Langley accepted the paper's argument that the revelations were in the public interest, because the couple presented themselves as blissfully happily married, and the nanny's revelations suggested that this impression was false. No injunction was ordered and, in 2006, the couple agreed a settlement with the newspaper; no details of the settlement were revealed.

In *Loreena McKevitt* v *Niema Ash and Purple Ink Press* (see above), the author claimed that the personal values Ms McKennitt presented herself as holding were not always reflected in her behaviour, and her book corrected this false impression. However, Mr Justice Eady rejected this argument, and said that while revelations of serious misbehaviour by a celebrity might be justified in the public interest, relatively trivial matters would not:

> the mere fact that a celebrity falls short from time to time, like everyone else, could not possibly justify exposure, in the supposed public interest, of every peccadilo or foible cropping up in everyday life.

Public interest in government stories

Where the claimant is the Government or another public body, the courts have said that a stricter public interest test should be imposed. In all other areas, the media must show that disclosure is in the public interest, but for disclosures of government information, the Government has to show that disclosure would cause harm to the public interest.

In *A-G* v *Guardian Newspapers (No 2)* (1988) (part of the *Spycatcher* litigation; see earlier), the House of Lords approved the approach of the Australian High Court in a case about government secrecy, which had said that in a democratic society, disclose of information that sheds light on the workings on government will usually be in the public interest and should be allowed. It should only be restrained if disclosure would cause harm to the public interest. That could not be the case here, because the information the Government sought to suppress was already available to the public from so many sources that further disclosure could not make any difference. The injunction against publication was lifted. However, the *Sunday Times* had published material from the book before it was even published, so the same argument could not be used for it, and it was ordered to pay the Government an account of profits (see p. 248).

The same approach may be applied to private companies when they are carrying out functions which might usually be fulfilled by a public body.

In 1994, the accountancy firm KPMG Peat Marwick sought an injunction preventing the *Liverpool Echo* from publishing information from a report it had prepared for Liverpool City Council. The report concerned a cable-laying contract which had lost the council a lot of money. The judge held that as the report might just as well have been prepared by the council's own people, it had to satisfy the same public interest test as for government information. On the facts, it was clear that this test was satisfied.

REMEDIES FOR BREACH OF CONFIDENCE

These remedies apply – as far as we know at this stage – both to traditional breach of confidence actions and claims involving misuse of private information.

▇ Injunction

As explained earlier, the main remedy for breach of confidence is an injunction. Claimants can apply for an injunction to prevent publication in the first place or to prevent further publication if the material has already been published. In either case, the injunction may be an interim one, which is designed to put the situation on hold until the issue is tried, or a permanent one, which is issued if a claimant proves their case at trial (in some cases an interim injunction will be issued before trial, and then if the claimant wins, it becomes a permanent one).

In practice, as explained at the beginning of this chapter, an interim injunction can often effectively kill a story without the defendant needing to prove their case at trial. A further problem is that they can be issued at very short notice (judges will do this over the phone, even at night), and it is not impossible for an injunction to be ordered just before a paper goes to press or even after printing has started. On the other hand, in many cases, if the media can successfully fight off an interim injunction, the claimant may not bother taking the matter to trial, because to do so would only give even more publicity to the information.

When considering either type of injunction, the Human Rights Act 1998 makes it clear that the courts must take into account the potential effect on press freedom. Section 12 of the Act states that if a court is asked to give any order which could affect freedom of expression, with regard to journalistic material, they must take into account the importance of the right to freedom of expression, and must consider the extent to which the material concerned is already in the public domain and any public interest in publication. Although this merely recognises defences which exist in English law, it makes it clear that the possibility of such defences applying must be considered even in the application for an interim injunction, and not just at trial. The court also has to consider 'any relevant privacy code'. This means that if a case involves the press, the courts are likely to look at whether, during work on the story, the journalists have behaved in accordance with the PCC Code, while in cases involving broadcast, they will look at the Ofcom Code or the BBC's own codes of practice. The overall effect of these provisions, as accepted by the Court of Appeal in *Douglas*, is that the courts must assess the merits of the case before they allow publication to be suppressed.

Special rules for interim injunctions

As seen in Chapter 14 on defamation, an injunction which prevents material being published in the first place is viewed as a serious restriction on freedom of expression, and although the courts are more willing to grant such injunctions in confidentiality cases than defamation ones, they still have to take into account some extra restrictions which the Human Rights Act puts on such injunctions. Section 12 provides that injunctions which restrain publication before trial should only be granted where the claimant can show that they are 'likely' to prove a breach of confidence if the case goes to trial. In *Cream Holdings* v *Banerjee* (2004), the House of Lords said this meant that in most cases, an interim injunction should only be ordered if the claimant could prove that it was more likely than not that they would win at trial. However, an injunction might also be granted in exceptional situations where the claimant could not prove they were likely to win, but where the consequences of disclosing the information would be especially serious for them.

In addition, s12 provides that a court should not grant an injunction unless:

- the journalist is present; or
- the claimant has taken all practical steps to notify the journalist; or
- there are compelling reasons why the journalist should not be notified.

In practice, these restrictions are often not difficult to get round; in the *Douglas* case (see p. 232), the initial temporary injunction was granted over the phone, late at night, after *OK!* said that it had tried to contact the editor of *Hello!*, but the only person available at its offices at that time of night was a security guard.

As with defamation cases, a claimant seeking an injunction to prevent publication before trial must also prove that their loss could not be equally well compensated by damages. This is not usually difficult with confidentiality cases involving secret information, since no amount of money can make the information secret again. There are cases where monetary compensation may be sufficient however, and there an injunction will be refused.

 In ***Douglas* v *Hello!***, the court refused to stop the circulation of *Hello!* on the grounds that, on the facts, the couple's loss could be adequately compensated without suppressing publication. The harm done by *Hello!* was that it had compromised the Douglas's right to sell pictures of themselves, and this was something that money could compensate for.

The party seeking an interim injunction has to give what is called a cross-undertaking in damages, which means that if the matter goes to trial, and the court holds that there was no breach of confidence, the claimant has to pay damages to the defendant, and may have to pay costs as well.

Extent of injunctions

If a court imposes an injunction preventing publication, that injunction applies to all media organisations which know about the injunction, and not just the newspaper named in the case.

 In the long-running *Spycatcher* litigation (see earlier), the *Sunday Times* first published information from Peter Wright's book, and the Government successfully secured an injunction preventing the paper from publishing further material. When other papers then published material from the book, they were held in contempt of court because, the court said, the purpose of the injunction was to prevent publication and they had frustrated that purpose. This ruling was later confirmed by the House of Lords.

In some cases, an injunction may be so widely drafted that it not only prevents publication of the material concerned, but also bans the media from mentioning that action has been taken to prevent publication. The late media magnate Robert Maxwell, for example, used injunctions in this way to completely suppress reporting of problems with his company.

Order for delivery up

If the information is in a physical form (such as documents), a court can order it to be handed back to the owners (this is known as 'delivery up'). This can cause problems for the media, in that in some cases, the documentation will identify the source who leaked it, if, for example, copies are numbered, a distribution list is attached or the source has made any notes on the material. In the case of very secret (usually government) documents, there may be tiny differences between copies which the untrained eye would not spot, but which experts can use to trace the source. Destroying or altering documents once an order has been made can be contempt of court, so if it looks as though a situation might end up in court, it may be best to destroy documentation beforehand.

A court can also order the media to disclose the source of information which has been given in breach of confidence, but this power is subject to the protection of sources provided by the Contempt of Court Act 1981 (see Chapter 6).

Damages

Although most breach of confidence cases concern claimants who are trying to get an injunction to prevent publication, there are also cases where confidential information is published before the claimants have a chance to try to prevent it. In this situation, they can go to court to try to get damages (and if necessary an injunction against further publication). However, damages for breach of confidence tend not to be as high as in defamation actions, for example.

 In *Campbell* v *MGN* (2004), the House of Lords upheld an award for £3,500 for model Naomi Campbell, after the *Mirror* published photos and details of her visits to Narcotics Anonymous.

Account of profits

The nature of stories built on confidential information means they are often the kind that sell newspapers and magazines. Therefore, if a breach of confidence is found, and the publishers have made money as a result of it, they can be ordered to give an 'account of profits' to the claimant, which is an amount of money based on the profits the defendant has made as a result of using the confidential material (it is an alternative to damages, not an addition). In cases involving books, publishers can be ordered to pay the whole of the profit on a book, but with newspapers or magazines, the court would have to calculate how much of the profit made on that issue was due to use of the confidential information.

Law in practice Confidentiality and defamation

Stories based on confidential information can also raise a dilemma with regard to defamation. Documents can be forged, sources may be wrong or bear a grudge, and by their nature, these kinds of stories will often be defamatory if they turn out not to be true. In this situation, journalists are often concerned that if they go to the owner or subject of the information to check the facts, and that person or organisation realises the story is based on confidential information, the story may be stopped by an injunction for breach of confidence. Rod Dadak, Head of Defamation at solicitors Lewis Silkin, has this advice:

- If you go ahead and use confidential information without checking the facts, you are taking a big risk. Judges don't look at these issues from the journalist's point of view, and they disapprove of any failure to give the other side a chance to see the allegations.

- If possible, try to get the same information from other sources, so that you can then check it with the subject without revealing that you have the confidential material.

- It's worth bearing in mind that the Article 10 rules on injunctions (see p. 246) is making it harder for claimants to get pre-publication injunctions where material is in the public interest, so the risk of an injunction will not always be as high as it might have been in the past.

CLAIMS UNDER THE HUMAN RIGHTS ACT (HRA)

As noted earlier, Article 8 of the European Convention on Human Rights 1998 states that people are entitled to 'respect for their private and family life'. Does that mean that a person could bring an action against a newspaper or broadcaster based directly on that right, rather than suing for breach of confidence/misuse of private information? The answer, unfortunately, is not entirely clear. The Act makes it unlawful for 'public authorities' to act in a way that breaches rights protected by the Act, and that means that a person who believes their Article 8 right has been violated by a public authority can go to court with a claim based directly on the Act. They can only do this if English law offers no other way to get a remedy: so if, for example, their breach falls within the rules of breach of confidence, they would have to sue that way, and could only bring a case based directly on the Act if that claim failed. If there is no possible remedy in English law that could fit the circumstances of the case, they can go directly to a claim based on the HRA.

 In *Peck v UK* (2003), the European Court of Human Rights ordered the UK Government to pay almost £8,000 in compensation to a man whose suicide attempt was captured on the local authority's CCTV cameras, and given to the BBC for a TV programme. The court found that there had been a 'serious interference' with his rights under Article 8 and, at that time, there was no other remedy for him in English law (today, the Data Protection Act 1998 would apply).

What does this mean for claims against the press? During the passage of the HRA, it was suggested in Parliament that the BBC counts as a public authority and Channel 4 might too; this means actions could be brought against them based directly on a breach of Article 8. Other media organisations are private organisations rather than public bodies, so the Act does not directly make it unlawful for them to act in a way that breaches Article 8. However, a court is a 'public authority', and it is therefore unlawful for a court to act in a way that breaches Article 8. Some legal academics therefore believe that if a court failed to apply Article 8 in a relevant case, the court would be in breach of the HRA. So far, the courts have done this by applying Article 8 to existing English law and, as we have seen, have stated that there is no separate action for breach of privacy, but it remains to be seen whether this will continue to be the position.

It is also possible that organisations such as the Press Complaints Commission (PCC) or Ofcom could be considered to be 'public authorities', and this would mean that they could be the subject of a claim based directly on Article 8, if, for example, an individual felt they had failed to protect his or her Article 8 rights.

■ Privacy and the PCC Code

The PCC Code of Practice contains a number of provisions concerning privacy:

- Everyone is entitled to respect for his or her private and family life, home, health and correspondence, including digital communications.
- It is unacceptable to photograph people in private places without their consent (private places are defined as places where there is a reasonable expectation of privacy, and this may include public property as well as private).
- Editors may not use the fame, notoriety or position of a parent or guardian as sole justification for publishing details of a child's private life.
- The press should not publish material acquired by using hidden cameras or listening devices, intercepting phone calls or emails, or unauthorised removal of documents or photos.

Breach of these rules may, however, be allowed under the Code where it can be demonstrated that the action is in the public interest. The Code lists some situations where the public interest may apply, though it is made clear that these are not necessarily the only ones. The listed situations are where the breach relates to:

- exposing crime or detecting crime or 'serious impropriety';
- protecting public health and safety;
- preventing the public from being misled by the words or actions of an individual or organisation.

In cases involving children, the Code warns, the public interest will have to be 'exceptional' in order to justify the breach. The PCC website (see *Online resources* at the end of the chapter) gives full details of all its adjudications, and the cases give a useful guide to the way in which the provisions are interpreted.

CHAPTER SUMMARY

Background to the law

There are now two types of confidentiality claim:
- traditional breach of confidence;
- misuse of private information.

Breach of confidence

A claim for breach of confidence must prove:
- the information 'has the necessary quality of confidence'; and
- it was obtained in circumstances which impose an obligation of confidence; and
- it was or is intended to be used in an unauthorised way.

Misuse of private information

Claims involve a two-stage test:
- Does the claimant have a reasonable expectation of privacy? and if so,
- is their right to privacy more important than someone else's right to freedom of expression?

Defences

There are three defences to either kind of claim:

- consent;
- information in the public domain;
- public interest.

Remedies for breach of confidence

A successful claimant may win:

- an injunction (interim or permanent);
- order for delivery up;
- damages;
- account of profits.

Claims under the Human Rights Act (HRA)

- Direct claims under the HRA can be brought against public authorities.
- Courts must apply the HRA in all relevant cases.

TEST YOUR KNOWLEDGE

1 What are the three elements of a traditional breach of confidence action?

2 What is the test for misuse of private information?

3 A well-known author is about to publish the final instalment of a series of novels, and there has been a lot of publicity about how the story will end. You get a call from someone who works at the book's printers saying he can tell you what happens on the last page. Can you use the information?

4 You work on a trade magazine for the construction industry, and have recently written about a new process which can halve the time it takes for cement to dry. After publication, you are sent what seems to be an internal memo from the company concerned, in which one of their technical staff suggests there may be a possibility that the substance used in the process can cause cancer. You do not know who sent the memo. Can you use the information?

5 You work on a celebrity magazine. A well-known film star holds a birthday party for his wife, to which 1,000 guests are invited. No press are invited, and the couple have hired a security firm to keep out anyone without an invitation. After the party, one of the security guards offers you pictures taken with a secret camera. Can you use them?

6 You receive a press release stating that a local company is about to make 100 of its workers redundant; the press officer confirms the figures and you run the story. It turns out that the press officer is one of the people on the list to be made redundant, and has released information which was supposed to be kept secret for another two weeks as an act of revenge. Are you in breach of confidence?

7 You work on a local paper, and have been working on a story about a prominent local business's disregard for health and safety. Just as you get the last piece of information you need to run the story, you hear that a national paper was also about to publish it, but was prevented by an injunction. Can you go ahead with your story?

ONLINE RESOURCES

Campbell v *MGN* can be read at:
www.publications.parliament.uk/pa/ld200304/ldjudgmt/jd040506/campbe-1.htm

Von Hannover v *Germany* can be read at:
www.worldlii.org/eu/cases/ECHR/2004/294.html

Venables and Thompson v *News Group Newspapers and Others* can be read at:
www.hmcourts-service.gov.uk/judgmentsfiles/j640/
Venables_and_Thompson_v_NewsGroup.htm

The Press Complaints Commission website gives details of complaints about invasion of privacy and their outcome:
www.pcc.org.uk

For further resources and updates please go to the Companion Website for this book at www.pearsoned.co.uk/practicaljournalism

Trespass and harassment

In Chapter 17, we looked at situations where the media might be said to invade privacy because of what they publish. However, there are also situations where people feel their privacy has been invaded by the way the media behaves when gathering information or pictures for a story: doorstepping interviewees, for example, or pursuing celebrities to get a photo of them. In this chapter, we look at the law on trespass, which concerns being on someone else's land without permission; harassment, which can be a criminal offence; and electronic eavesdropping (phone tapping).

As well as the legal provisions regarding these issues, they are also covered in the codes of practice of the PCC and Ofcom. In many cases, people will turn to these rather than legal action (because it is easier and costs them nothing), so it is important to be aware of their provisions in this area (see Chapter 29, and Appendix I).

TRESPASS

There are clearly many cases when in order to get a story – or even a comment for one – journalists go onto other people's property without an invitation. In such situations, it is not uncommon for the unwilling interviewee to threaten to have reporters 'done' for trespass, but in fact trespass is a civil, rather than a criminal offence.

Trespass is committed by 'unlawful interference' with someone else's land (land includes buildings, such as someone's house or office) or their property. 'Unlawful interference' can be as little as going onto the land without permission, or staying there after being asked to leave, and it also applies where you have permission to be on the land, but while there, you do something which goes beyond what you have permission to do. For example, if someone agrees to let you in to their house and answer a few questions, you might commit trespass if, while they are out of the room, you search a drawer or go and wander about upstairs. If you gain entry to somewhere by deception (e.g. by claiming you are someone else), then you will be considered to have entered the land without permission, even if the owner asks you in.

It is, therefore, fairly easy to commit trespass, but it is not common for journalists to be sued for it, simply because the law offers a few useful remedies in these situations. Trespass is not (with one exception, discussed below) a criminal offence, but a civil wrong, so you will not find yourself arrested and escorted off the premises simply for trespassing. The police can help the landowner to use reasonable force to get you off the premises, but they are not obliged to.

The landowner can go to court to get an injunction to stop you trespassing again, but unless you are following the same story over a long period of time, this clearly offers them no practical help, especially as the courts have shown themselves to be very reluctant to prevent publication of material gained through trespass. A landowner can also sue for damages, but unless you have actually caused damage to their land, these will not amount to much. However, if a journalist had behaved extremely badly during a trespass, for example by forcing their way into someone's home, or searching through private property, a court might show its disapproval by ordering exemplary damages, which means an additional sum designed to punish a claimant who has behaved very badly.

Only the landowner or the person who is in 'immediate possession' of the land can sue for trespass. This would include, for example, the tenant of a house or office, but not someone who is a guest or visitor.

 In *Kaye* v *Robertson* (1991), the case involving the actor 'interviewed' in his hospital bed (see p. 223), Mr Kaye could not sue for trespass, as he was effectively only a guest or visitor.

Trespass to land can only be committed by going onto land, or throwing or putting something on it; it cannot be committed, for example, by standing in a public place (or somewhere you have permission to be) and photographing someone on private land, or standing outside someone's front garden and waiting for them to leave the house (though where a large group of journalists and/or photographers gather, the police can use powers under the Highways Act 1980 to move them on – see p. 391).

 In *Bernstein* v *Skyviews and General Ltd* (1978), Lord Bernstein, then chairman of Granada TV, went to court to try to get damages from a company which took photos of his house using aerial photography. As the plane was never less than several hundred feet above the land, the court held that there was no trespass.

As stated above, there is one criminal offence related to trespass: aggravated trespass under the Criminal Justice and Public Order Act 1994. It is committed by entering land where a lawful activity is taking place, and doing anything intended to disrupt or obstruct that activity. It is aimed at situations such as protests and hunt sabotage, and is unlikely to be committed by journalists, even when they are present to report such events.

HARASSMENT

The Protection from Harassment Act 1997 was primarily designed to deal with the problem of stalkers, but given the activities of some journalists, it was always possible that it could also be used against the media, and this has proved to be the case (see below). The Act creates two criminal offences.

The first offence, defined in s1, is committed where someone:

- pursues a course of conduct which amounts to harassment of another; and
- knows or ought to know that that course of conduct amounts to harassment.

The Act does not specifically define harassment; the only explanation given, in s7, is that it includes behaviour which alarms the victim or causes them distress. This would seem to cover more than just physical violence or threats, and might, for example, include doorstepping, constant phone calls or photographers chasing someone in the street, but as so far very few cases have been reported, we do not know for certain exactly what might qualify as harassment, nor how severe the distress or alarm would need to be. The behaviour must take place as part of a 'course of conduct', which is defined as something which happens on at least two occasions. This offence can be punished with up to six months' imprisonment and/or a fine.

In *Thomas* v *News Group Newspapers Ltd* (2001), the *Sun* carried a story about an incident which took place in a police station. A Somali asylum seeker came into the station asking for directions to an asylum centre, and after the woman left, Ms Thomas, who was a clerk at the police station, overheard another officer making a joke which she considered to be racist. She complained and the officer was demoted. The *Sun*'s initial story referred to Ms Thomas as 'a black clerk', and the paper then published several readers' letters criticising her. A second article then invited readers to give their views on the decision to discipline the officer who made the joke. As a result, Ms Thomas received hate mail, and became afraid to go to work. She brought a case against the *Sun* under the Protection from Harassment Act. The paper tried to have the claim struck out, but the Court of Appeal held that Ms Thomas had an arguable case, and the newspaper would have to show that its conduct was reasonable. The court said that where a harassment case involved publication, the test would be whether publishing material that was likely to cause someone distress was an abuse of the freedom of the press.

The second, more serious offence, defined in s4, is committed when someone puts another person in fear of violence on at least two occasions, and they know or ought to know they are putting that person in fear of violence. It is punishable by up to five years' imprisonment and/or a fine.

If someone is convicted of either of the offences, a court can, in addition to punishing them, impose a restraining order to prevent the harassment being repeated. There is a defence to both offences if the person said to have harassed the claimant can show that, in the circumstances, their behaviour was reasonable, or was for the purposes of preventing or detecting crime.

In *Majrowski* v *Guys and St Thomas NHS Trust* (2006), the House of Lords held that an employer could be prosecuted for harassment carried out by its employees, so it would seem that publishing and broadcasting companies can be charged, as well as the journalist who actually carries out the harassment.

Someone who is a victim of the behaviour described in the s1 offence can bring a civil action against the person responsible (regardless of whether that person has been charged with the criminal offence). They can claim damages for the anxiety caused and for any financial loss.

ELECTRONIC EAVESDROPPING

Section 1 of the Regulation of Investigatory Powers Act 2000 makes it an offence to intercept someone's phone calls (except, for example, where the interception is done by the police or security services, within rules laid down in the Act). It is also banned under the PCC Code of Practice.

In 2007, the Royal Editor of the *News of the World*, Clive Goodman, was convicted of offences under s1, relating to allegations that he had intercepted calls to various members of the Royal Family, by accessing their voicemail messages. He was sentenced to six months imprisonment.

Intercepting is defined as modifying or interfering with a telecommunications system, so the Act does not prohibit straightforward taping of a phone call, for example, if you are interviewing someone, unless the tape will be passed on to someone else or broadcast (in which case you would need their consent to the taping). However, it is considered ethical to inform someone if you are taping them.

The Wireless Telegraphy Act 1949 bans the unauthorised use of 'wireless apparatus' with intent to obtain information about the contents of any message, and also disclosure of such information. This means it is an offence to listen in to police messages in the hope of getting information about an investigation.

The PCC Code

The Code states that journalists must not:

- engage in intimidation, harassment or in persistent pursuit;
- persist in questioning, telephoning or photographing individuals once asked to stop;
- remain on someone's property after being asked to leave;
- follow people.

Editors should take care not to use material acquired through the kind of behaviour referred to above.

CHAPTER SUMMARY

Trespass

Trespass can committed by:

- entering someone's land (or building) without permission;
- staying when asked to leave;
- doing something you have no permission to do.

Harassment

The Protection from Harassment Act 1997 creates two offences:

- pursuing a course of conduct which amounts to harassment of another;
- putting someone in fear of violence on at least two occasions.

The Act also creates a civil right to sue for harassment.

Intercepting phone calls

The Regulation of Investigatory Powers Act 2000 makes it an offence to intercept phone calls.

TEST YOUR KNOWLEDGE

1 Who can sue for trespass?

2 You are reporting a case in which a child was murdered, and want to get an interview with her parents. In which of these situations might you commit trespass:

    (a) You wait outside the front gate of her house, for her parents to come out. They ask you to leave, but you stay where you are.

    (b) The father agrees to an interview and invites you in. You ask to use the toilet, so that you can have a look at the child's bedroom and describe it in your story.

    (c) You stand opposite the house and look through the window, so that you can describe the parents in your story.

3 What is the definition of harassment under the Protection from Harassment Act 1997?

4 What can you use as a defence if sued for harassment?

ONLINE RESOURCES

www

The Protection from Harassment Act 1997 can be read at:
www.opsi.gov.uk/acts/acts1997/1997040.htm

The Regulation of Investigatory Powers Act 2000 can be read at:
www.opsi.gov.uk/Acts/acts2000/20000023.htm

Thomas v *News Group Newspapers* can be read at:
www.freebeagles.org/caselaw/CL_hs_Thomas_full.html

For further resources and updates please go to the Companion Website for this book at www.pearsoned.co.uk/practicaljournalism

18

Trespass and harassment

Chapter

19

Protecting sources and source material

Many of the most important stories the media carry involve publishing information which someone else does not want to be known: allegations of crime or corruption in high places, for example, or facts which suggest an individual or organisation has lied to or misled the public. In many such cases, the information on which the story is based will come from a source who is only willing to provide it on the understanding that they will remain anonymous. Sometimes this is because their position simply makes it awkward for them to be seen to have talked to the press; often it is because they risk losing their job, or even being prosecuted if they are revealed as the source of the information.

Whatever the reason, it is a basic rule of journalistic ethics, laid down in the ethical codes of the NUJ, the Press Complaints Commission (see Appendix I) and Ofcom (see Chapter 29), that a journalist who agrees to keep a source's identity confidential should honour that promise. The reason for this is not only fairness to that particular source, but also a wider public interest; if sources could not trust the media to protect their identity, an enormous amount of information that the public ought to know would never be revealed.

English media law recognises that public interest in some circumstances will protect the journalist's right to keep their sources secret. However, this protection is far from absolute, so a journalist needs to know under what circumstances they can be ordered to reveal their sources.

A related issue covered in this chapter is that of when you can be forced to hand over to the police (and certain other organisations) research material that you use in your work, and when they can search for it themselves, or even intercept your emails. There is some special protection for journalistic material in this context, particularly if it is confidential, but again, this protection is limited.

There are four main legal provisions under which a journalist can be required to reveal their sources, or allow access to their research material:

- the Contempt of Court Act 1981,
- the Police and Criminal Evidence Act 1984 (PACE),
- the Official Secrets Acts,
- the Terrorism Act 2000.

In addition, there are other acts which give investigative powers to the police and other agencies with regard to specific types of offence.

THE CONTEMPT OF COURT ACT 1981

The Contempt of Court Act details when a journalist can be ordered by a court (or some kinds of tribunal) to disclose a source or information which would reveal a source.

Usually, if a person refuses to answer a question put to them in court, they will be in contempt of court. However, if the person is a journalist, and the answer to the question would reveal the source of a story, the Contempt of Court Act provides that a refusal to answer will not be contempt of court, except in three situations. These situations are where the court is satisfied that disclosure is necessary for one of the following reasons:

- in the interests of national security;
- in the interests of justice;
- for the prevention of crime or disorder.

On the face of it, this sounds like fairly strong protection for the media, but unfortunately the way in which the courts have interpreted the three categories means that there are in fact a wide range of situations in which disclosure may be ordered. In 1996, the English law on protection of sources was examined by the European Court of Human Rights, in the case of **Goodwin v United Kingdom** (1996) (see below). The court criticised the approach of the English courts, and stressed that failing to give adequate protection to journalists' sources could breach the Article 10 right to freedom of expression. It stated that a court could only be justified in ordering a journalist to reveal their sources if there was an overriding public interest in the source being revealed. That ruling should be taken into account by any court judging a case on protection of sources, but as the cases discussed below show, there does not appear to have been any radical change of emphasis as a result.

Of course, even where one of the three conditions referred to above applies, the court cannot physically compel you to disclose your source, but if you fail to do so when ordered to, you can be found in contempt of court and fined or even put in prison.

Interests of national security

Case law suggests that where national security is involved to any degree, the courts are likely to decide that disclosure is necessary; in fact in *X Ltd* v *Morgan Grampian* (1991), the court stated that the decision would be 'almost automatic':

In *Secretary of State for Defence* v *Guardian Newspapers* (1985), the *Guardian* published a confidential memo from the Secretary of State for Defence, regarding the arrival of Cruise missiles in Britain. The Government went to court to get the document back, and the paper realised that returning it would enable the Ministry of Defence to identify the civil servant, Sarah Tisdall, who had leaked it. The *Guardian* argued that it was protected by s10 of the Contempt of Court Act, because the information in the document did not actually threaten national security. However the Government claimed that the return of the document was necessary, because even if the revelation in question did not endanger national security, the interests of national security demanded that civil servants who had access to confidential information and were willing to leak it should be identified. It argued that such a person might well leak something more dangerous next time. The House of Lords accepted this argument and ordered disclosure; the *Guardian* complied and Ms Tisdall was sentenced to six months' imprisonment.

▧ Interests of justice

This is perhaps the most grey area in the legislation, and a category which has proved to be much wider than the media would like. At one time it was assumed that this category would only apply where disclosure of the source was vital to court proceedings which were already under way, or at least planned. However, in the key case of *X Ltd* v *Morgan Grampian* (1991), the facts of which are stated below, the courts gave the term a considerably wider definition. Disclosure, the court said, could be considered necessary in the interests of justice where it was necessary to enable someone to 'exercise important legal rights and to protect themselves from serious legal wrongs'.

In deciding whether this was the case, the court said that the relevant issues were:

■ the nature of the information obtained from the source. The greater the legitimate public interest in the information, the more likely a court would be to allow protection of the source.

■ the way in which the source obtained the information. A court would be more likely to protect a source who has got hold of the information legitimately, whereas if it was stolen or otherwise obtained illegally (which would include in breach of confidence – see Chapter 17), there would need to be a strong public interest in publication to persuade the court to allow the source to be kept secret. There would, however, still be cases where sources should be protected even though they had obtained information illegally: the court gave the example of a source acting to expose wrongdoing.

As a result, the 'interests of justice' category is capable of being a worryingly wide one, and it can be difficult to predict the results in individual cases.

In *X Ltd* v *Morgan Grampian* (1991), a then trainee reporter, Bill Goodwin, was working for the trade magazine *The Engineer* when he received a call from a source telling him that a company called Tetra was in financial difficulties. He called Tetra to get its reaction to the information, which alerted it to the fact that his source must have had access to a confidential company document, a copy of which had recently gone missing. Tetra applied for an injunction to prevent publication of the story; when that was granted, it then applied for an order requiring Mr Goodwin to disclose his source. Mr Goodwin claimed the protection of s10, but Tetra argued that disclosure was necessary 'in the interests of justice', because it would enable it to bring proceedings to get the document back. The case went all the way to the House of Lords, who decided in favour of Tetra. Bill Goodwin refused to disclose the source and was fined £5,000 for contempt of court. However, he took his case to the European Court of Human Rights and won (*Goodwin* v *United Kingdom* (1996)). The Court ruled that forcing him to disclose his source was a breach of the Article 10 right to freedom of expression, and that failing to give adequate protection to sources undermined the role of the press as a public watchdog. The public interest in protecting Goodwin's source outweighed Tetra's interest in identifying that person.

In *Camelot Group Plc* v *Centaur Communications Ltd* (1999), an employee of Camelot, which runs the National Lottery, sent the magazine *Marketing Week* a copy of the company's draft accounts, a week before they were due to be made public. The magazine ran a story based on the leaked material, which put the company directors on a bad light, and Camelot went to court to try to make the magazine give them the documents. This would have identified the source, so the magazine refused. The Court of Appeal supported Camelot's claim, ordering that the documents should be handed back because the disloyal employee posed an 'ongoing threat' to Camelot, and its interest in identifying that person outweighed the public interest in protecting sources.

In *Ashworth Security Hospital* v *MGN Ltd* (2002), the *Mirror* got hold of details about the medical treatment of Ian Brady, the notorious 'Moors murderer', who killed several children during the

1960s. Brady was in Ashworth Security Hospital, and was on hunger strike at the time in protest against his treatment there. The story revealed details of the way in which the hospital was dealing with the hunger strike, including force feeding of Brady. The paper had got the information from a journalist who had been paid for it; the paper did not know where he had got it from. The hospital went to court to get the *Mirror* to divulge its source, but the paper argued that to do so would reveal who the journalist's source was. Like Bill Goodwin's case, the matter went all the way to the House of Lords and, once again, it ruled that the source should be disclosed, because it was in the interests of justice that someone leaking confidential information from hospital records should be identified and punished by the hospital, in order to prevent further leaks from that person and deter others from doing the same. The journalist, a freelance called Robin Ackroyd, then came forward and identified himself voluntarily, but refused to divulge his source.

The hospital then took Ackroyd to court, but in *Ackroyd v Mersey NHS Trust* (2006), the High Court refused to order him to reveal his sources. The judge said that although the hospital had a legitimate interest in discovering the source, this was outweighed by the public interest in journalists protecting their sources. On the evidence, the judge said, Mr Ackroyd was a responsible journalist whose purpose was to act in the public interest, and over the time since the case was first examined, it had become clear that the original source had not been acting for financial reasons. In addition, the extent of material leaked was less than originally claimed, security procedures had been tightened, and there had been no further significant leaks. Taken together, these factors meant that the court could find no 'pressing social need' to order disclosure of the source.

In *Interbrew v Financial Times* (2002), stories had been published about the brewery company Interbrew, which led to a fall in its share price. The stories turned out to be based on false information and a forged document, and the company took several newspapers to court to try to find out the source of it. The Court of Appeal ordered disclosure, stating that this was in the interests of justice because the fact that the document was forged made it clear that the source had intended to cause problems for the company. The newspapers refused to hand over the information, and no contempt proceedings were brought. However, the Court of Appeal decision still stands as a precedent, so the newspapers are currently preparing to challenge it in the European Court of Human Rights (ECHR). In the meantime, Interbrew continued to try to get the documents back, by means including threats to go to court to have one newspaper's assets frozen (such an order means the individual or organisation cannot get access to their own money). However Interbrew has now agreed to suspend actions until the ECHR case is heard.

In 1996, a journalist on *The Journal* in Newcastle was taken to court by the local police over a story which alleged that local crime figures had been presented in a misleading way. However, the High Court refused to force the reporter to reveal her sources, stating that her story had raised a question of 'considerable public importance', and this outweighed the police argument that the source should be revealed in the 'interests of justice'.

The courts have, in two cases, suggested that they will be less likely to order disclosure in cases where claimants have turned straight to legal action, without making their own attempts to discover the source of information. The reasoning seems to be that if there is some other way of finding the source, it cannot be said to be 'necessary' to order disclosure by the media.

In 1994, the top-security Broadmoor Hospital went to court to try to force a news agency to reveal its source for reports that two convicted killers had escaped while on day trips. The court declined to make the order, because the hospital had not made any attempt to investigate the leak for itself.

In *John v Express Newspapers plc* (2000), the Court of Appeal refused to order Express Newspapers to divulge the source of a confidential document about the singer Elton John's financial affairs, partly because he had not made sufficient effort to find out the source of the leak before going to court.

Prevention of crime

Obvious examples of cases where disclosure is necessary for the 'prevention of crime' might be those where, for example, identifying a source would help the police stop that person or someone else from committing a planned crime. In practice, the courts have given the category a wide meaning, and in *X Ltd* v *Morgan Grampian* (1991), it was stated that disclosure in these cases, as in those involving national security, disclosure should be 'almost automatic'.

In *Re an Inquiry under the Company Securities (Insider Dealing) Act 1985* (1988), a journalist for the *Independent* was questioned by inspectors from the Department of Trade, who were investigating suspected insider dealing, resulting from leaks from government departments. The reporter had written stories which suggested he had sources in those departments, but he refused to reveal them. The inspectors were using disclosure powers granted under the Financial Services Act 1986, which does not give any protection to journalists' sources, but as it allows anyone who refuses to reveal information to be treated as though they were in contempt of court, the House of Lords ruled that s10 of the Contempt of Court Act should be considered.

The House of Lords found that the reporter was not protected by s10, because disclosure was 'necessary for the prevention of crime'. It had been argued that this category could only apply if revealing the source was necessary in order to prevent further insider dealing, but the House of Lords held that the meaning was wider than this. In this case, they said, the job of the inspectors was not just to prevent further insider dealing by the same people, but to investigate the case so that measures could be taken to deter insider trading generally. The identity of the source was 'necessary' for that process to take place, and that process would prevent crime.

PACE – INFORMATION REQUIRED BY THE POLICE

So far we have looked at situations where journalists can be ordered to divulge their sources by a court. In this section, we consider the related issue of when the police can demand access to information or material which they believe will assist in a criminal investigation. This may include material which identifies sources, but it can also extend to just about any kind of research and other material used in journalistic work. For example, the courts have frequently ordered the media to hand over footage and/or photographs of violent demonstrations. This has led to a belief among some groups that the press are on the side of the police, which can put photographers and reporters at risk, and clearly, taking photographs at such events becomes more difficult when the subjects know that the pictures might end up being used as evidence against them. Similarly, it is more difficult to make credible promises of confidentiality to a source in situations where the police have power to access material which could identify sources.

Answering police questions

With the exceptions of investigations related to terrorism and breaches of the Official Secrets Acts (see below), the law does not oblige anyone, including journalists, to answer questions put to them by the police. It is often believed (sometimes even by the police) that refusing to answer questions amounts to the offence of obstructing the police in their duties, but this is not the case. The Police Act 1996 defines this offence as 'wilfully' obstructing an officer, and in the key case of *Rice* v *Connolly* (1966), the High Court stated that to do something 'wilfully' meant to do it without legal excuse. In this country, it explained, we may have a moral and social duty to help the police, but there is no legal duty to do so, and so there is legal excuse for refusing to answer a police officer's questions. (Although *Rice* was decided before the Police Act 1966 was passed, similar wording was in use before; the case remains good law and was referred to, for example, in *Ashworth* v *MGN* (see earlier). Note, however, that this does not extend to giving false or misleading information.

This means that if the police want access to information that you have, they have to go to court to get it, usually under powers granted in the Police and Criminal Evidence Act 1984 (PACE). These only apply, however, to records and documents, and not to information which is not in any recorded form, such as the name of a source which you have not written down.

▣ Police search and seizure powers

The Police and Criminal Evidence Act 1984 (PACE) is the main piece of legislation governing police powers of search and seizure. It sets out special rules for police access to journalistic material, which are stricter than those which apply to most other material (e.g. the police must apply to a circuit judge for access to journalistic material, rather than to a magistrate, as they do for most other material).

PACE defines 'journalistic material' as records or documents 'acquired or created for the purposes of journalism'and held in the possession of the person who acquired or created it for those purposes. This can include research material as well as actual copy.

In *Commissioner of Metropolitan Police* v *Mackenzie* (1987), the Vice Squad attempted to obtain documents gathered by the *Sun* for an investigation into 'rent boys'. The warrant application was made against the then editor of the paper, Kelvin Mackenzie, and failed because the police could not prove that he personally had ever been in possession of the material.

PACE divides journalistic material into two different categories:

- **Excluded material** is defined as material which is held under an 'undertaking, restriction or obligation of confidence'. This would include any material which has been given to a journalist on the understanding that its source was not revealed. The requirement of confidentiality must have existed from the time when the material was acquired or created.

- **Special procedure material** is all other (non-confidential) journalistic material.

If the police wish to obtain material in either of these categories, they have to apply to a circuit judge, usually for a production order which requires the holder of the material to hand it over (though in some circumstances they can apply for a search warrant instead – see below). A production order should only be granted if the police can satisfy the requirements set out in Schedule 1 of PACE. The person or company who holds the material must be told about the application, and can put their arguments against it to the judge.

For excluded material an order should only be granted if the police can show that:

- there are reasonable grounds for believing that excluded material exists on the premises;

- a search warrant would have been granted under any legislation which existed before PACE.

There are very few pre-PACE provisions which would allow the police to obtain or search for excluded material so, in practice, journalists will only rarely be obliged to give up this kind of material. Two exceptions, however, are where the material has been stolen, as the Theft Act 1968 provides for such material to be seized (or searched for), or where the material relates to offences under the Official Secrets Acts.

For special procedure material, an order should only be granted if there are reasonable grounds for believing that:

- a serious offence has been committed;
- there is special procedure material on the premises;
- the material is likely to be of substantial value to the investigation of the offence;
- the material is likely to be admissible evidence; and other ways of obtaining the material have either failed, or not been tried because they were bound to fail;
- it is in the public interest for the order to be granted.

The last of these conditions would seem on the face of it to suggest a high degree of protection for journalistic material but, in practice, the courts have shown themselves to be very willing to accept that the public interest more often lies in helping the police than in protecting press sources, or press freedom generally. Nor are they especially strict in their application of the conditions laid down in Schedule 1.

 In 1994, the police were able to persuade a court to give them access to film and photographs of a demonstration against the controversial Criminal Justice and Public Order Bill, on the grounds that this would help them identify those who had committed public order offences. The press argued that this was not in the public interest, because demonstrators would come to see the press as being on the side of the police, making it extremely difficult to report similar events in future. This argument was rejected.

 In 1986, the *Western Daily Press* was ordered to hand over pictures of a disturbance which arose out of a police operation, even though the police had not specified what offence they believed had been committed or what value the pictures might be to the investigation.

 In 1990, the police successfully applied for production orders against 25 different papers and broadcasters after protests against the Poll Tax (a local tax which was the short-lived predecessor of the Community Charge) turned into a riot. Photos and film of the events were handed over, but a couple of weeks later, the police went back to court and asked for similar orders against four more companies. These were granted, even though the police admitted they had not yet looked at all the material supplied under the previous orders. The media argued that the police could not therefore know whether they needed the extra material, but the court said that the police needed to see that extra material before they could say whether it was relevant.

 In *Bright* v *Central Criminal Court* (2001), the police applied for a production order regarding correspondence between a newspaper reporter and David Shayler, an ex-employee of MI5 who had made a number of allegations of wrongdoing against the Security Services, and who had fled to France to avoid charges under the Official Secrets Act. The order was initially granted, but then overturned by the Divisional Court, which emphasised the importance of free speech, particularly with regard to allegations that might be embarrassing or inconvenient to public authorities. The court stated that where the media was conducting a genuine investigation into 'corrupt or reprehensible activities by a public authority' the courts should only allow access to their material where there was 'compelling evidence' that this would be in the public interest, and the material was genuinely relevant. That was not the case here.

If a media organisation or journalist refuses to comply with a production order, the police can apply to a circuit judge for a search warrant; they can also do this instead of applying for a production order. The holder of the material does not have to be told of the application for a search warrant, and even if they are told, or find out, they have no right to put their case against a warrant to the judge.

To get a search warrant (whether for excluded or special procedure material), the police must show that the Schedule 1 conditions which would be necessary for a production order (see above) are satisfied, and in addition, that *one* of the following four conditions applies:

■ it is not practicable to communicate with anyone who is entitled to grant entry to the premises;

■ it is not practicable to communicate with anyone who is entitled to grant access to the material;

■ the material contains information which is subject to a restriction on disclosure or obligation of secrecy imposed by statute (an example would be material which the Official Secrets Act 1989 makes it an offence to disclose – see Chapter 22) and is likely to be disclosed in a way that breaches that legislation if the warrant is not granted; or

■ serving notice of an order might seriously prejudice the investigation.

If the police enter premises with such a warrant, they can remove additional material not covered by that warrant without going back to court.

In 1987, the police used these powers to get a warrant to search the offices of the *New Statesman*, after it published an article by the investigative journalist Duncan Campbell about Zircon, a £500 million spy satellite that the Government was said to have concealed from Parliament. They were able to get a warrant because the offices were thought to have contained material which was subject to the Official Secrets Act.

Warrants under PACE have to be issued for specific premises, but the Serious Organised Crime and Police Act 2005 introduces a new 'all premises' warrant, which allows the police to search any premises occupied or controlled by the person named in the warrant. This could potentially mean that one warrant could cover not just a journalist's office, but their home as well. Before ordering such a warrant, the judge must be satisfied that it is not reasonably practical for the police to list all the premises they might need to search, and that there are reasonable grounds for searching premises not specified in the application.

Law in practice Dealing with documents

Once a media organisation or journalists has been served with notice that the police are applying for a production order, it becomes a potential contempt of court to destroy, hide or alter the material concerned. Before notice is served, however, this does not apply, so any journalist who thinks such an application might be made would be well advised to dispose of any unnecessary material in advance (e.g. in the cases concerning film and photography of demonstrations, much of the material demanded was unpublished extra footage and pictures, which could have been destroyed).

THE OFFICIAL SECRETS ACTS

Official Secrets legislation (see Chapter 22) provides extensive powers of investigation to the police. Section 6 of the Official Secrets Act 1920 (as amended by the Official Secrets Act 1939) states that where the chief officer of police has reasonable grounds for suspecting that an offence under s1 of the Act (these are spying offences) has been committed and that a person can supply information about the offence, the chief of police can authorise a senior police officer to require that person to reveal the relevant information. Before doing this, the chief of police must usually get the Secretary of State's permission, but in cases of 'great emergency', can go ahead without it.

It is a criminal offence to refuse to comply, or knowingly supply false information, and the provision applies to journalists and journalistic information just as to everyone else; there is no special protection.

Section 9 of the Official Secrets Act 1911 provides that, with a warrant from a magistrate, the police can enter any premises named in the warrant, at any time, and can use force to get in if they need to. They can search the premises and anyone there, and take any material which is evidence of an offence under the Act. In cases of emergency, the police need not even get a warrant: a superintendent can issue a written order which has the same effect.

Section 8 of the Official Secrets Act 1989 provides that if someone is in possession of documents or articles containing information which has been disclosed by a government employee, entrusted to someone in confidence by a government employee, or entrusted in confidence to other states or international organisations, it is a criminal offence not to hand over that information to a government official if asked to do so.

THE TERRORISM ACT 2000

Anti-terrorism legislation creates some widely-drawn offences concerning cooperation with police inquiries into terrorism, with perhaps the most significant development being that, where terrorist offences are concerned, the rule that no one is obliged to help the police with their enquiries does not apply.

These are the offences which are most likely to affect the media in their work:

■ Section 38b of the Terrorism Act 2000 (as amended by the Anti-Terrorism, Crime and Security Act 2001) makes it a serious offence to withhold information concerning suspected terrorist offences, and the offence can be committed not just by refusing to answer questions if asked, but also by failing to offer the information voluntarily, even if you are not asked for it and the police do not know you have it. The section states that it is an offence not to disclose to the police, as soon as reasonably practical, information which you know or believe might be of 'material assistance' in:

   ■ preventing someone from committing an act of terrorism; or

   ■ bringing about the apprehension, prosecution or conviction of someone in the UK, for committing, preparing or instigating an act of terrorism.

There is a defence where the person in possession of the information has a 'reasonable excuse' for not disclosing it (which is not defined in the Act). There is no special defence relating to the media. The maximum sentence for this offence is five years in prison.

■ A similar provision in s19 makes it an offence to withhold information about people who are involved in funding terrorism. It states that where someone, through their trade, profession, business or employment, acquires information that leads them to believe or suspect that someone else has committed an offence concerning the financing of terrorism, the person who has the information will commit an offence if they do not disclose their suspicion, and the information which prompts it, to the police as soon as reasonably practicable. Again, 'reasonable excuse' is a defence, but there is no specific media defence. The maximum sentence is five years' imprisonment.

- Section 58 makes it an offence to collect, record or possess information (including photographs) which is likely to be useful to someone preparing or committing an act of terrorism. The only defence in the Act is to prove reasonable excuse for collecting, recording or possessing the material. The maximum sentence is ten years' imprisonment.

- Section 39(1) makes it an offence for someone who knows or has reasonable cause to suspect that a terrorism investigation is being or will be conducted, to disclose anything which is likely to prejudice the investigation, or interfere with material likely to be relevant to it. Disclosure here could include publication.

- Section 39(2) applies when someone knows or has reasonable cause to suspect that information has been disclosed under s19 (see above), and discloses to another information which could interfere with any resulting investigation, or interferes with material which could be relevant to that investigation. For both s39 offences, there is a defence where the person did not know or have reason to suspect that a terrorist investigation was likely to be affected, or where there is reasonable excuse for the disclosure or interference.

The police have extensive investigatory powers in relation to offences of terrorism, which are contained in Schedule 5 of the 2000 Act. In additional to general powers to enter and search premises, search anyone in them, and seize and retain relevant material, paragraph 5 of Schedule 5 provides that the police can apply to a circuit judge for an order giving them access to journalistic material, in both the excluded and special procedure categories defined by PACE (see above).

The application has to relate to specific material, or material of a specific description, and the judge must believe that the person the order is made against has the material in their possession, custody or control. The order can require a person to hand over, or give the police access to, such material within seven days (or the judge can decide on a different period). If the person is not in possession of the material, they can be required to disclose, to the best of their knowledge, its location, again within seven days.

Where a judge makes an order giving access to journalistic material, they can also order any person who appears to be entitled to grant entry to the relevant premises to allow the police to enter the premises and access the material. This order can only be granted if the judge is satisfied that:

- The material is excluded or special procedure material.

- It does not include material subject to legal privilege (see the *Glossary*).

- The order is being sought for the purposes of a terrorist investigation.

- There are reasonable grounds for believing that the material is likely to be of substantial value to a terrorist investigation, either by itself or with other material.

- There are reasonable grounds for believing that it is in the public interest that the material should be produced or access given to it, taking into account the potential benefit to the terrorism investigation, and the circumstances in which the material is held.

Anyone who is ordered to hand over or make available material, or who has had material taken by the police under a warrant, can then be required to explain that material under paragraph 13 of Schedule 5. It is an offence, with a maximum sentence of two years, to give a false or misleading explanation.

◼ Additional provisions for Northern Ireland

Three additional important provisions for the media in the Terrorism Act 2000 apply to Northern Ireland only. Paragraphs 19–21 respectively allow the Secretary of State for Northern Ireland to issue orders:

- giving any police officer an authority equivalent to a search warrant, in respect of specific premises;
- requiring any person to produce or allow access to special procedure material or excluded material;
- requiring any person to provide an explanation of material seized as a result of actions taken under the two above provisions.

OTHER LEGISLATION

In addition to the legislation discussed above, there are statutes which provide powers to order disclosure of information on specific matters, or powers of search and seizure. These are some of the most important as regards the media's areas of work.

The Financial Services Act 1986 gives inspectors from the Department of Trade and Industry powers to summon people for questioning about any matter relating to their inquiries (which are usually into allegations of financial misconduct). Failure to attend without a reasonable excuse is an offence. Similar powers are given to the Financial Services Authority under the Financial Services and Markets Act 2000.

The Serious Organised Crime and Police Act 2005 gives the police, the Serious Organised Crime Agency, and officers of Revenue & Customs powers to issue a 'disclosure notice' to anyone they believe has information relating to investigation of one of the offences listed under the Act, which is likely to be of substantial value to the investigation. The notice can require the person to answer questions, supply information or hand over documents. It does not, however, apply to excluded material as defined by PACE.

The Criminal Justice Act 1987 permits the director of the Serious Fraud Office to order anyone whom they believe has information relevant to an investigation, to answer questions, provide information or supply documents. Refusing to do so is an offence, which can result in a prison sentence.

The Police Act 1997 allows police investigating serious crime to break into premises and plant bugs, where the chief constable thinks that this is necessary because evidence gained is likely to be of substantial value in the prevention or detection of serious crime, and the purpose cannot be achieved any other way. However, where the material sought is 'confidential journalistic material', the police must get the approval of a commissioner (one of a specially-appointed group of sitting or former High Court judges) first or, in urgent cases, as soon as possible afterwards. Serious crime in this context includes any offence involving violence, or substantial financial gain, or carried out by a large group of people.

The Regulation of Investigatory Powers Act 2000 allows the Home Secretary to issue a warrant allowing specified officials of the police, security services and Revenue & Customs to intercept emails, where they are satisfied that this would be proportionate to the purpose for which the warrant is sought, and the warrant is necessary for any of the following reasons:

- in the interests of national security;

- for the purpose of preventing or detecting serious crime;

- for the purpose of safeguarding the economic wellbeing of the UK;

- for the purpose of giving effect to the provisions of any international agreement on mutual assistance.

When considering requests for warrants, the Home Secretary must also look at whether the same information could be obtained in another way. The warrant can be issued secretly, and there is no way of finding out whether you are the subject of one (in fact your internet service provider, who would have to facilitate the intercepting, is not allowed to tell you).

The Act also provides for the police, Revenue & Customs and the intelligence services to have access to 'communications data', which does not include the content of emails, but does cover information such as phone numbers called, addresses emails have been sent to, and the time and date of calls/emails. Access to communications data is less restricted than access to the content of communications, and can be allowed for a wide variety of purposes, including in the interests of public safety, to prevent death or injury, to assess or collect any tax or duty, and for any other purpose specified by the Secretary of State. If you encrypt your email messages, you can be ordered to reveal the encryption code, and if you are ordered to reveal the code, it is an offence to tell anyone that you have done so.

CHAPTER SUMMARY

Contempt of Court Act 1981

Refusal to reveal a source is not contempt of court, except where disclosure is necessary:

- in the interests of national security;

- in the interests of justice;

- for the prevention of crime or disorder.

Information required by the police

Refusing to answer police questions is not an offence (except in terrorism and official secrets cases).

Court orders to give material to the police are made:

- for excluded material (confidential) only if a search warrant could have been issued pre-PACE;

- for special procedure material (non-confidential) if six grounds are satisfied.

The Official Secrets Acts

- Refusing to give information about an espionage offence is an offence.

- The police can search premises and seize potential evidence, with a warrant.

- Refusing to hand over certain types of leaked documents is an offence.

The Terrorism Act 2000

It is an offence to:

- withhold information about suspect terrorist offences, or information, acquired through work or business, about the funding of terrorism;

- collect, record or possess information likely to be useful in terrorism;
- disclose anything likely to prejudice a terrorism investigation.

Other legislation

Other legislation providing investigative powers that can be used against the media includes:

- the Financial Services Act 1986;
- the Serious Organised Crime and Police Act 2005;
- the Criminal Justice Act 1987;
- the Police Act 1997;
- the Regulation of Investigatory Powers Act 2000.

TEST YOUR KNOWLEDGE

1 In which three situations does the Contempt of Court Act 1981 require a journalist to reveal their sources, or risk being in contempt?

2 In which of these situations might a court order that you should reveal your source?

   (a) You have published a story about the temper tantrums of a well-known celebrity, based on information given to you by her chauffeur.

   (b) You are sent a secret document detailing plans to buy new nuclear missiles and publish a story based on information in the document. You do not know who sent it.

   (c) You publish details of plans by an animal rights group to kidnap the son of a high-profile model, known for her support of the fur trade. Your information comes from someone within the organisation.

3 You have recently published a story about alleged corruption within the local police force. Two police officers turn up at your workplace and ask you to tell them where you got the information from. Do you have to tell them?

4 What are the two types of journalistic material defined under PACE? How do police powers with regard to them differ?

5 You are researching a story about alleged sexual harassment of female police officers in your local force, comprising sexist remarks and jokes. You put the allegations to a senior officer, who asks you to hand over your evidence, threatening to get a production order if you do not. What should you do?

6 You have recently conducted an interview with a member of an extremist group, which is suspected to be involved with terrorism. The police ask to see your notes; in what circumstances can you be forced to hand them over?

ONLINE RESOURCES

www The full text of *Ashworth* v *MGN* can be read at:
www.parliament.the-stationery-office.co.uk/pa/ld200102/ldjudgmt/jd020627/ash-1.htm

The Terrorism Act 2000 can be read at:
www.opsi.gov.uk/ACTS/acts2000/20000011.htm

News stories about protection of sources are covered on the website of the Campaign for Press and Broadcasting freedom, at:
www.cpbf.org.uk

Reports on the state of the law in protection of sources in the UK and other countries can be found on the European Federation of Journalists website, at:
www.ifj-europe.org/default.asp?Issue=EFJsources&Language=EN

19

For further resources and updates please go to the Companion Website for this book at www.pearsoned.co.uk/practicaljournalism

Protecting sources and source material

The increasing use of computers over the past couple of decades has made it easy for organisations to hold a vast amount of information about individuals, to access and use that information, and to pass it on to others. As a result, legislation was passed to regulate the accumulation, storage and use of this information, and the current situation is governed by the Data Protection Act 1998. It creates rights for people who are the subject of stored information, and duties for those who hold the information.

Trainee journalists are often surprised to find out that they need to know about the Data Protection Act, which at first glance would seem to have more to do with the work of marketing departments and companies which send out junk mail. But in fact the Act affects the work of the media in two important ways:

■ Media organisations themselves (from the biggest newspaper company to the individual freelance journalist working from home) collect, store and use information on individuals, and this fact gives them responsibilities under the Act. The Act provides for the media to be exempt from most of these responsibilities in certain situations, but these are limited.

■ Organisations approached by the media for information will often use the Act as a reason to refuse disclosure. Sometimes they will be correct to do so, but in many cases the refusal is the result of a misunderstanding of the Act, or the Act is deliberately wrongly used as a reason to keep information secret. A good understanding of the legislation is the best way to deal with these situations.

The Act is overseen by the Information Commissioner, the same official who oversees the Freedom of Information Act (see Chapter 25).

INFORMATION COVERED BY THE ACT

The Data Protection Act 1998 applies to what it calls 'personal data'. In normal language, we might use 'personal data' to mean the kind of information which could prove embarrassing if disclosed, but the Act defines it much more widely than this. It uses a two-part definition, detailing what 'data' is, and which data is 'personal'.

Data is essentially any information held on computer, or in a non-computerised filing system where information is organised in such a way as to make specific information relating to a particular person readily accessible. This means that, for example, information written on a piece of paper in a pile on your desk with lots of other randomly-assorted pieces of paper would not be covered, and probably nor would interview notes in a notebook which covered lots of different stories in no particular order. However, if you filed the information so that you could easily access information about a particular person, the information held that way would be subject to the provisions of the Act. In practice of course, most of us now keep information on our computers, and this is all covered by the Act.

 In *Campbell* v *MGN* (2002) it was established that photographs could be classified as data for the purposes of the Act. This approach was confirmed in *Douglas* v *Hello!* (2005). The facts of both cases are discussed below.

Personal data is defined under the Act as information relating to a particular person, held in the above ways, from which that person can be identified, either from that piece of information alone, or in combination with other information which the holder has or is likely to get. It includes not just factual details about the person, but any expression of opinion about them, or any suggestion of anyone's intentions with regard to that person. In the case of *Durant* v *Financial Services Authority (Disclosure of Information)* [2003], the Court of Appeal clarified this definition, stating that it essentially meant 'biographical' information, which affects someone's privacy in relation to their personal or family life, business or profession. Merely mentioning someone in a document did not make that document 'personal data'. This means that notes of an interview with someone for a human interest story or personal profile, for example, would clearly be 'personal data', and so would a contacts list with people's names and phone numbers. On the other hand, incidental mention of a person's name in a document which did not relate in any way to their privacy would not qualify as 'personal data'.

There is also a special category of 'sensitive personal data', which is defined as information which relates to any of the following details about a person:

- race or ethnic origin;
- political views;
- religious beliefs or beliefs of a similar nature;
- membership of a trade union;
- physical or mental health or condition;
- sex life;
- having committed or being alleged to have committed any offence;
- legal proceedings related to the commission or alleged commission of an offence by the subject, the result of such proceedings and any sentence passed.

Sensitive personal data is subject to stricter rules about when and how it can be processed than other forms of information (see below).

 In *Campbell* v *MGM* (2002), the model Naomi Campbell brought a claim against the *Mirror* regarding publication of information and photographs concerning her treatment for drug addiction. The case is most often discussed in the context of privacy and breach of confidence (see p. 232), but Ms Campbell also said that the paper's use of the information breached the Data Protection Act. In this context the High Court found that the information published could be classifed as sensitive personal data, as it referred to her health, and this finding was not disturbed by the two later appeals in the case.

Terminology

There are three other terms which are worth explaining before we look at the provisions of the Act:

- **Data subject** means the person the information is about (in this chapter, the word 'subject' is used to mean the data subject).

- **Data controller** is the term used for the person or organisation which holds the information (defined as whoever 'determines the purposes for which and the manner in which' personal data is processed).

- **Processing** is widely defined, but in practice covers just about anything that a journalist would be likely to do with information, including obtaining it, recording it, holding it, looking at it, using it or disclosing it to anyone else.

MEDIA DUTIES UNDER THE ACT

As explained above, media organisations all process personal data, which makes them data controllers. Data controllers have three main obligations under the Act:

- to register their status as a data controller;
- to comply with the Act when processing personal data.
- to act in accordance with the rights the Act provides for the subjects of personal data.

As stated above, in some cases, the media are exempt from some of these duties, and these exemptions are discussed at p. 277.

Registration

All data controllers are required to register with the Office of the Information Commissioner and each data controller must supply their name and address, and details of the purposes for which they process data, the category of people they hold information on, and the kind of information held. These details need not be especially precise: for example, the Information Commissioner's Office suggests that for the media, the stated purpose should be:

> Processing by the data controller of any journalistic, literary or artistic material, made or intended to be made available to the public or a section of the public.

This information is published on the Information Commissioner's public register of data controllers. Data controllers also have to provide a security statement detailing measures taken to protect against unlawful use of the data by others; this is not made public.

There is no journalistic exemption from the obligation to register, and failure to do so is a criminal offence.

Law in practice **Freelances and data protection**

Journalists who work for a company will be covered by the company's registration under the Act, but if you are freelance, and you process data, the law requires you to register personally as a data controller. This can be done online at the website of the Information Commissioner's Office (see *Online resources* at the end of the chapter). Registration currently costs £35 per year.

■ Processing personal data

The Act sets out eight principles which should be followed when data is processed. Data must be:

1 processed fairly and lawfully;

2 processed for limited purposes;

3 adequate, relevant and not excessive;

4 acccurate and up to date;

5 kept no longer than necessary;

6 processed in accordance with the data subject's rights;

7 kept with an appropriate degree of security;

8 not transferred outside the European Economic Area (EEA), except to countries which have adequate protection for the data subject. (The EEA comprises the EU, plus Iceland, Liechtenstein and Norway.)

In order for data to be fairly processed, at least one of a number of conditions have to be met. The conditions are laid out in Schedule 2 of the Act, and those most likely to apply in situations where information is processed by the media are:

■ The subject has consented to the processing.

■ Processing is necessary for the performance of a contract with the subject (e.g. many publications use contracts when organising an interview with a celebrity or the subject of a human interest story, though in these cases there will be consent as well).

■ Processing is necessary in order to pursue the legitimate interests of the data controller or third parties. The media might argue, for example, that processing certain data is necessary in order for it to pursue its legitimate interests of publishing journalistic material. This provision will not apply where pursuing the defendant's legitimate interests unjustifiably prejudices the interests of the subject (see the *Douglas* case, below).

The fact that one of these conditions has been met does not, however, necessarily mean that the data has been processed fairly and lawfully. They are minimum standards, and it is quite possible for a data controller to meet one of these conditions and yet still deal with the information in a way which is unfair or unlawful. The Act makes it clear, for example, that if information is obtained by deception, including where the subject is deceived about the purpose to which it will be put, any subsequent processing of it cannot be considered fair.

In *Douglas* v *Hello!* (2005), the court considered the claims of film stars Catherine Zeta Jones and Michael Douglas that publication of unauthorised photos of their wedding represented a breach of the Act's provisions on fair and lawful processing. The High Court found that the fact that the pictures were obtained surruptitiously (the photographer sneaked in to the wedding and took the pictures secretly) meant that the processing could not be fair. In addition, it was clear that none of the conditions in Schedule 2 had been satisfied. The only potentially arguable condition was that the use of the photos was necessary in order for *Hello!* to pursue its legitimate interests, but the court held that this was not applicable because publication would unjustifiably prejudice the interests of the couple.

■ Processing sensitive personal data

Processing of data which fulfills the definition of 'sensitive personal data', as explained above, can only be fair and lawful if at least one of the conditions listed in Schedule 2 are met, plus at least one of a list of extra conditions listed in Schedule 3 to the Act, or in the Data

Protection (Processing of Sensitive Personal Data) Order 2000. The conditions most likely to be of use where the media are processing information are:

■ The subject has given their explicit consent.

■ The information has been deliberately made public by the subject.

■ The processing is in the public interest, is necessary for the detection or prevention of any unlawful act (or failure to act), and has to be carried out without the subject's consent being sought, in order not to prejudice that purpose.

■ The processing is in the public interest, and is necessary for the discharge of any function which is designed to protect the public from dishonesty, malpractice, incompetence, seriously improper conduct, or mismanagement of or failure in services provided by any organisation, and has to be carried out without the subject's consent being sought, in order not to prejudice that purpose.

■ Disclosure of the information is for the purposes of journalism, with a view to publication, and is in the public interest, and is in connection with:

    ■ the commission or alleged commission of any unlawful act; or

    ■ alleged or proven dishonesty, malpractice, seriously improper conduct, incompetence or unfitness of any person; or

    ■ alleged or proven mismanagement of or failure in services provided by any organisation.

(The first two conditions come from Schedule 2; the rest are contained in the 2000 Order.)

■ Rights of the data subject

The Act gives data subjects a series of rights; some of these have no relevance to the work of journalists, but the following may:

■ The right to access: Data subjects are entitled to find out what information about them is being processed by or on behalf of a specific data controller. They have to pay the data controller a fee (currently no more than £10), and the information must be provided within 40 days.

■ The right to prevent processing: Anyone can ask a data controller to stop (or not start) processing data relating to them if it is causing, or could cause, unwarranted substantial damage to the data subject or someone else. The data controller has 21 days to respond, and can either agree to comply, or argue that the request is unjustified. In the latter case, the subject can go to court to apply for an order.

■ The right to rectification or destruction: If personal data is inaccurate, or contains expressions of opinion based on inaccurate data, the subject can apply to a court to order the data controller to rectify or destroy the data.

■ The right to compensation: If a media organisation breaches any provision of the Act and a person suffers loss and/or distress as a result, the organisation can be liable to pay compensation (though so far this does not seem to offer a way for people to prise huge payouts from the media; Catherine Zeta Jones and Michael Douglas were only awarded £50 for their claim under the Act). It is a defence in this situation to prove that the organisation has taken all reasonable care.

■ The right to an assessment: Anyone who believes personal data on them has been processed in ways that breach the Act can ask the Information Commissioner to make an assessment. If the Commissioner agrees, and the matter cannot be settled voluntarily, the Commissioner can serve an enforcement notice.

EXEMPTIONS FOR THE MEDIA

Having read the provisions detailed above, it will be obvious that there are many situations in which the media cannot comply with the Data Protection Act and still do their jobs effectively. For example, no form of investigative journalism would be possible if reporters had to tell the subjects of their stories every bit of information that they held on them, and the subject had to consent before the material could even be looked at, let alone published. Recognising this, s32 of the Act contains a special exemption for material (including sensitive personal data) that is processed for journalistic purposes, which allows the media to breach some provisions of the Act.

However, the exemption does not apply automatically in every situation where information is processed for journalistic purposes. It will only apply where all three of the following conditions are satisfied:

- the processing is undertaken with a view to publication of journalistic or literary material (these are not defined in the Act);
- the data controller reasonably believes that, having regard to the special importance of the public interest in freedom of expression, publication would be in the public interest;
- the data controller reasonably believes that, in all the circumstances, it is impossible to comply with the provision in question.

In deciding whether publication is in the public interest, the Act states that the data controller can take into account the publisher's compliance with any relevant code of practice (examples would be the Ofcom codes for broadcast journalists, and the Press Complaints Commission Code for print media).

If (and only if) these conditions are satisfied, the media need not comply with any of the following provisions:

- all of the provisions on fair and lawful processing, except the seventh, which requires safe storage of information;
- the requirement to allow data subjects access to the information held on them;
- the requirement to stop (or not start) processing information where it is causing or could cause them damage or distress;
- the requirement to rectify or delete inaccurate data or expressions of opinion based on inaccurate data.

In addition, if someone goes to court to try get an order giving them access to information held on them by the media, or to stop or prevent processing of that information, and the media organisation claims they are covered by the journalistic exemption, the proceedings can be 'stayed' (meaning suspended, so that no order can be given), while the Commissioner decides whether or not the exemption conditions are satisfied. This only applies if the information concerned has not yet been published. Without this provision, someone being investigated by the press could use the Act to find out what information was held on them, and then prevent it being reported by claiming that disclosure would cause them distress or damage.

 In *Douglas v Hello!* (2005), the court roundly rejected the magazine's claim to the exemption, because it was impossible to establish any public interest reason for publishing the photographs. Mr Justice Lindsay commented that the fact that the public would be interested in the pictures 'is not to be confused with there being a public interest'.

In *Campbell* v *MGN*, the Court of Appeal held that the journalistic exemption did apply, because the *Mirror* could demonstrate that there was a public interest in publication of the story: Ms Campbell had lied when she previously denied having a drug problem, and the story was correcting the false impression those denials gave. The Court of Appeal also specifically stated (overturning a ruling given in the High Court) that the exemption applied both before and after publication of the story. Although Ms Campbell then appealed to the House of Lords and won her case, the House of Lords' decision was based purely on the issues of breach of confidence and privacy, and the Data Protection Act claim was not discussed. This would seem to suggest that the Court of Appeal's view on the application of the defence still applies, but we will not know this for sure until it is tested again in the courts.

In *Stone* v *South East Coast Strategic Health Authority* (2006), a convicted murderer called Michael Stone tried to use the Data Protection Act to prevent publication of a report into his treatment for mental health problems and drug abuse. Mr Stone was undergoing the treatment at the time, in 1996, when he attacked Lin Russell and her daughters Megan and Josie, killing Lin and Megan and leaving Josie seriously injured. An independent inquiry was ordered to try to find out if there was anything that could have been done to prevent the killing, and Mr Stone cooperated with the inquiry, but objected to the report being made public on the grounds that it would divulge his private medical details. However, the High Court found that there was a clear public interest in publishing the report in full.

Protecting sources

The right of access to information could potentially be a route for people to find out who has supplied information to the media. Take, for example, a situation where an employee tells a paper about misconduct by a senior member of management in the firm where they work. If the senior manager learns that they are being investigated, they could make a request for the information held by the paper, from which they could very probably work out who the source was.

However, some protection against this scenario is provided by s7(4) of the Act, which provides that where access to information cannot be given without disclosing information relating to another individual, from which that individual can be identified, the data controller need not comply with the request unless that person gives consent, or it is reasonable in all the circumstances to do so without consent. In deciding whether or not compliance is reasonable without consent, the data controller can take into account any duty of confidentiality owed to the person who supplied the information, and any express refusal of consent by that person.

The journalist may nevertheless be obliged to give the subject access to as much of the material is possible without divulging the source's identity, for example by withholding names and other identifying details.

INVESTIGATION AND ENFORCEMENT

The Act provides for the Information Commissioner to issue enforcement notices, requiring people or organisations who are in breach of the Act to comply with it. This provision is backed up with powers of entry and inspection for which a warrant from a judge is required. However, a warrant should not be granted if the data controller claims that the data concerned is being processed for the purposes of journalism, until the Commissioner has determined whether the journalistic exemption applies.

Where a data controller claims the journalistic exemption, an enforcement notice cannot be issued until the Information Commissioner has assessed whether the exemption applies, and a court has given leave for the enforcement notice to be issued. A court should only give this leave where it is satisfied that the Information Commissioner has reason to suspect that the breach of the Act is of substantial public importance.

Failure to abide by an enforcement notice, or persistent breaches of the Act, can be prosecuted as a criminal offence, punishable with a fine of up to £5,000.

PROBLEMS WITH GATHERING INFORMATION

So far we have looked at the implications of the Act when media organisations act as data controllers, but as mentioned in the introduction to this chapter, the Act also has an impact on journalists' research activities, in that organisations may, rightly or wrongly, use it as a reason not to reveal information. The Newspaper Society's 2004 Press Freedom Survey found widespread concern about the way in which the Act was used to stifle newsgathering, with 43 editors naming it as the single greatest obstacle to reporting. As well as deliberate misuse of the Act to avoid answering difficult questions, editors complained that in many organisations, the Act was misunderstood, or used as an excuse when officials simply could not be bothered to collate the information required.

Local authorities, hospitals and councils were all mentioned as problem areas, but the two areas where most difficulty seems to be caused are the police, particularly with regard to information about crime and accident victims; and schools, many of which seem to believe (wrongly) that the Act absolutely prevents them from revealing the names of children photographed by the press at events such as sports days. Both these areas have now been addressed by guidelines, which are discussed below; a good knowledge of these may help reporters get the information they need.

In general terms though, the best defence against obstructive and unnecessary use of the Act is to have a thorough knowledge of its provisions, and to be able to explain them when you believe a refusal of disclosure is based on a misunderstanding.

20
Data protection

Law in practice Challenging use of the Data Protection Act

As the Newspaper Society's 2004 Press Freedom Survey shows, the Data Protection Act is widely misunderstood, and organisations will often cite it as a reason for refusing information in situation where the Act does not actually prevent the information being released. If you suspect this to be the case, it can be useful to ask them to explain why they think the Act prevents disclosure, as you may be able to clarify the misunderstanding.

For example, organisations will often refuse to reveal the name or contact details of an individual because they do not have the subject's consent to do so, but the Act does not say that they may not ask for that consent. In some cases, of course, the subject will not give consent, but often organisations will refuse to put you in touch with someone even in the most innocuous of circumstances when the subject would actually be quite happy to be contacted. In that case explaining that the Act allows them to ask for the person's consent may solve the problem.

The Information Commissioner also issues Good Practice Notes and other guidelines from time to time, to help correct situations where the Act seems to be being misinterpreted; new ones are published on the Office of the Information Commissioner's website (see *Online resources* at the end of the chapter).

▩ Information from the police

The Association of Chief Police Officers (ACPO) has a Code of Practice on data protection, and its Media Advisory Group has produced further guidelines covering the effect of the Data Protection Act on the release of information to the media (see *Online resources* at the end of the chapter). The guidelines specifically state that 'the Police Service should be supportive of a free flow of information to the media', as well as ensuring that people's rights under the Act are respected. To assist officers in striking the right balance, the guidelines make these specific points:

- The Act provides for situations in which personal information can be released without the subject's consent, where that would be in the public interest. Whether a particular situation falls within this category must be assessed on a case-by-case basis; the guidelines give the example of a major accident involving a large number of casualties, where it would be in the public interest to give out information about the victims without having to wait and get consent from them or their next of kin, in order to minimise public alarm and distress. ACPO's Code of Practice on Data Protection gives a further example, stating that information may be disclosed without consent where it is the public interest because police are appealing for witnesses.

- In general, however, personal details of victims, witnesses or anyone who is next of kin to a victim should not be released to the media without that person's consent. Before deciding how to publicise a crime or accident, the police should ask for the views of the victim, witnesses or next of kin, and where juveniles are involved, it would be good practice to consult the parents or guardians, even though this is not specifically required by the Act. However, personal details can be released to the media even if the subject says they do not want them to be, if the police feel that in the specific case, there is an 'exceptional reason' to do so.

- The Act does not give victims the right to prevent any details of the incident from being released, as long as doing so does not make it possible to identify them.

- When someone's consent is sought for release of information, the question should be put in a balanced way (the suggested wording is 'We often find it helpful in our enquiries to pass on someone's details to the media. Do you object if we do that in your case?'). In other words, the police should not aim to discourage people from having their details released.

- Where victims of crime agree to have their details released, but to do so might make them vulnerable to further crime, the police are justified in refusing to release the details (the guidelines give the example of an elderly person living alone). In this situation, police officers should explain the reason for the refusal, so that journalists who happen to find out the victim's name another way will take this issue into account when deciding whether to publish it.

- The guidelines also address situations where journalists ask the police for further details on stories they have obtained from other sources, but the subject of the information has not consented to its release. In this situation, the police should consider whether releasing the information would provide an opportunity to correct inaccuracies or speculation. They should not volunteer the name of anyone who is under investigation but has not been charged, but if the media already has the name, the police can confirm it.

- In some cases, the victim of an accident may subsequently be charged with a crime (e.g. where a stolen car is involved in a crash). In such situations, if an arrest is imminent, the identity of the person should not be released, even if they consent to it, until they have been charged. If it turns out that no charge is brought, the identity can be released then. Where the person is a juvenile, their identity should not be disclosed even after they are charged.

■ Information from schools

Twenty-five of the editors surveyed for the Newspaper Society's 2004 Press Freedom Survey said schools were refusing either to allow press photography of school events at all, or more commonly allowed photography but then claimed that the Data Protection Act prevented them from supplying the names of the children in the photo. This was the case even though the pictures were often taken for stories which celebrated the school's achievements. Many schools were also reluctant to release exam results. Other organisations dealing with children, such as sports clubs, were also imposing restrictions on photography and/or caption information. As one editor quoted in the survey commented, 'These restrictions are hampering local newspapers reporting on the many positive stories, and preventing a whole generation of children from being proud to appear in their local newspaper.'

In answer to these criticisms (and also to press stories that even parents were being prevented from taking pictures at school events), the Information Commissioner produced a Good Practice Note on the subject (see *Online resources* at the end of the chapter). It states that as long as the school agrees to the press taking photographs, and the parents are informed that photos taken may be used in the press, there is no breach of the Act in allowing photographers to take pictures in school or at school events. As far as information for captions is concerned, the Department for Education and Skills has released guidance on this, which contains advice from the Information Commissioner. It states that schools can simply ask parents whether they mind the information being released, and if this consent is given, schools can give out the information without breaching the Act.

With regard to exam results, guidelines from the Information Commissioner explain that, under the Act, schools have to inform parents and pupils about the data they they process. This is usually done at the start of a child's time in the school, using a template form produced by the Office of the Information Commissioner, and on this form, the purposes for which data may be used includes disclosure to the press. As well as being given this form, parents should also be told that they can object to publication. If this has been done, there is no problem with releasing results to the press, and no need to get further consent (unless a particular child or parent has objected, which the school will know about).

Law in practice School photography

One of the few editors in the Newspaper Society's 2004 Press Freedom Survey who reported no problems with getting caption information for school photos explained that schools in the local area sought blanket permission from parents at the start of each school year, so that there was no need to do so every time a photographer attended a school event. Far from refusing consent, parents were usually more anxious to make sure their children were not left out. It may therefore be useful for local papers to suggest this course of action to schools in their area.

OBTAINING INFORMATION FROM OTHERS

What is the situation where a journalist obtains information from someone else, and that person's disclosure is in breach of the Act? Section 55 of the Data Protection Act 1998 makes it an offence to knowingly or recklessly, without the consent of the data controller, obtain, disclose or procure the disclosure of personal data or the information in it. There is a defence where the person procuring, obtaining or disclosing the information believed doing so was justified in the public interest. The offences are not imprisonable, but if prosecuted in the Crown Court, can lead to an unlimited fine.

No journalist has yet been charged with any of these offences, but according to author Mark Watts, it may not be long before this happens (see *Online resources* at the end of the chapter). He investigated the activities of private detectives and others who gather data for (among others) national newspapers, including unauthorised disclosure of information from the police national computer, and supply of information from phone accounts or in connection with vehicle registration, and claims that at least one police force has 'long lists' of the media clients of detective agencies who illegally obtain personal information.

CHAPTER SUMMARY

Information covered by the Act

The Act covers personal data, defined as information held on computer or in a filing system, from which an individual can be identified.

Media duties under the Act

Media organisations and journalists who process personal data must:

- register with the Information Commissioner;
- process data fairly and lawfully, in accordance with the eight principles stated in the Act;
- comply with others' rights under the Act.

Stricter rules apply to 'sensitive personal data' covering issues such as race, political views, health or religious beliefs.

Exemptions for the media

The media can be exempt from most of the Act's provisions, but only where it can prove that:

- data was processed for the purpose of publication;
- publication was in the public interest;
- it was impossible to comply with the Act.

Investigation and enforcement

The Information Commissioner has powers of investigation and enforcement, but use of these against the media is restricted.

Problems with gathering information

The Act is often used to deny the press information. This can be challenged by:

- knowledge of the Act;
- understanding guidelines from the Information Commissioner;
- understanding guidelines issued by ACPO, for information from the police.

Obtaining information from others

Knowingly or recklessly obtaining, disclosing or procuring personal data without the consent of the data controller is an offence.

TEST YOUR KNOWLEDGE

1 What do these terms mean:

(a) data controller

(b) data subject

(c) processing?

2 Which of these falls within the definition of 'personal data' under the Data Protection Act?

(a) Photographs of individuals held on computer.

(b) Hand-written notes from interviews with individuals, stored in paper files labelled with each interviewee's name.

(c) Notes of interviews for a series of personal profiles, typed up and held on computer.

(d) Business cards of regular contacts, stored in a card index.

(e) A box full of press cuttings, unsorted.

(f) Files of press cuttings, sorted into files on different people.

3 You are holding information about a celebrity, which details their mental health problems. What is the minimum you have to do to make sure you process this information in compliance with the Data Protection Act?

4 You are researching a story about a local businessman paying bribes to council officials. The businessman submits a written request, citing the Act and requiring you to disclose the information you hold about him. Do you have to comply?

5 You are researching a story about the marital difficulties of a very well-known actor. He submits a written request, citing the Act and requiring you to disclose the information you hold about him. Do you have to comply?

6 You and a photographer visit a local school to report on a carol concert. Photographs are taken, but when you call to get information for the picture captions, you are told that the Data Protection Act prevents the school disclosing the name of any pupil. Is this true?

20

Data protection

ONLINE RESOURCES

www The Data Protection Act can be read at:
www.opsi.gov.uk/ACTS/acts1998/19980029.htm

The Office of the Information Commissioner's website is at:
www.ico.gov.uk

The Association of Chief Police Officers Media Advisory Group Code of Practice on Data Protection can be read at:
www.acpo.police.uk/asp/policies/Data/magguidelines.pdf

The Newspaper Society's 2004 Press Freedom Survey can be read at:
www.newspapersoc.org.uk/Documents/Publications/pr2005/press-freedom.htm

The Freedom of Information Centre website contains articles by journalist Mark Watts, on illegal information gathering by the media, at:
www.foiacentre.com

For further resources and updates please go to the Companion Website for this book at www.pearsoned.co.uk/practicaljournalism

Copyright

The law of copyright is part of a branch of law known as intellectual property, and gives those who create something – from a magazine article, to a novel or a piece of music – the power to protect the work they have done from being copied or used by other people. If you own the copyright on something, the law states that others cannot copy it or use it as if it were their own work, without your permission. So if, for example, you hold the copyright on a feature which has been published in a magazine, and it is then reproduced without permission on an unrelated website, you could sue for damages.

There are two reasons why a journalist needs to know about copyright: first, because in some instances you will own the copyright on your own work; and second, because you will often want to quote other people's words or use other people's work during your research, and you need to know how far the law allows you to do this.

Most of the English law on copyright comes from the Copyright, Designs and Patents Act 1988.

WORKS PROTECTED BY COPYRIGHT

The Copyright, Designs and Patents Act 1988 states that copyright applies to three types of work:

- original literary, dramatic, musical or artistic works;
- sound recordings, films or broadcasts;
- the typographical arrangements of published editions.

If a piece of work does not fall into one of these categories, it is not protected by copyright.

Literary, dramatic, musical and artistic works

The key requirement here is that work must be original. However, this does not mean it has to be strikingly imaginative, unusual or new, simply that it is the copyright holder's own work and not merely copied from something else.

 In *Independent Television Publications Ltd v Time Out Ltd* (1984), a court found that the programme listings carried by *TV Times* could be counted as an original literary work, because although they were only a compilation of information from different sources, some work and effort had been put in to compiling and organising the information. (Television companies are now obliged under the Broadcasting Act 1990 to supply listings to any publisher that wants them, but they still retain copyright and can charge for the listings.)

In *Ladbroke (Football) Ltd* v *William Hill (Football) UK Ltd* (1964) the court found that football fixture lists were protected by copyright, which was owned by the Football Association.

The fact that two pieces of work may be very similar does not mean that they cannot both be subject to copyright, so long as the similarity is accidental and not the result of copying.

The two types of work in this category that are most relevant to journalists are literary and artistic works. Literary works are defined in s3(1) as: 'any work, other than a dramatic or musical work, which is written, spoken or sung'. 'Literary' in this context really means capable of being written down; it does not mean that the work has to have any literary merit or be capable of being considered 'literature', or even that it has to be comprised of words. Common examples are books, newspaper and magazine features and stories, interviews, speeches and song lyrics, but the category also includes computer programs, databases and tables: so the South East Trains timetable is protected by copyright in exactly the same way as the latest Booker Prize-winning novel.

However, there must be some sort of substance to the work: slogans and catchphrases are too brief to be covered by copyright. (They can be registered as trademarks if the originator wants to protect them, but copyright does not arise automatically as it would for an article or book.)

Artistic works include photographs, maps, graphics and drawings, and again, there is no need for any great creative merit; even a very simple sketch may be covered. However, there must be some tangible item as a result of the work.

In *Kenrick & Co* v *Lawrence & Co* (1890) a simple drawing of a voting paper and a hand making a pencilled cross against the name of a candidate was held to be covered by copyright. However, as it was so simple, it was only protected against exact or near-exact copies; a slightly different picture with the hand in a different position was not a breach of copyright.

In *Creation Records Ltd* v *News Group Newspapers* (1997), the band Oasis was involved in a photo shoot at a country hotel. The pictures had been set up with the band members positioned around a pool, and a Rolls-Royce apparently rising out of the water. A photographer for the *Sun* got a room in the hotel, and from the window, was able to photograph the scene. The record company which had organised the shoot tried to sue for breach of copyright, arguing that the arrangement of the scene itself (even before any photos were taken) constituted an artistic work, comparable to a collage. The court disagreed; the scene was too impermanent to amount to an artistic work (it was, however, protected by the law on confidentiality; see Chapter 17).

In 2001, the AA was sued by the map makers Ordnance Survey, after it used Ordnance Survey maps as the basis for producing its own maps. Ordnance Survey was able to prove the plagiarism, because they had deliberately put tiny mistakes in their own maps, and these were reproduced in the AA material. The case was settled out of court, with the AA paying £20 million.

Sound recordings, films and broadcasts

Sound recordings include any recording of sounds, regardless of how it is made. Film covers any recording of a moving image. Broadcast is defined as an electronic transmission of images, sounds and information to the public, but does not include internet transmission unless it is a concurrent transmission of a live event, or part of a programme service transmitted at scheduled times, or a transmission that also takes place at the same time by other means. The Act specifically provides that taking a photograph of a TV screen while a programme is broadcast (sometimes known as a 'screen grab') can be a breach of copyright.

Typographical arrangements

This category covers the way in which a printed page is laid out and protects against unauthorised photocopying.

Copyright and ideas

Section 3(2) of the 1988 Act provides that, in order to be covered by copyright, literary, dramatic and musical works have to be recorded in a tangible form, such as writing or a tape recording. This means that mere ideas which have not been put into a permanent form will not be protected by copyright, and nor will words which have been spoken but not recorded or written down. The main implication of this for journalists comes in the area of commissioning. If, for example, a freelance writer suggests a feature idea to a magazine, that idea is not protected by copyright, and an unscrupulous commissioning editor may be able simply to take it and give it to another writer, or produce the feature in-house (in this situation, however, there will sometimes be protection from the law of confidentiality – see p. 231).

In *Green* v *Broadcasting Corp of New Zealand* (1989), the host and creator of 'Opportunity Knocks', a popular TV talent show at the time, sued a New Zealand TV company for copying the show. Their programme used the same title and had a very similar format, including using a device called a 'clapometer' which measured the audience's applause for each act, but the court said that these were too imprecise to amount to a 'dramatic work' that could be protected by copyright.

In *IPC Media Ltd* v *Highbury Leisure Publishing* (2004), IPC sued rival publishers Highbury, alleging that its new magazine *Home* infringed IPC copyright on its title *Ideal Home*. IPC alleged that *Home* copied *Ideal Home*'s design, pointing out the similarities between the two title's cover formats, inside layouts and subject matter of features. The court rejected the claim, saying that all the features and techniques mentioned were commonly used throughout the magazine industry, and that in a highly competitive market, it was inevitable that designers would use similar tricks and techniques, and subject matter would coincide. The similarities IPC had pointed to were really at the level of ideas, themes and styles, which copyright law did not protect.

In *Baigent* v *Random House* (2006), two of the three authors of a book called *The Holy Blood and The Holy Grail* sued the publishers of the best-selling novel *The Da Vinci Code*. The claimants' book was a non-fiction work, advancing the theory that Jesus married Mary Magdelene and had children. *The Da Vinci Code* uses this theory as the basis for a thriller, in which the hero tries to find evidence that would prove it to be true, while those who want to keep it secret try to stop him. The author of *The Da Vinci Code* admitted that *The Holy Blood* had been used as part of his background research, and had one of his characters refer to it in the book. The claimants argued that he had breached their copyright by copying the 'central theme' of their book. The court rejected this argument, saying that there had been no copying of a central theme, and that even if there had been, that central theme was essentially a collection of ideas, and as such could not be protected by copyright. Only the expression of those ideas could be copyrighted, and the court found no evidence of substantial copying of the text.

News and information

Because of the requirement that copyright material has to have some tangible form, news and information are not covered by copyright, only the words used to express them in a particular news story. This means that if you uncover a scoop about, for example, a local politician having an affair, the actual story that you write about it will be copyright, but other papers can still report the facts in different words, even if the only information they have comes from your story and they would not otherwise have known about it. Equally, of course, you can do the same with stories in rival papers.

However, this does not amount to a wholesale licence to lift stories from other publications. Where the lifting goes beyond the basic facts, and reproduces a substantial amount of either the original writer's words, or quotations used in the original piece, without acknowledging that they came from the copyright holder, there may be a breach of copyright.

 In *Express Newspapers plc v News (UK) Ltd* (1990), the *Daily Express* sued the *Today* newspaper for breach of copyright, after *Today* ran a story about Pamela Bordes, who at the time was in the news for being what the tabloids like to call a 'high class call girl'. The *Express* had had the story as an exclusive in its first edition, and the facts and quotes were lifted by *Today* for its second edition. *Today* then counter-sued the *Express* for lifting one of its stories on the Royal family. In both cases, the judge refused to accept that publishing the facts of the stories was a breach of copyright. He pointed out that it was (and still is) standard practice for newspapers to pick up stories from each other and rewrite them, and said that to accept that this practice was a breach of copyright would allow individual newspapers to claim a monopoly in particular news stories, which would not be in the public interest. However, both newspapers were liable for breach of copyright for reproducing the other's quotes, because getting the quotes in the first place demanded skill and effort and was therefore work which could be protected.

 In *Walter v Steinkopf* (1892), Rudyard Kipling had been writing news dispatches for *The Times*, and a paper called the *St James Evening Gazette* began regularly printing substantial parts of them in its own coverage. *The Times* sued. The court confirmed that there was no copyright in news itself, but that there was copyright in the way that news was expressed in a story. It observed that the *Gazette* had used large amounts of copy from *The Times*, had done so regularly and deliberately, and had not made any effort to rewrite the reports at all; what the *Gazette* had done was described as 'a mechanical operation with scissors and paste'. The *Gazette* was taking advantage of someone else's labour at no cost to itself and, the court held, what it had done amounted to breach of copyright.

 In *Walter v Lane* (1900), a *Times* reporter was granted damages after a rival newspaper copied word for word a speech which he had taken down in shorthand and used in a news story. As with *Walter v Steinkopf*, what appeared to influence the court was that the *Times* reporter had used skill and effort in taking the speech down in shorthand, whereas the other paper was getting something for nothing. (Obviously, had the rival paper's reporter attended the speech, they could have made their own notes and used those without breaching *The Times*' copyright).

As some of the judgments above point out, it is in the public interest that news is reported as widely as possible, and Parliament specifically recognised this when passing the 1988 Act, which creates a special defence which, within limits, can allow use of copyright material (such as quotes) in reporting current events, provided the copyright holder is acknowledged (see below).

Speeches and interviews

A speech which has previously been written down is covered by copyright, because it exists in a tangible form before it is spoken; the copyright belongs to the speaker. Someone who records that speech (on sound or film) would own the copyright to the recorded words, so both the person who wrote the speech, and the person who recorded it could sue for breach of copyright.

Where a speaker talks off the cuff, or gives an interview, there is no copyright in their words until they are written down or recorded by someone else (such as a reporter), whether with or without the speaker's permission. Where a journalist makes an accurate note or recording of words spoken off the cuff or in an interview, the copyright for the words belongs to the speaker, but the journalist will own the copyright to the tape or notes. A defence under the 1988 Act allows words recorded in these circumstances to be used for reporting current events, or in a broadcast or cable programme, without the speaker's permission (see p. 297).

What does copyright protect?

Protected	Not protected
Original literary, dramatic, musical and artistic works, including almost anything written down in words, plus photos, maps and drawings	Ideas (though these may be protected by confidentiality; see Chapter 17)
Sound recordings, films and broadcasts	Facts
Typographical arrangements	News and information

◼ Official information

Documents published by or on behalf of the Government are covered by what is called Crown copyright, so they cannot simply be copied or reproduced without permission. In most cases, where the media wants to publish extracts from a government document which is publicly available, a licence is issued allowing publication of small amounts of material without charge. However, there are some categories where Crown copyright is waived. Copying material which by law must be available to public inspection is not usually a breach of copyright.

Reporting words spoken or read during parliamentary or court proceedings is not an infringement of copyright.

ESTABLISHING COPYRIGHT

The copyright on a piece of work comes into existence as soon as the work is created, and gives the holder (usually, though not always, the creator of the work) the right to sue anyone who uses the work unlawfully.

It is often believed that in order to establish the copyright to a work, you have to mark it with the copyright symbol and/or post it to yourself or someone else so that the date of creation is confirmed. This is not the case. Copyright comes into existence automatically when a work is created, and does not need to be registered in any way; nor does the work have to be published in order for copyright to exist. The posting technique can be useful as a way to prove the date that copyright arose, in case of a dispute later, but the copyright will exist anyway.

OWNERSHIP OF COPYRIGHT

The 1988 Act provides that the first owner of any work is the person who creates it, unless the work is created in the course of employment. In that case, unless you have agreed otherwise in your employment contract, the employer owns the copyright. So, for example, if you are on the staff of a magazine or newspaper, your employer will usually own the copyright to everything you write as part of your job, and can use it for any purpose. A freelance journalist, on the other hand, owns the copyright to all their work, unless they agree otherwise with the company that commissions it.

Once the work is created, the copyright holder can transfer ownership to someone else. For example, when magazines and papers commission a freelance to write for them, they quite often buy the copyright to that article from the freelance as part of the deal. This then enables them to sell on the work to other publications if they wish to, without paying any more money to the freelance, or asking their permission; this is often called buying 'all rights'. Freelances can, of course, refuse to work on this basis and negotiate to keep the copyright, simply allowing the work to be used on a one-off basis (or to allow further use, but be paid for it).

If a reader sends a letter to a newspaper and does not state that it is not to be published, they are effectively giving permission to publish that letter (in legal terms, this is issuing a licence – see below). However, the writer of the letter retains copyright in it.

Ownership of photographs

If a photograph was taken after the 1988 Act came into force on 31 July 1989, the original copyright belongs to the person who takes the photo; this applies as much to a family snapshot as to a shot taken by a famous photographer. For photos taken before the Act came into force, copyright belongs to the person who commissioned them, so in the case of a wedding photo, for example, it would usually be the couple themselves or one of them.

In addition to the copyright issue, privacy rights attach to pictures commissioned for 'private and domestic purposes' (see p. 229).

Law in practice   Using photos

One area to be careful of is illustrating stories about ordinary people with school, college or wedding photographs, or any other pictures which have been taken by a professional photographer. People are often happy to hand these over to a reporter, but in fact they may not own the copyright, even if they paid for the photograph; in most cases it remains with the photographer, whose permission should be sought before publishing.

Transferring copyright

Someone who owns copyright in a work can give (or more commonly, sell) all or part of that right to someone else in one of two ways:

- assignment
- licence.

Assignment

Assigning copyright is the equivalent to selling it, or part of it. For example, as stated above, many publishers buy copyright as part of the deal when they commission a feature. In that case, the writer is assigning the copyright to the publisher, who can then use the feature as many times as it wants to, and can also sell it to other publishers; effectively, the feature becomes the publisher's property. Assignment of copyright must be in writing to be legally binding. In some large publishing companies, regular freelances are asked to sign a form stating that all commissions are on an all rights basis unless otherwise agreed; in others, a commissioning form is sent out when each job is ordered.

Licence

A licence is a way of giving someone permission to use the work in a particular way or for a particular length of time. If, for example, a freelance writer only grants a licence – for example, the right to publish the article once in a particular magazine – the copyright remains with the writer and if the publisher wants to use the piece elsewhere or again it must get permission. A licence granting exclusive use of material must be in writing to be legally binding (and in fact it is good practice to get any agreement involving copyright in writing).

Law in practice Commissioning work

If you commission work – whether copy or photographs – from someone else, and you (or your company) may at some point want to use that work for something other than the original use, you need to agree this with the freelance, either at the time of commissioning or when you want to reuse the material. If, for example, you commission someone to write a feature for your magazine, that does not give you the right to put it on your website as well, unless you agree that with the freelance in advance. Similarly, if you commission a photographer to take pictures for a particular feature, you do not automatically have the right to use them on a later occasion, even in the same magazine. Many large publishing companies, particularly magazine companies, now use printed commissioning forms, which are sent out to the freelance, confirming the rights that have been bought; this is a useful way to make sure both sides are clear on what is being bought. To have legal effect, however, the freelance needs to be informed of the terms at the time the commission is agreed; sending a form after the job is done is not legally binding, although it is common practice in many companies.

21

Copyright

INFRINGING COPYRIGHT

There are several ways in which copyright can be infringed, but for journalistic purposes, the most important is copying, which includes reproducing all or part of someone else's work as though it were your own work, or publishing it without permission, even if you acknowledge it as the copyright holder's work (there are however some situations in which this is permitted; see p. 293).

In order to count as an infringment of copyright, the 1988 Act provides that there must be use of a 'substantial part' of the original work. There is no set rules on what proportion of a work will be considered substantial, but the quality of what is reproduced (in terms of its importance to the original work) can be as important as the quantity.

In *PCR Ltd* v *Dow Jones Telerate Ltd* (1998) a business reporter used information from a private report on the world cocoa market, including sets of figures, in an article of her own. Although the amount of information used was not large, it included more or less all the significant points in the market report, and as a result, her article was held to be a breach of copyright.

Exact copies are obviously a breach of copyright, while taking a set of facts from a story and expressing them in a completely different way is not. In between the two, however, lies a grey area. The basic test is whether the person doing the second piece of work has contributed a significant degree of work and skill over and above that already in the original work so, obviously, just changing the odd word in a feature and then reproducing it is very likely to be a breach of copyright; however, if the original work is genuinely only the basis, and significant skill and effort has gone into the second piece of work, the courts are less likely to find a breach. The amount of effort and skill which went into the original work is also a factor; as the case of *Kenrick* v *Lawrence* (see earlier), about the drawing of a hand, shows, less protection is given when the original work itself requires little skill.

In *Warwick Film Productions* v *Eisinger* (1969), the courts were asked to decide whether the compiler of one anthology of quotations had breached the copyright of another, published earlier. Although some of the quotations were the same, the court found that the material had been arranged differently, and used with material from other sources. This involved a sufficient degree of work to ensure that there was no breach of copyright.

▦ Parodies

Parodying a piece of work (meaning making a humorous imitation of it) can be breach of copyright, if the parody is sufficiently similar to the original. The courts tend to be more lenient about parodies which are created for political or topical comment than those used for commercial purposes.

In *Williamson Music* v *Pearson Partnership Ltd* (1987), an advertising agency produced a jingle for a bus company, which used the tune of the song 'There is Nothing Like a Dame'. Although the words were different, the tune was exactly the same, and the holder of copyright for the tune was granted an injunction.

Parodies can also cause problems with the moral right of protection against false attribution of authorship (see p. 300).

▦ Embargoes

When a copyright holder gives permission for their material to be used (in legal terms, issues a licence – see above), they may put certain conditions on that use, such as an embargo, which states that the material cannot be used before a stated date. If this is ignored, the resulting publication may be a breach of copyright.

In 1992, the *Sun* published the Queen's Christmas message two days before Christmas. It is usual practice for the message to be issued to all national papers before Christmas, with an embargo prohibiting publication until after the Queen's broadcast on Christmas Day, and this happened as usual, but the *Sun* ignored the embargo. The Queen began an action for breach of copyright, and the case was settled out of court with the paper agreeing to pay a substantial sum to charity.

▦ Length of copyright

Before the 1988 Act, copyright could last for ever, but now the Act lays down limits for how long copyright in different types of work lasts. When these periods come to an end, the work goes out of copyright, and is said to be 'in the public domain'. It can then can be used by anyone, in any way, without charge.

The table below shows the lengths of copyright for different types of work, under the Act. However, it only applies to works created since the Act was passed; older works may be subject to different time periods, and specialist legal advice may need to be sought regarding these.

Work	Length of copyright
Literary, dramatic, musical and artistic works	70 years from the end of the calendar year in which the author/composer/artist dies.
Sound recordings	50 years from the end of the calendar year in which they were made.
Broadcast	50 years from the end of the calendar year in which it was made.
Film	70 years from the end of the calendar year which sees the death of the last among the principal director, screenplay writer, writer of the dialogue or composer of music created especially for the film.
Published editions (layouts, design and so on – see p. xx)	25 years from the end of the calendar year in which it was first published.

DEFENCES

The Copyright, Designs and Patents Act 1988 allows some use of copyright-protected works without permission from the copyright owner, and these can provide defences to an action for breach of copyright. The five which are most relevant to the media are:

- fair dealing;
- incidental inclusion;
- public interest;
- reproduction of speeches and interviews;
- acquiescence.

In *Ashdown* v *Telegraph Group* (2001) (see later), the Court of Appeal looked at the question of whether the HRA right of freedom of expression could provide a defence to breach of copyright, and concluded that it did not give the media any extra protection over and above that provided by the defences listed above.

■ Fair dealing

This allows parts of copyright works to be quoted, reproduced or used for the purposes of criticism or review, or in the course of reporting current events. This means that if you are writing a review of a book, for example, you can quote parts of it word for word, while in reporting a news story, a broadcaster could use parts of another channel's broadcast. The defence applies where:

- the material is used for the purpose of criticism or review; or in reporting current events;
- the copyright holder receives 'sufficient acknowledgement' (though this is not always necessary for TV and film clips; see below);
- the amount of material used is fair;
- the material used has already been made available to the public.

What material can be used?

The defence of fair dealing applies to written or spoken words, to film clips and 'artistic works'. This means that, for example, if a celebrity hits the news, BBC news could use excerpts from an ITN interview with that person, and newspapers can quote from each other's stories. As well as material from other publishers and TV companies, the defence can allow the media to use other copyright material, such as government and local authority reports and private papers (though they must have been made available to the public; see below).

However, the defence does not apply to photographs used for reporting current events (though they can be used in criticism and review). If one paper holds the copyright on a particular photograph, others cannot publish it and then use the defence of fair dealing in reporting current events, even if they acknowledge where it came from.

In *Banier* v *News Group Newspapers* (1997), the case concerned stories about Princess Caroline of Monaco, who was suffering from alopecia (hair loss). Pictures of her had been taken by a French photographer, and several papers had bought permission to use the pictures from him. The *Sun* did not seek permission, but printed some of the pictures anyway. The paper claimed that it intended to negotiate a licence fee after publication, and that it was common practice to print without permission and pay afterwards where a story needed to be published quickly in order to remain newsworthy. The court rejected this argument, stating the publication was unlawful. It ordered an injunction and awarded damages to the photographer.

It is important to be aware that a newspaper or magazine may hold copyright to photos even if it has not taken or commissioned them. Where an ordinary person is involved in a high-profile news story, a paper may pay relatives or friends for the copyright to family snaps, which means that other papers will be breaching copyright if they publish them.

Stills taken from TV or film do not count as photographs for the purpose of fair dealing, and their use can therefore be covered by the defence.

Criticism and review

Clearly this covers specific reviews of the work concerned, but it is wider than this, covering situations where copyright material is used to illustrate the theme of a feature or programme.

In *Pro Sieben Media AG* v *Carlton UK Television Ltd* (1999), Pro Sieben, a German TV company, had the rights to a TV interview with Mandy Allwood, a British woman who had hit the news when she was pregnant with octuplets. It used the interview on a daily news programme. Carlton then used clips of the same interview in a programme of its own, about chequebook journalism, and this was found to be within the limits of fair dealing, since Mandy Allwood had been paid by newspapers for her story (see later for more details on this case).

In *Time Warner Entertainments Co* v *Channel Four* (1994), Channel 4 made a TV programme about the fact that the film 'A Clockwork Orange' had been withdrawn from public showings because of the violence in it. Using clips from the film in the programme was covered by the defence of fair dealing (see later for more details on this case).

In *Fraser-Woodward* v *BBC* (2005), a photographic agency sued the BBC for showing its photographs, without permission, in a programme about the tabloid press. The pictures were seen in shots of the pages of newspapers. Mr Justice Mann ruled that they were used for the purpose of criticism of the practices of the tabloid press and therefore could fall within the defence.

Reporting current events

The fair dealing defence also allows broadcasters and newspapers to use each other's material where it is fair to do so for the purpose of reporting current events. This means that, for example, if one TV company has footage of a key event in the news, others can use clips from it to illustrate the story, and where one newspaper has broken a story, others can use excerpts from it. As with reviews, the copyright holder should be given sufficient acknowledgement, but this is waived for sound recordings, film or broadcasts where it would be impossible 'for reasons of practicality or otherwise' to acknowledge the copyright holder.

The Act does not define current events, and there seems to be no set time limit on whether an issue will be considered current; it is clear, however, that the defence is not limited to coverage of events happening at or just before the time of reporting.

 In *Hyde Park Residence Ltd* v *Yelland* (2000) the Court of Appeal considered whether a story about the relationship between Princess Diana and Dodi Fayed could count as reporting current events, considering that they had both been dead for a year when it was published. The court held that it could, taking into account the fact that news stories about the relationship had continued appearing since the car crash which killed the couple, and that Dodi's father had recently issued press statements about it (though the case failed for other reasons; see later).

 In *Ashdown* v *Telegraph Group* (2001), the Court of Appeal held that a story about a meeting between Tony Blair and Paddy Ashdown, then leader of the Liberal Democrats, could be considered reporting of current events, even though the meeting had taken place a couple of years earlier. The issue, the court said, was whether the report in question was informing the public about 'matters of current concern' (the defence in fact failed on other grounds).

The requirement for the reporting to be of current events only applies to the report which uses the copyright material; the material itself need not be a report of current events. For example, where a celebrity hits the headlines, fair dealing would allow use of excerpts from an old interview with that person.

Sufficient acknowledgement

To be covered by fair dealing, the review must contain 'sufficient acknowledgement' of the copyright work. This means that it must be clear who the copyright holder of the work is, unless it is published anonymously or is not published, and it is impossible to find out the copyright owner by reasonable inquiry. The acknowledgement must identify the source properly, so words such as 'a book on the subject says' or 'an academic report stated' would not be sufficient. However, as long as the source is clearly identified, it is not necessary to thank them for use of the material.

 In the *Pro Sieben* case mentioned above, the clips carried the Pro Sieben logo in one corner of the screen, and it was suggested that this could not count as 'sufficient acknowledgement' because the symbol was meaningless to most UK viewers. However, the Court of Appeal held that this was irrelevant; the symbol was the way in which the company habitually identified itself, and therefore amounted to sufficient acknowledgement.

Fairness

The courts will look at whether the usage of material was 'fair', but it is important to realise that fairness here relates to the amount of material used, not the way in which is was used. There is no problem, for example, with using quotes in a book review even if the review concludes that the book is terrible. The issue of fairness is simply whether the amount of material used was reasonable given the purpose of the work it was used in; if the amount used is excessive for that purpose, the defence will not apply. There is no set amount of copyright material that can be used in this way, but it must not amount to 'illegitimate exploitation' of the work. The courts will also consider whether the purpose could have been achieved without using the copyright material, and whether the use of the material had a commercial impact on the copyright holder, for example if it represented competition to the original work.

In the 'Clockwork Orange' case referred to above, the TV programme used 12 clips from the film, which it was found amounted to around 8 per cent of its length, and 40 per cent of the TV programme. It acknowledged the film company as copyright holders. However, the film company claimed that fair dealing could not apply because in selecting only violent scenes, Channel 4 had misrepresented the film. The Court of Appeal held that the fact that the clips were unrepresentative of the work was not relevant, as long as the purpose of using them was genuinely criticism or review. The main issue was the amount of material used, and the court ruled that it was within the limits of fair dealing, so the defence applied.

In *BBC v British Satellite Broadcasting Ltd* (1992), British Satellite Broadcasting (BSB) had paid a lot of money for rights to show World Cup matches played in 1990, and owned the copyright for those broadcasts. The BBC showed clips from them in its news broadcasts, and was sued by BSB. The court held that the usage was fair, even though the clips comprised the most important parts of each match, and also held that sports reports were included within the definition of current events. (As a result of this decision, most UK TV companies made a voluntary agreement setting out when and how clips from other broadcasters' sports coverage could be used.)

In the *Pro Sieben* case (see earlier), the fact that the extract used was just 30 seconds out of an original nine-minute interview contributed to the court's finding that Carlton was covered by the fair dealing defence. The court was also swayed by the fact that the Carlton's documentary did not represent any commercial competition to Pro Sieben.

In *Hyde Park Residence Ltd v Yelland* (2000) (see earlier) the story about Princess Diana and Dodi Fayed was illustrated with stills taken from security cameras at Villa Windsor, a house in Paris. Mr Fayed's father had claimed the couple were engaged and had viewed the house as a possible marital home. The *Sun*'s story sought to disprove this by demonstrating that Dodi and the Princess had only spent half an hour there, hence the use of the security cameras. The Court of Appeal held that the paper could have conveyed this information adequately without using the copyright material and, in any case, the length of the couple's stay at the house did not prove whether or not they planned to marry.

In *Ashdown v Telegraph Group* (2001) (see earlier), the court was influenced by the fact that the use of the leaked document had a commercial value to the paper, in attracting more readers, and also had a potentially adverse impact on the economic interests of Mr Ashdown, the copyright holder, because it might diminish the value of his memoirs, which he intended to publish at some point.

Defendants often argue that if material was obtained in an underhand way, use of it cannot be fair. The courts however, draw a distinction between unauthorised obtaining of material, and actual stealing.

In the 'Clockwork Orange' case, Channel Four had gone abroad to get a copy of the film (which was banned in the UK) rather than going through the copyright holders, and the copyright holders claimed that this meant the usage could not be fair. However, the court stated that the way in which material was obtained would seldom, if ever, be relevant to the issue of fair dealing.

In the *Hyde Park* case, the court specifically mentioned the fact that the security film had been stolen as one of the reasons why fair dealing did not apply.

Available to the public

The work concerned must be one which has been made available to the public. Essentially, this means that the defence will not cover use of a copyright work which has become available by means of a leak. For example, when the sixth episode in the Harry Potter saga was published in 2005, some copies were stolen before publication. If a newspaper had quoted from one, it would not have been covered by the defence of fair dealing.

In the past, the courts have held that material could be considered to be 'available to the public' without actually being published in the normal sense of the word: the fact that it has been seen, legitimately, by a number of people may be sufficient. However, the Copyright and Related Rights Regulations 2003 state that the fair dealing defence will not apply to material used for criticism or review, which has been made available by an 'unauthorised act'. This does not apply to material used for reporting current events.

In *Sun Printers Ltd* v *Westminster Press* (1982) the court held that a company memo which had been sent to top executives and union officials could be said to be available to the public for the purposes of the fair dealing defence.

In *Fraser* v *Evans* (1969), a secret document written for the Greek Government was leaked to the *Sunday Times*. The paper wanted to use quotes from the report in a story about its contents, and the Court of Appeal agreed that it had an arguable defence of fair dealing, even though only very few people had seen the report. The Court pointed out, however, that the defence was arguable in the case of publishing extracts, but said that an injunction might have been granted if the paper had wanted to publish the whole report.

Incidental inclusion

Section 31 of the 1988 Act provides a defence where copyright material is used 'incidentally' in an artistic work, sound recording, film, broadcast or cable programme. 'Incidental' is not defined, but the defence is generally thought to apply to inclusion that is not deliberate, and might be difficult to avoid, such as, for example, picking up background music when filming a news event in the street.

Spoken words

The Act acknowledges that once spoken words are recorded (on tape, film or in writing), copyright applies, and belongs to the person who said the words. However, s58 provides that where the media records spoken words (in writing or otherwise), for the purpose of reporting current events, broadcasting or including in a cable programme service, they can then use the material recorded, provided five conditions are met:

- the record was made directly from the speech or interview, not taken from a previous recording;
- the speaker has not said that a recording should not be made;
- the words themselves do not breach any existing copyright;
- the speaker has not prohibited the use that is made of the words, before they were recorded;
- the person who has lawful possession of the record (e.g. the person who made the notes) consents to the use made of the words.

This basically means that when reporting current events, you are permitted to use any spoken words, unless the speaker has specifically said that they do not want them noted down and/or published. This applies regardless of whether the words are spoken in public or not.

Public interest

The 1988 Act does not specify a defence of public interest, but the courts have recognised over the years that there are situations where the subject of a report, story or programme is important enough to override the protection of copyright.

In *Hyde Park Residence Ltd* v *Yelland* (2001) (see earlier), the *Sun* claimed that it was covered by the public interest defence, because the issue of whether the mother of the future King of England had planned to remarry was a matter of public interest. The court acknowledged that the events surrounding Princess Diana's death were a matter of public importance, but said there was nothing about the stills themselves that justified removing copyright protection from them.

 In *Lion Laboratories* v *Evans* (1985), a court allowed publication of copyright material about a machine used to test whether motorists were above the drink-driving limit; the material suggested that the device might not be completely accurate. The *Daily Express* successfully raised the public interest defence, and this use of the defence was specifically approved by the Court of Appeal in *Hyde Park*.

▨ Acquiescence

Where the owner of copyright knows that their work is being used, and allows this to go on without complaint, they may find it difficult to make a claim for breach later on.

 In *Film Investors Overseas Services SA* v *Home Video Channel Ltd* (1996), the copyright holder on a collection of porn films had granted a licence for their use to the Home Video Channel. However, the use made of the films went further than the licence allowed; the copyright holders were aware of this from early 1993, but did nothing about it. The court held that where a copyright holder is aware of a breach and does not complain, it had effectively consented to the use and so had no claim.

▨ Innocent infringement

This is not strictly speaking a defence, but can affect the remedy claimed. If a breach of copyright is committed, but the publisher or broadcaster did not know, or have any reason to suspect that the work was subject to copyright, the copyright owner can claim an account of profits (see below), but not damages. This could apply, for example, where a publisher wrongly believed that material was out of copyright.

▊ REMEDIES FOR BREACH OF COPYRIGHT

Breach of copyright can be dealt with by:

- interim injunctions, which are granted before publication, and prevent it going ahead (the Human Rights Act limits the situations where these can be used);
- permanent injunctions, which prevent further publication;
- damages;
- account of profits.

An award will often include both an injunction and damages, or an injunction and an account of profits; however damages and account of profits are alternatives, and are not both ordered in the same case.

If damages are awarded, the amount will depend on the circumstances of the case. In some situations, a court will consider that it is only necessary to compensate the copyright holder for their financial loss, in which case what are called 'infringement damages' will be ordered, which normally amount to the price the publisher would have had to pay if use of the copyright material had been agreed in advance. However, a court can also impose what are called 'flagrant damages', where it believes the justice of the case demands this. These are higher damages, aimed at marking the court's disapproval of the defendant's conduct, and deterring them (and others) from breaching copyright again. They might be ordered, for example, where a copyright holder has refused permission to publish their work, and the defendant has gone ahead and published it anyway, or in a situation where the copyright holder would never have given permission and so was not asked.

 In *Williams* v *Settle* (1960) a photographer sold some wedding photographs to the media after the bride's father-in-law was murdered. She would never have given permission for this, and under the law as it was at this time, she owned the copyright because she had paid for the photos. The court ordered flagrant damages of £1,000 against the newspaper which published them.

 In *Nottinghamshire Healthcare NHS Trust* v *News Group Newspapers* (2002), the *Sun* published a photograph taken from the medical records of a convicted killer, who was being kept in a secure mental hospital; the picture was used to illustrate a story about the killer being let out on day release. The NHS Trust sued for breach of copyright, and the court awarded flagrant damages of £10,000.

 In 2005, photographer Chris Tofalos accepted damages of £45,000, after English Basketball, the sport's regulating body, used his pictures without authorisation on over 200 occasions.

Instead of damages, a claimant may ask for account of profits, which means that instead of claiming the amount that they lost through the breach of copyright, they base their claim on the amount that the defendant has made as a result of using the material. This is most often done in cases concerning books, as with newspapers, magazines and broadcast programmes, it is clearly very difficult to assess the amount of profit which can be attributed to use of the copyright material.

MORAL AND PRIVACY RIGHTS

While copyright is essentially about the economic value of a person's work, moral rights address the fact that the kind of work which is protected by copyright tends to involve a certain amount of creativity and self-expression, and for that reason, the people who produce it usually want to be acknowledged for it, and to have some say in how it is used or altered. The Copyright, Designs and Patents Act 1988 therefore includes rules about people being credited for the work they produce, which is called the right of paternity, and about what is done with the work after completion, called the right of integrity.

For journalists, these rights are very limited, as we shall see, but it is still important to know about them, as often journalists assume they have moral rights over work when in fact they do not. You need to know both what your rights over your own work are, and if you commission work from others, what rules cover your use of that work.

The Act also creates moral rights which protect against use of some private photos, and false attribution of authorship. With all these rights, do not be deceived by the term 'moral rights'; they may sound like no more than rules which nice people abide by, but they are legal rights like any others, and breach of them can result in a claim for damages and/or an injunction.

Right of paternity

The 1988 Act provides that the creator of a literary, dramatic, artistic or musical work has the right to be identified as its author. Unlike copyright though, this right does not arise automatically, and must be 'asserted' by a statement from the creator of the work. (This is the reason why many books contain a statement that 'The author has asserted her moral right . . .'.) Photographers and journalists are not covered by this provision, and so there is no automatic right to a byline in newspapers or magazines.

Where copyright work is used in a situation covered by the fair dealing defence, it is not necessary to identify the author of the work concerned, unless they are the copyright holder.

Right of integrity

Under the 1988 Act, the author of a literary, dramatic, artistic or musical work has the automatic right not to have that work undergo 'unjustified modification', and any changes made to the work have to be 'reasonable in the circumstances and not prejudicial to the honour or reputation' of the author. As with the right of paternity, however, work produced for newspapers and magazines is exempt from this provision, so photographers and journalists have no right under the Act to object to a feature being rewritten, or a picture cropped in a way they do not like.

False attribution of authorship

In the chapter on defamation, we saw that saying something untrue about a person could not lead to liability for libel unless the statement damaged their reputation; the fact that it was untrue is not enough in itself. However, there is one situation where publishing a false statement, even if not defamatory, can break the law, and that is what is called false attribution of authorship. It applies where words are published in such a way as to suggest that a particular person said or wrote them, when that is not the case. It could apply, for example, to making up quotations, or to substantially rewriting an article which gives the writer's personal opinion.

 In *Moore* v *News of the World* (1972), the *News of the World* interviewed the writer Dorothy Squires, and on the basis of that, published an article which it said she had written. Ms Squires said she had not used the words that the paper printed, and the court awarded her £100 in damages.

 In *Clark* v *Associated Newspapers Ltd* (1998), the publishers of the London *Evening Standard* were sued over a piece which was written as a parody of the diaries published by MP Alan Clark. The piece carried the name of its author, Peter Bradshaw, and it was explained in the heading that this was an imaginary entry in Mr Clark's diary. The court said that the rule of false attribution did not prevent publication of parodies like this, but that to stay within the law, the publisher had to make it very clear that the article was a parody and not the real thing. This had not been made sufficiently clear in this case, where the overall impression given was that this was Mr Clark's work.

 In 1988, Godfrey Cannon, a nutrition expert, was awarded substantial damages after the *Today* newspaper falsely attributed authorship of an article to him. The paper had commissioned him to write an article, but did not use the copy he supplied, and instead printed another piece with his name on it, which contained views with which Mr Cannon completely disagreed.

Unlike the rights of paternity and integrity, the right not to have authorship falsely attributed does apply to journalists, and to material used in newspapers and magazines.

Unauthorised use of pictures

As well as moral rights for the creators of copyright work, the Act provides that where someone has commissioned pictures for 'private and domestic purposes' (such as wedding photos, for example), they have a moral right not to have copies issued to the public, which includes the press, even if the person issuing the picture owns the copyright. This means that even if you get hold of someone's wedding picture via the photographer who took it, and the photographer consents to its use, publishing the photo may be in breach of the rights of the person who commissioned the photography in the first place (usually the couple).

CHAPTER SUMMARY

Works protected

Copyright protects:

- original literary, dramatic, musical and artistic works;
- sound recordings, films and broadcasts;
- typographical arrangements.

Establishing copyright

Copyright comes into existence when works are created; it does not have to be registered.

Ownership

Copyright is owned by the creator of the work or their employer, but can be assigned to others.

Infringing copyright

Copyright is breached by copying a substantial part of it, or breaking the conditions of a licence.

Defences

There are five defences:

- Fair dealing permits fair use of published material for reporting current events or in criticism or review, with acknowledgment.
- Incidental inclusion allows use that is incidental, such as part of a background.
- Public interest allows use where the material is such that copyright protection would be against the policy of the law.
- Speech can be reproduced in reporting current events
- Aquiescence applies where the copyright holder knows of the breach and takes no action.

Remedies

Any of three remedies may be ordered:

- injunctions, temporary or peramanent;
- damages;
- account of profits.

Moral and privacy rights

The 1988 Act also gives moral rights and a privacy right:

- the right of paternity, which is the right to be identified as author of a work; this does not apply to journalists or photographers;
- the right of integrity, which protects against 'unjustified modification' of work; this does not apply to work for magazines and newspapers;
- the right not to be falsely identified as the author of published words;
- the right for someone who has commissioned private photographs not to have tbem released to the public.

TEST YOUR KNOWLEDGE

1 Which of these is likely to be a breach of copyright?

(a) You need a map to illustrate a feature, so your designer finds one in a book, then redraws it, using different colours and typefaces.

(b) You are writing a feature on reality TV, and to illustrate it, you use a screen grab from 'Big Brother'.

(c) You work on a magazine for the building industry, and one of your rival titles features an interview with an important architect. You use the quotes given in the feature, but with completely different copy.

(d) You work on a woman's magazine, and a rival title does a feature on women who leave their children. You think this a really interesting idea, so you cover the same subject in your magazine.

(e) You attend a speech given by a local businessman. Before he begins his speech, he says that he does not wish any of his words to be reported in the press. The speech turns out to reveal that he is planning to close a local factory, which is an important employer in the area, so you write a news story, quoting from his speech.

(f) You are reporting a story about a young girl who has gone missing, and her parents give you a school photograph, which you publish.

(g) You work on a local weekly paper and receive the text of a very newsworthy speech by a local politician, which is under an embargo until the following week. Your rival paper comes out earlier in the week than you, so if you respect the embargo, it will get the story first. You publish the speech.

(h) You report a court case, in which one witness gives a long answer about the scientific explanation behind a particular piece of evidence. You print the answer verbatim.

2 You are on the staff of a magazine. Who owns the copyright on the stories you produce?

3 What does selling 'all rights' mean?

4 Who owns the original copyright on photographs?

5 What are the four elements of the defence of fair dealing?

6 In which of these situations could you be in breach of a moral right provided by the 1988 Act:

(a) You are a features editor and you receive a feature which you do not think is up to scratch, so you completely rewrite it, leave out some of the case histories, and add a new one which you have found yourself.

(b) You commission a photographer to do a fashion shoot on raincoats. Six months after using the pictures in the fashion feature, you need a picture to illustrate a piece on the weather, so you use one of the fashion shots.

(c) A local politician has been exposed as having an affair with his secretary. You publish a humorous piece, presented as the secretary's diary.

(d) You are reporting on a murder case which has just finished, and a local wedding photographer rings to say she took the defendant's wedding photos and is willing to supply copies for a fee. You agree, and publish one of the pictures.

ONLINE RESOURCES

The Copyright, Designs and Patents Act 1988 can be found at:
www.opsi.gov.uk/acts/acts1988/Ukpga_19880048_en_1.htm

The UK Patent Office (responsible for intellectual property in the UK) has a useful guide to copyright law at:
www.intellectual-property.gov.uk

The Office of Public Sector Information gives information on copyright for official documents, at:
www.opsi.gov.uk/advice/crown-copyright/copyright-guidance/copyright-in-public-records.htm

The National Union of Journalists has useful practical advice on copyright for commissioning editors and freelance journalists, at:
www.nuj.org.uk/inner.php?docid=56

21

Copyright

For further resources and updates please go to the Companion Website for this book at www.pearsoned.co.uk/practicaljournalism

REPORTING GOVERNMENT AND BUSINESS

As the title suggests, this section deals with laws which apply specifically to writing about government (and other public bodies), and about businesses. The law dealt with in these chapters is of two different kinds: as well as restrictions on what the press can write, these chapters also cover laws which help journalists, because they oblige organisations to make certain types of information available to the public.

Chapter 22 covers the law on publishing particular types of government information, such as material relating to national security or defence, while Chapter 23 explains the law on press access to the decision-making meetings of local government, and also details other laws under which local public bodies must make information public. During elections, laws come into play which restrict what can be written about candidates and the election, and these are covered in Chapter 24.

Chapter 25 covers the Freedom of Information Act 2000, which provides a right to access information from a wide range of public bodies. The chapter explains how journalists can use the legislation, and how to proceed if a request for information is refused.

Finally, Chapter 26 covers laws which relate specificially to writing about businesses. It contains details of the kinds of information which certain types of company must, by law, make public, and where to find it. It also covers the law on insolvency, a key area for any journalist who covers a specific industry or business in general.

Chapter

22

Official secrets

Certain types of official information, such as material related to issues such as defence and national security, are subject to stringent laws which make it a criminal offence not just to publish that information, but in some cases even to receive it. The reason for such strict protection is that it is considered necessary to keep such information secret because it could be useful to enemies of the UK, whether these might be other states or, for example, terrorists. In practice, however, governments have frequently tried (sometimes successfully) to keep such information secret even when its disclosure poses no real threat, and could even be considered to be in the public interest.

The main restrictions are contained in two Acts: the Official Secrets Act 1911 and the Official Secrets Act 1989. Although prosecutions of journalists under the Acts are rare, they can happen. In addition, the Acts criminalise many situations in which official information is passed to journalists, which means protection of sources is very important in these cases (the law on this issue is covered in Chapter 19).

THE OFFICIAL SECRETS ACT 1911

Section 1 of the Act makes it an offence if:

any person for any purpose prejudicial to the safety or interests of the state –

(a) Approaches, inspects, passes over or is in the neighbourhood of or enters any prohibited place [this is defined in the Act, and essentially covers any government or military building, any site concerned with essential services such as gas or electricity, and anywhere related to communications, such as railways and roads]; or

(b) Makes any sketch, plan, model or note which is calculated to be or might be or is intended to be or could be directly or indirectly useful to an enemy; or

(c) Obtains, collects, records or publishes, or communicates to any other person any secret official code word or password, or any sketch, plan, model, article or note, or other document or information which is calculated to be or might be or is intended to be directly or indirectly useful to the enemy.

A person convicted of doing any of these things could be liable to up to 14 years in prison.

For the media, the most likely source of problems comes from s1(c) of the Act, but in practice the case below is the only one in which a journalist has been prosecuted under s1 in over 50 years.

 In 1978, two journalists who had interviewed an ex-soldier about what the source described as security 'scandals' were prosecuted under the Act, in what became known as the 'ABC case' after the initials of the defendants. However, the judge criticised the prosecution as 'oppressive', pointing to the fact that the Act required that a defendant had acted 'for any purpose prejudicial to the safety or interests of the state'. The government had suggested that the intention to publish the information in a magazine was sufficient to meet this requirement, but the judge found that the words meant that the Act was really intended to deal with people who were in league with a foreign power. Although he did not rule out use of s1 against the media, he said that it should be reserved for cases where there was an accusation of collusion with a foreign power and, as a result, the Attorney-General withdrew that part of the prosecution.

OFFICIAL SECRETS ACT 1989

The 1911 Act originally had a s2, which concerned the publication or receipt of pretty much any official information. It was so widely drawn that it effectively made it an offence to publish even the most harmless and trivial details of government activity, such as the brand of paperclips used in the Foreign Office, or whether the apple pie in the Department of Employment canteen was served with cream or custard. It was widely criticised, and eventually the then government passed the 1989 Act, which abolished s2 of the 1911 Act, and replaced it with a series of specific offences related to particular types of information. The Act is quite complicated and creates a number of different offences relating to different types of information, disclosed by different types of government employee, so the sections below can only be a summary of the provisions, but will give you a basic understanding of the kind of behaviour that is prohibited.

Offences of disclosure

The 1989 Act makes it an offence for anyone who is or has been employed by the Crown (which covers the armed services, the Civil Service and Ministers), and government contractors to disclose information in relation to:

- security and intelligence (s1);
- defence (s2);
- international relations (s3);
- crime (s4);
- details of government phone-tapping, interception of mail, or other communications (s4);
- information on security, intelligence, defence or international relations, which has been communicated in confidence to other states or international organisations (s6).

By narrowing the law down to these specific categories, the Act makes it plain that material will not be protected by the Official Secrets Act merely because it is secret and comes from the government; it must fall within one of these classes.

 In 2000, a former MI5 agent called David Shayler wrote about the activities of the security services in the *Mail on Sunday*, alleging, among other things, that MI5 kept secret files on a number of Labour MPs. He was convicted under s1 and s4 of the 1989 Act, and sentenced to six months' imprisonment.

It is often assumed that there must be a public interest defence for government employees who leak information which it is in the public's interest to know. The Act however, contains no such defence for this offence, and in the *Shayler* case, the House of Lords confirmed that it did not exist.

The offences created by s1–4 and s6 means that, if a source employed by, or under contract to, the Crown, passes information in one of these categories to you, they could be convicted under the Act. Protecting your sources obviously then becomes an issue in this situation (see Chapter 19). However, there is a further implication for journalists in this section of the Act, in that it is also possible for a journalist to be charged with aiding and abetting, or inciting, these offences if, for example, the source has been paid for the information, or helped or encouraged to get or disclose it. This could be the case even if, in the event, the material was never published.

■ Offences concerning publication

Section 5 of the Act makes it an offence for any person to disclose (which includes publishing), without lawful authority:

- any information, document or other material that falls within the categories detailed in s1–4; and
- which has been disclosed without authorisation by a Crown employee or government contractor; or
- which has been disclosed without authorisation by someone to whom the information was properly entrusted, in confidence, by a Crown employee or government contractor; or
- which has been disclosed by a Crown employee or government contractor; in circumstances where it was intended to be kept confidential.

In addition to proving the above facts, if the information is covered by s1–3 of the Act, the prosecution also has to prove that:

- the disclosure was damaging to the public interest; and
- the person disclosing it knew, or had reasonable cause to know, that it was protected information under the Act, that the disclosure was unauthorised and that its publication was damaging.

The issue of whether a disclosure was damaging to the public interest is to be judged on the facts of the case, and would be a question for a jury to decide if a person was prosecuted. Note that this provision is not the same as a public interest defence. A public interest defence would allow the press to avoid conviction if it could be shown that it had published material which it was to the public's benefit to know, but under the 1989 Act, this defence is not available and so it makes no difference that a publication might disclose, for example, government wrongdoing or incompetence. The reference to the public interest in s5 simply means that there will be no liability for revelations that are harmless (e.g. because the information is trivial, or does not reveal any real secret).

Section 6 makes it an offence to disclose, without lawful authorisation, information on security, intelligence, defence or international relations, which has been communicated in confidence to other states, or international organisations. Again, the disclosure must be damaging, and the person disclosing it must know, or have reason to know it was damaging, and to know that the material was obtained in circumstances prohibited by the Act. However, this section contains a defence which is not applicable to the other classes of information, which states that there will be no offence if the information or material has previously been made available to the public with the authority of the nation or organisation concerned, or if the person making the disclosure is a member of that organisation.

■ Penalties and prosecutions

The maximum sentence under the 1989 Act is two years' imprisonment. Prosecutions under the 1989 Act can only be brought with the consent of the Attorney-General, or in the case of information relating to crime, with the consent of the Director of Public Prosecutions. Although there have been some attempts to prosecute journalists, none has so far resulted in a conviction, probably because in political terms, no government wants to be seen to be trying to suppress press freedom. However, sources who have supplied information to the press have been successfully convicted.

In 1998, journalist and defence expert Tony Geraghty wrote a book called *The Irish War*, which discussed surveillance techniques used in Northern Ireland. Although the Government knew about the book, and made no attempt to prevent its publication, shortly after it was published Mr Geraghty was arrested and his home searched. However, a year later, the Attorney-General discontinued the prosecution, without giving a reason.

In 1999, an officer in the Royal Navy was sentenced to 12 months in prison for leaking information about a possible biological weapon attack by Iraq to the *Sun*. The paper paid him £10,000, and ran the story, but no one from the *Sun* was prosecuted.

In 1997, a former MI6 officer was sent to prison for a year, for sending a synopsis of a book about his work to a publisher.

■ Investigation powers

Although prosecutions of journalists under the Official Secrets Acts are rare, the special investigatory powers provided to the police under the Acts can bring their own problems for the media, even if no charge is brought. If the police suspect that a crime under the Acts has been committed, or is about to be committed, and can prove reasonable grounds for that suspicion, a magistrate can authorise a warrant entitling them to search premises and seize evidence. In an emergency, where the police believe that the interests of the state demand immediate action, a police superintendant can sign the warrant.

Under the usual law on search and seizure for investigating crime (see p. 263), material which is held in confidence for the purposes of journalism is called 'excluded material' and cannot usually be seized. However, in exceptional circumstances, such material can be seized with a warrant from a circuit judge, and the Police and Criminal Evidence Act 1984 allows police to get such a warrant where an offence under the Official Secrets Acts is suspected. They can also get a warrant to seize what is called 'special procedure material', which includes material for journalistic purposes that is not within the category of 'excluded material' (this would include, for example, pictures or documents that had not been received under circumstances of confidentiality).

Journalists can be questioned in court about the sources of information protected under the Acts. As we saw in Chapter 19, the Contempt of Court Act 1981 places some limits on this questioning, because of the importance of journalists protecting their sources; however, this does not apply when national security is at issue.

■ Official secrets and breach of confidence

Using the Official Secrets Act is not the only way to suppress publication of official secrets; in some cases, the Government will instead use the law on breach of confidence, which concerns disclosure of information that was obtained in circumstances of confidentiality. This is discussed in Chapter 17.

DEFENCE ADVISORY NOTICES

Defence Advisory Notices (usually referred to as DA Notices) are part of a system which allows the Government of the day to warn the press in advance that publishing information on certain subjects is considered to be damaging to the national interest, or likely to put lives at risk. A DA Notice is not a legally enforceable order, but a request that the press do not publish information on the matters listed, without first seeking advice from the DA Notice Secretary, who can be contacted at any time.

The notices are issued by the Defence, Press and Broadcasting Advisory Committee (DPBAC), which is made up of representatives from the Foreign Office, Ministry of Defence, the Home Office and the media, and meets twice a year. They are sent to newspaper editors and to their equivalents in the broadcasting sector, and also posted at the DPBAC website (see *Online resources* at the end of the chapter).

Currently there are five DA Notices in place, which cover defence and security issues. DA Notice 3, for example, concerns weapons, and requests that information is not published on issues such as the design of nuclear weapons and the technology behind them; security arrangements for their transport and storage; or the design details, capabilities or areas of vulnerability of non-nuclear weapons.

According to the Committee's website, the idea of the system is not to censor information, but to promote negotiation between the Government and the media, so that as much as possible of a story can be published without revealing genuinely secret and harmful information. Breach of a DA Notice is not a criminal offence, and the DA Notice system does not have any sanctions of its own; however, there is clearly potential for overlap between the issues cited in DA Notices, and the sort of material which is protected from disclosure by the Official Secrets Acts and the law on breach of confidence, and legal action can be taken using these routes. According to the website, this should not happen as a result of discussions with the DA Notice Secretary, which are confidential, but the media law experts Robertson and Nicol suggest that it may be unwise to trust this assertion. They cite a 1985 case in which a publisher submitted an advance copy of a book, assuming that it would receive useful guidance on making sure it contained no harmful material, and instead found itself on the receiving end of an injunction, which meant that the book could never be published.

Law in practice DA Notices

The DA Notice system encourages journalists to contact the DA Notice Secretary before publishing anything covered by a DA Notice and, in some cases, discussions with the Secretary may mean that, rather than abandoning a story, you can find an approach that tells the story without revealing harmful information. The Secretary can be contacted at any time; contact details are published on the DA Notice website (see *Online resources*, at the end of the chapter).

22

Official secrets

CHAPTER SUMMARY

The Official Secrets Act 1911

It is an offence to, for a purpose prejudicial to the safety or interests of the state:

- be in or near a prohibited place;

- make a sketch, plan or note that could be useful to an enemy;

- obtain or publish anything that could be useful to an enemy.

The Official Secrets Act 1989

It is an offence for government employees and contractors to disclose information on:

- security and intelligence;

- defence;

- international relations;

- crime;

- interception and phone-tapping;

- confidential information given to other nations or international organisations.

It is also an offence to publish information in these categories, if unlawfully disclosed by a government employee or contractor.

The Act also gives police wide powers of search, seizure and arrest.

Governments also use breach of confidence laws to stop leaks of information.

Defence Advisory Notices

The DA Notice system is a voluntary system for protecting information which could harm the national interest or put lives at risk.

TEST YOUR KNOWLEDGE

1 List the six categories of information that are protected under the Official Secrets Act 1989.

2 Which of these situations could mean you are guilty of an offence under the Official Secrets Acts?

   (a) A computer consultant working for a company which is installing new systems for the Ministry of Defence gives you a document detailing weaknesses in the system that could expose it to hackers. You publish a story based on the document.

   (b) A civil servant gives you a secret document, which should only have been seen by top NHS officials, that details plans to halve the number of intensive care departments in hospitals. You publish a story revealing the plans.

   (c) A former member of the security services contacts you with a story about phone taps on well-known public figures. Your paper pays £10,000 for the evidence, but in the end decides not to run the story.

3 You have been working on a story given to you by a top civil servant, about problems with security at a naval base. Before the story can be published, the police arrive at your office, and state that you are suspected of being about to commit an offence under the Official Secrets Act 1989. What powers do they have with regard to:

(a) your research material

(b) you.

ONLINE RESOURCES

www

The website of the Defence, Press and Broadcasting Advisory Committee, with details of how the DA Notice system works, and current DA Notices, is at:
www.dnotice.org.uk

The full text of the Official Secrets Act 1989 is at:
www.opsi.gov.uk/acts/acts1989/Ukpga_19890006_en_1.htm

Details of some high-profile cases brought under official secrets legislation can be read at:
news.bbc.co.uk/1/hi/uk/216868.stm

News stories about the effect of official secrets legislation on the media are featured on the website of the Campaign for Press and Broadcasting freedom, at:
www.cpbf.org.uk

Details of the case against David Shayler can be found at his website:
www.thememoryhole.org/spy/shayler/welcome.htm

For further resources and updates please go to the Companion Website for this book at www.pearsoned.co.uk/practicaljournalism

Reporting local government

The decisions made by local authorities, from the London Assembly right down to the smallest parish council, can have important implications for local communities, and are a rich source of stories for local – and sometimes national – papers and broadcasters. In this chapter we look at the rules on access to council meetings and documents, including the resources available for investigating the standards of behaviour of council members.

ACCESS TO MEETINGS AND DOCUMENTS

The rules on access to the meetings in which decisions are made, and the documents associated with them, are contained in four separate pieces of legislation:

- the Local Government Act 1972;
- the Local Government Act 2000;
- the Local Government (Access to Information) Act 1985;
- the Public Bodies (Admission to Meetings) Act 1960.

The rules that are applicable depend on the type of council, with different rules applying to:

- principal authorities;
- authorities operating cabinet-style government;
- parish councils and other bodies covered by the the Public Bodies (Admission to Meetings) Act 1960.

(These three categories are explained in the sections below.)

Access to other local authority records is provided by the Freedom of Information Act 2000 (see Chapter 25) and the Audit Commission Act 1998.

Principal authorities

Principal authorities include county, district and London Borough councils, the London Assembly and combined police or fire authorities (but not parish or community councils). The rules on access to their meetings are contained in the Local Government Act 1972 and the Local Government (Access to Information) Act 1985. The legislation provides that members must sit in public for full council meetings, meetings of committees and sub-committees, and any other formal meeting involving councillors, except where confidential or exempt information (see p. 315) is being discussed.

Confidential information is information which:

- has been supplied by a government department, under an obligation not to disclose it to the public; or
- which is prohibited from being disclosed, either by law or by a court order.

When confidential information is being discussed, the council must exclude the public and the press.

Exempt information covers a range of types of information, which has recently been extended by the Local Government (Access to Information) (Variation) Order 2006. It includes:

- information relating to any individual;
- information likely to reveal the identity of any individual;
- information relating to the financial or business affairs of any particular person (including the authority holding the information);
- information relating to consultations or negotiations on any labour relations matter between the council and its employees or officers;
- information relating to any action taken or to be taken in connection with the prevention, investigation or prosecution of crime.

(For the full list, plus extra categories relating only to Wales, the regulations can be consulted online – see *Online resources* at the end of the chapter.)

Councils are not obliged to exclude the public when exempt information is being discussed, but they may; if they want to do this, the councillors must vote on whether to do so. Councils in England are required to consider the public interest and should not exclude the public unless the public interest in doing so outweighs the public interest in disclosing the information (this defence is not specifically included for Wales). The public cannot be excluded where the exempt information relates to a proposed development for which the council can grant itself planning permission, nor if the information is required to be registered under other legislation listed in the regulations (such as the Companies Act and the Charities Act).

If a council meeting excludes the public because confidential or exempt information is being discussed, it should only do so for as long as it takes to discuss that information, and not for the whole meeting (such items are therefore usually put on the agenda either at the beginning or end of the meeting). Neither the public nor the press can be excluded from meetings for any reason other than that confidential or exempt information is being discussed.

Law in practice **Exempt information**

The categories of exempt information under the Local Government Acts are wider than the categories of information which councils can refuse to disclose under the Freedom of Information Act. This means that if a council excludes the press while it is discussing exempt information, you may be able to get access to the information by making a request under the Freedom of Information Act 2000 (see Chapter 25).

Access to documentation

A Council must usually give five clear days' notice of a council meeting, by posting a notice at its office, and copies of agendas and reports have to be open to public inspection for at least five days before the meeting. If a meeting is called at shorter notice, the documentation must

23

Reporting local government

be available for inspection from the time it is called. In either case, the meeting should stick to the published agenda. Matters which are not on the original agenda can only be discussed if the chairman states that the matter is urgent; a reason must be given for this.

Where officers are to present reports at the meeting, the report must contain a list of any background papers which were used in preparing the report and have played a significant role in shaping the conclusions the report puts forward. These background papers have to be made available to the public, and remain so for four years.

As long as a meeting is open to the public, the authority must also provide specific facilities for the press. Accredited representatives from newspapers and news agencies should be given an agenda and any further documentation needed to explain the items on the agenda, and the council must make available sufficient facilities for the press to report on the meeting and telephone the story in (at the reporter's own expense). Copies of other documents given to council members may be supplied as well, but this is at the discretion of the relevant council official. The council can charge for the cost of copying and sending documentation to the press.

After the meeting, minutes, reports and summaries of any discussions that took place in private must be made available to the public, and remain so for six years. It is a criminal offence to try to stop anyone from inspecting or copying this documentation. Exempt or confidential information is not covered by these provisions.

■ Councils operating cabinet-style government

The Local Government Act 2000 set up a new way of working for councils who are responsible for areas with over 85,000 inhabitants, sometimes called 'executive' arrangements. Under the old arrangements, most important decisions were taken by the full council, or by committees made up of members of the council, and the meetings at which these decisions were taken were held in public. The new system, however, sets up 'cabinet-style' working, in which either the council leader or a directly elected mayor takes decisions with a cabinet of two to ten councillors, or a council manager. Councils must also set up at least one oversight and scrutiny committee, which is made up of council members who are not part of the cabinet. These committees, which must reflect the overall political balance of the authority, can review council policies, and examine decisions made and actions taken; access to their meetings is governed by the Local Government Act 1972, as above. However the actual decision-making power now lies with the cabinet, who may all come from the party which has a ruling majority. Decisions can also be delegated to specific council officials.

The rules on when the press (and public) will be allowed access to cabinet meetings are contained in regulations called the Local Authorities (Executive Arrangements) (Access to Information) (England) Amendment Regulations 2000, as amended by the Local Authorities (Executive Arrangements) (Access to Information) (England) Regulations 2002 and 2006. They apply to London borough councils, county councils, district council and unitary authorities that are operating the cabinet-style system. (Unitary authorities are local authorities which, in some areas, replace the old city and county authorities with a single body.) There are differences between the rules in England and in Wales.

Access to meetings in England

Under this regime, only decisions classified as 'key decisions' have to be taken in public. 'Key decision' is defined in the Local Government Act as a decision that is likely to either:

- lead to the local authority spending or saving a significant amount of public money, judged by reference to its budget for the service or function being discussed (the amount which will be considered significant is decided by the official making the decision, but to inform this process, councils have to agree and publish the amounts above which they consider expenditure or savings to be significant); or

■ have a significant effect on people living or working in at least two wards or electoral divisions.

Guidelines issued in February 2001, however, make it plain that where possible, decisions should also be treated as 'key' whenever they are likely to have a significant effect on the community, even if only in one ward; an example would be the decision whether or not to close a school.

Meetings on key decisions: The regulations require local councils to issue a 'forward plan', updated monthly, which lists the 'key decisions' the cabinet intends to make over the next four months, and any reports which are to be considered as part of the process of making any of the decisions listed. The forward plan is usually published on the council website, as well as being available for inspection at council offices. Reports which are to be considered must be available for public inspection for at least five days before the decision is made, as well as a list of any background papers used for the report, copies of which must be available in sufficient numbers to meet requests from the public.

The forward plan also has to include:

■ the names of the official(s) who will make each decision;

■ the main organisations who will be consulted about it and how;

■ details of how people can make their views on the matter known.

At least five days before a meeting in which a key decision is to be discussed or put to a vote, the council must issue an agenda and any reports relating to the business on it (if a meeting has to be held at short notice, the agenda must be available from the time the meeting is set up). Copies of all these documents must be provided to the press on request, though the council may charge for the costs of photocopying and sending the material.

The meeting itself must then be held in public, unless confidential or exempt information (as defined above) is to be discussed, or where discussions are likely to include details of advice given by a political adviser or assistant. If the council wants to exclude the public because exempt material or advice given by a political advisor or assistant is to be discussed, it has to pass a resolution to that effect. The public and press may only be kept out of the meeting during discussion of the exempt or confidential information itself.

Once a decision is made (whether in public or in private, by the cabinet or an individual), a written record of it, detailing the reasons for it, any alternatives that were discussed and any conflicts of interest, must be made available to the public at the council offices 'as soon as reasonably practicable'. Any reports which were considered as part of the decision-making process should be made available at the same time. Copies of these documents must be supplied to the press on request.

Non-key decisions: Where a decision to be taken is not classified as 'key', the matter can be handled in a private meeting and, in addition, key decisions which are taken by individual officers rather than the council executive are not subject to the provisions above. The constitutional campaigning organisation Charter 88, among others, has expressed concern that this means councils can avoid public scrutiny by setting a very high financial limit for when expenditure or saving will be considered significant (and so classifying fewer decisions as key ones) and/or formally delegating decisions to individual officers.

In councils operating executive arrangements in Wales, there are no special provisions regarding key decisions. Meetings must be held in public unless:

- the nature of the matters to be discussed make it likely that confidential information would be disclosed if the public were present;
- the council passes a resolution excluding the public because exempt information is to be discussed (as explained above, the categories of exempt information in Wales contain additional categories – see *Online resources* at the end of the chapter).

The Public Bodies (Admission to Meetings) Act 1960

This Act is sometimes known as the Thatcher Act, as it was sponsored by the former Prime Minister Mrs Thatcher, early in her career. It covers the meetings of:

- parish and community councils;
- parish meetings;
- health authorities;
- primary care trusts.

The Act states that full meetings of these bodies, and meetings of their committees, must generally be held in public, but the public can be excluded where publicity would be against the public interest because of the confidential nature of the business to be discussed, or for another reason. The council has to pass a resolution in order to exclude the public in this way, and it must state the reason.

Exclusion from council meetings

As we have seen, all three pieces of legislation allow councils to exclude the public where exempt information is being discussed. According to the media law experts Geoffrey Robertson and Andrew Nicol (see *Media Law*, p. 619), this provision is sometimes used to cover up matters that might embarrass the authority or an official, rather than being used in the public interest. As a result, they suggest that journalists should challenge use of the secrecy provisions, and ask that the press be allowed to stay, even if the public have to be excluded.

A case which can be used in support of this argument is *R v Liverpool City Council, ex p Liverpool Taxi Fleet Operators Association* (1975). It concerned a council meeting to discuss raising the number of local taxi licences, where a number of taxi drivers and others wanted to attend and have their say. The room was too small for all of them, so the council ruled that the public would be excluded, but the press could stay. The decision was challenged in court, but the Divisional Court held that it was reasonable, partly because the council had not deliberately chosen too small a room, but also because it had allowed the press to stay. This suggests that the decision was acceptable because it was not a deliberate attempt to avoid publicity, which in turn implies that if such an attempt was made, it could be successfully challenged.

Defamation and local government

As we saw in Chapter 15, public meetings of local authorities and their committees are covered by qualified privilege, so it is safe to report anything said during them, so long as you make sure you are within the rules of that defence. Qualified privilege also covers fair and accurate copies or extracts of any material issued by a local authority for the information of the public, or of any register or other document which is required by law to be open to public inspection.

Remember though that this protection does not extend to everything said by local councillors; only what they say in public meetings or the specified classes of document. Local councils cannot, as a body, sue for libel, but individual councillors can (see p. 187).

ACCESS TO LOCAL GOVERNMENT RECORDS

All local authorities are covered by the Freedom of Information Act 2000, the operation of which is discussed in Chapter 25. In addition, there are other legal provisions which require them to make specified types of information available to the public.

Accounts

Section 15 of the Audit Commission Act 1998 provides a right for 'any person interested' to see a local authority's accounts and 'all books, deeds, contracts, bills, vouchers and receipts relating to them' for 20 working days before the council's annual audit (this also applies to fire, police and civil defence authorities). Copies must be supplied if requested (there may be a charge for this). There is some debate about whether journalists qualify as a 'person interested', but it is clear that if the journalist is on the local electoral roll, they will qualify, so as long as there is someone on the staff who lives in the area, access should be feasible. Alternatively, if your employer is based in the area and pays business rates to the relevant council, a representative of that company will count as an interested person.

The case of *Hillingdon LBC* v *Paullsson* (1977) establishes that the right of access exists even in relation to documents described as confidential, with the exception of personal information about staff in connection with their employment. It is not necessary to specify the exact document you want; you can ask to see a complete class of documents (such as all contracts), and the request can only be refused if the amount of paperwork would be of an unmanageable size (*Evans* v *Lloyd* (1962)). But if you do know you want a particular document, it must be made available; you do not have to accept only being shown the relevant entry in the records.

Councils do not always welcome journalists using the Act with open arms, but they cannot avoid its provisions: refusing a request for a copy of any document covered by the Act or obstructing lawful access to the records is a criminal offence. The 20-day period must be advertised by the council, usually on its website and in a local paper.

The Act also allows local electors, at any time of the year, to see a council's statement of account (the document prepared by the auditor which shows income and expenditure for the preceding year). Many authorities now post this on their websites. In addition, the Local Government Act 1972 provides a right for local electors to see all orders for payment by a council, and the Local Authorities (Members' Allowances) Regulations 1991 allow local electors to see details of allowances and expenses claimed by councillors.

Planning and development

Applications for planning permission have to be open to public inspection, and there are also public registers of enforcement notices (issued when work is done without planning permission) and breach of condition notices (issued when work does not comply with planning permission conditions).

Local councils also have a duty to carry out strategic planning for their area, and their draft plans must be open to public inspection, along with the supporting documentation.

In the case of some large construction projects (such as roads or airports), it may be necessary for Parliament to pass a private bill to make the work possible (see p. 4). The text of such bills has to be lodged with the local authority, along with detailed plans of the proposed development. These documents must be available to the public for inspection and copying.

Register of interests

Under the Local Government Act 2000, all local authorities must draw up a register of the financial and other interests of council members, which must be available for public inspection. Council members must inform the monitoring officer (who is responsible for the register) of the following interests:

- their jobs and the name of their employers;
- the names of any firms in which they are a partner or companies of which they are a director;
- the name of any company in which they own more than £25,000 worth of shares, or more than a 1/100th share of the company;
- any contracts for goods, services or works between the council and the member themselves, any firm they are a partner in, or any company they are a director of, hold more than £25,000 worth of shares in, or own more than a 1/100th share in;
- any land held in the area governed by the council;
- any land leased or licensed from the council;
- membership of and/or positions of control or management in:
    - other bodies where they represent the council;
    - other public authorities;
    - companies, industrial and provident societies and charities;
    - private clubs;
    - trade unions and professional organisations;
    - any organisation whose main purpose is to influence public opinion or policy.

Conflicts of interest

The main interest of the register to journalists is obviously in making it possible to spot when council members have failed to declare a conflict of interests. The rules on this are contained in a code of conduct, which the Act requires all local authorities to draw up for its members. It must be available for public inspection and is supervised by a standards committee. Councils have a certain amount of discretion over the code they draw up, but some mandatory provisions are set down in the Act, including a rule that members must declare any personal interests which are relevant to business under discussion by the council.

Guidance on the Act issued by the Standards Board (which oversees operation of the codes of conduct) states that the register can act as a trigger to tell members when they have an interest that should be disclosed, but such interests are not limited to those details which have to be entered on the register. Members are told to ask themselves whether any of the following people would be more affected by the council's decision on the matter under discussion than other people in the area:

- the member;
- their partner, a relative, or a close friend;
- an organisation which employs any of the above people;
- any company in which the member holds more than £25,000 worth of shares, or owns more than a 1/100th share of.

If any of these people or organisations would be more affected by the decision than others in the local area, the member has a personal interest. They must then consider whether this interest is prejudicial: the test for this is whether a member of the public, knowing all the facts, would judge that the member's interest was important enough to affect their judgement of the issue.

If there is a personal interest (whether prejudicial or not), the member must declare the interest before the issue is discussed, or as soon as the conflict of interest comes to light. If the interest is prejudicial, the member must withdraw from the discussion, unless the standards committee votes to allow them a dispensation to stay. If they are an executive member, they cannot take part in any decision on the issue. There are two exceptions to the rules on prejudicial interests:

- members can still take part in overview and scrutiny committees, unless the prejudicial interest is a financial one, or concerns a decision they have taken at an area committee or joint committee meeting;
- they can take part in area or joint committee meetings, unless the interest is a financial one, or the meeting is taking a decision on the matter which has been delegated from the executive or council.

If a member has a personal interest that is not prejudicial, they can still take part in the meeting and any vote, as long as the interest has been declared.

OTHER LOCAL PUBLIC BODIES

Most local public bodies are subject to the provisions of the Freedom of Information Act 2000, but additional provisions on access to information apply to certain important types of local body.

Schools

Legislation imposes a number of duties on schools with regard to publicly available information:

- All schools (state and private) must make available details of their exam results, rates of truancy, numbers of pupils staying on after 16, admission arrangements and policies, and appeal procedures for refusal of admission (Education Acts 1996 and 1997).
- The governing bodies of every county, controlled or maintained school must keep a written statement of their position on policy matters, which the head teacher must make available to any interested person (Education (No 2) Act 1986).
- The governing bodies of grant-maintained schools must make an annual report available to the public.
- Meetings of school governing bodies can be open to the public, but do not have to be; however, in most cases their minutes must be open to inspection (Education (School Information) Regulations 1998).

Police authorities

Police authorities are required by the Police and Magistrates Courts Act 1994 to produce plans for local policing, detailing their priorities and objectives for the year ahead. The authorities have discretion to publish these plans in whatever way seems most appropriate to them (most now do this on their websites).

Each local police authority also has to produce and publish an annual report as soon as possible after the end of the financial year. The report must include an evaluation of how well the policing plan was carried out over the previous year.

Social services departments

Local social services departments must produce an annual Children Services Plan, detailing how they intend to develop services for children with disabilities over the coming year. The report is available to the public.

Magistrates' courts committees

Magistrates' courts committees must hold a meeting in public at least once a year, and the minutes of their meetings must be available for inspection (confidential information can be excluded from the minutes, but this must be made clear, and a reason given).

NHS Trusts and health authorities

Health authorities have to publish annual statistics on waiting times for each area of medicine, numbers of complaints and the time taken to deal with them, and performance relative to national and local standards established by the Department of Health.

Access to meetings of health authorities and NHS Trusts is covered by the Public Bodies (Admissions to Meetings) Act 1960 (see above), and a circular from the Department of Health, issued in 1998 (Health Service Circular 1998/207) (see *Online resources* at the end of the chapter) makes it clear that both the public and press should be allowed into meetings as far as possible, and that meetings should only be held in private where the business being discussed creates a risk of real harm to individuals if discussed in public.

CHAPTER SUMMARY

Access to meetings and documents

The rules on access to local government meetings vary with different type of council.

Principal authorities

These include county, district and London Borough councils.

Members must sit in public except in two situations:

- councils must exclude the public where confidential information is being discussed.
- they may exclude the public where exempt information is being discussed.

Access to documentation

- Five days' notice of a meeting should given.
- Agendas and reports are open to inspection beforehand.
- Background papers must be available to the public.

Councils operating cabinet-style government

Decisions can be taken by cabinets or individuals.

Meetings in England

- Key decisions must be taken in public, unless confidential or exempt information, or advice from a political advisor, is to be discussed;
- Non-key decisions can be taken in private.

Meetings in Wales

Meetings must be held in public unless confidential information would otherwise be disclosed.

The Public Bodies (Admission to Meetings) Act 1960

Covers other local authority meetings and stipulates that:

- meetings should generally be public;
- the public can be excluded for confidentiality or other reasons.

Access to local government records

- All local authorities are covered by the Freedom of Information Act 2000.
- The Audit Commission provides rights to see council accounts and other financial information.
- Planning permission applications and notices are open to public inspection.
- All councils must have a publicly-available register of members' interests.

Other local public bodies

Duties to make information public apply to:

- schools;
- police authorities;
- social services departments;
- magistrates' courts committees;
- NHS Trusts and health authorities.

23

Reporting local government

TEST YOUR KNOWLEDGE

1 What is the definition of a 'key decision' under the Local Government Act 2000?

2 Which types of council does the 2000 Act apply to?

3 In what circumstances can the public be excluded from a local council cabinet meeting?

4 In what circumstances can the public be excluded from a parish council meeting?

5 You want to report on a meeting of your local county council, but are told that the meeting will discuss exempt information. What arguments could you use to gain access to the meeting?

6 During a meeting of your local council, one of the councillors accuses another of corruption. The chairman forbids her from saying any more, but when you ring the councillor later, she gives you all the details behind her allegations. What is the position on using the information, with regard to defamation?

7 Who has the right of access to local council accounts under the Audit Commission Act 1998?

ONLINE RESOURCES

www

The Local Government (Access to Information) (Variation) Order 2006 can be read at:
www.opsi.gov.uk/si/si2006/20060088.htm

The Local Government Act 2000 can be read at:
www.opsi.gov.uk/Acts/acts2000/20000022.htm

Health Service Circular 1998/207 can be read at:
www.dh.gov.uk/PublicationsAndStatistics/LettersAndCirculars/HealthServiceCirculars/fs/en

The Local Government Association website is at:
www.lga.gov.uk

The Orchard News Bureau website has examples of the kind of story that can be investigated through use of the laws described in this chapter:
www.orchardnews.com

For further resources and updates please go to the Companion Website for this book at www.pearsoned.co.uk/practicaljournalism

Reporting elections

The reporting of elections – whether local, national or European – is governed by special rules, under the Representation of the People Acts, and the European Parliamentary Elections Act 1978. The reason for this legislation is to ensure that the press is not able to mislead voters and unfairly influence election results, as could happen if, for example, a major newspaper published an untrue and damaging story about a candidate just before polling day.

It is important to be aware that the law of defamation also applies to coverage of elections – see below. In addition, broadcasters are subject to extra provisions, which are explained in Chapter 29.

OFFENCES RELATED TO ELECTION REPORTING

The Representation of the People Acts and the European Parliamentary Elections Act 1978 create four main offences with regard to press reporting of elections:

- making false statements about candidates;
- falsely reporting a candidate's withdrawal;
- publishing exit polls before voting ends;
- published unauthorised advertisements.

False statements about candidates

Section 106 of the Representation of the People Act 1983 makes it an offence to publish any false statement about an election candidate, before or during an election. In such a case, the prosecution need to prove four elements:

- the statement was one of fact, not opinion;
- the words referrred to the character or behaviour of the candidate concerned;
- the statement was made with the purpose of damaging the candidate's chances in the election;
- the statement was untrue.

Fact or opinion?

To fall within the offence, that statement made must be presented as a statement of fact; mere expression of an opinion is not enough. In each case, the judge will decide whether the statement is one of fact or comment, and clearly there will be times when the distinction is a difficult one to see.

 In *Ellis v National Union of Conservative and Constitutional Associations* (1900), describing someone as a 'radical traitor' was deemed an expression of opinion.

 In *Pirbhai v DPP* (1995), a leaflet which said of the politician Jack Straw that he 'hates Muslims' was considered to be presenting those words as a statement of fact, because nothing in the leaflet qualified the statement or indicated that it was merely the writer's opinion. As it was found to be false, the offence had been committed.

Referring to character

The false statement must refer to the candidates 'personal conduct or character'; statements about someone's political beliefs or performance as a politician do not fall within the offence.

 In *Burns v Associated Newspapers* (1925), a newspaper described the leader of the Labour Party as a Communist, on the eve of an election. The courts refused to issue an injunction against the paper, on the grounds that the claim concerned political allegiance and not personal behaviour.

 In 1998, a journalist was prosecuted under the Act for falsely claiming, on a website, that a particular candidate was homosexual. In this case the Act could apply because the allegation referred to the candidate's personal behaviour, not his political beliefs.

The statement does not have to be in any way defamatory; merely making a false accusation about the candidate's character or conduct is enough. This is because a false statement which might not be defamatory can still have an effect on someone's political prospects: for example, to say that someone does not recycle their rubbish would not be defamatory, but it would clearly have the potential to influence voters if the person spoken of was a Green Party candidate. If the statement happens to be true, there is no problem, of course.

Purpose of the statement

The statement must be made with the intention of damaging the candidate's chances in the election. This is effectively judged on the content of the statement itself, and whether it appears to have been calculated to influence voters against the candidate. The statement does not have to be proved to have caused actual damage to the candidate's chances (which in any case would probably be impossible to prove).

Falsity

The candidate does not have to prove categorically that the statement is false; according to the leading media lawyers Geoffrey Robertson and Andrew Nicol, in their book *Media Law*, an affadavit (see the *Glossary*) from the candidate stating that the words are false will be enough (but see *Defences*, below).

When does the Act apply?

The Act refers specifically to 'candidates' and, according to Robertson and Nicol, this means it only applies after an election campaign has formally started, since before then there are technically no candidates. There may of course be people who everyone knows will stand (including those currently in the seats to be voted for), but until the election campaign has formally begun, they are not candidates. Parliamentary elections begin with the dissolution of Parliament, the announcement that the Government intends to dissolve Parliament, or the issue of a by-election writ. Local election campaigns run from five weeks before polling date or from publication of notice of the election.

Defences

There is one defence available, where the person who made or published the statement can show that they had reasonable grounds for believing the words were true. A court is unlikely to grant an injunction where the publisher or maker of the statement says this is the case.

Penalties

The courts can issue an injunction preventing publication or further publication of the false statement. The maker or publisher of the statement, if convicted of the offence, can be fined and disqualified from voting for up to five years.

■ False statements about withdrawal

Section 75 of the Representation of the People Act 1983 makes it an offence knowingly to publish a false statement that a candidate has withdrawn from an election, in order to benefit another candidate.

■ Exit polls

Under the Representation of the People Act 2000, it is an offence to publish any results of an exit poll before the official polls close. An exit poll is defined as any forecast about the result of an election or statement about the way that voters have voted, where the forecast or statement is, or seems to be, based on information supplied by voters, after voting. The reasoning behind this is that publishing such results could dissuade people from bothering to vote, if they see that their favoured party already has a good lead. Anyone who publishes such a poll before official polls have closed can be fined up to £5,000.

In 2004, the European Parliament elections were, in some areas, run using all-postal ballots. On the day of the election, *The Times* published an opinion poll which had asked people in the all-postal areas how they had voted. The Electoral Commission (an independent organisation which regulates UK elections) complained that this amounted to an exit poll and should not have been published. The issue was not tested in the courts, but may have to be in the future, as the use of postal ballots increases.

■ Unauthorised advertisements

Paid advertisements for or about a particular election candidate may only be published with the authorisation of the candidate concerned, or their agent. This is the case whether the advertisement praises or attacks a particular candidate, and publishing an unauthorised advertisement is an offence. The measure only applies to paid advertisements: there is nothing to stop a publication praising or attacking a candidate in its editorial space (so long as the coverage does not amount to a false statement as described above, or to defamation).

OTHER LEGAL CONSIDERATIONS

When reporting elections, you also need to bear in mind the law on defamation and incitement to racial hatred.

Defamation and elections

Defamation law (as explained in Chapter 14) applies to election candidates just as it does to anyone else. Journalists often assume that reports of remarks made by election candidates must be automatically covered by absolute privilege, just as remarks made in Parliament are, but this is not the case. Section 10 of the Defamation Act 1952, states that:

> A defamatory statement published by or on behalf of a candidate in any election to a local government authority to the Scottish Parliament or to Parliament shall not be deemed to be published on a privileged occasion on the ground that it is material to a question in issue in the election, whether or not the person by whom it is published is qualified to vote at the election.

This means that you can be sued for reporting remarks made by one candidate about another, as well as making (and publishing) defamatory remarks yourself.

Fair comment may apply to remarks made by election candidates, under the normal rules of the defence (see p. 198).

However, in *Culnane* v *Morris* [2005], the High Court held that s10 did not mean that statements made by an election candidate could never be covered by qualified privilege. The judge held that the provision merely meant that the fact that a statement was 'material to a question in issue in the election' did not by itself mean privilege applied. Where a statement fell within the requirements of the common law defence of qualifed privilege (see p. 204), the defence could apply.

Race relations law

If you are reporting speeches or literature from extremist candidates, or public meetings held by them, it is important to be aware of the provisions of the Public Order Act 1986, regarding incitement to racial hatred, and of the new offence of inciting religious hatred, once it is brought into force (see Chapter 27).

Law in practice Covering election meetings

During election campaigns, public places such as schools have to be made available to candidates, so that they can hold public meetings to publicise their campaigns. This being the case, Robertson and Nicol suggest that there can be no legitimate reason for excluding the press from such meetings, and any reporter who is asked to leave should point out that the meeting is a public one and insist on their right to stay. If ejected, say Robertson and Nicol, a reporter could sue for assault.

CHAPTER SUMMARY

Offences related to election reporting

There are four statutory offences:

- false statements about candidates;
- false reporting of withdrawal;

- publishing exit polls before voting ends;
- unauthorised advertisements.

Other legal considerations

Reporters also need to consider:

- defamation law – statements made by or on behalf of election candidates are not covered by privilege;
- laws on racial and religious hatred.

TEST YOUR KNOWLEDGE

1 Making a false statement about an election candidate is an offence under the Representation of the People Act 1983. What are the four elements of this offence?

2 Assuming all the following statements are false and all the people mentioned are election candidates, which of the statements could amount to an offence under the Act?

(a) John Black is a complete womaniser and unfit for public office.

(b) Mary Brown was a member of the Communist Party at university.

(c) Jane White is a lesbian.

(d) Terry Green may be a Tory, but his real sympathies lie with the National Front.

3 It is widely thought that a general election will be called in May. Your local MP has already announced his intention to stand again, despite a number of recent scandals about him being made public. During April, you write a stinging criticism of him, arguing that his performance has been abysmal, and voters would be crazy to vote him in again. Two of the accusations you made against him are untrue. Have you committed an offence under s160 of the Representation of the People Act 1983? Are there any other legal problems you should worry about?

4 On the morning of a local election, you do a vox pop in the local shopping centre, asking people whom they have voted for. When can you publish the material?

ONLINE RESOURCES

www

The Electoral Commission has a media handbook covering local elections, which can be downloaded at:
www.electoralcommission.org.uk

The National Union of Journalists has advice on reporting on extremist election candidates, at:
www.nuj.org.uk/inner.php?docid=704

For further resources and updates please go to the Companion Website for this book at www.pearsoned.co.uk/practicaljournalism

Reporting elections

24

Chapter
25

Freedom of information

Most of the chapters in this book concern laws which restrict the material you can publish; by contrast, this chapter explains an area of the law which can help you in your job. Freedom of information (FOI) legislation gives both the press and the public the right to see information about the workings of government and public authorities, and can provide a rich source of stories.

In Sweden, FOI rights have existed for centuries, while the USA has had FOI legislation since the 1960s, and Canada, Australia and New Zealand since the early 1980s. In the UK, however, right up until the end of the 20th century, there was a culture of secrecy about government information, and public records, even on the most trivial of subjects, generally remained closed to both public and press for 30 years after they were produced.

In 2000, however, the Government passed the Freedom of Information Act, which introduces a general right for the public to see official information held by the government and public authorities, subject to exceptions for certain types of information. Although there have been numerous complaints about public bodies being slow to release information (or refusing to do so at all), the Act has allowed the press to uncover a vast amount of information which would once have been kept secret (see below).

THE FREEDOM OF INFORMATION ACT 2000

The Act came into force on 1 January 2005, but it applies to all records held by public authorities, regardless of whether they were created before or after that date. It gives any person (not just UK citizens or UK residents) the right to request access to all types of recorded information from a public authority in England, Wales or Northern Ireland (a separate, rather more media-friendly act applies to Scotland). The provisions apply to the press just as they do to everyone else; journalists have the same rights, but no extra ones.

The right of access has two elements:

- the right to be told whether a particular piece of information exists (e.g. you might want to know whether statistics are kept on a particular subject); and
- the right to be given that piece of information.

The Act exempts certain categories of information from the right of access, and also lists a further set of categories to which access need only be granted if it is in the public interest to do so. Authorities can also refuse to fulfil a request for information if the cost of doing so is above a specified limit. Outside these categories, however, if a piece of information exists in recorded form, the public authority must release it, even if doing so might reveal information that the authority would prefer not to make public (e.g. if it would embarrass officials).

The legislation imposes duties on public authorities to make their information easier to access. It also creates an appeal procedure, by which someone whose request has been turned down can have it reviewed by the Information Commissioner, an independent watchdog set up to oversee the working of the Act and, after that, by the independent Information Tribunal.

▨ Public bodies covered by the Act

The Act covers around 100,000 different public authorities, both national and local, including all government departments, the Houses of Parliament, all local authorities, the NHS, schools, the armed forces and the police, plus a vast number of individual organisations ranging from the Civil Aviation Authority to the Potato Council. A full list of the bodies covered can be found in Schedule 1 of the Act (see *Online resources* at the end of the chapter), and is updated monthly. The only public bodies specifically excluded from the Act are MI5, MI6 and Government Communications Headquarters (GCHQ).

As well as the public bodies listed in Schedule 1, the Act also covers companies which are wholly owned by any public body on that list. In addition, the Act allows for the Secretary of State to designate private organisations as public bodies for the purposes of certain aspects of their work, which would mean that there was a right of access to information on that work. This power might be used, for example, to designate a private company contracted to deal with social security claims, for example, or a private hospital which was being paid to treat NHS patients. No such designations have been made yet.

▨ Types of information

The Act provides access to all types of recorded information, including written documents, letters, memos, emails, computer records, audio and video cassettes, microfiche, maps, photographs and handwritten notes. If the information you want has been recorded somewhere, you should be allowed access to it (unless one of the exemptions allowed under the Act applies).

In 2005, the *Sunday Herald* used the Act's Scottish counterpart to prove that the leader of the Scottish Conservatives, David McLetchie, was claiming expenses for taxis used on private business, including trips to the dentist. The *Herald*'s Scottish Political Editor Paul Hutcheon was able, after a long fight, to get access to the politician's taxi receipts, which were initially refused, but later ordered to be released by the Scottish Information Commissioner. The resulting stories eventually led to McLetchie's resignation.

In 2006, journalist Malcolm Prior used the Act to uncover a catalogue of errors by local councils concerning planning permission for mobile phone masts. A legal loophole allows companies to assume that planning permission for masts below 15m high has been granted if they do not get a response to their planning application within 56 days. FOI requests to 41 local councils found that 68 applications had gone through because of mistakes, such as sending out mail by second class post instead of first, using the wrong date stamp and calculating deadlines incorrectly.

Stories uncovered by the *Guardian* using FOI requests during 2006 have included:
- the release of documents held by West Yorkshire police, showing that the serial killer Peter Sutcliffe (known as the Yorkshire Ripper) probably attacked many more victims than the public was told;

- the £900 per day fee paid by the Government to Sir David Henshaw to find a solution to problems with the Child Support Agency;

- the fact that almost all Britain's local councils hold investments in the arms trade.

In 2006, the BBC used FOI requests to reveal, among other things, that an average of one prisoner per day was absconding from Britain's open prisons, that UK hospitals were each charging patients up to £1.5 million per year for parking, and that the UK secretly sold plutonium to Israel during the 1960s.

If the piece of information you want does not exist in any recorded form, the public body is not obliged to create it: so, for example, if you want to know the number of times your local hospital ward is cleaned each week, and the hospital does not collect this information, you cannot insist on it being put together for you. Although the Act gives a right to the information you ask for (if it exists), this does not necessarily mean that you will be allowed to see the record from which the information comes.

What if the information you want has been deleted from a computer system, but could be retrieved? In 2005, the Information Tribunal considered such a case, and decided that there might be situations where the authority could be expected to try to retrieve the information. Where the information was merely in a computer's recycling bin, or was deleted from the original machine but held on the back-up tape, it could be considered as material the authority still held, and should therefore be supplied. Where retrieving the information demanded specialist skills, an authority might still be expected to do so, depending on how much that process would cost; if the cost of retrieval would go over the standard cost limit (see below), the request can be refused.

The Act includes access to personal information, but where such information concerns people other than the person making the request, it will only be released where to do so would not breach the Data Protection Act 1998 or the Human Rights Act 1998.

▧ Publication schemes

The Act requires public bodies to produce what it calls a publication scheme, which specifies the classes of information it intends to publish, what form the information will be published in, and whether it will be available free of charge or subject to a fee. In most cases, details of the publication scheme will be published on the organisation's website, and before making a request under the Act, it is obviously sensible to check first whether the information is available through the publication scheme, which will be a quicker way of getting it than making an FOI request. The fact that a certain piece of information is not included in the publication scheme does not, however, mean it is not available, only that it is not published as a matter of course.

▧ Exemptions under the Act

Although the general principle of the Act is that information should be made available, it lists a number of situations, known as exemptions, in which a public authority can refuse to supply information.

There are two classes of exemptions:

- absolute exemptions;

- qualified exemptions.

In addition, s14 of the Act gives authorities the right to refuse 'vexatious' requests; this is not defined in the Act, but the government website which explains the Act (see *Online resources* at the end of the chapter) suggests that it would apply to requests designed to disrupt the authority's work. In addition, where an authority has complied with a request for a particular person, s14 allows it to refuse a subsequent request by the same person for the same, or 'substantially similar', information unless a reasonable time has elapsed since the previous request.

Absolute exemptions

Where information is covered by one of the absolute exemptions listed in the Act, a public authority is not obliged to allow access to it, nor even to confirm or deny whether it exists. The absolute exemptions cover the following.

Information already accessible: Section 21 gives authorities the right to refuse to supply information which is 'reasonably accessible' to the applicant in another way. Information will be considered 'reasonably accessible' if a public authority would be obliged by any other law to give it to the public on request, regardless of whether or not the public is required to pay for such access. For example, the information contained on anyone's birth certificate can be obtained on request by paying a fee, so it is not possible to use the Freedom of Information Act to obtain the same information from another source which might supply it free of charge.

Information which is given voluntarily to the public on request, for a fee, can also be considered 'reasonably accessible', but only if it is made available under the relevant authority's publication scheme (see below), and the charges are in accordance with this scheme. Material which is simply made available for inspection does not count as being 'reasonably accessible'.

Security matters: Section 23 exempts information which refers to any of a list of organisations dealing with security matters, including MI5, MI6, the SAS and Government Communications Headquarters.

Court records: Section 32 exempts information which is only held in a document:

- created by a court for the purpose of its proceedings;
- served on or by the relevant authority for the purpose of court proceedings;
- filed with or in the custody of a court;
- created or held by someone conducting an inquiry or arbitration, for the purposes of those proceedings.

Parliamentary privilege: Section 34 provides an exemption where to disclose the information requested would infringe parliamentary privilege. A certificate to that effect, signed by the Speaker of the House of Commons or the Clerk of the Parliaments, is to be taken as conclusive proof that the exemption is necessary.

Conduct of public affairs: Section 36 exempts information held by the House of Commons or House of Lords, where 'in the reasonable opinion of a qualified person' disclosure could:

- prejudice the operation of collective ministerial responsibility (this is the convention by which ministers publicly support decisions made by the Cabinet, regardless of their personal views);
- prejudice the work of the Executive Committee of the Northern Ireland Assembly or the National Assembly for Wales;
- inhibit the free and frank provision of advice, or exchange of views for the purposes of deliberation;
- prejudice the effective conduct of public affairs in any other way.

25

Freedom of information

The 'qualified person' will be the Speaker in relation to information held by the House of Commons, and the Clerk of the Parliaments for information held by the House of Lords.

Section 36 also applies to information held by government departments, but in this case it is subject to the public interest qualification (see below).

Qualified exemptions

Where information falls under one of the following qualified exemptions, the authority which holds it can refuse to disclose it, but before making this decision, it must consider whether disclosure would be in the public interest. This means that it has to balance the public interest in disclosure against the public interest in keeping the information secret; if the public interest in disclosure is stronger, the information should be supplied. The Act does not define 'public interest', but the Information Commissioner has issued guidance on how the test should be applied – see *The public interest test* box later.

If the authority concludes that the public interest would be better served by refusing to disclose the information, it must give the applicant its reasons, unless doing that would effectively result in disclosing the information. It can also refuse to confirm or deny whether the information even exists.

The categories of qualified exemption are as follows.

Information intended for publication: Section 22 exempts information which the relevant authority intends to publish in the future if, in the circumstances, it is reasonable to refuse access until the date of publication, even if that date is not yet decided. The exemption only applies if the authority had already planned to publish the material when the request was made.

National security: Section 24 allows authorities to refuse access to information where it is necessary for the purpose of safeguarding national security. A certificate signed by a Cabinet Minister, the Attorney-General, the Advocate General for Scotland or the Attorney-General for Northern Ireland saying that this exemption should apply is regarded as conclusive proof that it is necessary.

Defence: Section 26 states that information is exempt from the Act if its disclosure is likely to prejudice the defence of this country or any colony, or compromise the effectiveness of our armed forces or any forces 'cooperating' with them.

International relations: Section 27 provides that authorities need not disclose information which could prejudice:

- relations between the UK and another state, or any international organisation or international court;
- UK interests abroad;
- the promotion or protection of UK interests abroad.

Section 27 also exempts from the Act confidential information obtained from another state, or an international court or organisation.

Domestic relations: Section 28 exempts information which could prejudice relations between any of the following:

- the UK government;
- the Scottish Administration;
- the Executive Committee of the Northern Ireland Assembly;
- the National Assembly for Wales.

Economic interests: Section 29 exempts information which could prejudice:

- the economic interests of the UK;
- the financial interests of the government, the Scottish Administration, the Executive Committee of the Northern Ireland Assembly or the National Assembly for Wales.

Criminal investigations and proceedings: Section 30 exempts information held for the purpose of a criminal investigation or criminal proceedings.

Law enforcement: Section 31 exempts information which could prejudice specified aspects of law enforcement, including:

- prevention or detection of crime;
- offenders being caught or prosecuted;
- the administration of justice;
- tax assessment or collection;
- operation of immigration controls;
- security and order in prisons.

It also exempts information concerning the relevant authority exercising its functions for a stated list of purposes, including:

- investigating accidents;
- securing health and safety at work;
- protecting charities from mismanagement;
- investigating improper or illegal conduct.

Auditing: Under s33, a public authority which has the job of auditing other public authorities, or otherwise examining the way in which they use their resources, can refuse access to information which could prejudice that role.

Formation of government policy: Section 35 provides an exemption for information held by a government department, or the National Assembly for Wales, that relates to:

- the development of government policy;
- ministerial communications;
- advice provided by or requested from any of the law officers;
- the operation of any ministerial private office.

Conduct of public affairs: Section 36 exempts information held by public authorities where 'in the reasonable opinion of a qualified person' disclosure could:

- prejudice the operation of collective ministerial responsibility (this is the convention by which ministers publicly support decisions made by the Cabinet, regardless of their personal views);
- prejudice the work of the Executive Committee of the Northern Ireland Assembly or the National Assembly for Wales;
- inhibit the free and frank provision of advice, or exchange of views for the purposes of deliberation;
- prejudice the effective conduct of public affairs in any other way.

The 'qualified person' will vary according to which authority is holding the information, but will be a senior person within that organisation.

Communications with royalty: Section 37 exempts information relating to communications with the Royal family or the Royal Household, or to the award of honours.

Health and safety: Section 38 exempts information which, if revealed, could threaten the physical or mental health or safety of any person.

Environmental information: Certain types of environmental information is already subject to its own rules on disclosure under a separate Convention, and s39 exempts such information from the provisions of the Freedom of Information Act (see p. 341 for more detail about accessing environmental information).

Personal information: Section 40 exempts disclosure of personal information about any individual – including the person making the request – where that disclosure would breach the Data Protection Act 1998.

Legal professional privilege: Section 42 exempts information which is covered by legal professional privilege, which means documents containing legal advice which pass between a lawyer and their client, and documents produced for the purposes of litigation.

Commercial interests: Section 43 exempts information which amounts to a trade secret, or could prejudice anyone's commercial interests, including those of the organisation which holds the information.

The public interest test

As we have seen, certain categories of information need only be revealed if it is in the public interest to do so. The Information Commissioner's Office has produced a guidance note, *Freedom of Information Act Awareness Guidance No 3*, explaining how it expects the public interest test to be operated, and it is well worth familiarising yourself with this advice, as it can be used to challenge authorities which operate the test incorrectly. The guidance gives the following advice:

- The right to get access to information, and the right to know whether the information exists are two separate rights. This means that the fact that it is not in the public interest to release the information itself does not necessarily mean that it is not in the public interest to say whether it even exists (though sometimes that may be the case).

- The 'public interest' is quite simply something which serves the interests of the public. The guidance gives the following examples of situations where there is likely to be a strong public interest in disclosure:

  - Where it would further understanding of and participation in public debate about current issues. This would be the case, for example, where disclosure would allow a more informed public debate about something which the Government or a local authority was considering doing.

  - Where it would promote accountability and transparency with regard to the decisions public bodies take, and/or the way they spend public money. For example, where the private sector is used to deliver publicly-funded services, it is likely to be in the public interest to disclose information which ensures greater competition and better value for money. Disclosing details about gifts to or expenses claimed by public officials is also likely to be in the public interest, according to the guidance.

- – Where it would help individuals and companies to understand decisions made by public authorities that affect them, and in some cases, to challenge those decisions.

- – Where it would bring to light information affecting public health or safety. An example would be where prompt disclosure of information might contribute to the prevention of accidents or disease.

■ The fact that something is interesting to the public will not necessarily mean that disclosing it is in the public interest; there has to be some benefit to the public which outweighs the benefits to the public of withholding the information.

■ There is a clear distinction between the public interest in withholding information, and private interests in doing so, and only the public interest justifies refusing an FOI request. For example, there is obviously a public interest in not revealing details which would compromise the country's ability to defend itself. However, where disclosure would reveal corruption or incompetence, or would simply embarrass the authority or someone working in it, the interests protected by non-disclosure would be private ones, and authorities should not take these kinds of issues into account when deciding whether information should be released in response to an FOI request. In some cases, private and public interests might coincide, but only the public interest should be a factor in the decision.

■ The fact that information might be too complicated for the applicant to understand is not a valid reason for refusing an FOI request. Nor is the fact that disclosure might mislead the public because the information does not give the complete picture (e.g. if the information reveals a policy recommendation that was never actually followed). In both cases, according to the Commissioner, the solution is to provide explanation or set the information in its context, not to suppress it.

■ Applying for information

A request under the Act must be made in writing, but it need not be on any particular form, even if the organisation has produced one, and the Freedom of Information Act website specifically states that it can be done by email. The request should state clearly what information is required, and give the name of the applicant and an address for correspondance; it is not, however, necessary to identify yourself as a member of the press.

You can also specify what form you want the information in: you can ask, for example, for a summary of it, or copies of a specific document, and can specify whether you want it provided in paper or electronic form. The Act requires the authority, as far as possible, to accommodate such requests.

The authority you apply to should reply as soon as possible, but in any case not later than 20 days after receiving the request. Section 16 of the Act places a duty on public authorities to assist and advise applicants, so if they do not understand the request, they should contact you for clarification. The reply should either:

■ tell you that they do not hold the information you want;

■ supply the information;

- refuse the application, and give reasons for doing so (a refusal should cite which exemption the information falls under);

- state that the information may be subject to one of the public interest exemptions, and that the authority is extending the time limit in order to consider this issue.

If a fee is payable (see below), the authority must let you know before going ahead with supplying the information; when they do this, the 20-day period is suspended until the fee is paid, when it begins again.

Delay in considering public interest exemptions is one of the biggest difficulties with using the Act for journalistic purposes. In this situation, the Act only requires authorities to release the information within a 'reasonable' time, which in practice means they can (and sometimes do) go on extending the time limit for months. This can be a useful delaying tactic as, in many cases, the story will eventually stop being newsworthy (but see p. 340 for advice on speeding the process up).

Law in practice Using the information

The Act does not lay down any restrictions on using the information supplied through it, so you do not need permission to publish the results of your application. However, the document in which the information is found may be subject to copyright, and the Act does not lift this, so checks may need to be made before publishing direct copies of such documents.

It is also important to be aware of the risk of defamation when using information obtained under the FOI Act. In letters, emails and internal memos, people may well say things about other individuals or organisations that could be defamatory, so you need to make sure that if you publish these statements, you are covered by a defence (see Chapter 15).

Challenging refusals

If your request is refused, in most cases the organisation concerned will have a procedure for challenging this, and details of that procedure should be supplied when you are notified of the refusal. If the request is still refused after using that procedure, you can apply to the Information Commissioner's Office, an independent review body, which can look at it again, and if it agrees that the decision was wrong, order the public authority to release the information. However, the Commissioner's Office has become notorious for delay, and in practice this step will only be worth taking if the story you are chasing will still be newsworthy in several months' time.

Where the information in question is held by a department of central government, and the Commissioner has ordered it to be released on public interest grounds, the Cabinet Minister in charge of that department can veto the Information Commissioner's order, and the veto can only be challenged by judicial review (see p. 49). No other public body can refuse the Information Commissioner's order, and a Minister's veto cannot be extended to information held by any body other than its own department.

If the Information Commissioner does not order the information to be released, there is a final right of appeal to the independent Information Tribunal. This right also applies to an authority who has been ordered by the Commissioner to release requested information; it can go to the tribunal to try to get that decision reversed. It is also possible to seek judicial review (see p. 49), if you believe that the Commissioner or the Tribunal have misinterpreted the Act.

In 2000, *Which?* magazine requested details from local councils of resturant hygiene inspections made at events such as the Ideal Home Show and the Cheltenham Festival. One of the councils, Hammersmith and Fulham in London, refused the request, but after appealing to the Information Commissioner, the magazine was given access to the information. The Information Commissioner said it was in the public interest to release this kind of information, and there was no good reason not to: well-run restaurants had nothing to lose from public scrutiny.

In 2005, the Information Tribunal upheld a request from a taxpayer to the Inland Revenue, after the Revenue had claimed it did not have the information he asked for. The applicant's wife had experienced severe delays in getting back tax which she had overpaid, and he requested details of what action the Revenue was taking to deal with its failure to reach acceptable standards when dealing with such refunds. The Revenue replied that it did not accept that it had not met the required standards, and so it had no information with regard to any failure to do so. The Information Commissioner upheld this view, but the Information Tribunal found that the Revenue had publicly apologised for problems with refunding overpayments, and that the failings it had apologised for were obviously those that the requester was asking for information on. The Tribunal stated very firmly that public bodies could not pick and choose which requests to fulfil on the basis of whether they approved of the terms of the request.

In 2005, the Information Commissioner ordered Corby Borough Council to reveal information on how much it had paid to a temporary finance officer. The Council had claimed an exemption under s40, claiming that the information was personal, and releasing it would breach the Data Protection Act 1998, and that disclosure would cause damage and distress to the employee concerned. The Information Commissioner rejected these claims. The ruling pointed out that there had been controversy over the way in which the officer was appointed, because it was known that he had been paid a significantly higher rate than was usual (although the salary was known, the FOI request was for the total amount paid, including various allowances). It said that the payment made to senior council officials was a matter of legitimate public interest, and such officials had to be prepared for a certain degree of public scrutiny, which was part of the process of holding them accountable for their actions. The officer could not, therefore, have expected the information to remain confidential, and prejudice to his interests was therefore not a sufficient reason to refuse disclosure.

In 2006, the *Guardian* was successful in getting the Ministry of Defence to reveal the names of 500 arms sales officials. The Ministry had initially refused to supply the information, claiming that disclosure would lead to the officials being harassed by peace campaigners. The *Guardian* had to take its case to the Information Commissioner, who found that there was no evidence that disclosure would result in a threat to the officials' safety.

■ Costs

Authorities are allowed to charge for providing information requested under the Act. If the information falls within the authority's publication scheme, the scheme will give details of any charges. For other information, the Act states that:

■ Information which costs an authority up to £450 to answer (or £600 for information held by central government) should be provided free.

■ If your request will cost the authority more than this, it can refuse to answer it, or can answer it and charge anything from no fee up to the full cost of the work involved.

In 2007, the Government announced plans to include in the cost the time taken by officials to decide whether an exemption applied; if put into practice the NUJ estimates 17,000 more requests a year could be rejected on the grounds of costs.

Law in practice

Journalist and campaigner Heather Brooke runs courses for journalists on how to use the FOI Act effectively. She offers these tips:

■ The key to successful searches is being as precise as possible. 'Journalists often imagine they can go on a big fishing expedition, order all an authority's records for the past ten years and then trawl through and find a big story. But that kind of request will instantly be refused on cost grounds, so you need to narrow it down.'

■ Most larger authorities now have a person designated to handle FOI requests, whose name can be found on their websites or by calling the organisation. Try to develop a relationship with the FOI Officer at any public authority you deal with regularly. They can help you make your requests more precise, by giving you information on what records they hold, and how the information in them is broken down. 'For example, I wanted to find out some statistics going back across five years, and the FOI officer I dealt with was able to tell me that they'd only held that information electronically for part of that time, and searching through the paper records would go over the cost limit. By narrowing my search to the records they held electronically, I avoided having the request refused, and still got enough information for a really good story.'

■ Section 16 of the Act gives authorities a duty to assist people requesting information, so if an authority is not very forthcoming about how it holds information, it can help to remind it politely of s16.

■ If you are unable to narrow your request down, you can avoid a rejection on cost grounds by breaking it up, and making separate, smaller searches. So instead of asking for a certain figure going back over ten years, for example, you could make separate requests for smaller chunks of time. You can also break information up by geographical area, or ask for all the correspondance relating to one person, and then make another request relating to another person. The Act does allow authorities to aggregate costs, so if you make a lot of searches over a short period, they can add them together and reject them on cost grounds. In practice, no one seems to be doing this, but if it looks as though it might be a problem, either space your requests out (a space of two months prevents aggregation), or get colleagues to submit requests in their names. 'In theory, you could even use a false name, but that could cause problems if your request is refused and you have to go through the process of challenging it.'

■ If the information you want is not held centrally, check whether it is held regionally. For example, people often want to find out information about the police as a whole, but there is surprisingly little information held that way, However, if you make a separate request to each police force, you might get the same information that way.

■ The Act is not only useful for investigating individual stories; it can be used to open up whole categories of information which will be useful for everyday news gathering. For example, once you have successfully requested information from a food safety inspection, you know you can go back and get that kind of information every time you write a relevant story, because the precedent is established.

■ Delay is the biggest problem with using the Act, but there are ways to speed things up. When an authority extends the 20-day period on a request to consider whether disclosure is in the public interest it has to have a set of criteria by which it measures the public interest, so as soon as you are notified of the extension, write and ask to be informed of the criteria by which it is deciding the question. 'Firstly, it shows that you are serious and you know your rights, and secondly, you'll often find that they'll mention criteria which aren't allowed under the Act, such as embarrassment to officials, which you can obviously then challenge.'

■ The Information Commissioner has signed a memo of understanding with the Department of Constitutional Affairs stating that he would give requesters updates on the progress of their requests every 28 days, so it's worth writing and asking for those. The Commissioner has also said that he will make more effort to recognise that some types of information are perishable, so stress the importance of timeliness to your story.

ENVIRONMENTAL INFORMATION

As we saw earlier, information about the environment is covered by one of the FOI Act exemptions, but this does not mean it is inaccessible. The reason for the exemption is that access to this type of information is covered by a separate set of Regulations, which work in a similar way to the FOI Act, and in fact give greater access because they cover more organisations and contain fewer exemptions.

The Environmental Information Regulations 2004 were passed to put into effect an EU Directive establishing a common standard of openness about environmental matters across the EU. They create a right of access to information about the environment held by public bodies, and also private companies which carry out a public function, such as water, electricity and gas suppliers. Like the FOI Act, the right is open to everyone, not just journalists, and journalists have no special rights of their own. A person requesting information is not obliged to say why they want it.

As with the FOI Act, the Regulations are enforced by the Information Commissioner.

■ Information covered

The Regulations apply to environmental information which is held in some recorded form, which includes anything written down, drawn, recorded on tape or kept in the form of a computer file. 'Environmental' is defined as covering:

■ the 'state of the elements of the environment', including air, water, soil, landscape, natural sites, biological diversity and its components, including genetically modified components, and the interaction between these various elements;

■ factors which are likely to affect the elements of the environment, such as noise, energy, radiation or waste;

■ measures likely to affect the elements of the environment, including legislation, policies and plans, and cost-benefit analyses used to assess such measures;

■ reports on the implementation of environmental legislation;

■ the state of human health and safety, including contamination of the food chain and conditions of human life; and cultural sites and built structures as far as they are affected by the state of the elements of the environment.

■ Making a request

Requests for information can be made orally or in writing (including by email), although the Information Commissioner's Office recommends that a written note of oral requests is kept.

They can be made to any employee of the relevant organisation but, as with FOI, most bodies covered by the Regulations have designated a specific person to deal with such queries. The Regulations impose a duty to assist people wanting information, so if your request is too general, the organisation should come back to you and ask for it to be narrowed down.

Requests must be responded to as soon as possible, and within 20 days at most, unless they involve a particularly large amount of information or are very complex. In that case, the deadline can be extended by another 20 days.

If the organisation does not hold the information you want, but knows or believes that another body does, it should either pass on your request, or tell you where it believes the information is held.

■ Exemptions

The Regulations allow organisations to reject requests for certain types of information, but only where doing so would be in the public interest; there are no absolute exemptions as in the FOI Act.

The categories are:

- personal information where disclosure would breach the Data Protection Act;
- 'manifestly unreasonable' requests (guidance from the Information Commissioners suggests this covers requests designed to disrupt the work of the authority, or which would be so expensive that the cost outweighs the public interest in disclosure);
- requests which are too general (but before rejecting such requests, the body must try to help the requester narrow them down);
- unfinished or incomplete information;
- internal communications;
- information which, if disclosed, would adversely affect:
    - international relations;
    - national security;
    - defence;
    - public safety;
    - the course of justice;
    - a person's ability to get a fair trial;
    - the ability of a public body to conduct a criminal or disciplinary enquiry;
    - intellectual property rights;
    - the confidentiality of proceedings of any public body, where confidentiality is provided by law;
    - confidentiality of commercial or industrial information;
    - the interests of the person supplying the information;
    - protection of the environment.

(The last four categories do not apply where the information sought concerns emissions.)

The public interest test works in the same way as for the FOI Act, and the Information Commissioner's guidance stresses that even where information falls within the above categories, it can only be withheld if the public interest in keeping it secret outweighs the public interest in disclosure.

■ Challenging refusals

If a request is rejected, you can challenge this through the relevant body's appeal procedure. If the information is still not released, you can appeal to the Information Commissioner and the Information Tribunal, as for FOI requests.

■ Charges

Public authorities cannot charge for access to any public registers or list of environmental information, nor for allowing someone to inspect a particular record at a place of the authority's choice. For other requests (such as supplying a copy or summary of a particular record) they can make a reasonable charge. Charges should be published in advance.

CHAPTER SUMMARY

The Freedom of Information Act

The act applies to all information held by public authorities.

It gives any person the right to:

- be told whether requested information exists; and
- be given that information.

Exemptions

There are two categories of exempted information:

- absolute exemptions – information covered can be withheld;
- qualified exemptions – information can be withheld if it is in the public interest to do so.

Challenging refusals

There are four ways to challenge refused requests:

- the authority's own procedure;
- the Information Commissioner;
- the Information Tribunal;
- judicial review.

Environmental information

The Environmental Information Regulations provide a right of access to environmental information held by public bodies and private companies carrying out public functions.

Types of information

'Environmental information' includes information on:

- the state of air, water, soil, landscape and biological diversity;
- noise, energy, radiation and waste;
- legislation and policies which affect the environment;
- human health and safety;
- cultural sites and buildings as affected by the state of the environment.

Exemptions

Sixteen classes of information can be withheld if doing so would be in the public interest.

Challenging refusals

Routes for challenge are the same as for FOI requests.

TEST YOUR KNOWLEDGE

1 How long does a public body have to deal with an FOI request?

2 You apply to your local council for details of the price paid for the rather spectacular floral displays it has placed outside the town hall. Your request is refused, on the grounds that the material is covered by a qualified exemption. Can you challenge the refusal and, if so, how?

3 You ask your local hospital for details of expenses claimed by senior managers over the past year. Which of these reasons is grounds under the Act for refusing a request for information?

(a) The information cannot be revealed because the officials concerned regard their expenses as private.

(b) Putting together the information would cost £200, and the public body believes this is not a good use of its budget.

(c) The hospital considers that all expenses claimed are fair and reasonable, and chooses to make no comment on your story.

(d) The public would not understand the nature of the expenses claimed, and might be misled.

(e) The hospital will not release the figures unless you agree to include corresponding figures from other hospitals, so as to put the sums in context.

4 Which bodies are covered by the Environmental Information Regulations 2004?

5 Your local authority has recently switched to a new company for collecting waste in the area, after going through a process of tendering. You apply to see the contract between them, but the council says it is exempt from the Environmental Information Regulations because disclosure would adversely affect commercial confidentiality. Can you challenge the refusal, and if so, how?

ONLINE RESOURCES

www

The Freedom of Information Act can be read at:
www.opsi.gov.uk/ACTS/acts2000/20000036.htm

Schedule 1 of the Act, incorporating regular updates, can be found at:
www.foi.gov.uk/coverage.htm#schedule1

The Office of the Information Commissioner has a website at:
www.ico.org.uk

The Department of Constitutional Affairs has a useful website about the Act, at:
www.foi.gov.uk

Your Right to Know, run by FOI campaigner and journalist Heather Brooke, is full of examples of the way in which the Freedom of Information Act can be used to get access to official information:
www.yrtk.org

The Campaign for Freedom of Information website includes a user guide to the Act, and over 500 examples of press stories based on disclosures made under it:
www.cfoi.org.uk

For further resources and updates please go to the Companion Website for this book at www.pearsoned.co.uk/practicaljournalism

25

Freedom of information

Chapter

26

Writing about business

If you are one of the hundreds of journalists who work for trade magazines, you will spend most of your time writing about businesses, as will many newspaper journalists. In this area the law offers both opportunities and problems. On the plus side, the law obliges companies to make public a considerable amount of information about themselves, and knowing your way around these sources is an essential tool for a business journalist. On the minus side, companies, especially big ones, tend to employ expensive lawyers, which means they are often prone to threaten legal action if they do not like something you write. Obviously that does not mean you should never write anything that might upset a company, but you do need to be absolutely certain of your legal ground. In addition to this chapter, therefore, business reporters need to make sure they are very familiar with the law on defamation, covered in Chapter 14, and breach of confidence, in Chapter 17.

This chapter also covers the various types of insolvency proceedings. As these usually (though not always) involve the failure of a company, they are an area where inaccurate reports can cause real problems, so a business reporter needs to have a good understanding of the types of proceeding and their implications.

THE LAW ON BUSINESS INFORMATION

English law recognises several different types of business, and the type of information which must legally be made available to the public varies with each type of business.

Limited companies (also known as incorporated firms) are a legal concept, which is used as a way of giving what is called 'legal personality' to a group of people who are running a business together. Having legal personality means that an organisation has a legal existence which is separate from the people who make it up, and can make contracts, own property, and sue or be sued in its own name.

In addition, a limited company has what is called limited liability, which essentially means that any debts run up by the company are legally the responsibility of the company, and not of the individuals who run or own the company. (The practical result of this is that, if the company fails, the individuals who own the company can only lose the amount of money they have invested in the company; they cannot be sued personally or have any of their own assets taken, even if the company does not have enough money to pay its debts.) New limited companies are formed by registering with the Companies' Registrar (usually known as Companies House, this is not, as often believed, a specific building, but an agency of the Department of Trade and Industry which has centres in London and Cardiff.) In exchange for the benefits of limited liability, they have to submit to strict rules about the way they are set up and operated, including disclosing certain information for public inspection. The idea behind making this information available is that it allows the public to make informed decisions about companies that they may wish to invest in or do business with (see below), but it can also be very helpful to journalists.

Limited companies can be private or public, the main difference being that public companies can raise money by selling shares in the company to the public in general. A company which has 'plc' after its name is a public company.

Sole traders are the simplest type of business, and consist of one person in business by themselves. There are no legal requirements for setting up as a sole trader, beyond the fact that the sole trader must register as self-employed with Revenue & Customs so that they can be properly taxed. A sole trader has what is called unlimited liability, which means that any debts incurred in the course of trading are the sole trader's personal responsibility. If they go out of business owing money, their creditors may have a claim on the sole trader's assets and personal possessions, just as they would if the debts had been run up for personal purposes. Sole traders are not required to publish any information about their business, so the only real way to get useful information, other than from the sole trader themselves, is from clients or suppliers.

Partnerships work in a similar way to sole trading, but involve two or more people in business together. Like sole traders, they can simply set up and trade, without needing to register with Companies House, but the Business Names Act 1985 requires that the names of partners must be open to public inspection at the partnership's main place of business. In most cases partners will also draw up a legal document called a Partnership Agreement, which details who owns what and who does what, but this is not required to be open to public inspection. In some cases, both or all the partners share the work of the partnership, but it is also possible to have sleeping partners, whose role is to put money into the business, rather than to take part in the work it does. Partners usually have unlimited liability, and each one of them is personally liable for all the debts of the partnership.

Limited liability partnerships are a relatively new form of business, created in the Limited Liability Act 2000. They allow partners to benefit from limited liability, very much as the directors of limited companies do, and are subject to many of the same formalities as limited companies regarding setting up and operating. The main difference is that the partners have more freedom to decide (and change) their rights and responsibilities within the partnership than directors of a limited company do.

INFORMATION ON LIMITED COMPANIES

As mentioned above, limited companies are subject to a number of legal provisions covering the way they operate, many of which require them to make particular types of information available to the public and/or shareholders.

Law in practice Company information

The information which, by law, limited companies have to make available can be a useful source of stories, or at least leads, for journalists who write about business and business people. The information will be kept either at the relevant company's registered office or by Companies House. Information held by Companies House can be accessed online (though there is a small charge for all but the most basic information about a company), as well as at its centres in London and Cardiff (see *Online resources* at the end of the chapter).

26

Writing about business

Initial documentation

When a new limited company is set up, it must register with Companies House and lodge four documents: the Memorandum of Association, the Articles of Association. Form 10 and Form 12. These are as follows:

- The Memorandum of Association details the company name, the initial shareholders, whether the registered office is in England, Wales or Scotland, and the purpose of the company (this need not be at all precise; Companies House advises that vague wording such as 'to carry on business as a general commercial company' is adequate).

- The Articles of Association state how the company will be run, including the respective powers of the directors, managing director and shareholders, the arrangements for meetings between shareholders and the board, and the rules on selling shares in the company. (In some firms, for example, there may be a rule that shares can only be sold with the consent of the rest of the board, and/or that members of the board get first refusal on shares to be sold; in this way, the directors can keep control of the ownership of the company.) Companies can draw up their own Articles or simply elect to state that they will adopt a model system devised by Companies House.

- Form 10 gives details of the first director(s), the company secretary and the intended address of the registered office. As well as their names and addresses, the company's directors must give their date of birth, occupation and details of other directorships they have held within the past five years (currently, home addresses must be given, but new legislation being debated as this book went to press may allow the use of business addresses instead).

- Form 12 is a statement that the directors have complied with all the legal formalities.

Ownership and finance

Most limited companies are financed by a combination of long-term loans, which are called debentures, and what is called ownership capital. The ratio of ownership capital to loans is known as the company's 'gearing', and can be an important factor in measuring its general health and prospects.

Debentures are usually secured, which means that the person (or organisation) making the loan has a legal interest in the asset which the money was used to buy (such as machinery or buildings), and while the loan still exists, the company cannot dispose of that asset without the debenture holder's consent.

Ownership capital (also called equity capital) comes from the sale of shares. When a company issues shares, it divides the value of the company into smaller units, which can then be bought and sold; all the people or organisations who own shares own a proportion of the company. If the company makes a profit, shareholders are usually given a payment called a dividend.

Under the Companies Act 1985, every shareholder's interest must be registered, and this register is open to public inspection at the company's registered office, as is a register of all holders of debentures. In some cases, however, the name that appears will not be the person who in reality owns the shares. Shares can be held by a nominee, which means that the shares are legally held in that person's (or company's) name, but someone else has what is called 'beneficial ownership'. 'Beneficial ownership' means being entitled to any dividends from them and to the proceeds if they are sold. This may sound suspicious (and it can be used for devious purposes) but in practice it is often merely a device which allows stockbrokers, banks and other financial institutions to deal efficiently and quickly with clients' shares.

The Companies Act 1985 provides that if anyone acquires a beneficial interest in 3 per cent (or more) of the shares in a public company that carry unrestricted voting rights, the company must be told who that person (or organisation) is within two days, and any subsequent important changes in their holding must also be disclosed. The same applies where several shareholders agree to acquire 3 per cent or more between them. The company has to keep a register of information (often called the 3 per cent register) received in connection with these provisions, which must be indexed and open to public inspection for at least two hours a day.

Public companies can also make their own investigations into nominee shareholdings, and the results of their enquiries must also be shown in the 3 per cent register, and made available to the public for six years.

Company directors have to register all the shares and debentures they hold in their company, and the prices paid when they are bought or sold. This includes holdings through nominees, or by directors' spouses or children, or in a parent or subsidiary company. They also have to register any increase or decrease in their holdings. This information must be indexed and open to the public, at the company's registered office.

◼ Information on directors

In addition to information on their holdings in a company, directors have to submit certain other details to public and/or shareholder scrutiny. Copies of a director's contract of service with the company have to be made available to shareholders, and companies quoted on the London Stock Exchange must, under its rules, make service contracts available for public inspection at their registered offices, and for at least 15 minutes before its Annual General Meeting. The documentation must include details of the directors' salaries and other remuneration, any provisions for early retirement, and any compensation to be paid for ending directors' contracts. The chairman's earnings also have to be stated in the annual accounts.

If a director has a financial interest in contracts their company has made, or if the company has made a loan or any other credit transaction to a director, that must be disclosed in the company's annual accounts. Companies also have to list any directorships which their directors hold in other companies, or have held over the past five years. This information must be available to public inspection.

These requirements can, with some clever digging, yield some very interesting stories. Robertson and Nicol (*Media Law*, 2002) cite the examples of one service contract which revealed that a particular director was required to take his wife along on every overseas trip, and a set of accounts which disclosed that a company had loaned a director £140,000 to buy a £200,000 house, allowing him to pay just £23 a week to live there. Because directors' home addresses must be disclosed, a *New Statesman* journalist was able not just to report the story but to get a photo of the rather luxurious residence.

Law in practice **Ownership of buildings**

Sometimes it can be useful to find out whether a business, or one of its directors, owns a particular building or piece of land. For the vast majority of buildings and land in the UK, this information has to be registered with the Land Registry when land is bought or sold, and then becomes publicly available (only land which has not changed hands since 1925 is not included in the Register). The information held includes the price paid, and details of what are called 'restrictive covenants' on the property, which may limit what can be done there.

26

Writing about business

These details can be accessed via the Land Registry website (see *Online resources* at the end of the chapter), on payment of a small fee. The usual way to search is by looking up individual properties. If you want to find out all the property that a company owns, there is also an index which can be searched this way, but only at the discretion of the registrar. It is not usually possible to search for property owned by an individual in this way.

Accounts

Limited companies have to prepare annual accounts, which are sent to Companies House and can be inspected by the public. All but the smallest companies must have their accounts checked by auditors, whose job is to verify, for the benefit of shareholders, that the picture painted in the accounts is true.

The information that must be included in accounts depends on the size of the company.

Large companies and all public companies must include:

- a profit and loss account (or income and expenditure account if the company is not trading for profit);
- a balance sheet signed by a director;
- an auditors' report signed by the auditor (if appropriate);
- a directors' report signed by a director or the secretary of the company;
- notes to the accounts;
- group accounts (if appropriate);
- an operating and financial review signed by a director or secretary.

Medium-sized companies need only deliver an abbreviated profit and loss account, plus:

- a full balance sheet;
- a special auditor's report;
- the directors' report;
- notes to the accounts.

Companies are classified as medium-sized if they meet at least two of the following criteria: annual turnover of £22.8 million or less; balance sheet total of £11.4 million or less; average number of employees 250 or fewer.

Small companies need only deliver an abbreviated balance sheet and notes, plus an auditor's report (and some very small companies are exempt from the requirement to be audited). A company qualifies as small if it fulfils at least two of the following criteria: annual turnover of £5.6 million or less; balance sheet total of £2.8 million or less; average number of employees 50 or fewer (these and the limits for medium-sized companies are increased from time to time; the figures quoted here were set in 2004).

Where a directors' report is required, it must include:

- any important changes in the assets the company holds;
- any interests held by the directors in the company's shares at the end of the financial year;
- any donations over £200 made to political parties or any EU political organisation during the financial year;

- the total amount donated to charity, if this is over £200;
- details of the company's policies on hiring disabled people, and consulting employees (this requirement only covers firms with over 250 employees).

Companies which plan to issue shares to the public also have to make available information documenting their recent performance, and expectations for the future.

Annual general meetings

All public limited companies must hold an Annual General Meeting (AGM) of their members (some private companies also do so, but do not have to). In most cases, annual general meetings are fairly bland, stage-managed events, with little important discussion, but in situations where it is known there are problems with a company, they can be much more useful to journalists. The meetings include a vote on the director's remuneration, which shareholders may use to show their displeasure at the company's performance: in 2002, for example, the Prudential was forced to backtrack on its planned executive pay scheme after shareholders refused to support it.

AGMs must also provide an opportunity for shareholders to question directors, and this too can provide some useful copy. As well as 'ordinary' shareholders showing their displeasure at the way a company is performing, question and answer sessions may feature representatives of pressure groups, who can gain access to the meeting by buying just one share.

Companies are not obliged to admit the press to AGMs, though many do. If press access is denied, buying one share in the company turns you into a shareholder with a right to attend; alternatively, a shareholder can nominate someone to attend in their place (known as a proxy), and if shareholders want publicity for something they feel is going wrong at the company, you may be able to get one to let you attend as their proxy. AGMs of public (but not private) companies are covered by qualified privilege under the Defamation Act 1996 (see p. 209), as is publication of fair and accurate extracts from any document that the board of the public company makes available to its members, or any document circulated to the members of a public company which concerns the appointment, resignation, retirement or dismissal of the company's directors. The events at an AGM of a public company will usually be a matter of public interest, so the defence of fair comment may also apply.

INSOLVENCY PROCEEDINGS

The idea of insolvency proceedings is that a person or company who cannot pay their debts can have their assets fairly shared among their creditors and, after a period, have any remaining debts cancelled. This can be done voluntarily or at the request of a creditor. An individual who becomes insolvent is described as going bankrupt, while for companies or partnerships the term used is going into liquidation. There is also a way of winding up a company which occurs for reasons other than being unable to pay debts (and often involves no fault or failure), which is called members voluntary liquidation (see below).

Bankruptcy

Bankruptcy proceedings begin with the filing of a petition for a bankruptcy order. This can be done by the company which is going bankrupt (known as the debtor), or one of the people or companies they owe money to (known as creditors), either at the High Court in London or the county court nearest where the debtor works or lives. The debtor must owe at least £750 in unsecured debts. A petition from a creditor can be refused if the debtor has already made an offer and it has been unreasonably refused.

Where a debtor has assets worth over £2,000, and debts of £20,000 or less, the district judge can make an interim bankruptcy order and refer the case to a licenced insolvency practitioner, who will try to make voluntary payment agreements with the creditors, so that the debtor can avoid bankruptcy. This is called an individual voluntary arrangement.

If the bankruptcy order goes ahead, the person is legally bankrupt from the time the order is made. Legal control of all the debtor's property is then taken over by the Official Receiver (an officer of the court) or a licensed insolvency practitioner (the latter being most likely in cases where there is a good chance of the creditors getting a large proportion of what they are owed). This person is known as the trustee in bankruptcy. Notice of the bankruptcy is advertised in the *London Gazette* and also in a local or national newspaper (sometimes both).

The official then examines the debtor's assets and liabilities, which must be laid out in a statement within 21 days. A creditors meeting may then be held to inform creditors of the full situation. The Official Receiver can allow journalists into a creditors meeting, but is not obliged to do so.

If the debtor does not cooperate fully with the Official Receiver, a public examination in bankruptcy (often referred to as the PE or bankruptcy court) can be held, which takes place before a district judge. It can also be held at the request of at least 50 per cent of the creditors. Anyone, including the press, may attend, and fair and accurate reports of a public examination are protected by absolute privilege.

The public examination is designed to satisfy the court that it has full information on the debtor's financial situation, and to clarify why they have been unable to pay their debts, including an assessment of whether the situation involves any criminal offence. It also considers whether any assets of the debtor which have been transferred to someone else should be recovered; any transaction from the past two years can be declared void, unless it is a standard trading transaction. This period can be extended to ten years, if it can be proved that transfers were made in order to deprive creditors of money.

The procedure is that the debtor is questioned on oath by the Official Receiver or their assistant; refusal to answer is contempt of court and punishable as a criminal offence. Questions can also be asked by the trustee in bankruptcy (or a lawyer representing them), and by creditors. The information divulged will usually include:

■ the debtor's liabilities (debts);

■ the debtor's assets;

■ whether there are secured creditors (often banks or building societies, these will be creditors who loaned money against security, for example via a mortgage).

If the court is satisfied that all questions have been answered, the public examination will usually be concluded, but in some cases it may be adjourned for further inquiries to be made.

From this you can build up a picture of the scale of the bankruptcy (i.e. how much of the money will not be paid back), who will be affected by it and to what degree. After the costs of bankruptcy are accounted for, secured creditors are generally the first to be paid, since they have the right to be paid from the sale of the property used as security. Assuming there is some money left, the group with next claim on it are what are called 'preferential creditors'. This group now mostly comprises employees of the bankrupt person; it used to include certain government departments but this 'Crown preference' was abolished under the Enterprise Act 2002. Unsecured creditors are only paid if there is money left over after these two groups have been paid.

What it means to be bankrupt

An individual going through the bankruptcy process must declare all assets to the Official Receiver, right down to their household goods and clothes. The Official Receiver then decides what they can keep – usually just clothes and household necessities, and equipment or vehicles needed for work. Everything else that the bankrupt owned comes under the legal control of the Official Receiver and can be sold to pay the creditors. If the bankrupt still has an income, deductions can be made from it, though they must be left with enough to meet their family's normal domestic needs.

A person who is bankrupt must disclose this fact if applying for a bank account or credit of more than £500; not doing so is a criminal offence. The bankrupt can still trade as a self-employed person, but is not allowed to trade under a different name from that which they were made bankrupt under, unless they tell everyone they do business with that this is the case. Bankrupts are barred from acting as company directors, and from some professions, but are no longer automatically banned from holding public offices such as MP, local councillor or magistrate.

The names of people who are currently bankrupt are held on a register which is open to the public (see *Online resources* at the end of the chapter).

How does bankruptcy end?

Bankruptcy is usually imposed for a year, after which the bankrupt is automatically discharged (until the Enterprise Act 2002 it was usually three years). This releases the individual from their former debts (except any arising from fraud), and the restrictions of bankruptcy. It can happen earlier if the Official Receiver finishes their investigations earlier and files a notice with the court. If the debts and bankruptcy costs are paid before the date of discharge, the bankruptcy can be lifted immediately. The discharge can be postponed if the Official Receiver considers that the person has not carried out their duties under the bankruptcy order.

If, during their enquiries, the Official Receiver concludes that the individual has been dishonest before or during the bankruptcy, or is otherwise to blame for their situation, the Official Receiver can apply to the court for a Bankruptcy Restrictions Order, which keeps the individual under the bankruptcy restrictions for a longer than usual period, which can be up to 15 years. Alternatively the individual can agree to such restrictions by giving a bankruptcy restrictions undertaking, which means the matter does not have to go before the court.

◼ Liquidation proceedings

Liquidation means the closure of a company. It can take place because the company cannot meet its debts, but this is not always the case, so it is important to know the difference between the following three types of liquidation:

Members voluntary liquidation: This takes place when the directors of a solvent company decide to close it down. An example might be where the directors of a small family firm are all retiring. A liquidator is appointed, but creditors do not have to be notified. This procedure can only be used where the company is able to pay its debts within 12 months; if the liquidator finds this not to be the case, the procedure becomes a creditors voluntary liquidation.

Creditors voluntary liquidation: Despite the name, this procedure is initiated by the directors of a company, rather than the creditors, because the company cannot meet its debts or its assets are worth less than its liabilities. The procedure can only go forward if company shareholders with 75 per cent of the shares agree to it. They appoint a liquidator, who will then meet the creditors to examine why the situation has arisen and assess the assets and liabilities. Only after these meetings have been held can the company be said to be in liquidation.

Compulsory liquidation: In this case, the liquidation is initiated by a creditor, who petitions the court to wind up the debtor company on the grounds that it cannot meet its debts (technically, compulsory liquidation can also arise because a company has failed to file its statutory report, or hold its statutory set-up meeting, has suspended or not even started doing business, or does not have the number of members required by law; however, most cases are concerned with insolvency). If the court grants a winding-up order, the Official Receiver then takes over the company, closes it down, and supervises the distribution of assets to the creditors.

OTHER PROCEEDINGS FOR COMPANIES IN TROUBLE

There are other routes which a company facing insolvency may take, and if you write about businesses, it is essential to know the difference between them.

Administration: This process is used as an alternative to liquidation, where either the directors of a failing company or its creditors believe it can either continue as a going concern, or be sold for more than would be raised from going into receivership. Either the company directors, or a creditor, can apply to the court for an administration order.

If the court is satisfied that the business cannot pay its debts (or is likely to become unable to), an insolvency practitioner is appointed as administrator, either to sell the company or put into effect a rescue plan. The effect is to give the business a breathing space: while the company is in administration, the creditors cannot take legal action to wind up the company or appoint a receiver. The process is known as being 'in administration'.

Receivership: The process of administrative receivership (usually known as being 'in receivership') is not a court process, and takes place when a major creditor (usually a bank) appoints an insolvency practitioner as receiver, to recover money owed to it. The receiver does not make payments to unsecured creditors.

Voluntary agreements: A company in trouble may be able to avoid liquidation by applying to the court to make a corporate voluntary arrangement. If the court agrees, it will make an interim order, which has the effect of suspending all proceedings by creditors against the company. A liquidator prepares a proposal for repayment, which is put to the creditors; if 75 per cent of them (calculated by the value of their debts) agree to it, the agreement is binding on all other creditors who know about it. If the creditors do not agree, the interim order lapses and the creditors can take legal proceedings.

Director disqualification orders

When a company has failed (whether it goes into liquidation, administration or receivership), the Official Receiver or the appointed Insolvency Practitioner must send the Secretary of State a report on the conduct all the directors who ran the company during the three years before its failure. As well as people officially named as directors, this includes anyone who has in practice carried out the function of a director. On the basis of this report, the Secretary of State for Trade and Industry may seek a director disqualification order under the Company Director Disqualification Act 1986, which disqualifies the individual concerned from:

- acting as a director of a company;
- taking part, directly or indirectly, in the promotion, formation or management of a company;
- being a liquidator or an administrator of a company;
- being a receiver or manager of a company's property.

Each order specifies the period it is to last, which may be from two to 15 years.

The kind of conduct which would prompt the Secretary of State to apply for an order includes:

- continuing to trade to the detriment of creditors at a time when the company was insolvent;
- failure to keep proper accounting records;
- failure to prepare and file accounts or make returns to Companies House;
- failure to submit tax returns or pay tax or other money due to the Crown;
- failure to cooperate with the Official Receiver or the appointed Insolvency Practitioner.

If an order is to be sought, the Official Receiver makes a report to the court, which is also supplied to the directors concerned. They can challenge the allegations (usually by means of written statements) and other evidence may be called for or against the order. The court then decides whether the order should be imposed. At any stage during the process, a director can give a voluntary undertaking to abide by the restrictions, in which case the matter does not have to go before the court.

A public register of disqualified directors is held by Companies House; almost 10,000 directors have been disqualified since the 1986 Act came into force.

26

Writing about business

Law in practice **Defamation and insolvency**

Clearly, neither businesses or individuals take kindly to being reported as being in financial difficulties, so reporting insolvency can easily land you in trouble with the libel lawyers if you are not careful. These are some of the traps to watch out for:

- Saying that someone is bankrupt when they are not is defamatory. You should never describe someone as bankrupt until a bankruptcy order has been made, even if one has been filed. Unless the debtor has themselves filed for bankruptcy, it is unwise to report that an order has been applied for at all; if is refused (e.g. if the creditor has rejected an offer from the debtor which the court feels was reasonable), the debtor may sue on the basis that you were implying they were bankrupt.

- A public examination in bankruptcy is a court proceeding which is covered by absolute privilege. This is not, however, the case with a creditors meeting, so if any possibly defamatory allegations are made at such a meeting (as they often will be when angry creditors are involved) you need to be sure that you are covered by another defence, such as justification, if you report them.

- The distinction between members voluntary liquidation and creditors voluntary liquidation is very important. A members voluntary liquidation does not generally involve any

→

fault or failure on the part of a company, so if you describe a firm going through this process using the wrong term, you are saying (falsely) that it cannot pay its debts, which is obviously defamatory.

- Technically, a company going into administration reflects less badly on its management than going into liquidation, since there is still some value left in it. Whether this distinction would be enough to found a libel action if you used the wrong term is unclear, but it is safest (and obviously better practice) to make sure you clarify which type of proceedings is involved before you report a story. Certainly the terms are not, as some reporters assume, interchangeable.

CHAPTER SUMMARY

The law on business information

There are four main types of business under English law, each covered by different rules on the information they must publish

- limited companies;
- sole traders;
- partnerships;
- limited liability partnerships.

Information on limited companies

Limited companies have a legal duty to make public:

- documentation created when a company is started;
- details of shareholders and debenture holders;
- information about directors, including their remuneration package;
- annual accounts.

Insolvency proceedings

Insolvency proceedings (except for members voluntary liquidation) occur when an individual or company cannot pay their debts.

- Bankruptcy applies to individuals;
- liquidation applies to companies.

Other proceedings for companies in trouble

There are three other routes:

- administration, where a failing company may still have a future as a business;
- receivership, where a major creditor appoints an insolvency practitioner to recover money owed to it;
- voluntary agreements, where court proceedings are suspended while a failing company and its creditors try to make their own agreement regarding payment.

TEST YOUR KNOWLEDGE

1 What are the four main types of company recognised in English law?

2 You are writing about a limited company, and want to find out if its directors have been linked to any other companies. What information is publicly available and where would you find it?

3 What is a debenture holder?

4 You want to attend the Annual General Meeting of a public company in the industry you write about, but you are told that the press is not invited. What can you do?

5 What is the difference between bankruptcy and insolvency?

6 What is a Bankruptcy Restrictions Order?

7 A local company has gone into members voluntary liquidation. Which of these sentences is it safe to use when writing the story?

    (a) Anderson Brothers have gone into members voluntary liquidation.

    (b) Anderson Brothers have gone bust.

    (c) Anderson Brothers have gone into liquidation.

    (d) Anderson Brothers have gone into compulsory liquidation.

    (e) Anderson Brothers have gone into receivership.

8 You suspect that a local businessman may have been disqualified from holding directorships. How can you check?

26

Writing about business

ONLINE RESOURCES

www

Companies House has a website where you can access information on limited companies:
www.companieshouse.gov.uk

The Land Registry website is at:
www.landreg.gov.uk

The Insolvency Service website is at:
www.insolvency.gov.uk

The Individual Insolvency Register lists the names of people who are currently bankrupt or have made individual voluntary agreements. It can be searched online at:
www.insolvency.gov.uk/bankruptcy/bankruptcysearch.htm

For further resources and updates please go to the Companion Website for this book at www.pearsoned.co.uk/practicaljournalism

RACE, RELIGION AND PUBLIC ORDER

This section covers legal restrictions on publishing material which, broadly speaking, have the potential to stir up hatred, extreme offence or disorder. The first chapter covers restrictions on publishing material which could encourage racial and religious hatred. It includes details of the Public Order Act, which makes it an offence to publish certain types of material which could stir up racial hatred, and the new legislation against stirring up religious hatred (which is not yet in force). The chapter also covers a related offence, blasphemy, which deals specifically with publications which concern the Anglican faith.

The second chapter in this section deals with three very old criminal offences, which can be committed by publication of material which, in different ways, could be said to disturb public order or morals. As you will see when you read the chapters, the offences are clearly out of tune with modern thinking on freedom of expression, and it is unlikely that prosecutions would be brought for any of them today, but as they still form part of the law, they are included for the sake of completeness.

Race and religion

Legislation against stirring up racial hatred has existed for several decades, and though its main target is those who publish words (or pictures) with the intention of causing racial hatred, the wording of the legislation also makes it possible for journalists reporting such words to be guilty of an offence, which is why you need to know about it. Until 2006, similar protection was not available for religious groups which were not also racially defined (so Jews and Sikhs, for example, were covered by the legislation, but Muslims, Catholics and Buddhists were not).

The current government was keen to introduce new legislation in this area, and after a long parliamentary struggle, passed the Racial and Religious Hatred Act 2006. However, widespread opposition to the legislation meant the government's initial bill was very much watered down in the Lords, and the resulting Act does not offer the same degree of protection as that regarding racial hatred. At the time this book went to press the 2006 Act was not yet in force, but was expected to come into force early in 2007. A further offence relating to religion is blasphemy, discussed at the end of this chapter.

INCITEMENT TO RACIAL HATRED

The law on inciting racial hatred is contained in the Public Order Act 1986. This states that it is an offence to do any of the following with the intention of stirring up racial hatred, or in circumstances where racial hatred is likely to be stirred up:

- use threatening, abusive or insulting language or display abusive or insulting written material;
- publish or distribute abusive or insulting written material, perform plays, distribute or present visual images or sounds, or produce a programme containing abusive or insulting written material;
- possess written material or recordings of images or sounds that are threatening, abusive or insulting, with a view to displaying or publishing them (this provision does not make it an offence to receive unsolicited racist material, or keep it, for example as background research, as long as you do not plan to publish it).

The Public Order Act 1986 was amended by s164 of the Broadcasting Act 1990, so that the offence can also be committed by broadcasting a TV or radio programme. The broadcaster, the programme maker and the person shown or heard using the threatening, abusive or insulting language can all be prosecuted.

Racial hatred

Section 17 of the Public Order Act 1986 defines 'racial hatred' as 'hatred against a group of citizens in Great Britain defined by reference to colour, race, nationality (including citizenship) or ethnic or national origins'.

Intention and circumstances

The offence can be committed with two different states of mind:

- where the defendant deliberately stirs up racial hatred;
- where the defendant does not have this intention, but does any of the prohibited acts in circumstances where racial hatred is likely to be stirred up.

The latter provision means that a publication could potentially be guilty of the offence if it reports, for example, inflammatory speeches given or leaflets issued by a politician with racist views. It was also made clear, during the process of the Bill that became the Act, that publishing readers' letters which use threatening, abusive or insulting words may be an offence. The Home Office stated that if such letters were published, merely including other letters putting the opposing view, or adding an editorial comment to that effect, would not necessarily be enough to avoid committing the offence. However, if a court was called upon to decide such a case, it would (the Home Office said) look at the whole context of the publication and not just the offending words in isolation.

This somewhat inconclusive position has the potential to make it difficult for the media to examine the issue of racism, since it is impossible to expose racist statements to public criticism if you cannot repeat them or show them being made. However, some support for the media's position has come from a decision of the European Court of Human Rights, in **Jersild v Denmark** (1995). The case was brought by Danish broadcasters, who had produced a documentary discussing the issue of growing racial hatred among the country's young people. The programme included interviews with racists, in which they put forward their views. The broadcasters were not seeking to promote those views, only to report on the fact that they seemed to be held by an increasing number of young people, but they were prosecuted and convicted under Denmark's anti-racism laws (as were the people interviewed). They brought an action against the Danish Government on the grounds that their right to freedom of expression had been breached, and the Government argued that, within the programme, they should have included opposing views, or in some other way refuted the statements made. The Court of Human Rights disagreed. It said that the interviewees were not protected by Article 10 because of the nature of the statements they made, and so their convictions were not a breach of the right to freedom of expression. However, the broadcasters were merely showing the statements in the context of a serious investigation into an important issue, and to convict them for doing this was a serious violation of Article 10.

This suggests that if a TV programme or press report shows or repeats words which would be caught by the Act, as part of a serious examination of a subject of public interest, prosecuting the media for incitement to racial hatred would be a breach of Article 10.

 In 2004, the Crown Prosecution Service (CPS) announced it would not be prosecuting the broadcaster Robert Kilroy Silk over an article in which he criticised Arab states. The CPS said that the offence of incitement to racial hatred had not been committed, because there was no evidence that Mr Kilroy Silk intended to stir up racial hatred against Arabs; his purpose had been to criticise the regimes in particular countries. Nor were the words 'likely' to stir up racial hatred. The

CPS said that in this context, 'likely' meant more than 'liable to'; it had to be shown that the probable result of the words would be to create extreme dislike of a racial group, to such an extent that public order could be affected. As the article had previously been published a year earlier without complaint, it did not appear likely that the second publication would have this effect.

Threatening, abusive or insulting

These words carry their ordinary, everyday meaning; there is no special definition and in each case, it is for the court to decide whether the words used were threatening, abusive or insulting. However, decided cases have made it clear that to justify a conviction, the words need to be more than merely rude or unpleasant.

In 2006, a Muslim preacher called Abu Hamza was convicted of incitement to racial hatred (and other offences, including incitement to murder), after a jury watched videos of him telling congregations that killing Jews was their religious duty, describing Jews as 'cursed by Allah', traitorous and dirty, and saying that Hitler was sent by Allah.

Law in practice Reporting racist remarks

When reporting inflammatory racist remarks made by someone, it will often be safer to paraphrase them, rather than quoting directly, so that the words you publish are not themselves 'threatening, abusive or insulting'.

Defences

Section 19(2) of the Public Order Act 1986 provides a defence where the person accused of the offence is not shown to have intended to stir up racial hatred, and was unaware and did not suspect or have reason to suspect, that the material concerned was threatening, abusive or insulting.

In addition, the Act does not apply to words used in a fair, accurate and contemporaneous report of public proceedings in a court or tribunal, or fair and accurate reports of proceedings in Parliament.

Investigation and prosecutions

The Public Order Act 1986 allows the police to get a search warrant from a magistrate, in order to search premises where they suspect that someone is in possession of material that would be unlawful under the Act. Prosecutions can only be brought with the consent of the Attorney-General. In 1987, the Attorney-General said that if asked to consider a prosecution concerning the media, he would take into account the type of publication and its circulation and potential readership, and any special circumstances which existed at the time and might have influence on the effect of the published material.

All the offences mentioned above can result in a sentence of up to two years' imprisonment and/or a fine.

RELIGIOUS HATRED

The Racial and Religious Hatred Act 2006 makes it an offence to do any of the following with the intention of stirring up religious hatred:

- use threatening words or behaviour, or display any threatening material;
- publish or distribute written material which is threatening to the public or a section of the public;
- distribute, show or play a recording of sounds or images which are threatening;
- possess written material or recordings which are threatening, with a view to it being shown, published, displayed, distributed, played or included in a programme service (defined in the Broadcasting Act 1990 as any television or radio service).

Note that the words must be threatening; in contrast to the law on racial hatred, insulting or abusive words are not enough. In addition, the acts must be committed 'with the intention of stirring up racial hatred', rather than, as with racial hatred, in circumstances where it is likely to be stirred up; this gives better protection to responsible media reports of racist views held by others.

The 2006 Act defines religious hatred as 'hatred against a group of persons defined by religious belief or lack of religious belief'. This is potentially a very wide definition, since 'religious belief' would appear to extend further than actual membership of a recognised religion.

Defences

The 2006 Act provides a potentially wide defence to protect freedom of expression, stating that:

> Nothing in this Part shall be read or given effect in a way which prohibits or restricts discussion, criticism or expressions of antipathy, dislike, ridicule, insult or abuse of particular religions or the beliefs or practices of their adherents, or of any other belief system or the beliefs or practices of its adherents, or proselytising or urging adherents of a different religion or belief system to cease practising their religion or belief system.

This was added as a response to critics of the Bill, who argued that the planned legislation was an unjustified interference with freedom of speech, and would prevent everything from reasoned discussion of religious issues to jokes about religion. Until the 2006 Act comes into force and is tested in court, it will not be clear how much protection the defence gives.

The 2006 Act does not apply to words used in a fair, accurate and contemporaneous report of public proceedings in a court or tribunal, or fair and accurate reports of proceedings in Parliament.

Investigation and prosecutions

The 2006 Act allows the police to get a search warrant from a magistrate to search premises when they suspect someone is in possession of material that would be unlawful under the Act. Prosecutions can only be brought with the consent of the Attorney-General. A successful prosecution carries a sentence of up to seven years in prison and/or a fine.

Race, religion and the PCC Code

The PCC Code provides that :

- the press must avoid prejudicial or pejorative reference to an individual's race, colour or religion;
- details of an individual's race, colour or religion should not be given unless genuinely relevant to the story.

BLASPHEMY

Blasphemy is an old offence, which is committed by vilifying or ridiculing God, or the Anglican religion, or indecency related to God or the Anglican religion. It does not apply to ordinary criticism of or humour about these subjects, only to material which is outrageously offensive or indecent. It only applies to material concerning the Anglican (Church of England) faith, and not to any non-Christian religions. Other Christian faiths, such as Catholicism, have some protection under the blasphemy laws, but only in so far as their beliefs coincide with those of the Church of England (so, for example, offensive remarks about the Pope would not be covered, but offensive remarks about God can be).

 In *R v Bow Street Magistrates' Court, ex p Choudhury* (1991), a group of Muslims sought to have the author Salman Rushdie prosecuted for blasphemy, because he had written a book, *The Satanic Verses*, which they felt was offensive about their faith. The High Court held that blasphemy was not applicable to faiths other than the Church of England.

In practice, prosecutions for blasphemy are thought to be very unlikely today, and there have been several instances in recent years where material that was said to be highly offensive to Anglicans (and other Christians) has been published, and no prosecution has resulted. In fact there has been only one prosecution for blasphemy since 1922, and that one, the case of *Whitehouse* v *Lemon* (see below), was a private prosecution brought without official support from the Anglican church.

 In *Whitehouse* v *Lemon* (1978), the magazine *Gay News* published a poem which described Christ engaging in homosexual acts. Mary Whitehouse, who at the time was a well-known campaigner against obscenity, brought a private prosecution against the editor and the publishers of *Gay News*, and won her case.

 The British Board of Film Classification took the unusual step of asking the Director of Public Prosecutions (DPP) to watch the film 'The Last Temptation of Christ' (1988), and give an opinion as to whether it was blasphemous, after nearly 2,000 people complained to the Board in advance of the film's release in the UK. The film included a scene in which Christ on the cross fantasises about making love to Mary Magdelene, and the Board admitted that it could be offensive to Christians, but said the subject of Christ's life was approached sincerely and reverently, and was in no way contemptous; the controversial scene was actually used to highlight the enormity of Christ's sacrifice, as represented by Christian belief. The DPP agreed that the necessary ingredients for a blasphemy charge were not present, and no prosecution was brought.

CHAPTER SUMMARY

Racial hatred

It is an offence to use, possess, distribute of publish threatening, abusive or insulting words, sounds of pictures with the intention of stirring up racial hatred, or in circumstances where racial hatred is likely to be stirred up.

There is a defence for anyone who did not intend to stir up racial hatred, and had no reason to suspect the relevent material was abusive, threatening or insulting.

Religious hatred

It is an offence to use, publish, show or display material which is threatening, with the intention of stirring up religious hatred. The offence is not supposed to restrict criticism or discussion of religion.

A defence protects criticism which is not threatening.

Exceptions

Neither offence applies to fair, accurate and (for court reports) contemporaneous court or Parliamentary reports.

Investigation and prosecution

Both offences carry search powers for the police; neither can be prosecuted without the Attorney-General's consent.

Blasphemy

Blasphemy is committed by vilification, or ridicule of, or indecency relating to God or the Anglican religion.

TEST YOUR KNOWLEDGE

1 To which of these groups does the law on inciting racial hatred apply:

   (a) Black people

   (b) Asians

   (c) Italians

   (d) Jews

   (e) Catholics

   (f) Welsh people?

2 You attend a public meeting in which your local MP makes a speech, which is extremely abusive about Asian people in the area. Can you report what he says?

3 The same MP repeats his allegations in Parliament. Can you report them?

4 You are attending a court case in which the accused is charged with a racially motivated attack. While being cross-examined, he launches into a tirade of racist language and threats against the family of his victim. Can you report this?

5 How is 'religious hatred' defined in the Racial and Religious Hatred Act 2006?

ONLINE RESOURCES

www   The Racial and Religious Hatred Act 2006 can be read at:
www.opsi.gov.uk/acts/acts2006/20060001.htm

The Crown Prosecution Service statement about the Kilroy Silk case can be read at:
www.cps.gov.uk/news/pressreleases/archive/2004/131_04.html

Jersild v *Denmark* can be read at:
www.worldlii.org/eu/cases/ECHR/1994/33.html

For further resources and updates please go to the Companion Website for this book at www.pearsoned.co.uk/practicaljournalism

27

Race and religion

Chapter 28

Criminal, seditious and obscene libel

This chapter covers three criminal offences, which share the term 'libel', but differ from the civil action of the same name. None of the three is likely to make a huge impact on your journalistic life: the first two are very old offences that are unlikely to be the subject of prosecutions today; the third is still active but not in practice likely to be used against many journalists. However, as they are all still part of media law, they are included here for the sake of completeness.

CRIMINAL LIBEL

In the previous chapters, we have looked at the civil action for libel, where a person who claims to be libelled sues the maker or publisher of the offending statement for damages and/or an injunction. There also exists a criminal offence of libel, which can be committed by making an extremely damaging statement about someone. In practice, the offence appears to have fallen out of use in this country (though several other European countries still use criminal libel laws). Only two prosecutions have been brought in the UK during the 20th century, and as we shall see at the end of this chapter, it may be that any prosecution brought now would fail, because of the effects of the Human Rights Act 1998. Since it has not officially been repealed, however, it is worth at least being aware of the offence of criminal libel.

What is criminal libel?

Criminal libel began as an offence which was designed to protect public order, and was traditionally thought to be committed only by making a statement that was likely to cause a breach of the peace. More recent case law makes it clear that it can be committed in two ways:

- publication of a statement that is likely to cause a breach of the peace; or
- publication of a statement that has an extremely serious effect on the reputation of the person concerned. The effect would have to be serious enough to make it in the public interest for a prosecution to take place.

In some cases of course, the same statement might fulfil both criteria, so that the publisher of the statement could be sued for libel, and prosecuted for criminal libel. There is one big difference, however, in that truth is not necessarily a defence for criminal libel.

 In 1975, the businessman Sir James Goldsmith took out a private prosecution for criminal libel against *Private Eye*, over a story which he claimed presented him as the leader of a conspiracy to obstruct a police search for Lord Lucan, who famously went missing after his family's nanny was found murdered. Sir James said that the story was part of a campaign against him by *Private Eye*, and said that as a result of this campaign, there had been bomb scares at the offices of his solicitors, and therefore the article could be said to be likely to provoke a breach of the peace. In the event, the case did not go to trial; Sir James settled with *Private Eye* after it agreed to withdraw its allegations and pay for an apology to be printed in a national newspaper.

In 1977, a convicted sexual offender called Roger Gleaves brought a private prosecution for criminal libel against several journalists who had written about his criminal activities, including the authors of a book on him, and three reporters from the *Sunday People*. All five were committed to trial by a magistrate, and the three newspaper reporters were actually remanded in custody because the magistrate felt they were likely to commit further offences. They were released the following day on the order of a judge, and the Director of Public Prosecutions (DPP) later took over the case against them, and offered no evidence. The book authors, however, were tried, and had to prove the truth of their allegations, even though Gleaves had been convicted of the offences they had reported. (In a civil action this would not have been necessary, as a criminal conviction is accepted as proof that the relevant offences were committed.) After a two and half week trial, the authors were acquitted.

Publication

For the purposes of criminal libel, the offending words must be written, or in some other permanent form, but unlike in a civil libel case, they need not be published to a third party; addressing the remarks to the person concerned is enough. This is because of criminal libel's roots as a public order offence, since it was quite likely to be the person the words were about who would create a breach of the peace.

Who can be the subject?

Criminal libel can be committed against any individual and, unlike civil libel, the offence can also be committed against groups of people, if the purpose of the offending remark is to excite hatred against that group of people (though in practice this kind of behaviour would be more likely to be dealt with today by using race relations legislation, or possibly the new legislation on inciting religious hatred). It is also possible to commit criminal libel through a remark about someone who is dead, if it can be proved that the remark was likely to make that person's relatives commit a breach of the peace. (This contrasts with civil actions for libel, which cannot be based on defamation of a dead person.)

Defences

In civil libel, proving that words were true is a complete defence. This is not the case with criminal libel; in fact, it used to be said of criminal libel that 'the greater the truth, the greater the libel', on the grounds that a statement that was true was more likely to cause a breach of the peace than one which was false. In order to have a defence, the maker of the statement must instead prove that the words were both true and published for the public benefit.

It is also a defence to criminal libel if the words were published under absolute or qualified privilege. Some academics suggest there may also be a defence of fair comment, but there are no decided cases on this point.

Punishment for criminal libel

A person who publishes a criminal libel can be sent to prison for up to 12 months, and/or fined.

Restrictions on prosecutions

The Law of Libel Amendment Act 1888 established restrictions on prosecutions for criminal libel, stating that proprietors and editors could only be prosecuted with permission from a High Court judge. In order to allow a prosecution of a proprietor or editor, the judge must be satisfied that there is an exceptionally strong case, that the libel is extremely serious and that the public interest justifies criminal proceedings.

 In *Desmond* v *Thorne* (1983), a man described by the *Sunday People* as a 'violent and drunken bully' sought leave to bring a prosecution for criminal libel against the paper. Having heard evidence provided by the newspaper, which undermined the man's claims, the judge refused leave for the prosecution, stating that the case was not 'so clear as to be beyond argument', and that in addition, the public interest did not demand a prosecution.

 In *Hilliard* v *Penfield Enterprises* (1990), a woman sought to prosecute magazine publishers over a story claiming that her late husband had been a member of the IRA. She was refused leave, on the grounds that criminal libel regarding a dead person required that the maker of the statement intended to injure surviving relatives by denigrating the memory of the deceased person.

The Act does not, however, require judicial permission for prosecutions against journalists, and this loophole was exploited in the cases brought by Roger Gleaves (see above), who prosecuted journalists rather than proprietors and therefore did not need judicial permission (which in the circumstances would probably have been refused). However, if a prosecution against a journalist was brought today, the Act would have to be read in the light of the Human Rights Act 1998, and it is likely that a court would find that the same protection should now be extended to journalists.

Criminal libel today

The Law Commission recommended in 1982 that the offence of criminal libel should be repealed, and although this has not happened, many lawyers now believe that the advent of the Human Rights Act 1998 means that a prosecution for criminal libel may be impossible, as it would be considered too strong a restriction on the right to freedom of expression. In *Lingens* v *Austria* (1986), the European Court of Human Rights held that the Austrian government was in breach of the European Convention on Human Rights by using criminal libel laws against a journalist who had criticised a politician.

SEDITIOUS LIBEL

The criminal offence of seditious libel, also known as sedition, is committed by publishing words that are likely to disturb the internal peace and government of the country. It was originally an offence that protected established authority from challenge, and the much greater tolerance for public debate that we have today means that in practice, a prosecution for sedition is extremely unlikely. In theory, however, words that do any of the following could be considered seditious:

- promote hatred or contempt of the sovereign or her family, the Government or constitution of the UK, one or both Houses of Parliament, or the administration of justice in the UK;
- incite British subjects to use unlawful means to change any matter relating to the Church or the state;

- promote discontent or dissatisfaction among British subjects;
- Stir up ill-will between members of different social classes.

However, merely publishing such words is not, by itself, sedition, however forceful the criticism; it is also necessary to prove that the publisher of the words intended to disturb legal authority.

In *R* v *Aldred* (1909), a man was prosecuted for seditious libel after publishing statements, addressed to Indian students, which argued that as part of the fight for Indian independence, assassinating political figures should not be considered murder.

In 1990, a group of Muslims tried to bring a prosecution against the author Salman Rushdie, arguing that his book *The Satanic Verses* had created discontent among British subjects, by causing hostility between Muslims and non-Muslims. The courts decided that even if the book had caused such hostility, this did not amount to the offence of sedition, which required that the words complained of incited violence against the state and democratic institutions.

Defences

Printers and distributors of seditious material have a defence if they can prove that they were unaware, and had no reason to suspect, that the contents were seditious. There is also a defence of privilege, which applies to newspaper reports of parliamentary and judicial proceedings, provided they are fair and accurate.

Punishment for sedition

The possible range of punishments for publishing seditious material include life imprisonment but, in practice, any sentence of imprisonment is extremely unlikely.

Sedition today

The last prosecution for sedition took place over 50 years ago, and though the offence still remains part of English law, most lawyers believe it is very unlikely that such a prosecution would be brought today, given that our society now expects a much more free and open debate about political issues.

OBSCENE LIBEL

The offence of obscene libel, sometimes known just as obscenity, is defined in the Obscene Publications Act 1959 as being committed by publishing 'matter' (which could include pictures as well as words), the effect of which 'tends to deprave and corrupt those who are likely, having regard to all the relevant circumstances, to read, see or hear' it. It can also be committed by possessing obscene material for commercial publication.

The effect of such 'matter' has to be judged by the standards of today, and to be considered obscene it would have to go beyond being tasteless or explicit, and actually have a potentially harmful effect on those who see it.

◾ Defences

The Obscene Publications Act 1959 introduced a defence which applies where the publication of obscene material is 'for the public good . . . in the interests of science, literature, art or learning, or of other objects of public concern'. This defence was successfully used by the original publishers of the novel *Lady Chatterley's Lover* when they were prosecuted for obscenity.

◾ Penalties

Publishers may be fined and/or imprisoned, but in practice prison sentences are only likely to be applied to those who are commercially exploiting harmful pornography.

CHAPTER SUMMARY

Criminal libel

- Committed by publishing, in writing, a statement that is likely to create a breach of the peace, or have an extremely serious effect on the subject's reputation.
- Truth is not a defence.

Prosecutions of editors and proprietors (and probably journalists) require permission from a High Court judge; prosecution for this offence is now extremely unlikely, and could be challenged under the Human Rights Act 1998.

Seditious libel

- Committed by publishing words likely to disturb the peace and government of the country, with the intention of disturbing legal authority.
- The last prosecution took place over 50 years ago, and it is unlikely to be prosecuted today.

Obscene libel

- Committed by publishing matter which 'tends to deprave and corrupt' those who are likely to read it.
- It must have a potentially harmful effect rather than being merely distasteful or explicit.

In practice it is only likely to apply to the commercial production of harmful pornography.

TEST YOUR KNOWLEDGE

1. Describe the two ways in which criminal libel can be committed.

2. What are the main differences between libel and criminal libel?

3. What is seditious libel?

4. Define obscene libel.

For further resources and updates please go to the Companion Website for this book at www.pearsoned.co.uk/practicaljournalism

Section

7

BROADCASTING AND PHOTOGRAPHY

The two chapters in this section deal with specific provisions which apply to two branches of the media: TV and radio journalists, and photographers. Chapter 29 covers the Broadcasting Code issued by Ofcom, which regulates the broadcast media on general principles such as privacy and accuracy, and on reporting of specific types of story, such as those on elections or involving children.

Chapter 30 examines the law as it applies to photographers, covering restrictions on when and where photographs can legally be taken.

Television and radio journalism

Broadly speaking, TV and radio journalists are covered by the same legal rules as print journalists, and everything you have read in the preceding chapters will apply if you work, or hope to work, in broadcasting. However, television and radio journalism are also covered by a set of restrictions which do not apply to print journalists, namely the Broadcasting Code issued by Ofcom, the body which regulates broadcasting in the UK. Although the Code is not law, it is not, like the other journalistic codes, a purely voluntary scheme. Broadcasters in the UK have to have a licence, issued by the Government, and a broadcaster who seriously breaches the Ofcom Code could potentially have their licence revoked, making it unable to continue broadcasting. In practice this has not happened, but Ofcom also has a range of other sanctions for breaches of the Code, such as fines, which are regularly used (see below). The full Code can be found on the Ofcom website (see *Online resources* at the end of the chapter) but in this chapter, you will find the main provisions that are applicable to journalists.

In addition to the Ofcom Code, BBC journalists are covered by the BBC's own Editorial Guidelines, overseen by the BBC Board of Governors (see *Online resources* at the end of the chapter).

THE OFCOM BROADCASTING CODE

The Code was published on 25 May 2005, and came into force on 25 July 2005. It replaces six previous codes issued by the organisations which regulated broadcasting before Ofcom was created: the Broadcasting Standards Commission, the Independent Television Commission, and the Radio Authority. Programmes broadcast before 25 July 2005 are covered by the relevant previous codes, but where a programme was originally shown before that date, and is repeated after it, the new Code applies to the repeat(s), as well as to all new programmes shown after that date.

The Code covers all UK broadcasters, but the BBC is only covered by six of the sections (the subject matter of the other sections are covered by its own guidelines, with complaints dealt with by the BBC governors' complaints committee). The Code works retrospectively, in that broadcasters can only be disciplined once they have broadcast a programme which breaches the Code. There is no provision for Ofcom to see programmes in advance and prevent those which breach the Code from being broadcast, nor to get offending sections removed before first broadcast.

Issues covered by the Code include:

■ protecting the under-18s;

■ harm and offence;

- crime;

- religion;

- impartiality and accuracy;

- elections and referendums;

- fairness;

- privacy;

- sponsorship;

- commercial references.

Not all the provisions in the Code will have direct relevance to the daily work of journalists; the following sections discuss only those that do.

Protecting the under-18s

This section covers both the effect of broadcasting content on the under-18s, and the treatment of under-18s by broadcasters. Key provisions include the following:

- The under-18s must be protected from content which could seriously impair their physical, moral or emotional development, and the under-15s from content which is unsuitable for them. In this context, TV companies must respect the 9pm 'watershed', and radio broadcasters must take particular care over what is broadcast at times when children are likely to be listening, such as at breakfast time. Clear information should be given about content likely to distress children if broadcast on radio at these times, or before the watershed on TV.

- When reporting sexual offences involving under-18s (whether as defendants, victims or witnesses, in the criminal, civil or family courts), broadcasters should take care not to breach inadvertently any statutory rules preventing identification, for example by broadcasting details which could lead to identification when pieced together with material from elsewhere.

- When covering any pre-trial investigation into an alleged criminal offence, broadcasters should pay particular regard to the vulnerable position of any victim, witness or defendant who is not yet adult, before publishing their name, address, school, college, place of work, or any picture of them.

- Violence, dangerous behaviour, offensive language and sexual content should not be shown before the watershed or when children are likely to be listening, unless justified by the context.

Harm and offence

This section is a mixed bag of provisions, ranging from rules about the use of flashing lights which could trigger epilepsy attacks, to preventing audiences from being put into a trance by a TV hypnotist. The most relevant to journalists include the following:

- TV programmes must meet 'generally accepted standards' of protection for the public against harmful and offensive material. If offensive material is used, it must be justified by its context.

- Factual programmes or items should not 'materially mislead' viewers or listeners.

- Methods of suicide or self-harm should not be included unless justified editorially and by their context.
- If simulated news is broadcast (e.g. in a documentary), broadcasters must make sure the audience is not misled into thinking they are watching actual news.

■ Crime

This section deals with material which could encourage crime or lead to disorder. The following should be noted:

- Descriptions or demonstrations which could show how to commit crime should not be used unless editorially justified.
- Convicted or self-confessed criminals must not be paid or promised payment of any kind for interviews or other programme contributions concerning their criminal activities, except where the payment would be in the public interest.
- No payment should be made to anyone who is or is likely to be a witness in criminal proceedings, while those proceedings are active, nor should any payment be suggested or made dependent on the result of a trial. Loss of earnings and expenses can however be reimbursed.
- Where future criminal proceedings are foreseeable, no payment should be made to anyone who might reasonably be expected to be a witness, unless there is a clear public interest in that person giving information (such as for the purposes of investigating crime), and the information could not be obtained without the payment.
- Broadcasters must 'use their best endeavours' to ensure they do not broadcast anything which could endanger lives, or compromise attempts to deal with a kidnapping or a hostage situation.

■ Religion

This section covers 'religious programmes', but as this is defined as 'a programme which deals with matters of religion as the central subject, or a significant part, of the programme', it would appear that it could equally well apply to, for example, a documentary about the Catholic church or Islam, as to 'Songs of Praise' or the 'Morning Service'. The main provision applicable in a documentary context would be that the views of people who belong to a particular religion or religious denomination must not be subject to 'abusive treatment'.

■ Impartiality and accuracy

This is an important section for journalists, as it specifically covers news. It does not apply to the BBC, as these matters are regulated by the BBC governors. The section provides that:

- News 'in whatever form', must be reported with 'due accuracy' and presented with 'due impartiality'. Impartiality is defined as not favouring one side or the other, but the Code makes it clear that 'due impartiality' means a level of impartiality that is appropriate to the programme in question, and the subject. It does not require that each side is given exactly equal airtime, or that every argument has to be represented.
- Significant errors should be corrected promptly, on air, and at an appropriate time (i.e. so that people who saw or heard the mistake are also likely to see or hear the correction).

29

Television and radio journalism

- No news programme should use a politician as an interviewer, newsreader or reporter, unless editorially justified. In that case, the politician's political allegiance must be stated.

Special rules apply to coverage of 'matters of politicial or industrial controversy, and matters relating to current public policy'. Matters of political or industrial controversy are defined as political or industrial matters on which politicians, industry and/or the media are 'in debate'. Matters relating to current public policy are policies under discussion, or already adopted by local, regional or national Government, or bodies which make policy on their behalf, such as quangos. Where coverage relates to any of these issues:

- Programmes must not include expressions of the broadcaster's own opinion (unless they are speaking in a court of law or a legislative forum). The exception to this rule is where the matter under discussion concerns the provision of programme services.

- Due impartiality must be observed. However, this need not be done in a single programme, but can be achieved by the combined effect of a series of programmes. 'Series' in this context includes not just the usual meaning of the word in broadcasting terms, but also, for example, a cluster or season of programmes on the same subject, or two programmes, such as a drama and a documentary, covering the same issue. To gain this protection, however, it should be made clear on air that the programmes are linked.

- Views and facts must not be misrepresented, and should be presented 'with due weight over appropriate timeframes'.

- If a presenter or reporter has a personal interest which could call into question the due impartiality of the programme, this should be made clear to viewers.

- Presenters and reporters (other than those on news programmes), and chairs of discussion programmes can put forward their own points of view, but these must be balanced with adequate representation of other views, either in the same programme or in the series as a whole.

- Presenters who appear regularly must not use this advantage in such a way as to compromise the requirement for due impartiality.

- Phone-in presenters must encourage alternative views.

- 'Personal view' programmes must be indicated as such from the outset. The Code defines such programmes as those which 'present a particular view or perspective', ranging from the highly partial views of campaigners on a particular issue, to the opinion of a journalist, author or academic with experience or knowledge of a particular subject. The requirement that the nature of such programmes should be made clear is described as a minimum standard, and in some cases it may be necessary to do more than that to ensure a programme does not breach the impartiality requirements (the Code does not suggest what these extra measures might be).

- On local radio, local digital sound services and radio licensable content services, a further rule prohibits programmes from giving 'undue prominence' to the views of particular persons or bodies on these subjects. 'Undue prominence' is defined as 'a significant imbalance of views' in a station's coverage of an issue as a whole over a relevant period of time.

Two extra rules apply where coverage concerns matters of political or industrial controversy, or matters relating to current policy, which are of national or international significance, or which carry a similar weight of importance within a smaller broadcast area. Where programmes concern these kinds of issues:

- 'An appropriately wide range' of views must be presented, and given due weight, either in a single programme or across a range of clearly linked programmes.
- Views and facts must not be misrepresented.

Elections and referenda

This section, which does not apply to the BBC, covers broadcasts during an 'election period' or 'referendum period'. The Code defines the start of these periods as follows:

- for a general election or Scottish Parliament election, when Parliament or the Scottish Parliament is dissolved;
- for parliamentary by-elections, when the writ is issued, or on any earlier date published in the *London Gazette*;
- for by-elections to the Scottish Parliament, when the vacancy occurs;
- for the Welsh National Assembly, the Northern Ireland Assembly, the London Assembly and local government elections, on the last date for publication of notices of the election;
- for referenda held under the Northern Ireland Act 1998, when the draft of an Order is laid before Parliament;
- for other referenda, at the time stated in the Act which authorises the referendum.

In all cases, the period ends when the polls close.

During an election or referendum period, these rules apply:

- During a referendum period, coverage must give due weight to 'designated organisations'. These are organisations which the Electoral Commission designates as the lead campaigners for one of the possible outcomes. Broadcasters must also consider giving appropriate coverage to other 'permitted participants'; these are organisations that have registered with the Electoral Commission, which allows them to spend more than £10,000 on their campaign, but obliges them to comply with the Commission's regulations.
- Candidates in UK elections, or representatives of 'permitted participants' in a referendum must not act as newsreaders, presenters or interviewers in any type of programme.
- Appearances of candidates in UK elections, or representatives of 'permitted participants', on non-political programmes can go ahead if they were planned before the election period, but new appearances should not be arranged after the period starts.
- Reports or discussions about a particular constituency or electoral area must observe due impartiality, and candidates representing parties with significant previous electoral support or evidence of significant current support must be invited to take part, as must independents with significant support. If one candidate agrees to take part, the candidates from other major parties in that area should then be invited to do so as well. (In either circumstance, if one or more candidates refuse or cannot take part, the item/programme can still go ahead.)
- Any report or discussion of a constituency or electoral area must include a list of all the candidates, giving their first and last names, and the party they represent (or stating that they are independent). For larger regional elections (e.g. to the Scottish Parliament, European Parliament or London Assembly), the list need not mention every candidate in a region by name, just the parties and the names of any independent candidates. If a radio item is broadcast more than once on the same day, the list need not be repeated, but listeners/viewers should be told where they can find out this information (e.g. on a website).

- If a candidate takes part in a programme on any subject, they should not be allowed to make points about the constituency or electoral area, unless other candidates will be given a similar opportunity.

- All discussion and analysis of issues related to the election or referendum must end when the polling stations open.

- The results of opinion polls must not be broadcast on polling day, until the polls close.

▨ Fairness

This section deals with the way in which broadcasting companies treat the people who are directly affected by programmes, such as those mentioned, shown or interviewed. The overall rule of the section is that broadcasters must avoid unjust or unfair treatment of individuals in programmes, and it sets out practices with should be followed in this respect. Failing to follow any of these practices will only be a breach of the Code if it results in unfairness to an individual or organisation. However, the Code points out that it cannot prescribe a set of practices that, if followed, would absolutely prevent all unfairness, and so a company may be in breach of the rule on fairness even if it has followed all the specified breaches, if it is nevertheless unfair or injust in some other way.

The practices to be followed are:

- Broadcasters and programme makers should be fair in their dealings with potential contributors to programmes, though there may be exceptional cases where they are justified in not being fair.

- When someone is invited to take part in a programme (unless the subject is trivial and/or their role very minor), they should be informed, at an appropriate stage, about:
  - the nature, subject and purpose of the programme;
  - why they have been asked to contribute;
  - when and where the programme will be broadcast;
  - what kind of contribution they are expected to make (e.g. whether an interview or discussion, live or recorded);
  - the areas of questioning, if appropriate, and the nature of other contributions;
  - any significant changes to the programme during the process of making it, which might affect their decision to participate, and/or cause material unfairness;
  - the nature of their contractual rights, and those of the programme maker/broadcaster;
  - whether they will be able to have changes made to the programme if they are to be shown a preview.

  If, having been given all this information, a person or organisation consents to take part in a programme, their consent is known as informed consent (see *Privacy* below). It may however be fair to withhold some or all of this information when it is justified in the public interest, or because of other provisions in this section.

- If a contributor is under 16, permission should be obtained from a parent, guardian or other person over 18 who is *in loco parentis*. Contributors who are under 16 should not be asked for their views on matters which it is not within their capacity to answer properly without this consent.

- If a person over 16 is not in a position to give consent, it should be sought from someone aged 18 or over who has primary responsibility for their care. Contributors in this position should not be asked for their views on matters which it is not within their capacity to answer properly without this consent.

■ If a programme is edited, contributions should be represented fairly.

■ If contributors are given any kind of guarantee (e.g. of anonymity or confidentiality, or relating to the content of a programme), these promises should normally be honoured.

■ If material produced for one programme is later reused in another (whether by the same company or a different one), the broadcaster should make sure this reuse does not create unfairness.

■ Before broadcasting a factual programme, broadcasters should ensure that material facts have not been presented, disregarded or left out in such a way as to be unfair to an individual or organisation, and if someone has been left out in circumstances which could cause unfairness, they should be offered a chance to contribute.

■ No programme should present facts, events, people or organisations in a way that is unfair to any individual or organisation.

■ If a programme makes allegations of wrongdoing or incompetence, or any other serious allegations, the subject of the allegations should normally be given an 'appropriate and timely' chance to respond.

■ If someone is asked to contribute to a programme, but chooses not to appear or give a comment, the programme should state this, and give their explanation (if any), if it would be unfair not to do so.

■ Where a person or organisation chooses not to take part in a programme, and it is appropriate for the programme to include that person or organisation's view, this must be done fairly.

The section also contains a set of rules on 'Deception, set-ups and wind-up calls', which states that broadcasters and programme makers should not normally obtain information, sound, film or consent to contribute to a programme through deception, which includes surreptitious filming or recording. However, there are three situations where the Code says it may be legitimate to use material obtained through deception or misrepresentation, without the subject's consent:

■ where it is in the public interest to do so, and the material could not be obtained in any other way;

■ where the subject is not clearly identifiable;

■ where the subject is a person in the public eye. However, in this case, unless there is also a public interest justification, this material should not be used where it would result in unjustified public ridicule or personal distress.

■ Privacy

This section works in a similar way to the previous one, with a basic rule and a set of practices to be followed. Failing to follow one or more of the practices will only be a breach of the Code where it results in an unwarranted invasion of privacy, but as with the previous section, following the practices is not a guarantee that a broadcaster will not be found in breach, if it has in some other way committed an unwarranted invasion of privacy. The Code recognises that in some situations – particularly emergencies – there may be difficult decisions to be made on the spot about whether privacy is being infringed. It also acknowledges that there is a clear

29

Television and radio journalism

public interest in such situations being reported, and promises that Ofcom will take both factors into account when judging complaints about privacy.

The basic rule stated in this section is that any infringement of privacy, whether it is a result of the process of making a programme, or of the content of a programme, must be 'warranted'. The Code explains that in order for an invasion of privacy to be warranted, the programme maker must be able to justify it, in the particular circumstances of the case. If the justification offered is in the public interest, the broadcaster must be able to show that this outweighs the right to privacy. Examples of the public interest, the Code says, would be where the invasion of privacy is justified in the cause of revealing or detecting crime, protecting public health or safety, exposing misleading claims or revealing incompetence that affects the public.

The practices to be followed are:

■ The location of a person's home or family should not be revealed without their consent, unless warranted.

■ Broadcasters should recognise that people who are caught up in newsworthy events still have a right to privacy, unless it is warranted to infringe it. This applies both when reporting current events, and for later programmes looking at those events.

■ Broadcasters should ensure that words, pictures or actions filmed or recorded in public places are not so private that their inclusion in a programme should require consent from the people featured, unless broadcast without consent is warranted.

■ Any material which infringes privacy should only be used with the person's informed consent, or where it is warranted, as defined above (callers to phone-in shows are considered to have given consent by the act of phoning in).

■ If a person or organisation's privacy is being infringed, and they ask for filming or recording to stop, the programme maker should normally comply with their request, unless continuing is warranted.

■ When filming or recording takes place inside the premises of an organisation, institution or other agency, permission should be obtained from the relevant authority, unless it is warranted to go ahead without permission. It is not normally necessary to get consent from employees or members of the public whose appearance is incidental.

■ Material obtained by surruptitious filming or recording should not be used unless it is warranted. This includes material obtained by using long lenses or recording devices; by leaving a camera or recorder unattended on private property, without the informed consent of the owner of the property; by taping a phone conversation without telling the other person; or by deliberately continuing to record when the subject believes you have stopped.

■ Broadcasters should not film, record, or use footage or tape of, people involved in an emergency, accident victims, or anyone suffering a personal tragedy, where to do so would be an infringement of privacy, unless it is warranted or the people concerned have given informed consent. This applies whether the events are in a public place or not.

■ People who are distressed should not be pressurised to give interviews or otherwise take part in a programme, unless this is warranted.

■ Broadcasters should take care not to broadcast the names of anyone who has died, or been involved in an accident or violent crime, unless they are sure that the next of kin have already been told or unless it is warranted.

■ When covering past events that have caused trauma to individuals (including crime), broadcasters should try to reduce the potential distress to victims and/or relatives, unless not doing so is warranted. As far as possible, surviving victims and/or close relatives of victims should be told when such programmes are made and broadcast.

- Broadcasters should take special care not to infringe the privacy of people under 16, and should recognise that the fact that they do not lose their right to privacy because their parents may be famous, or because newsworthy events have happened at their school.

- Where a programme features someone under 16 in such a way that their privacy is infringed, consent should be obtained from the person themselves, if possible, and also from their parent, guardian, or someone over 18 who is *in loco parentis*, unless the subject is trivial, the person's participation is minor, or the invasion of privacy is warranted.

- People under 16 should not be questioned about personal matters without the consent of their parent, guardian, or someone over 18 who is *in loco parentis*, unless it is warranted to do so without consent.

- People who are over 18, but vulnerable in some way, should not be questioned about personal matters without the consent of someone over 18 who has primary responsibility for their care, unless it is warranted to do so without consent. As examples of vulnerable adults, the Code cites the bereaved, people with learning difficulties, people with mental problems or dementia, and people who are traumatised, sick or terminally ill.

Sponsorship

The main relevant provision here is that news programmes may not be sponsored. The Code includes within this category news bulletins and news desk presentations on radio, and news and current affairs programmes on television. Current affairs programmes are defined as those carrying explanation and analysis of current events and issues.

Commercial references

This section provides that broadcasters must maintain editorial control over their programmes and ensure that advertising and programme content are kept separate. The main provisions which could potentially affect journalists are:

- Undue prominence should not be given to a product or service in any programme. 'Undue prominence' is defined as the presence of a product in a programme where there is no editorial justification for it, or the manner in which it is referred to.

- Advertising must not appear within programmes, unless editorially justified.

- Wherever possible, the broadcast of charity appeals, over a period of time, should benefit a broad range of charities.

COMPLAINTS UNDER THE CODE

Complaints about privacy or fairness can only be brought by 'persons affected', or someone who they authorise to make a complaint. 'Persons affected' are defined as:

- a person who took part in the programme and may have been the subject of the alleged unfairness;

- a person who has a 'sufficiently direct interest' in the subject matter of the alleged unfairness;

- a person whose privacy may have been invaded, either by the content of a programme or the process of making it.

29

Television and radio journalism

'Person' in this sense can include a company or other organisation. In exceptional cases, a relative or someone else who is closely connected can bring a complaint without the affected person's authorisation (e.g. if the person is a child).

Other complaints can be brought by anyone, and investigations can also be instigated by Ofcom itself. While it does not have to investigate every complaint, Ofcom is obliged to look into complaints where the complainant raises evidence that there is a case to answer. During investigations, broadcasters are given the chance to respond to the allegations made.

Sanctions for breach

If a breach is found, Ofcom can:

- issue a Direction forbidding repeat broadcast of a programme;
- issue a Direction to broadcast a correction, or a statement of Ofcom's finding in the case;
- impose a fine;
- shorten a company's licence to broadcast;
- revoke a licence;
- find that the matter is resolved and no further action need be taken.

The last is usually only done where the breach was hard to avoid or accidental, and the company has put in place prodecures to make sure nothing similar happens again (as in the *Radio Sheffield* case, below).

The Code in practice

Although the Code is relatively new, there have already been many complaints brought under it, which shed light on how it works in practice. In addition, during the first two years of its existence, Ofcom oversaw enforcement of the Codes used by the previous regulators (the Broadcasting Standards Commission, the Independent Television Commission and the Radio Authority), and as those codes contained many broadly similar provisions to those of the current Code, Ofcom's decisions on them are also a useful guide to how it operates.

The following illustrate Ofcom's treatment of some of the key points in the Code, but broadcast journalists may find it useful to spend some time on the Ofcom website (see *Online resources* at the end of the chapter), where all the regulator's decisions are reported fully. In addition to full details of the complaints and verdicts, these reports often include useful points of guidance on the interpretation of the Code.

 In 2006, satellite channel ATN Bangla was the subject of a complaint about footage of a minibus crash in Bangladesh, which included shots of dead bodies and an interview with a distressed child, who was filmed identifying her parents' bodies. Ofcom found that the footage of dead bodies, while disturbing, was 'not overly graphic in the context of a valid news report about such an horrific accident'. The shots were either at medium distance or, where they were closer, were partly obscured by electronic blurring techniques, which Ofcom said lessened the impact, with the result that there was no breach of the Code. Ofcom was not able to judge the footage concerning the child as ATN Bangla could not supply a copy; this failure was itself a breach of the Code, which provides that broadcasters must keep copies for specified lengths of time (these vary depending on the type of broadcaster, and are detailed on the Ofcom website).

Also in 2006, Ofcom examined a complaint against BBC Radio Sheffield, after a caller to a phone-in on football used highly offensive language about a particular player. The radio station agreed that the language was unacceptable, but said that the caller had not shown any sign that he might be abusive when talking to the production team before being put on air, that the team regularly warned callers to avoid strong language, and that the presenter had closed down the call quickly, apologised to listeners and made it clear that the station found the caller's words unacceptable. Ofcom agreed that it was very difficult for the station to have anticipated the incident, and acknowledged that it had taken further steps to prevent a repeat. It held that the matter was resolved.

In 2005, the satellite channel Bloomberg TV was found to have breached the Code provisions on impartiality. During the 2005 General Election, it broadcast live coverage of the launch of the Labour Party's 'Business Manifesto', followed by in-depth interviews with Tony Blair and two other members of the party. No other political party was featured. Bloomberg argued that the interviews had not been uncritical, and that other parties had been invited to take part, but declined. Ofcom, however, found that no other political party had been featured in this depth at any point in the campaign, and held that Bloomberg was in breach of the Code. Bloomberg was ordered to broadcast the Ofcom finding three times.

In 2005, a 'Dispatches' programme was the subject of a complaint about fairness from a company featured in it. The programme concerned parking charges, and contained allegations about incompetence and unfairness in the way these charges were imposed. One of the companies criticised in the programme, Capita, complained that, although it had provided a statement in response, it was not given an adequate chance to prepare this, because it was only made aware of the allegations two weeks before broadcast, and was not allowed to preview the programme. Ofcom rejected this part of the complaint, as Channel 4 had provided full information about the programme and the allegations made, and was not obliged to allow previewing of the film; given the nature of the allegations, two weeks was enough time to respond. Capita also complained that the response it supplied was not included, and that no explanation was given for this. It appeared that this was because Channel 4 had refused to broadcast the full statement, and therefore Capita had withdrawn it rather than have part of it broadcast. Ofcom found that even so, Channel 4 remained aware of Capita's position on the allegations, and should have represented it fairly. In addition, failing to supply any explanation for the lack of a statement could have given a negative impression of Capita, given that statements from the two other companies mentioned were included. Therefore, in these two respects, Channel 4 had been unfair and was in breach of the Code.

In 2005, Ofcom upheld a complaint from drugs company Novartis, about a Channel 4 programme concerning their leukaemia drug, Glivec. The company had been contacted several months before the broadcast and told that it would be given the opportunity to comment, but it was then only given the chance to answer detailed questions a month before the programme was shown. Ofcom found that it had been treated unfairly. The discrepancy between the time considered fair for a response here, and in the Capita case, illustrates that there is no set time limit; it will depend on the nature of the allegations.

In 2004, a Mrs Josephine Merrick, a descendent of the 'Elephant Man' Joseph Merrick, complained that her privacy had been invaded by a programme which showed her name, and her husband's and daughter's on a family tree diagram. The programme was examining the possible cause of Joseph Merrick's deformities and, in particular, whether there was any genetic basis for them. Ofcom found that there had been no invasion of privacy, because the family tree was shown so briefly that it was unlikely that she could be identified from it. In addition, there was a clear public interest in showing that descendants had nothing to fear from their genetic inheritance.

29

Television and radio journalism

CHAPTER SUMMARY

The Ofcom Broadcasting Code

The Code covers all UK broadcasters, but only certain sections apply to the BBC.

Breaches of the Code can only lead to sanctions after broadcast; it is not used to ban or censor programmes in advance.

Protecting the under-18s

Restrictions apply to:

- broadcasts containing sex, violence, offensive language and other content which could be damaging or unsuitable;
- reporting crime involving the under-18s, especially sexual offences.

Harm and offence

Under the Code, broadcasters:

- must not 'materially mislead';
- must meet 'generally accepted standards';
- should not include details of self-harm or suicide unless justified;
- should not use simulated newscasts in a misleading way.

Crime

Restrictions apply to:

- payment to criminals and witnesses;
- descriptions of how to commit crime;
- material which could endanger lives, especially in hostage or kidnap situations.

Religion

Programmes dealing with religion must not subject religious views to 'abusive treatment'.

Impartiality and accuracy

News must be reported with 'due accuracy' and 'due impartiality'.

Elections and referendums

Regulations apply to ensure that no one party is favoured by a broadcaster's coverage during elections and referendums.

Fairness

People interviewed, shown or mentioned in programmes should usually be:
- given full information about the programme;
- fairly represented;
- given a fair chance to respond to detrimental allegations.

Privacy

Invasions of privacy must be warranted, and special rules apply to:

- home and family details;
- people in newsworthy events;
- surruptitious filming and recording;
- people affected by past traumatic events;
- children and vulnerable people.

Sponsorship

News and current affairs programmes may not be sponsored.

Commercial references

- Products and services must not be given undue prominence.
- Advertising should not be shown in programmes.
- Charity appeals should benefit a range of organisations.

Complaints under the Code

Complaints about privacy and fairness must be brought by someone affected or their representative; others can be brought by anyone or instigated by Ofcom.

Sanctions for breach include:

- fines;
- prevention of repeat broadcast;
- broadcasting corrections;
- cutting short or revoking a licence.

TEST YOUR KNOWLEDGE

1 What powers does Ofcom have to censor programmes before transmission?

2 You are covering a story about identity theft, and you have an interview with a former fraudster, who explains exactly how she goes about getting the information needed to set up a bank loan in someone else's name. Would using the interview breach the Ofcom code?

3 You work for a local radio station, and report a dispute between two local organisations. One of them rings up complaining that you only used two short quotes from him, whereas his opponent was heard for approximately twice as long. Does he have a case under the Ofcom Code?

4 How does the Code define 'matters of political and industrial controversy'?

29

Television and radio journalism

5 You work for a local TV station, and are reporting on the possible closure of a local school. The local council says it has to be closed because of falling numbers, but parents are opposing the plan. Your child attends the school. Can you report the story without breaching the Code?

6 When does the 'election period' for a local government election begin? When does it end?

7 What information does the Code require contributors to a radio or TV programme to be given?

8 In what situations does the Code allow film or sound obtained by deception to be broadcast?

ONLINE RESOURCES

www The Ofcom Code is published in full, along with reports of adjudicated cases, at: www.ofcom.org.uk

The BBC Editorial Guidelines can be read at www.bbc.co.uk/guidelines/editorialguidelines/advice/

For further resources and updates please go to the Companion Website for this book at www.pearsoned.co.uk/practicaljournalism

Chapter

30

Photography

Much of the law already explained in this book applies to photographers as well as those who write the words that go with their pictures. However, there are some restrictions which apply specifically to photographers and photojournalists, and they are the subject of this chapter. Photographers should also make sure they are familiar with the law on harassment (Chapter 18); defamation (Chapter 14); and the Data Protection Act (Chapter 20).

PRIVATE PROPERTY

As we saw in Chapter 18, being on someone else's land without their permission, or refusing to leave when asked to, is trespass. Trespass is also committed by any 'interference' with land, which could include, for example, climbing onto a fence to get a view into someone's garden, even if no damage is done. There is no law against standing outside a private place and taking photographs, unless the pictures taken stray into the area of confidentiality (see below).

If you are on someone's land (which includes being in their house, shop or office) with their permission, there is no general law against taking photographs, but the person in control of the land (usually the owner or tenant) can impose conditions on what you will be allowed to do there. This means that they have the right to ban the taking of photographs, and if you ignore this and take them, you then commit trespass, because you are acting outside your permission to be on the land.

This rule applies even in private places which are open to the general public (such as stately homes or shops). Even if there is no general ban on taking photographs on the property which applies to everyone, the land owner or tenant can require an individual photographer to stop taking pictures, and/or order them to leave. They can also use reasonable force if a trespasser refuses to leave; however this would not permit, for example, physically attacking a photographer. In some cases, a landowner or tenant (or more often, employees such as security guards) may demand that film is handed over, but they have no legal right which backs up such a demand. Neither film nor cameras can be legally confiscated, or damaged, even if the photographer is trespassing.

Chapter 18 explains the remedies which can be ordered against a person who is liable for trespass. It is theoretically possible that a court could issue an injunction preventing publication of photographs obtained by trespassing, but in practice this is unlikely.

Photographs taken in a private place may however be caught by the law of confidentiality. As explained in Chapter 17, the law on this issue is currently in a slightly uncertain state, but in cases such as *Campbell* v *MGN* (2004) (see p. 239), it was stated that the question to be asked was whether the person photographed had 'a reasonable expectation of privacy'. The same would apply if the person taking the photograph was outside the private place, but the subject of the photograph was in the private place.

PUBLIC PLACES

Many apparently public places ban photography unless prior permission is obtained: this includes, for example, hospitals, most museums and galleries, stations and airports. Some public places run a paid permit system for commercial photographers: in London, for example, this includes Trafalgar Square and Parliament Square, the Royal Parks and anywhere on London Underground property. In these cases, photography may be allowed if you apply for permission and pay a fee, which is not very much use if you are covering news and need to take pictures on the spur of the moment.

The Official Secrets Act bans photography in a 'prohibited place', which includes:

- defence establishments;
- all factories, dockyards, ships and aircraft which belong to the Crown;
- any place where munitions are stored;
- any place which belongs to the Civil Aviation Authority;
- any telecommunications office owned by a public telecommunications operator;
- any place belonging to the Crown, or any railway, road, waterway, or gas, electricity or water works, which has been designated a 'prohibited place' by order of the Secretary of State.

The ban only applies to photographs which could be 'useful to an enemy' and are 'taken for a purpose prejudicial to the interests of the state', but photographers who are found in sensitive areas may find themselves quite closely questioned about what they are doing and why.

Section 58 of the Terrorism Act 2000 makes it an offence to take or possess a 'record of information' likely to be useful to a person committing or preparing an act of terrorism; a photograph can count as such as record. As we saw in Chapter 19, the Terrorism Act gives police wide powers to stop and search anyone who they reasonably suspect of an offence under the Act.

It is still unclear how far taking pictures of someone in a public place can be seen as a breach of confidence, or more accurately, the version of confidentiality which is described in Chapter 17 as 'misuse of private information'. In *Campbell* v *MGN* (2004) (see p. 239), the House of Lords said that a picture taken in a public place might be a misuse of private information where it showed a person in a particularly humiliating position, and the *Princess Caroline* case (see p. 240) states that public figures such as celebrities have a right not to be photographed when going about their private business. The 2006 case involving Elton John (see p. 241), however, suggests this does not prevent photography of activities that are not of a personal nature, as long as there is no harassment of the subject.

The PCC Code of Practice

In addition to the legal restrictions detailed above, the PCC Code has a number of things to say about photography:

- Photographs of individuals on private property should not be taken without permission.
- The use of long lens cameras to take pictures of people on private property is unacceptable.

- Children should not be photographed in relation to issues involving their welfare (or that of another child) without permission from a parent or 'similarly responsible adult'.

- Children should not be photographed at school without permission from the school authorities.

- The press should not obtain or publish material that is the result of using hidden cameras.

Courts

The Contempt of Court Act 1981 makes it a criminal offence to take any photograph within the 'precinct' of a court, and a further offence to publish such a picture, both offences punishable with a fine of up to £1,000. However, the Act does not define where the precincts of the court begin and end, and although taking pictures within a court building is clearly off limits, different courts apply different rules to, for example, pictures taken of people coming out of the door of a court, but still on court land. It is best to check with the individual court as to its policy before taking pictures outside the building. It is, however, permissible to take pictures of people leaving court, once both you and they are outside in the street.

As explained in the chapter on contempt of court, some tribunals are considered courts for the purposes of the Act, in which case photographs may not be taken within their 'precincts'. Again, it is sensible to check with the tribunal itself before taking pictures.

Even when it is legal to take a picture in connection with a court case, there may be restrictions on publishing it. This issue is dealt with in more detail in the chapters on reporting the courts, but the main restrictions are:

- Photographs of the victim of a sexual offence may not be published during that person's lifetime, if to do so would be likely to lead the public to identify the person as the victim of a sexual offence (see p. 121).

- People under 16 who are involved in youth court proceedings may not be identified, unless the court gives permission by lifting the statutory restrictions (see p. 129). This applies to victims and witnesses as well as defendants.

- In some cases, the courts may make discretionary orders preventing identification of certain witnesses or victims in a case. Publishing a photograph of that person will usually breach this order (see p. 125).

- No photograph of a defendant in a criminal case should be published if to do so would create a risk of serious prejudice to the court proceedings (see p. 73).

Obstruction and public order

Section 137 of the Highways Act 1980 states that an offence is committed when anyone 'without lawful authority or excuse, in any way wilfully obstructs the free passage along a highway'. For the purposes of the Act, 'highway' includes pavements as well as roads, so there is clearly potential in many situations for photographers to commit this offence.

The offence is potentially quite a wide one, and it can be difficult to pin down exactly what will amount to obstruction; simply standing on the pavement to take a photograph would usually not be, whereas a crowd of photographers blocking the road outside someone's house probably would be, but there are clearly many situations in between these two extremes.

Usually, if the police believe the highway is being obstructed, they will simply ask photographers to move on. However, a photographer who refuses to go, or continues to cause an obstruction, can be arrested.

Photographers may also run the risk of being arrested for obstructing the police in the execution of their duty, under s51 of the Police Act 1964. This is another very wide offence, and can be committed by doing anything which prevents the police from doing their job.

 In 2006, a Nottingham photographer was charged with obstructing the police after a police officer asked him to stop taking pictures of armed police officers in a public place, and he politely refused.

A situation which has caused particular problems for photographers is that of riots and demonstrations. In this situation, photographers have been arrested for breach of the peace, or under the Public Order Act 1986, which allows the police to arrest anyone behaving in a way that is 'likely to cause harassment, alarm or distress'. In several cases, photographers have been arrested, held for long enough to miss their news deadlines, and then had charges against them dropped; clearly, it is better to avoid being arrested in the first place if you can.

COPYRIGHT AND CONFIDENTIALITY

Taking a photograph of something that is protected by copyright can be a breach of that copyright. A common example arises in connection with human interest stories, where, rather than hand over precious original photographs, people may allow a photographer to shoot a direct copy of them. This is fine if the person who allows the photographer to do this actually owns the copyright, but in many cases (e.g. wedding or school photographs), they do not. Taking the photograph and publishing it will be a breach of copyright. The same applies to, for example, taking a photograph of an artwork, or a montage of headlines from other publications, unless the copyright holder(s) give permission.

Taking your own photograph of, for example, a scene that appears in someone else's picture will not be a breach of copyright. However, in some circumstances this may be a breach of confidentiality.

 In the 1997 case of *Creation Records* v *News Group Newspapers*, a photo shoot was organised for the cover of an Oasis album. Heavy security was in place around the set, but a press photographer managed to get in, and surruptitiously took some pictures, which were (not surprisingly) similar to the one that was chosen for the album cover. The record company sued, and the court found that publication was a breach of confidence.

 In *Douglas* v *Hello!* (2005) the film stars Catherine Zeta-Jones and Michael Douglas sued *Hello!* magazine for publishing photographs of their wedding, taken secretly by a photographer who had sneaked in. The Court of Appeal said that the right of celebrities to sell pictures of themselves was comparable to a trade secret, and was therefore protected by the law of confidentiality in the same way as the recipe for a soft drink, for example, would be.

For a more detailed explanation of the law on copyright and confidentiality, see Chapters 21 and 17.

CHAPTER SUMMARY

Private land

Entering and/or taking pictures without permission may be trespass and/or breach of confidence.

Public places

Permission may be needed; breaches of the Official Secrets Acts and Terrorism Acts are possible.

Courts

Photography within the precincts is banned; publication of pictures related to court cases may be restricted.

Public order

Photographers can be arrested for breach of the peace, obstruction of the highway and obstruction of the police.

Copyright and confidentiality

- Photographing a copyright work may be breach of copyright.
- Photographing a scene can be a breach of confidence.

TEST YOUR KNOWLEDGE

1 You are reporting a story about a local man who has built a huge extension on his house, without getting planning permission. You are standing on the pavement outside the house, taking pictures of the extension, when the owner comes out and demands you hand over your film. What are his legal rights?

2 You spot a well-known celebrity buying haemorrhoid cream in a shop, and manage to snatch a photo before the security guard escorts you from the premises. Can you publish the photo?

3 You work for a local paper, which is currently reporting a very high-profile rape case. You realise that the victim is someone who you photographed for an earlier, unrelated story. Can you publish that picture?

4 You are sent to photograph a family whose son has been killed in a hit and run accident. They do not want to hand over any pictures of their son, in case they are lost, but suggest that you photograph his old school photos. Can you do this?

5 A local stately home is hosting a birthday party for a major pop star; the press have been banned from the venue, but your sister is a waitress there, and offers to sneak in a camera and take some pictures for you. What legal issues do you need to consider?

30

Photography

ONLINE RESOURCES

www The Editorial Photographers UK and Ireland (EPUK) website has useful advice on copyright issues, at:
www.epuk.org

The PCC Code, and adjudications relating to photographs, can be read at:
www.pcc.org.uk

For further resources and updates please go to the Companion Website for this book at www.pearsoned.co.uk/practicaljournalism

Appendix 1
Press Complaints Commission
Code of Practice and Schedule

The Press Complaints Commission is charged with enforcing the following Code of Practice which was framed by the newspaper and periodical industry and was ratified by the PCC on 7 August 2006.

THE CODE

All members of the press have a duty to maintain the highest professional standards. This Code sets the benchmark for those ethical standards, protecting both the rights of the individual and the public's right to know. It is the cornerstone of the system of self-regulation to which the industry has made a binding commitment.

It is essential that an agreed code be honoured not only to the letter but in the full spirit. It should not be interpreted so narrowly as to compromise its commitment to respect the rights of the individual, nor so broadly that it constitutes an unnecessary interference with freedom of expression or prevents publication in the public interest.

It is the responsibility of editors and publishers to implement the Code and they should take care to ensure it is observed rigorously by all editorial staff and external contributors, including non-journalists, in printed and online versions of publications.

Editors should cooperate swiftly with the PCC in the resolution of complaints. Any publication judged to have breached the Code must print the adjudication in full and with due prominence, including headline reference to the PCC.

1 Accuracy

(i) The Press must take care not to publish inaccurate, misleading or distorted information, including pictures.

(ii) A significant inaccuracy, mis-leading statement or distortion once recognised must be corrected, promptly and with due prominence, and – where appropriate – an apology published.

(iii) The Press, whilst free to be partisan, must distinguish clearly between comment, conjecture and fact.

(iv) A publication must report fairly and accurately the outcome of an action for defamation to which it has been a party, unless an agreed settlement states otherwise, or an agreed statement is published.

2 Opportunity to reply

A fair opportunity for reply to inaccuracies must be given when reasonably called for.

3 *Privacy

(i) Everyone is entitled to respect for his or her private and family life, home, health and correspondence, including digital communications. Editors will be expected to justify intrusions into any individual's private life without consent.

(ii)   It is unacceptable to photograph individuals in private places without their consent.

Note – Private places are public or private property where there is a reasonable expectation of privacy.

4 *Harassment

(i)   Journalists must not engage in intimidation, harassment or persistent pursuit.

(ii)   They must not persist in questioning, telephoning, pursuing or photographing individuals once asked to desist; nor remain on their property when asked to leave and must not follow them.

(iii) Editors must ensure these principles are observed by those working for them and take care not to use non-compliant material from other sources.

5 Intrusion into grief or shock

(i)   In cases involving personal grief or shock, enquiries and approaches must be made with sympathy and discretion and publication handled sensitively. This should not restrict the right to report legal proceedings, such as inquests.

(*ii) When reporting suicide, care should be taken to avoid excessive detail about the method used.

6 *Children

(i)   Young people should be free to complete their time at school without unnecessary intrusion.

(ii)   A child under 16 must not be interviewed or photographed on issues involving their own or another child's welfare unless a custodial parent or similarly responsible adult consents.

(iii) Pupils must not be approached or photographed at school without the permission of the school authorities.

(iv)   Minors must not be paid for material involving children's welfare, nor parents or guardians for material about their children or wards, unless it is clearly in the child's interest.

(v)   Editors must not use the fame, notoriety or position of a parent or guardian as sole justification for publishing details of a child's private life.

7 *Children in sex cases

1 The press must not, even if legally free to do so, identify children under 16 who are victims or witnesses in cases involving sex offences.

2 In any press report of a case involving a sexual offence against a child –

(i)   The child must not be identified.

(ii)   The adult may be identified.

(iii) The word 'incest' must not be used where a child victim might be identified.

(iv)   Care must be taken that nothing in the report implies the relationship between the accused and the child.

8 *Hospitals

(i) Journalists must identify themselves and obtain permission from a responsible executive before entering non-public areas of hospitals or similar institutions to pursue enquiries.

(ii) The restrictions on intruding into privacy are particularly relevant to enquiries about individuals in hospitals or similar institutions.

9 *Reporting of Crime

(i) Relatives or friends of persons convicted or accused of crime should not generally be identified without their consent, unless they are genuinely relevant to the story.

(ii) Particular regard should be paid to the potentially vulnerable position of children who witness, or are victims of, crime. This should not restrict the right to report legal proceedings.

10 Clandestine devices and subterfuge

(i) The press must not seek to obtain or publish material acquired by using hidden cameras or clandestine listening devices; or by intercepting private or mobile telephone calls, messages or emails; or by the unauthorised removal of documents or photographs.

(ii) Engaging in misrepresentation or subterfuge, can generally be justified only in the public interest and then only when the material cannot be obtained by other means.

11 Victims of sexual assault

The press must not identify victims of sexual assault or publish material likely to contribute to such identification unless there is adequate justification and they are legally free to do so.

12 Discrimination

(i) The press must avoid prejudicial or pejorative reference to an individual's race, colour, religion, gender, sexual orientation or to any physical or mental illness or disability.

(ii) Details of an individual's race, colour, religion, sexual orientation, physical or mental illness or disability must be avoided unless genuinely relevant to the story.

13 Financial journalism

(i) Even where the law does not prohibit it, journalists must not use for their own profit financial information they receive in advance of its general publication, nor should they pass such information to others.

(ii) They must not write about shares or securities in whose performance they know that they or their close families have a significant financial interest without disclosing the interest to the editor or financial editor.

(iii) They must not buy or sell, either directly or through nominees or agents, shares or securities about which they have written recently or about which they intend to write in the near future.

14 Confidential sources

Journalists have a moral obligation to protect confidential sources of information.

15 Witness payments in criminal trials

(i) No payment or offer of payment to a witness – or any person who may reasonably be expected to be called as a witness – should be made in any case once proceedings are active as defined by the Contempt of Court Act 1981.

This prohibition lasts until the suspect has been freed unconditionally by police without charge or bail or the proceedings are otherwise discontinued; or has entered a guilty plea to the court; or, in the event of a not guilty plea, the court has announced its verdict.

(*ii) Where proceedings are not yet active but are likely and foreseeable, editors must not make or offer payment to any person who may reasonably be expected to be called as a witness, unless the information concerned ought demonstrably to be published in the public interest and there is an over-riding need to make or promise payment for this to be done; and all reasonable steps have been taken to ensure no financial dealings influence the evidence those witnesses give. In no circumstances should such payment be conditional on the outcome of a trial.

(*iii) Any payment or offer of payment made to a person later cited to give evidence in proceedings must be disclosed to the prosecution and defence. The witness must be advised of this requirement.

16 *Payment to criminals

(i)   Payment or offers of payment for stories, pictures or information, which seek to exploit a particular crime or to glorify or glamorise crime in general, must not be made directly or via agents to convicted or confessed criminals or to their associates – who may include family, friends and colleagues.

(ii)   Editors invoking the public interest to justify payment or offers would need to demonstrate that there was good reason to believe the public interest would be served. If, despite payment, no public interest emerged, then the material should not be published.

The **public interest**

There may be exceptions to the clauses marked * where they can be demonstrated to be in the public interest.

1. The public interest includes, but is not confined to:
   (i) Detecting or exposing crime or serious impropriety.
   (ii) Protecting public health and safety.
   (iii) Preventing the public from being misled by an action or statement of an individual or organisation.

2. There is a public interest in freedom of expression itself.

3. Whenever the public interest is invoked, the PCC will require editors to demonstrate fully how the public interest was served.

4. The PCC will consider the extent to which material is already in the public domain, or will become so.

5. In cases involving children under 16, editors must demonstrate an exceptional public interest to override the normally paramount interest of the child.

SCHEDULE 1

QUALIFIED PRIVILEGE

PART I

STATEMENTS HAVING QUALIFIED PRIVILEGE WITHOUT EXPLANATION OR CONTRADICTION

1. A fair and accurate report of proceedings in public of a legislature anywhere in the world.

2. A fair and accurate report of proceedings in public before a court anywhere in the world.

3. A fair and accurate report of proceedings in public of a person appointed to hold a public inquiry by a government or legislature anywhere in the world.

4. A fair and accurate report of proceedings in public anywhere in the world of an international organisation or an international conference.

5. A fair and accurate copy of or extract from any register or other document required by law to be open to public inspection.

6. A notice or advertisement published by or on the authority of a court, or of a judge or officer of a court, anywhere in the world.

7. A fair and accurate copy of or extract from matter published by or on the authority of a government or legislature anywhere in the world.

8. A fair and accurate copy of or extract from matter published anywhere in the world by an international organisation or an international conference.

PART II

STATEMENTS PRIVILEGED SUBJECT TO EXPLANATION OR CONTRADICTION

9. (1) A fair and accurate copy of or extract from a notice or other matter issued for the information of the public by or on behalf of –

    (a) a legislature in any member State or the European Parliament;
    (b) the government of any member State, or any authority performing governmental functions in any member State or part of a member State, or the European Commission;
    (c) an international organisation or international conference.

(2) In this paragraph "governmental functions" includes police functions.

10. A fair and accurate copy of or extract from a document made available by a court in any member State or the European Court of Justice (or any court attached to that court), or by a judge or officer of any such court.

11. (1) A fair and accurate report of proceedings at any public meeting or sitting in the United Kingdom of –

(a) a local authority or local authority committee;
(b) a justice or justices of the peace acting otherwise than as a court exercising judicial authority;
(c) a commission, tribunal, committee or person appointed for the purposes of any inquiry by any statutory provision, by Her Majesty or by a Minister of the Crown or a Northern Ireland Department;
(d) a person appointed by a local authority to hold a local inquiry in pursuance of any statutory provision;
(e) any other tribunal, board, committee or body constituted by or under, and exercising functions under, any statutory provision.

(2) In sub-paragraph (1)(a) –

"local authority" means –

(a) in relation to England and Wales, a principal council within the meaning of the Local Government Act 1972, any body falling within any paragraph of section 100J(1) of that Act or an authority or body to which the Public Bodies (Admission to Meetings) Act 1960 applies,
(b) in relation to Scotland, a council constituted under section 2 of the Local Government etc. (Scotland) Act 1994 or an authority or body to which the Public Bodies (Admission to Meetings) Act 1960 applies,
(c) in relation to Northern Ireland, any authority or body to which sections 23 to 27 of the Local Government Act (Northern Ireland) 1972 apply; and

"local authority committee" means any committee of a local authority or of local authorities, and includes –

(a) any committee or sub-committee in relation to which sections 100A to 100D of the Local Government Act 1972 apply by virtue of section 100E of that Act (whether or not also by virtue of section 100J of that Act), and
(b) any committee or sub-committee in relation to which sections 50A to 50D of the Local Government (Scotland) Act 1973 apply by virtue of section 50E of that Act.

(3) A fair and accurate report of any corresponding proceedings in any of the Channel Islands or the Isle of Man or in another member State.

12. (1) A fair and accurate report of proceedings at any public meeting held in a member State.

(2) In this paragraph a "public meeting" means a meeting bona fide and lawfully held for a lawful purpose and for the furtherance or discussion of a matter of public concern, whether admission to the meeting is general or restricted.

13. (1) A fair and accurate report of proceedings at a general meeting of a UK public company.

(2) A fair and accurate copy of or extract from any document circulated to members of a UK public company –

(a) by or with the authority of the board of directors of the company,

(b) by the auditors of the company, or

(c) by any member of the company in pursuance of a right conferred by any statutory provision.

(3) A fair and accurate copy of or extract from any document circulated to members of a UK public company which relates to the appointment, resignation, retirement or dismissal of directors of the company.

(4) In this paragraph "UK public company" means –

(a) a public company within the meaning of section 1(3) of the Companies Act 1985 or Article 12(3) of the Companies (Northern Ireland) Order 1986, or

(b) a body corporate incorporated by or registered under any other statutory provision, or by Royal Charter, or formed in pursuance of letters patent.

(5) A fair and accurate report of proceedings at any corresponding meeting of, or copy of or extract from any corresponding document circulated to members of, a public company formed under the law of any of the Channel Islands or the Isle of Man or of another member State.

14. A fair and accurate report of any finding or decision of any of the following descriptions of association, formed in the United Kingdom or another member State, or of any committee or governing body of such an association –

(a) an association formed for the purpose of promoting or encouraging the exercise of or interest in any art, science, religion or learning, and empowered by its constitution to exercise control over or adjudicate on matters of interest or concern to the association, or the actions or conduct of any person subject to such control or adjudication;

(b) an association formed for the purpose of promoting or safeguarding the interests of any trade, business, industry or profession, or of the persons carrying on or engaged in any trade, business, industry or profession, and empowered by its constitution to exercise control over or adjudicate upon matters connected with that trade, business, industry or profession, or the actions or conduct of those persons;

(c) an association formed for the purpose of promoting or safeguarding the interests of a game, sport or pastime to the playing or exercise of which members of the public are invited or admitted, and empowered by its constitution to exercise control over or adjudicate upon persons connected with or taking part in the game, sport or pastime;

(d) an association formed for the purpose of promoting charitable objects or other objects beneficial to the community and empowered by its constitution to exercise control over or to adjudicate on matters of interest or concern to the association, or the actions or conduct of any person subject to such control or adjudication.

15. (1) A fair and accurate report of, or copy of or extract from, any adjudication, report, statement or notice issued by a body, officer or other person designated for the purposes of this paragraph –

(a) for England and Wales or Northern Ireland, by order of the Lord Chancellor, and

(b) for Scotland, by order of the Secretary of State.

(2) An order under this paragraph shall be made by statutory instrument which shall be subject to annulment in pursuance of a resolution of either House of Parliament.

Glossary

Acquittal A verdict of not guilty in a criminal case.

Affadavit A written statement which has been sworn on oath by a witness, which can be used as evidence in court.

Appeal A case taken to a higher court by someone who believes the wrong result was reached in the original hearing.

Appellant The person who brings an appeal.

Attorney-General A Government Minister who acts as the Government's main legal advisor. Certain types of crime (such as offences under the Contempt of Court Act 1981 – see Chapter 6) require consent from the Attorney-General before prosecutions can be brought, and if this consent is given, the prosecution is brought in the name of the Attorney-General.

Bail The arrangement under which someone charged with a criminal offence can be allowed to remain free of custody until their trial.

Balance of probabilities The standard of proof in civil cases, where the claimant must prove that that there is a more than a 50 per cent chance that what they say is true (i.e. that is more likely than not).

Beyond reasonable doubt The standard of proof in criminal cases. The prosecution must prove to the magistrates or jury that it it beyond reasonable doubt that the defendant committed the offence they are charged with.

Bill A written proposal for a new law, which is debated in Parliament.

Caution A formal warning given by the police as an alternative to prosecution; can only be used when an offender admits guilt.

Claimant The person bringing a case in the civil courts.

Common law Law made by the decisions of judges in cases heard in the higher courts, which form precedents to be followed in later cases. Also known as case law.

Conditional fee agreement An agreement between solicitor and client in civil cases, under which the client pays nothing if they lose the case, and the solicitor gets an extra fee if they win. Often known as 'no win, no fee'.

Contemporaneous Published as soon as possible after an event (usually a court case).

Count Each one of the criminal charges faced by a defendant.

Damages An amount of money which may be awarded by a court to someone who wins a civil case.

Defence **1** A legal provision which allows someone who would otherwise be guilty of a crime or a tort to escape liability, if the circumstances of the defence are met (e.g. justification, fair comment and privilege in defamation).
2 The name given to the lawyers representing a person who is accused of a crime, or a person who is being sued in the civil courts.

Defendant Someone who is being prosecuted in the criminal courts or sued in the civil courts.

Double jeopardy An ancient rule which prevented someone acquitted of a crime from being charged again for the same offence; no longer an absolute rule in English law.

Family proceedings Hearings related to the care, custody, maintenance, paternity and adoption of children.

Green Paper A document issued by the Government when it is planning new legislation, setting out basic details of the area of law to be changed and inviting comment.

In camera In private. Used of hearings to which the press and public are not admitted.

In chambers (A hearing) held somewhere other than in an open court room, but not necessarily closed to the public or press.

Injunction A court order, which obliges someone to do or not to do something, either permanently or temporarily. Injunctions against the press usually prevent publication of particular material.

Journalistic material Material which has been 'acquired or created for the purposes of journalism'. This type of material has a degree of protection from search and seizure by the police.

Judicial review An action brought in the High Court, in which decisions made by official bodies can be reviewed; if the decision has been made unlawfully, or is completely unreasonable, it may be quashed.

Legal privilege The rule that communications between a lawyer and their client are confidential.

Ofcom The body which regulates broadcasting in the UK. It has a Code of Practice for broadcasters, breach of which can lead to fines and even loss of a broadcasting licence.

On remand Held in custody after being charged with a criminal offence, usually until the trial.

Plea The defendant in a criminal case's answer to the charge (i.e. guilty or not guilty).

Pleas in mitigation Arguments made by lawyers for a defendant who has been found (or pleaded) guilty to a crime, designed to give the court reason to treat them more leniently than they otherwise would.

Practice Direction An official document which contains detailed guidance for the courts on a particular issue, and supplements their ordinary rules of procedure.

Precedent A decision made in a legal case, which should be followed in later cases.

Press Complaints Commission (PCC) Independent body which deals with complaints from the public about the editorial content of newspapers and magazines. It has a Code of Practice, covering issues such as privacy and accuracy. Breaches are dealt with initially by trying to achieve a satisfactory resolution by negotiation between the complainant and the relevant publisher, but if this fails, the PCC can adjudicate on the complaint, and order the publisher to print a report of the result.

Private prosecution A prosecution brought by a private individual, if the Crown Prosection Service declines to take a case to court.

Prosecution 1 The process of bringing someone accused of crime before the courts.
2 The lawyers who represent that person.

Quash To declare invalid (usually used of a court order, verdict or sentence).

Reporting restrictions Legal provisions which prevent publication of some or all of the details of a court case, either temporarily or permanently.

Rule against prior restraint A traditional principle of English law which states that, as far as possible, the media should not be censored in advance, but dealt with after publication if material published is unlawful.

Settle out of court To agree a solution to a court case with the other party, without going to court. The majority of civil cases are settled in this way.

Striking-out application A preliminary hearing which decides whether, assuming the facts alleged by a party in a case are true, they would have an arguable case in law.

Tort A type of wrongdoing that is dealt with by the civil courts, rather than the criminal legal system.

Ward of court A person under 18 who, as a result of a legal order, is under the care of the Family Division of the High Court.

Youth Court A branch of the magistrates' courts, which deals with cases involving defendants aged under 18. The term describes a type of hearing, rather than a place.

Further reading

Section 1 Law and the legal system

Bradley, A. and Ewing, K. (2006) *Constitutional and Administrative Law*, Part I (14th edn), Harlow: Longman.

Berlins, M. and Dyer, C. (2000) *The Law Machine*, London: Penguin.

Elliott, C. and Quinn, F. (2005) *Tort Law* (5th edn), Harlow: Pearson.

Elliott, C. and Quinn, F. (2006) *Criminal Law* (6th edn), Harlow: Pearson.

Elliott, C. and Quinn, F. (2006) *English Legal System* (7th edn), Harlow: Pearson.

Section 2 Writing about the courts

Media Lawyer newsletter, published bi-monthly by Tom Welsh, 3 Broom Close, Broughton-in-Furness, Cumbria LA20 6JG.

Robertson, G. and Nicol, A. (2002) *Media Law* (4th edn), Chapters 7, 8 and 9, London: Penguin.

Welsh, T., Greenwood, W. and Banks, D. (2005) *McNae's Essential Law for Journalists* (18th edn), Chapters 11 and 12, Oxford; Oxford University Press.

Section 3 Defamation and malicious falsehood

Crone, T. (2002) *Law and the Media* (4th edn), Chapter 1, Oxford: Focal Press.

Mason, P. and Smith, D. (1998) *Magazine Law: a Practical Guide*, Chapter 2, 3, 5, 6 and 7, London: Routledge.

McBride, N.J. and Bagshaw, R. (2005) *Tort Law* (2nd edn), Harlow: Longman Law Series.

Price, D. (2003) *Defamation*, London: Sweet and Maxwell.

Robertson, G. (1999) *The Justice Game*, London: Vintage.

Robertson, G. and Nicol, A. (2002) *Media Law* (4th edn), Chapter 3, London: Penguin.

Section 4 Privacy, confidentiality and copyright

Bradley, A. and Ewing, K. (2006) *Constitutional and Administrative Law*, Part III (14th edn), Harlow: Longman.

McBride, N. and Bagshaw, R. (2005) *Tort Law* (2nd edn), Harlow: Longman Law Series.

Rozenburg, J. (2004) *Privacy and the Press*, Oxford: Oxford University Press.

Section 5 Reporting Government and business

Bradley, A. and Ewing, K. (2006) *Constitutional and Administrative Law*, Part III (14th edn), Harlow: Longman.

Brooke, H. (2006) *Your Right to Know: A Citizen's Guide to the Freedom of Information Act*, London: Pluto Press.

Pilger, J. (2005) *Tell Me No Lies: Investigative Journalism and Its Triumphs*, London: Vintage.

Robertson, G. and Nicol, A. (2002) *Media Law* (4th edn), Chapter 12, London: Penguin.

Thurlow, R. (1994) *The Secret State*, Oxford: Blackwell.

Section 6 Race, religion and public order

Fenwick, H. and Phillipson, G. (2006) *Media Freedom under the Human Rights Act*, Part 3, LexisNexis.

Robertson, G. and Nicol, A. (2002) *Media Law*, Chapter 4 (4th edn), London: Penguin.

Section 7 Broadcasting and photography

Cassell, D. (1989) *The Photographer and the Law*, London: BFP Books.

Index

The Longman Practical Journalism Series

'... invaluable in university journalism departments, on professional training courses, and in the broadcast newsroom itself. I would certainly adopt this for my students.'

Mike Henfield, University of Salford

This exciting text presents all the key practical skills required by today's broadcast journalist. Highly illustrated with examples from modern day newsrooms, the authors explain in detail the key techniques and theoretical context the broadcast journalist will need to know to succeed.

ISBN-10: 1-4058-2434-4
ISBN-13: 978-1-4058-2434-7

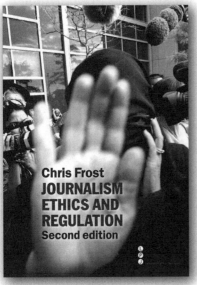

"Given the endless controversies around privacy, ethics and media regulation this book is a timely, comprehensive and indispensable handbook for journalists and a rallying cry for all those who believe ethical journalism is not just possible but an essential part of a free media in a democratic society."

Jeremy Dear, General Secretary of the National Union of Journalists (NUJ)

Journalism Ethics and Regulation provides journalism students and trainee journalists with the tools to make informed ethical decisions in their working lives. The text provides detailed coverage of the main codes of practice and regulatory bodies – PCC, Office of Communications, BBC, NUJ – in the UK and beyond.

ISBN-10: 1-4058-3536-2
ISBN-13: 978-1-4058-3536-7

Available from all good bookshops or order online at
www.pearsoned.co.uk/journalism

Longman Practical Journalism

PEARSON
Longman